HMH Georgia Science

This Interactive Student Edition belongs to

Kavya Rajkumar

Teacher/Room

Ms. McKie   F115

Houghton Mifflin Harcourt™

Consulting Authors

Michael A. DiSpezio

Global Educator
North Falmouth, Massachusetts

Michael DiSpezio has authored many HMH instructional programs for science and mathematics. He has also authored numerous trade books and multimedia programs on various topics and hosted dozens of studio and location broadcasts for various organizations in the U.S. and worldwide. Most recently, he has been working with educators to provide strategies for implementing science and engineering practices, including engineering design challenges. To all his projects, he brings his extensive background in science, his expertise in classroom teaching at the elementary, middle, and high school levels, and his deep experience in producing interactive and engaging instructional materials.

Marjorie Frank

Science Writer and
Content-Area Reading Specialist
Brooklyn, New York

An educator and linguist by training, a writer and poet by nature, Marjorie Frank has authored and designed a generation of instructional materials in all subject areas, including past HMH Science programs. Her other credits include authoring science issues of an award-winning children's magazine, writing game-based digital assessments, developing blended learning materials for young children, and serving as instructional designer and co-author of pioneering school-to-work software. In addition, she has served on the adjunct faculty of Hunter, Manhattan, and Brooklyn Colleges, teaching courses in science methods, literacy, and writing.

Acknowledgments for Cover

Front cover: *iceberg* ©Hans Reinhard/Corbis

Michael R. Heithaus

Dean, College of Arts, Sciences & Education
Professor, Department of Biological Sciences
Florida International University
Miami, Florida

Mike Heithaus joined the FIU Biology Department in 2003, has served as Director of the Marine Sciences Program, and as Executive Director of the School of Environment, Arts, and Society, which brings together the natural and social sciences and humanities to develop solutions to today's environmental challenges. He now serves as Dean of the College of Arts, Sciences & Education. His research focuses on predator-prey interactions and the ecological importance of large marine species. He has helped to guide the development of Life Science content in this science program, with a focus on strategies for teaching challenging content as well as the science and engineering practices of analyzing data and using computational thinking.

Georgia Reviewers

C. Alex Alvarez, EdD
Director of STEM and Curriculum
Valdosta City Schools
Valdosta, Georgia

Suzanne Salter Brooks
Teacher
Lee Middle School
Sharpsburg, Georgia

Cindy Brown
Teacher
Coffee Middle School
Douglas, Georgia

Monica Dyess, EdD
Pine Grove Middle School
Valdosta, Georgia

Felecia Eckman
Teacher
Carl Scoggins Middle School
Dallas, Georgia

Theresa D. Flanagan
Physical Science Instructor
Arnall Middle School
Newnan, Georgia

Toppy R. Gurley, EdS
Science Dept. Chair
P.B. Ritch Middle School
Dallas, Georgia

Angel James
Middle Grades Educator
Midway Middle School
Midway, Georgia

Keith A. Peterman
Life Science Teacher
Lewis Frasier Middle School
Hinesville, Georgia

Monique Prince, EdD
East Paulding Middle School
Dallas, Georgia

Melanie Smith, MEd
Physical Science Instructor
Arnall Middle School
Newnan, Georgia

Cynthia L. Tupper
Science Teacher
Lewis Frasier Middle School
Hinesville, Georgia

Content Reviewers

Paul D. Asimow, PhD
*Professor of Geology
and Geochemistry*
Division of Geological and Planetary Sciences
California Institute of Technology
Pasadena, CA

Laura K. Baumgartner, PhD
Postdoctoral Researcher
Molecular, Cellular, and Developmental
Biology
University of Colorado
Boulder, CO

Eileen Cashman, PhD
Professor
Department of Environmental Resources
Engineering
Humboldt State University
Arcata, CA

Hilary Clement Olson, PhD
Research Scientist Associate V
Institute for Geophysics, Jackson School of
Geosciences
The University of Texas at Austin
Austin, TX

Joe W. Crim, PhD
Professor Emeritus
Department of Cellular Biology
The University of Georgia
Athens, GA

Elizabeth A. De Stasio, PhD
*Raymond H. Herzog Professor
of Science*
Professor of Biology
Department of Biology
Lawrence University
Appleton, WI

Dan Franck, PhD
Botany Education Consultant
Chatham, NY

Julia R. Greer, PhD
*Assistant Professor of Materials Science and
Mechanics*
Division of Engineering and Applied Science
California Institute of Technology
Pasadena, CA

John E. Hoover, PhD
Professor
Department of Biology
Millersville University
Millersville, PA

William H. Ingham, PhD
Professor (Emeritus)
Department of Physics and Astronomy
James Madison University
Harrisonburg, VA

Charles W. Johnson, PhD
*Chairman, Division of Natural Sciences,
Mathematics, and Physical Education*
Associate Professor of Physics
South Georgia College
Douglas, GA

Tatiana A. Krivosheev, PhD
Associate Professor of Physics
Department of Natural Sciences
Clayton State University
Morrow, GA

Joseph A. McClure, PhD
Associate Professor Emeritus
Department of Physics
Georgetown University
Washington, DC

Mark Moldwin, PhD
Professor of Space Sciences
Atmospheric, Oceanic, and Space Sciences
University of Michigan
Ann Arbor, MI

Russell Patrick, PhD
Professor of Physics
Department of Biology, Chemistry, and Physics
Southern Polytechnic State University
Marietta, GA

Patricia M. Pauley, PhD
Meteorologist, Data Assimilation Group
Naval Research Laboratory
Monterey, CA

Stephen F. Pavkovic, PhD
Professor Emeritus
Department of Chemistry
Loyola University of Chicago
Chicago, IL

L. Jeanne Perry, PhD
Director (Retired)
Protein Expression Technology Center
Institute for Genomics and Proteomics
University of California,
Los Angeles
Los Angeles, CA

Kenneth H. Rubin, PhD
Professor
Department of Geology and Geophysics
University of Hawaii
Honolulu, HI

Brandon E. Schwab, PhD
Associate Professor
Department of Geology
Humboldt State University
Arcata, CA

Marllin L. Simon, PhD
Associate Professor
Department of Physics
Auburn University
Auburn, AL

Larry Stookey, PE
Upper Iowa University
Wausau, WI

Kim Withers, PhD
Associate Research Scientist
Center for Coastal Studies
Texas A&M University-Corpus Christi
Corpus Christi, TX

Matthew A. Wood, PhD
Professor
Department of Physics & Space Sciences
Florida Institute of Technology
Melbourne, FL

Adam D. Woods, PhD
Associate Professor
Department of Geological Sciences
California State University, Fullerton
Fullerton, CA

Natalie Zayas, MS, EdD
Lecturer
Division of Science and Environmental Policy
California State University, Monterey Bay
Seaside, CA

Contents

Contents *(continued)*

Contents (continued)

The Universe and Our Solar System

Big Idea

Our solar system is just one of many billions of solar systems in the universe.

S6E1., S6E1.a, S6E1.b, S6E1.c, S6E1.d, S6E1.e

Viewing the night sky from an observatory

What do you think?

A telescope can be used to observe the night sky. What observations can you make about the universe and our solar system from your own backyard? As you explore this unit, gather evidence to help you state and support claims to answer this question.

Using high-powered binoculars

Unit 1
The Universe and Our Solar System

CITIZEN SCIENCE

Galaxy Zoo

The human eye is far better at identifying characteristics of galaxies than any computer. So Galaxy Zoo has called for everyday citizens to help in a massive identification project. Well over a hundred thousand people have helped identify newly discovered galaxies. Now you can, too.

① Think About It

The scientists using the Sloan Digital Sky Survey telescope can gather far more information than they can review quickly. Humans are better at galaxy identification than computers. Why might this be a difficult task for computers?

_____

_____

_____

Sloan Digital Sky Survey Camera

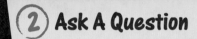
A galaxy seen edge-on

Spiral galaxy

② Ask A Question

How can people who aren't scientists help aid in galaxy identification?

With a partner, review the instructions on Galaxy Zoo's website and practice identifying galaxies. You will need to pay attention to the Galaxy Zoo classification system. Record your observations about the process.

_____

_____

_____

_____

_____

Things to Consider

Many different people review and classify each image of a galaxy at Galaxy Zoo. This way, scientists are able to control the mistakes that individuals may make.

✔ How can having many different people look at each galaxy help prevent errors?

③ Apply Your Knowledge

A List the characteristics you will be looking for when you examine a galaxy photo.

_____

_____

_____

_____

_____

_____

_____

B Review and classify galaxies on Galaxy Zoo's website.

C Create a classroom guide to the galaxies that you have identified.

Take It Home

What has the Citizen Science project known as Galaxy Zoo accomplished so far? Find out how many people have participated and compare that to the number of scientists working on the project.

Structure of the Universe

ESSENTIAL QUESTION

What makes up the universe?

By the end of this lesson, you should be able to describe the structure of the universe, including the scale of distances in the universe.

This image was taken from the Hubble Space Telescope. It shows just a small number of the galaxies that make up the universe.

S6E1.a Earth's position in the solar system and the universe's origins

S6E1.b Position of the solar system

S6E1.c Planets in the solar system

✋ Lesson Labs

Quick Labs
• Modeling the Expanding Universe
• Modeling Galaxies
• The Geocentric Model of the Solar System
• The Heliocentric Model of the Solar System

Field Lab
• Schoolyard Solar System

Engage Your Brain

1 Predict Check T or F to show whether you think each statement is true or false.

T   F

☐ ☐ You live on Earth.

☐ ☐ Earth orbits a star called the *moon*.

☐ ☐ Earth and the sun have the same composition.

☐ ☐ The sun is just one of many stars in the Milky Way galaxy.

☐ ☐ Distances in the universe are extremely large.

2 Draw When you look into the night sky, you are seeing only a very small part of the universe. Use the space below to draw what you see in the night sky.

Active Reading

3 Synthesize Many English words have their roots in other languages. Use the Latin words below to make an educated guess about the meaning of the word *universe*.

Latin word	Meaning
unus	one
vertere	to turn

Example sentence
Earth is part of the <u>universe</u>.

universe:

_____

_____

_____

Vocabulary Terms

• universe
• solar system
• planet
• star
• parallax
• nuclear fusion
• galaxy
• nebula
• light-year
• heliocentric
• geocentric
• supernova

4 Apply This list contains the key terms that you'll learn in this lesson. As you read, circle the definition of each term.

Our place in space

What makes up the universe?

You live on Earth, which is one of eight planets in the solar system that orbit the sun. As you probably know, the sun is a star. A *star* is a large celestial body that is composed of gas and emits light. Stars are grouped together in structures known as galaxies. A *galaxy* is a large collection of stars, gas, and dust. Based on observations by the Hubble Space Telescope, there are an estimated 100 billion or more galaxies in the universe. **Universe** is the word that scientists use to describe space and all of the energy and matter in it.

Active Reading

5 Identify As you read the text, underline those characteristics of Earth that make it a suitable place for life.

Earth—Our Home Planet

Earth is a special place. Imagine Earth without liquid water. There would be no vast, deep, blue oceans or broad, muddy rivers. The water would not evaporate and condense to form clouds in Earth's atmosphere. It would not fall to the ground again as rain or snow. Without water, there would be no plants to add oxygen to the atmosphere. And without oxygen, there would be no animal life on Earth.

Earth's atmosphere contains the combination of gases that animals need to breathe. The atmosphere also contains a thin layer of ozone gas. Ozone molecules in this layer absorb radiation from the sun that can be harmful to life. In addition, there are certain gases in the atmosphere that keep temperatures on Earth warm enough for life to exist.

The Sun

The sun appears to be much bigger and brighter than any of the stars you see at night. However, the sun is actually a medium-sized star. It seems bigger than other stars because it is the nearest star to Earth. The next-closest star to Earth is Proxima Centauri. It is 270,000 times farther away from Earth than the sun is.

From the moon, you can see Earth's continents, dark-blue oceans, and white clouds swirling in the atmosphere.

Visualize It!

6 Analyze What is the relationship between the sizes of the planets and their distances from the sun?

_____

_____

_____

Sun

Jupiter

Neptune

Uranus

Saturn

Earth   Mercury

Mars   Venus

The Solar System

Active Reading **7 Identify** As you read the text, underline the different bodies that make up the solar system.

The **solar system** is the collection of large and small bodies that orbit our central star, the sun. The contents of the solar system are numerous and stretch across a large area of space. For example, the solar system is so big that the distance from the sun to Neptune is 4.5 billion kilometers.

If you crossed the solar system beginning at the sun, you would encounter eight large bodies called *planets*. A **planet** is a spherical body that orbits the sun. Planets are generally larger than the other bodies in the solar system. The four planets that orbit nearest to the sun are the terrestrial planets. They are Mercury, Venus, Earth, and Mars. The terrestrial planets are all rocky, dense, and relatively small. The four planets that orbit farthest from the sun are the gas giant planets. They are Jupiter, Saturn, Uranus, and Neptune. These large planets have thick, gaseous atmospheres; small, rocky cores; and ring systems of ice, rock, and dust.

Orbiting most of the planets are smaller bodies called *moons*. Earth has only one moon, but Jupiter has more than 60. The rest of the solar system is made up of other small bodies. These include dwarf planets, comets, asteroids, and meteoroids. Altogether, there are up to a trillion small bodies in the solar system.

Sizes are roughly to scale. Distances are not.

Stars

A **star** is a large celestial body that is composed of gas and emits light. Like the sun, most stars are composed almost entirely of hydrogen and helium. Small percentages of other elements are also found in stars. Energy production takes place in the center, or core, of a star. Energy is produced by the process of **nuclear fusion**. In this process, stars fuse lighter elements, such as hydrogen, into heavier elements, such as helium. This energy leaves the core and eventually reaches the star's surface. There, energy escapes as visible light and other forms of radiation.

Stars vary greatly in size. Some small stars may be about the size of Earth. Giant and supergiant stars may be from 10 to 1,000 times as large as the sun is. The sun is a relatively cool star that is about 5,500 °C at its surface.

8 **Apply** Conduct research about one of the following aspects of stars:
• composition
• layers
• energy production
• size
Present your findings to the class in the form of an oral presentation or a poster presentation.

Think Outside the Book

Galaxies

Our solar system is located in the Milky Way galaxy. A **galaxy** (GAL•uhk•see) is a large collection of stars, gas, and dust that is held together by gravity. Small galaxies, called *dwarf galaxies,* may contain only a few million stars. Giant galaxies, however, may contain hundreds of billions of stars.

The Milky Way is a spiral galaxy. Spiral galaxies are shaped like pinwheels. They have a central bulge from which two or more spiral arms extend. Stars form in or near the spiral arms. The sun is located in a partial spiral arm of the Milky Way galaxy, near the edge of the galaxy. Elliptical galaxies and irregular galaxies are two other kinds of galaxies. Elliptical galaxies look like spheres or ovals, and they do not have spiral arms. Irregular galaxies appear as splotchy, irregularly shaped "blobs." Irregular galaxies are very active areas of star formation.

The Small Magellanic Cloud is an irregular dwarf galaxy that is located near the Milky Way. The blue stars are very young and are still surrounded by the gas and dust from which they formed.

Nebulae

A **nebula** (*plural,* nebulae) is a large cloud of gas and dust in space. Most stars form in nebulae. Nebulae are found in the arms of spiral galaxies and throughout irregular galaxies.

Nebulae may form from stars. Planetary nebulae form as stars like the sun age and push away their outer layer of material. Nebulae also form after supergiant stars that are much larger than the sun explode. A **supernova** is a gigantic explosion in which a high-mass star throws its outer layers into space. The nebulae that form from remains of these explosions are called *supernova remnants.*

There are three other main types of nebulae. Emission nebulae glow. Stars that are forming in these nebulae give off light and often have a red glow. The Orion Nebula is an emission nebula. Reflection nebulae reflect the light from other stars. These nebulae are often blue. The third type of nebulae are dark nebulae. Dark nebulae appear as dark regions in the sky because they block the light of stars behind them.

9 Compare How does a planetary nebula differ from other types of nebulae? Summarize the evidence that supports your claim.

_____

_____

_____

 Visualize It!

10 Describe Write the name of the correct type of nebula (dark nebula, emission nebula, or reflection nebula) under each of the three images below. Then, write a few words to describe each type.

A

_____

B

_____

_____

C

_____

_____

What is the structure of the solar system?

Our current model of the solar system is the *sun-centered* or *heliocentric* (hee•lee•oh•SEN•trik) model. In the **heliocentric** model, Earth and the other planets orbit the sun. The earliest models for the solar system assumed that the Earth was at the center of the solar system, with the sun, moon, and planets circling it. These models, which used Earth as the center, are called *Earth-centered* or **geocentric** (jee•oh•SEN•trik) models. The heliocentric model was not generally accepted until the late 16th to early 17th centuries.

Who proposed some early models of the solar system?

Until Galileo improved on the telescope in 1609, people observed the heavens with the naked eye. To observers, it appeared that the sun, the moon, the planets, and the stars moved around Earth each day. This caused them to conclude that Earth was not moving. If Earth was not moving, then Earth must be the center of the solar system and all other bodies revolved around it.

This geocentric model of the solar system became part of ancient Greek thought beginning in the 6th century BCE. Aristotle was among the first thinkers to propose this model.

Active Reading

11 Identify As you read the text, underline the definitions of geocentric and heliocentric.

Think Outside the Book

12 Research Use different sources to research a geocentric model of the solar system from either ancient Greece, ancient China, or Babylon. Before you begin, write down some questions you have about the model you have chosen. Then summarize your findings. Explain how new information has changed ancient models of the solar system and the universe.

Aristotle (384–322 BCE)

Aristotle

Aristotle (AIR•ih•staht'l) was a Greek philosopher. Aristotle thought Earth was the center of all things. His model placed the moon, sun, planets, and stars on a series of circles that surrounded Earth. He thought that if Earth went around the sun, then the relative positions of the stars would change as Earth moves. This apparent shift in the position of an object when viewed from different locations is known as **parallax** (PAIR•uh•laks). In fact, the stars are so far away that parallax cannot be seen with the naked eye.

of the Solar System?

Aristarchus

Aristarchus (air•i•STAHR•kuhs) was a Greek astronomer and mathematician. Aristarchus is reported to have proposed a heliocentric model of the solar system. His model, however, was not widely accepted at the time. Aristarchus attempted to measure the relative distances to the moon and sun. This was a major contribution to science. Aristarchus's ratio of distances was much too small but was important in the use of observation and geometry to solve a scientific problem.

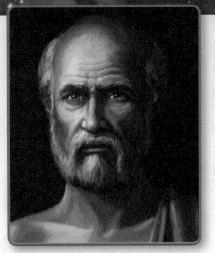

Aristarchus (about 310–230 BCE)

Aristotle thought that if Earth were moving, the positions of the stars should change as Earth moved. In fact, stars are so far away that shifts in their positions can only be observed by telescope.

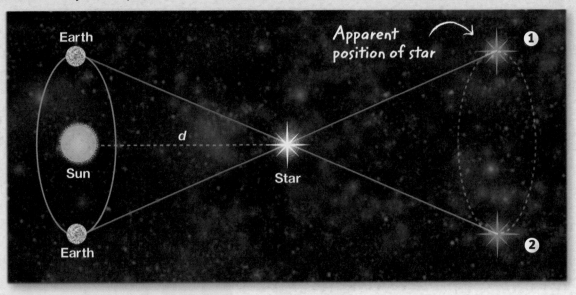

Diagram showing the shift in apparent position of a star at two different times of year seen from a telescope on Earth. A star first seen at point 1 will be seen at point 2 six months later.

Visualize It!

13 Predict If a star appears at position 1 during the summer, during which season will it appear at position 2?

_____

_____

_____

Ptolemy

Ptolemy (about 100–170 CE)

Ptolemy (TOHL•uh•mee) was an astronomer, geographer, and mathematician who lived in Alexandria, Egypt, which was part of ancient Rome. His book, the *Almagest*, is one of the few books that we have from these early times. It was based on observations of the planets going back as much as 800 years. Ptolemy developed a detailed geocentric model that was used by astronomers for the next 14 centuries. He believed that a celestial body traveled at a constant speed in a perfect circle. In Ptolemy's model, the planets moved on small circles that in turn moved on larger circles. This "wheels-on-wheels" system fit observations better than any model that had come before. It allowed prediction of the motion of planets years into the future.

Visualize It!

14 Describe Use the diagram at the right to describe Ptolemy's geocentric model of the solar system.

_____

_____

_____

_____

_____

Ptolemaic Model

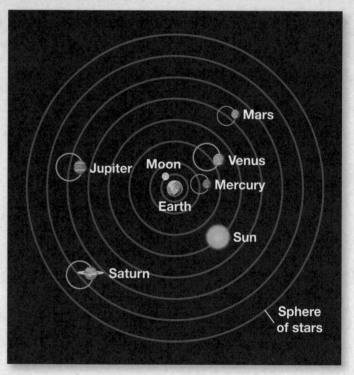

Mars

Jupiter Moon Venus

Mercury

Earth

Sun

Saturn

Sphere of stars

Think Outside the Book Inquiry

15 Defend As a class activity, defend Ptolemy's geocentric model of the solar system. Remember that during Ptolemy's time people were limited to what they could see with the naked eye.

Copernicus

The Polish astronomer Nicolaus Copernicus (nik•uh•LAY•uhs koh•PER•nuh•kuhs) felt that Ptolemy's model of the solar system was too complicated. He was aware of the heliocentric idea of Aristarchus when he developed the first detailed heliocentric model of the solar system. In Copernicus's time, data was still based on observations with the naked eye. Because data had changed little since the time of Ptolemy, Copernicus adopted Ptolemy's idea that planetary paths should be perfect circles. Like Ptolemy, he used a "wheels-on-wheels" system. Copernicus's model fit observations a little better than the geocentric model of Ptolemy. The heliocentric model of Copernicus is generally seen as the first step in the development of modern models of the solar system.

Nicolaus Copernicus (1473–1543)

Copernican Model

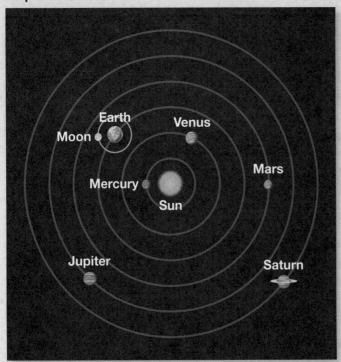

16 Compare How does Copernicus's model of the solar system differ from Ptolemy's model of the solar system?

Ptolemaic model	Copernican model

17 Describe In the boxes below, write your answers to each of the questions.

You live on Earth. What is Earth's place in the universe?

_____
_____
_____

Not to scale

Earth is part of the solar system. What is the structure of the solar system?

_____
_____
_____
_____
_____
_____
_____

The solar system is located within a partial spiral arm of the Milky Way galaxy. What is a galaxy?

_____
_____
_____
_____
_____
_____

How big is big?

How are distances in the universe measured?

Distances between most objects in the universe are so large that astronomers do not use kilometers to measure distance. Instead, astronomers measure distance using the speed of light. This unit of measure is known as a light-year. A **light-year** (ly) is the distance that light travels through space in one year. Light travels through space at about 300,000 km/s, or about 9.5 trillion km in one year. The closest star to the sun and Earth is Proxima Centauri. It takes light about 4.3 years to travel from Proxima Centauri to us. Therefore, the distance from Proxima Centauri to Earth is around 4.3 ly. Light from the sun travels to Earth in a little more than 8 minutes. Thus, the distance from the sun to Earth is around 8 light-minutes.

How do distances affect space travel? Our fastest interplanetary spacecraft, *Voyager 1,* travels through space at about 17 km/s. At this speed, it would take *Voyager 1* more than 70,000 years to reach Proxima Centauri.

The Voyager 2 spacecraft was launched in 1977. It explored Jupiter, Saturn, Uranus, and Neptune and is now close to moving out of the solar system and into interstellar space.

Do the Math

18 Compute If *Voyager 1* is now moving at 17 km/s, how far will it travel in one year?

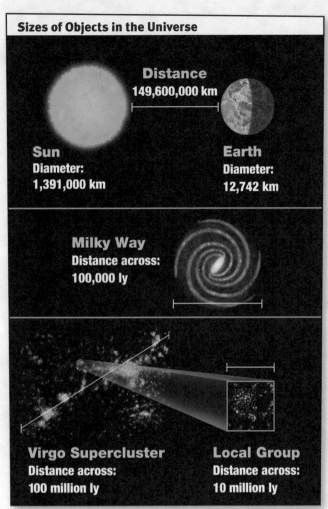

Sizes of Objects in the Universe

Distance
149,600,000 km

Sun
Diameter:
1,391,000 km

Earth
Diameter:
12,742 km

Milky Way
Distance across:
100,000 ly

Virgo Supercluster
Distance across:
100 million ly

Local Group
Distance across:
10 million ly

Images are not to scale

How are sizes in the universe measured?

The sizes of objects in the universe vary greatly. The units used to measure the size of an object in the universe depend on the object. The size of smaller objects, such as moons, planets, and stars, are often measured in kilometers. The size of these objects is often given as the diameter because they are close to being spherical. The diameter of Earth is about 12,742 km. The diameter of the sun is 1,391,000 km, making it about 109 times larger than Earth.

Light-years are used to measure the size of large objects in the universe, such as nebulae, galaxies, and galaxy clusters. The Milky Way galaxy has a diameter of about 100,000 ly across. Most of the other galaxies in the Local Group are smaller than the Milky Way. The Local Group is about 10,000,000 ly across. The Local Group is also part of the even bigger Virgo Supercluster. The Virgo Supercluster is about ten times wider than the Local Group, so it takes light 100,000,000 years to travel all of the way across.

What is the size of the observable universe?

Scientists still do not know the actual size of the entire universe. They only know the size of the universe that they can observe. Radiation from objects that formed early in the history of the universe has not yet reached Earth. And that takes time. Scientists have been able to take images of radiation that took around 14 billion years to reach Earth. These data tell scientists that the universe has a radius of at least 14 billion ly. However, the universe has been expanding in all directions since it formed. This means that objects are moving farther apart at an ever-increasing rate. Because the universe continues to accelerate outward, it is much larger than 14 billion ly in radius. Using the best current scientific techniques, it is estimated that the universe is around 93 billion ly in diameter and growing larger.

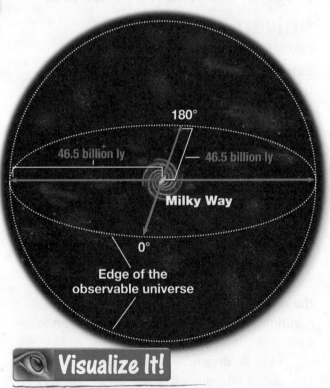

180°

46.5 billion ly   46.5 billion ly

Milky Way

0°

Edge of the
observable universe

👁 Visualize It!

19 Justify Use the model above to justify the current estimation of the diameter of the universe. Explain your reasoning.

What is the structure of the universe?

The universe can be defined as space and all the matter and energy in it. However, this definition does not tell us about the structure of the universe. Astronomers now know that throughout the universe there are areas where galaxies are densely concentrated. These are areas where galaxies are found in what are called *clusters* and *superclusters*. Clusters contain as many as several thousand galaxies. Superclusters can be made up of ten or more clusters of galaxies. There are also areas throughout the universe where very little matter exists. These are huge, spherical volumes called *voids*.

Astronomers have begun to think of the universe as having a structure similar to a three-dimensional web. Clusters and superclusters of galaxies make up the web. The large, empty volumes within the web are voids. It takes light hundreds of millions of years to cross the largest voids.

Active Reading **20 Describe** What is the general structure of the universe?

_____

_____

_____

_____

This supercomputer image is part of a simulation—the Bolshoi Simulation—of the evolution of the cosmos in a cube that is one billion light-years across.

© Houghton Mifflin Harcourt Publishing Company • Image Credits: (bg) ©Anatoly Klypin/New Mexico State University, Joel Primack/University of California, Santa Cruz

Think Outside the Book Inquiry

21 Apply Astronomers have begun to think of the universe as a system of clusters and superclusters of galaxies and voids. The clusters/superclusters of galaxies form the skeleton of the universe. Research the "cosmic web" of galaxies, and write a short essay or give a poster presentation about the structure of the universe.

Visual Summary

To complete this summary, fill in the blanks with the correct word or phrase. Then, use the key below to check your answers. You can use this page to review the main concepts of the lesson.

Structure of the Universe

Earth is a planet.

22 What star does Earth orbit?

_____

Bodies in our solar system orbit the sun.

23 What makes up our solar system?

_____

_____

The sun is a star.

24 Where do most stars form?

_____

The Milky Way is a galaxy.

25 What are galaxies made up of?

_____

26 Model Construct a model to show the position of our solar system in the Milky Way galaxy and in the known universe.

Lesson Review

Vocabulary

Fill in the blank with the term that best completes the following sentences.

1 A _____ is a large collection of stars, gas, and dust that is held together by gravity.

2 Space and all matter and energy in it is called the _____ .

3 A _____ consists of a star and all of the bodies in orbit around it.

Key Concepts

4 Identify What is a large celestial body that is composed of gas and emits light?

_____

5 Compare How does the size of the sun and its distance from Earth compare to the sizes and distances of other stars?

_____
_____
_____

6 Compare What is the difference between an emission nebula and a reflection nebula?

_____
_____
_____

7 Describe What is a light-year? Explain why light-years are used to measure distances and sizes in the universe.

_____
_____
_____
_____

Critical Thinking

Use the table to answer the following question.

Object	Distance from Earth
sun (nearest star)	8.3 light-minutes
Proxima Centauri (nearest star to sun)	4.3 light-years
center of Milky Way galaxy	25,000 light-years
Andromeda galaxy (nearest large galaxy)	2.5 million light-years

8 Claims • Evidence • Reasoning How far is the sun from the center of the Milky Way galaxy? State your claim along with evidence to support your claim and explain your reasoning.

_____
_____
_____
_____

9 Infer What question was prompted by the observations of Copernicus, and how did this lead to a change in our understanding of the solar system?

_____
_____
_____
_____

10 Deduce What do you think astronomers mean when they use the term *observable universe*? (Hint: Think of the time it takes for light from very distant objects to reach Earth.)

_____
_____
_____
_____

My Notes

Distances in the Universe

The second closest star to Earth is Proxima Centauri. Its distance from Earth is about 40,850,000,000,000 kilometers! Astronomers use a unit called a *light-year* to describe very large distances. A light-year (ly) is the distance that light can travel through space in one year. In space, light travels at about 300,000 km/s or close to 9.5 trillion km/year. So, Proxima Centauri is 4.3 ly from Earth.

Sample Problem

The following steps will teach you how to use conversion factors to convert between different units of measure and to understand which units are appropriate in a given situation.

A *conversion factor* is a fraction in which the numerator and the denominator represent the same amount or measurement but are in different units. When you multiply by a conversion factor, it is the same as multiplying by 1. Conversion factors are used to introduce the unit you need and to cancel the unneeded unit.

This image of the Whirlpool Galaxy was taken by the Hubble Space Telescope.

Calculate The Whirlpool Galaxy is located 294,500,000,000,000,000,000 kilometers (km) from Earth. Find the distance between Earth and the Whirlpool Galaxy in light-years (ly).

A Identify the units you have and the units you need. The current unit of measure is km. The unit of measure for the answer should be ly.

B Determine the conversion factor. We know from the introduction that there are 9,500,000,000,000 kilometers in a light-year. The conversion factor for converting km to ly is:

$$\frac{1 \text{ ly}}{9,500,000,000,000 \text{ km}}$$

Hint: The correct conversion factor will have the units you need in the numerator and the units you want to cancel in the denominator.

C Multiply the measurement by the conversion factor, and cancel the units.

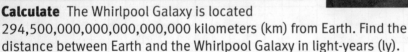

$$\frac{294,500,000,000,000,000,000 \text{ km}}{1} \cdot \frac{1 \text{ ly}}{9,500,000,000,000 \text{ km}}$$

D Simplify the fraction by dividing.

$$\frac{294,500,000,000,000,000,000 \text{ ly}}{9,500,000,000,000} = 31,000,000 \text{ ly}$$

E Answer.
The Whirlpool Galaxy is 31 million ly from Earth.

You Try It!

Distances within the solar system are also large but not large enough to use the unit of light-year. Instead, astronomers use the astronomical unit. An astronomical unit (AU) is the average distance between Earth and the sun. One AU is approximately 150,000,000 kilometers.

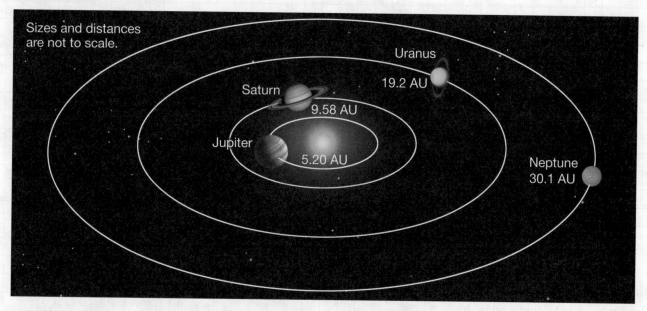

Sizes and distances are not to scale.

Uranus 19.2 AU

Saturn 9.58 AU

Jupiter 5.20 AU

Neptune 30.1 AU

1 Calculate Use a conversion factor and the diagram above to identify which planet is located 2,880,000,000 km from the sun.

A Identify the units you have and the units you need. The current unit of measure is km. The unit of measure for the answer should be AU.

B Determine the conversion factor. We know from the introduction that there are 150,000,000 kilometers in an astronomical unit. The conversion factor for converting km to AU is:

C Multiply the planet's distance from the sun by the conversion factor to find out how far the planet is from the sun in AU. Cancel the units.

D Simplify the fraction by dividing.

E Answer.

2 Synthesize What is an example of a distance that would appropriately be measured with the kilometer? The astronomical unit? The light-year?

_____

_____

_____

_____

_____

_____

_____

The Origin of the Universe

ESSENTIAL QUESTION

How did the universe begin?

By the end of this lesson, you should be able to summarize the evidence that has led scientists to accept the Big Bang theory to explain the origin of the universe.

The dark clouds in this image are part of the Eagle Nebula. Stars and the nebulae in which they form are part of the universe.

S6E1.a Earth's position in the solar system and the universe's origins

© Houghton Mifflin Harcourt Publishing Company • Image Credits: (bg) ©Digital Vision/Getty Images

Engage Your Brain

1 Predict Check T or F to show whether you think each statement is true or false.

T	F	
☐	☐	A galaxy is the largest structure in the universe.
☐	☐	Albert Einstein developed the law of universal gravitation.
☐	☐	The universe is between 13 and 15 billion years old.
☐	☐	The universe is expanding in all directions.

2 Describe In your own words, define the word *universe*.

_____
_____
_____
_____
_____
_____
_____
_____

Active Reading

3 Synthesize You can often define an unknown compound word if you know the meaning of the words it contains. Use the words and sentence below to make an educated guess about the meaning of the word *redshift*.

Word part	Meaning
red	the color of the visible spectrum with the longest wavelengths
shift	to move from one position to another

Example sentence
The wavelengths of a star that is moving away from Earth appear longer because of a <u>redshift</u>.

redshift:
_____
_____

Vocabulary Terms

• universe
• redshift
• Big Bang theory
• cosmic microwave background (CMB)
• wavelength
• electromagnetic spectrum
• spectrum

4 Apply As you learn the definition of each vocabulary term in this lesson, create your own definition or sketch to help you remember the meaning of the term.

The Stars at Night...

This string of galaxies may be made up of thousands of galaxies. Each galaxy contains millions to billions of stars.

What is the universe?

The **universe** is space and all of the matter and energy in it. That means you are as much a part of the universe as the sun and Earth are. Scientists can detect energy in the form of electromagnetic radiation from visible matter, such as stars. Scientists study this electromagnetic radiation to learn about the structures in the universe as well as to gather evidence of how the universe formed.

What large-scale structures make up the universe?

The universe is made up of several types of large-scale structures, each one larger than the last. A solar system is the smallest of the large-scale structures and consists of at least one star and the objects that orbit it. The next-largest structure is a star cluster, which is a group of stars bound together by gravitational attraction. Star clusters may contain a few hundred to many thousands of stars. A galaxy is larger than a star cluster. Galaxies contain millions to billions of stars. Still larger is a galaxy cluster, which is made up of dozens of galaxies. A supercluster is the largest structure. It is made up of hundreds of galaxies.

Active Reading

5 Identify As you read, underline each large-scale structure in the universe.

6 Identify The images below show a portion of the structures of the universe. Label each image with the correct term on the right.

solar system   galaxy

star cluster   galaxy cluster

A _____

B _____

C _____

D _____

On the Same

What is electromagnetic radiation?

Energy traveling as electromagnetic waves is called *electromagnetic radiation*. Each wave has a wavelength and a frequency. **Wavelength** is the distance between two adjacent crests or troughs of a wave. *Frequency* measures the number of waves passing a point per second. Frequency is inversely related to wavelength. This means that higher-frequency waves have a shorter wavelength.

How is electromagnetic radiation classified?

Active Reading **7 Identify** As you read, underline the name of each part of the electromagnetic spectrum.

All of the different wavelengths and frequencies make up what is called the **electromagnetic spectrum**. A **spectrum** (plural, *spectra*) is a continuous range of a single feature, in this case wavelength. The form of electromagnetic radiation with the longest wavelength and the lowest frequency is radio waves. Microwaves have shorter wavelengths and higher frequencies than radio waves. The next shortest wavelength radiation is called *infrared*. Visible light has a shorter wavelength than infrared. Even shorter in wavelength is ultraviolet radiation. The shortest wavelengths belong to x-rays and gamma rays.

How is spectral analysis used in astronomy?

Astronomers analyze spectra from all parts of the electromagnetic spectrum. Scientists can analyze spectra to learn about the motion and distance of objects. They can also learn about the properties of objects, such as composition and temperature.

Radio

8 Analyze Write the parts of the electromagnetic spectrum in order from lowest frequency to highest frequency.

_____
_____
_____
_____
_____
_____
_____

Microwave

LOWER FREQUENCY
LONGER WAVELENGTH

Wavelength?

Gamma rays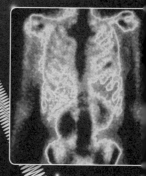

Infrared

9 Complete Electromagnetic _____ that has a shorter wavelength has a _____ frequency.

Ultraviolet

X-rays

Visible light

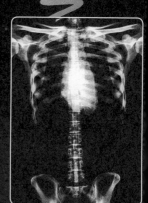

**HIGHER FREQUENCY
SHORTER WAVELENGTH**

Who's Who in the Universe?

Who are some scientists who contributed to our understanding of the universe?

People once thought that Earth was the center of the universe. The work of many scientists who followed changed our understanding of the universe. Scientists including Sir Isaac Newton, Albert Einstein, Georges Lemaître, Edwin Hubble, and George Gamow built upon the knowledge of earlier scientists. Our knowledge of the universe continues to grow as scientists today continue to build upon their work.

Active Reading

10 Identify As you read the next two pages, underline the contributions of each scientist.

Sir Isaac Newton

Newton's law of universal gravitation helps to explain the motions of objects in space.

Sir Isaac Newton (1643–1727) was an English scientist. He developed the law of universal gravitation. This law states that every object in the universe attracts other objects. It also states that the force of the attraction depends on the masses of the objects and the distance between them. Newton's law explains why objects fall toward the center of Earth. It also explains why planets orbit stars and stars are held together in galaxies.

Not all of Newton's ideas have stood the test of time. He thought that the universe did not change. He also believed that every star was fixed in one place in space and that stars were spread out evenly throughout the universe.

Albert Einstein

Albert Einstein (1879–1955) developed the theory of special relativity. This theory states that space and time are relative. *Relative* means that they depend on the motion of the observer and the object being observed. He also developed a new theory of gravity called *general relativity*. This theory explains how gravity causes space and time to curve. Although this seems like a strange idea, it is supported by many observations of the universe.

Newton's thinking still influenced Albert Einstein. Einstein's studies indicated that the universe was expanding. However, he adjusted his equations to fit Newton's idea that the universe stays the same over time.

Einstein won the Nobel Prize in Physics in 1921 for his contributions to science.

Lemaître's work convinced most astronomers that the universe was not unchanging, as Newton had thought.

Georges Lemaître

Belgian scientist Georges Lemaître (1894–1966) used Einstein's equations to show that the universe is expanding. Lemaître explained the relationship between the distances of galaxies and the speeds at which those galaxies are moving away from Earth. He proposed a hypothesis that was later developed into the currently accepted theory of the origin of the universe. He thought that if the universe was expanding, all matter must have been packed into a very small space—a "primeval atom"—at some time in the past.

11 Explain How did Lemaître's reasoning lead him to develop the concept of the "primeval atom"?

_____

_____

Edwin Hubble

American astronomer Edwin Hubble (1889–1953) was the first scientist to present observational evidence that supported the idea that the universe is expanding. Hubble observed a redshift in the light that was coming from distant galaxies. A **redshift** is an apparent shift toward longer (red) wavelengths of light in an object's spectrum. This shift is caused when the object moves away from an observer. His observations showed that most galaxies were moving away from Earth. Hubble also determined that the redshifts of galaxies depended on their distances from Earth. He discovered that the fainter and farther away a galaxy appeared, the greater its redshift. Therefore, the greater a galaxy's distance from Earth, the faster it is moving away from Earth.

Hubble's observations showed that the universe is expanding.

12 Explain How does the redshift of galaxies provide evidence that the universe is expanding?

_____

_____

George Gamow

George Gamow (1904–1968) outlined a theory that explained how elements formed in the universe. He knew that most of the visible matter in the universe is hydrogen and helium. Gamow and his student proposed that the isotopes of light elements, including hydrogen and helium, formed between 3 and 20 minutes after the universe began. In that brief period, no elements heavier than beryllium were formed. Heavier elements formed later in stars.

Gamow helped develop a mathematical explanation for the formation of light elements in the universe.

Getting Started with a Bang!

According to the Big Bang theory, the universe began with a rapid expansion.

What evidence supports the Big Bang theory?

The **Big Bang theory** states that the universe began with a tremendous expansion 13–15 billion years ago. It is the currently accepted scientific theory of the origin of the universe. According to the Big Bang theory, all of the contents of the universe existed in a tiny volume that suddenly began expanding in all directions. Scientific evidence that supports the Big Bang theory comes from several sources. Evidence includes the abundance of light elements in the universe, the redshift of galaxies, and the Cosmic Microwave Background (CMB).

Light Element Abundance

The Big Bang theory predicts certain percentages of light elements in the universe. These predictions are supported by data. The abundance of light elements in the early universe can be compared with the abundance of light elements in stars today. To do this, scientists study stars that are very far from Earth and in the early stages of development. Scientists analyze the spectral lines of these stars to determine the amounts of elements being produced within their cores. The percentages of light elements in these stars are very close to the theoretical values predicted by the Big Bang theory.

Active Reading

13 Identify As you read this page, underline the statements that describe the Big Bang theory.

Think Outside the Book

14 Claims • Evidence • Reasoning
Work with a partner to find out more about how scientific data provide evidence about the origin of the universe. Write an essay summarizing the evidence that supports the claim that the universe began with a big bang and has been expanding ever since. Explain your reasoning.

The Redshift of Galaxies

The expansion of the universe also supports the Big Bang theory. Edwin Hubble found redshifts, such as the example shown at the upper right, in the spectra of the galaxies he observed. The redshifts show that galaxies are moving away from Earth in all directions. Also, galaxies are moving at speeds proportional to their distance from Earth. The farther away a galaxy is, the faster it is moving. Hubble concluded that the distances between galaxies and galaxy clusters have been increasing over time. Because galaxies are moving apart, they must have been closer together in the past. This is consistent with the idea that the universe has been expanding since the Big Bang.

The most distant galaxies in the universe are shown in the background of this photo.

Visualize It!

15 Predict Which galaxies in this photo will have the largest redshift? Explain your reasoning.

_____

_____

_____

_____

Cosmic Microwave Background

The early universe was made of very hot particles. These particles absorbed and emitted visible and ultraviolet radiation. The universe cooled rapidly as it expanded. The radiation also spread out and cooled. Its wavelengths stretched into the microwave range. The universe today should be filled with traces of this early radiation, called the **Cosmic Microwave Background (CMB).**

The CMB can be detected by infrared and radio telescopes. In 1965, radio engineers Arno Penzias and Robert Wilson were using an antenna that transmitted telephone calls to orbiting satellites. They noticed a faint background signal from every direction in the sky. They discovered that they were picking up the CMB. The temperature of the radiation is a very cold 2.73 K. This temperature is similar to what scientists predicted the temperature would be after the universe cooled for billions of years.

Visualize It!

16 Explain What questions did scientists ask about the universe when they began studying data such as the WMAP temperature map?

_____

_____

_____

_____

_____

_____

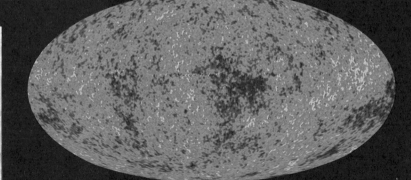

This sky map was made by NASA's WMAP (Wilkinson Microwave Anisotropy Probe) mission. It shows the temperatures of the CMB increasing from dark blue to red. Small temperature differences indicate the first major structures in the universe, such as galaxies and superclusters.

© Houghton Mifflin Harcourt Publishing Company • Image Credits: (tr) ©ESA, NASA, J.-P. Kneib (Caltech/Observatoire Midi-Pyrénées) and R. Ellis (Caltech); (br) ©NASA/WMAP Science Team

In the Beginning...

What were the conditions of the early universe?

Immediately after the Big Bang, the universe was no bigger than an atom. It was extremely dense and hot. It had an estimated temperature of about 1×10^{32} K. Matter and energy began to spread out rapidly in all directions. The temperature and density of the universe decreased quickly. This brief period of very rapid expansion immediately after the Big Bang is called *inflation*. Inflation lasted only a few fractions of a second. After inflation, the universe began to expand at a slower rate.

Scientists use particle accelerators to model the conditions in the early universe. Data from experiments have provided evidence of the particles that first existed in the universe. Scientists are also trying to find out how those particles combined to form atoms.

Active Reading

17 Identify As you read, underline the conditions that existed at the very beginning of the universe.

Scientists use particle accelerators to model conditions that existed during the Big Bang. The image to left shows a high-energy particle collision, similar to collisions scientists think happened during the Big Bang.

Inquiry

18 Compare How does a model of the Big Bang differ from the actual event?

_____

_____

_____

_____

_____

This is an artist's concept of how the universe may have looked when the first stars were forming some 200 million years after the Big Bang.

How can scientists estimate the age of the universe?

You can use the speed of a car to determine the time it takes the car to reach its current position from its starting point. Similarly, scientists can estimate the age of the universe by using the present rate of expansion of the universe. To determine this rate, scientists measure how fast distant galaxies are moving away from Earth. Current data show that the rate of expansion is increasing, or accelerating. Scientists use the present rate of expansion to estimate past rates of expansion. Then, they use these rates to determine the distances between galaxies in the early stages of the universe. Current estimates place the age of the universe at between 13 and 15 billion years old. The most widely accepted estimate is 13.75 billion years.

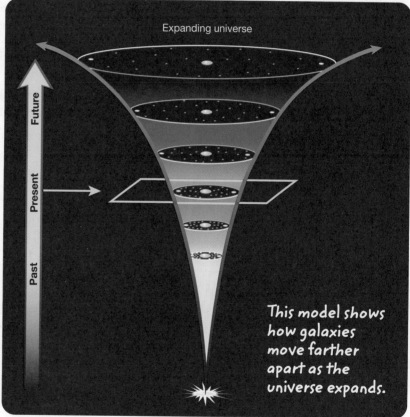

This model shows how galaxies move farther apart as the universe expands.

19 Explain How do scientists use the rates of expansion of the universe to estimate the age of the universe?

_____

_____

_____

_____

Visual Summary

The **Origin** of the **Universe**

To complete this summary, circle the correct word. Then, use the key below to check your answers. You can use this page to review the main concepts of the lesson.

Large-scale structures make up the universe.

20 A supercluster / solar system is made up of many galaxies.

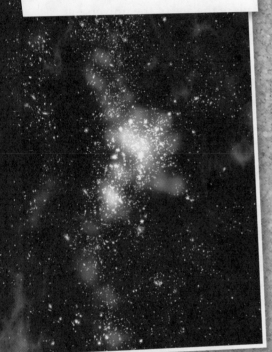

Evidence indicates that the universe is expanding in all directions.

21 Albert Einstein / Edwin Hubble was the first scientist to discover observational evidence that supported the concept of an expanding universe.

The Big Bang theory is the most widely accepted scientific theory about the origin of the universe.

22 The Big Bang theory is supported by the abundance of heavy / light elements in the universe.

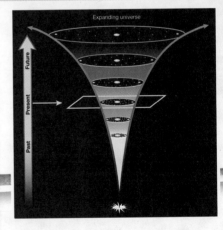

Answers: 20. supercluster; 21. Edwin Hubble; 22. light

23 Summarize Relate the contributions of scientists to our understanding of the universe. Include the names of at least two scientists and how their research had an impact on scientific thought about the universe.

36 Unit 1 The Universe and Our Solar System

© Houghton Mifflin Harcourt Publishing Company • Image Credits: (l) ©NASA

Lesson Review

Vocabulary

Fill in the blanks with the terms that best complete the following sentences.

1 According to the _____, the universe began as a tiny volume that suddenly and rapidly began expanding.

2 The _____ _____ is the remnant of the early radiation that filled the universe.

3 The _____ is space and all energy and matter in it.

4 A _____ is an apparent shift toward longer wavelengths of light caused when an object moves away from an observer.

Key Concepts

5 Describe Which statement best describes how scientific thought about the universe has changed over time? Circle your answer.

A. Scientists now know that Earth, not the sun, is the center of the universe.

B. Scientists now know that the universe changes over time rather than remaining unchanging.

C. Scientists now know that a solar system, not a star, is the largest structure in the universe.

D. Scientists now know that the universe was made of only matter, not matter and energy.

6 Identify Who discovered that hydrogen and helium formed during the early stages of the Big Bang?

_____

7 Describe What was Georges Lemaître's major contribution to the current understanding of the universe?

_____
_____
_____

Critical Thinking

Use the map to answer the following question.

8 Apply What does this map of the CMB show about radiation from the Big Bang? Describe the evidence that supports your claim and explain your reasoning.

_____
_____
_____
_____

9 Summarize What evidence other than the CMB provides support for the Big Bang theory?

_____
_____
_____
_____
_____
_____

10 Explain How does Newton's law of universal gravitation help scientists describe the universe?

_____
_____
_____
_____
_____
_____
_____
_____

My Notes

Mean, Median, Mode, and Range

You can analyze both the measures of central tendency and the variability of data using mean, median, mode, and range.

Tutorial

Orbit eccentricity measures how oval-shaped the elliptical orbit is. The closer a value is to 0, the closer the orbit is to a circle. Examine the eccentricity values below.

Orbit Eccentricities of Planets in the Solar System			
Mercury	0.205	**Jupiter**	0.049
Venus	0.007	**Saturn**	0.057
Earth	0.017	**Uranus**	0.046
Mars	0.094	**Neptune**	0.011

Mean The mean is the sum of all of the values in a data set divided by the total number of values in the data set. The mean is also called the *average*.	$$\frac{0.007 + 0.011 + 0.017 + 0.046 + 0.049 + 0.057 + 0.094 + 0.205}{8}$$ **1** Add up all of the values. **2** Divide the sum by the number of values. **mean** = 0.061
Median The median is the value of the middle item when data are arranged in numerical order. If there is an odd number of values, the median is the middle value. If there is an even number of values, the median is the mean of the two middle values.	0.007 0.011 0.017 0.046 0.049 0.057 0.094 0.205 ⟶ ⟵ **1** Order the values. **2** The median is the middle value if there is an odd number of values. If there is an even number of values, calculate the mean of the two middle values. **median** = 0.0475
Mode The mode is the value or values that occur most frequently in a data set. Order the values to find the mode. If all values occur with the same frequency, the data set is said to have no mode.	0.007 0.011 0.017 0.046 0.049 0.057 0.094 0.205 **1** Order the values. **2** Find the value or values that occur most frequently. **mode** = none
Range The range is the difference between the greatest value and the least value of a data set.	0.205 − 0.007 **1** Subtract the least value from the greatest value. **range** = 0.198

You Try It!

The data table below shows the masses and densities of the planets.

Mass and Density of the Planets		
	Mass (× 10²⁴ kg)	**Density (g/cm³)**
Mercury	0.33	5.43
Venus	4.87	5.24
Earth	5.97	5.52
Mars	0.64	3.34
Jupiter	1,899	1.33
Saturn	568	0.69
Uranus	87	1.27
Neptune	102	1.64

The "Mass" column header reads **Mass (× 10^{24} kg)**.

①

Using Formulas Find the mean, median, mode, and range for the mass of the planets. How do these masses compare to the mass of Earth?

②

Using Formulas Find the mean, median, mode, and range for the density of the planets.

③

Analyzing Data Find the mean density of the inner planets (Mercury through Mars). Find the mean density of the outer planets (Jupiter through Neptune). Compare these values.

Mean density of the inner planets: _____

Mean density of the outer planets: _____

Comparison:

_____

④

Evaluating Data The mean mass of the outer planets is 225 times greater than the mean mass of the inner planets. How does this comparison and the comparison of mean densities support the use of the term *gas giants* to describe the outer planets? Explain your reasoning.

_____

_____

Gravity and the Solar System

ESSENTIAL QUESTION

Why is gravity important in the solar system?

By the end of this lesson, you should be able to explain the role that gravity played in the formation of the solar system and in determining the motion of the planets.

Gravity keeps objects, such as these satellites, in orbit around Earth. Gravity also affects the way in which planets move and how they are formed.

 S6E1.d Gravity, inertia, and the motion of objects

© Houghton Mifflin Harcourt Publishing Company • Image Credits: ©NASA/National Geographic/Getty Images

Lesson Labs

Quick Labs
- Gravity's Effect
- Gravity and the Orbit of a Planet

Exploration Lab
- Weights on Different Celestial Bodies

Engage Your Brain

1 Predict Check T or F to show whether you think each statement is true or false.

T F

☐ ☐ Gravity keeps the planets in orbit around the sun.

☐ ☐ The planets follow circular paths around the sun.

☐ ☐ Sir Isaac Newton was the first scientist to describe how the force of gravity behaved.

☐ ☐ The sun formed in the center of the solar system.

☐ ☐ The terrestrial planets and the gas giant planets formed from the same material.

2 Draw In the space below, draw what you think the solar system looked like before the planets formed.

Active Reading

3 Synthesize You can often define an unknown word if you know the meaning of its word parts. Use the word parts and sentence below to make an educated guess about the meaning of the word *protostellar*.

Word part	Meaning
proto-	first
-stellar	of or having to do with a star or stars

Example sentence
The <u>protostellar</u> disk formed after the collapse of the solar nebula.

protostellar:

_____

_____

Vocabulary Terms

- gravity
- orbit
- aphelion
- perihelion
- centripetal force
- solar nebula
- planetesimal

4 Apply This list contains the key terms you'll learn in this section. As you read, circle the definition of each term.

Gravity

What is gravity?

5 Identify Underline the definition of and the effects of gravity.

Gravity is a force of attraction between objects that is due to their masses and the distances between them. Every object in the universe pulls on every other object. Objects with greater masses have a greater force of attraction than objects with lesser masses have. Objects that are close together have a greater force of attraction than objects that are far apart have.

Gravity is the weakest force in nature. A toy magnet can overcome the gravitational force acting on a paperclip by the entire mass of Earth. Yet, gravity is one of the most important forces in the universe. It accounts for the formation of planets, stars, and galaxies. It also keeps smaller bodies in orbit around larger bodies. An **orbit** is the path that a body follows as it travels around another body in space. For example, the moon orbits Earth, and Earth orbits the sun.

When astronauts are in orbit, Earth's gravity still pulls them downward toward the planet. However, they appear to be weightless and floating. They "float" because everything around them is falling at the same speed.

What are Kepler's laws?

The 16th-century Polish astronomer Nicolaus Copernicus (nik•uh•LAY•uhs koh•PER•nuh•kuhs) (1473–1543) changed our view of the solar system. He discovered that the motions of the planets could be best explained if the planets orbited the sun. But, like astronomers who came before him, Copernicus thought the planets followed circular paths around the sun.

Danish astronomer Tycho Brahe (TY•koh BRAH) (1546–1601) built what was at the time the world's largest observatory. Tycho used special instruments to measure the motions of the planets. His measurements were made over a period of 20 years and were very accurate. Using Tycho's data, Johannes Kepler (yoh•HAH•nuhs KEP•luhr) (1571–1630) made discoveries about the motions of the planets. We call these *Kepler's laws of planetary motion*.

Kepler found that objects that orbit the sun follow elliptical orbits. When an object follows an elliptical orbit around the sun, there is one point, called **aphelion** (uh•FEE•lee•uhn), where the object is farthest from the sun. There is also a point, called **perihelion** (perh•uh•HEE•lee•uhn), where the object is closest to the sun. Today, we know that the orbits of the planets are only slightly elliptical. However, the orbits of objects such as Pluto and comets are highly elliptical.

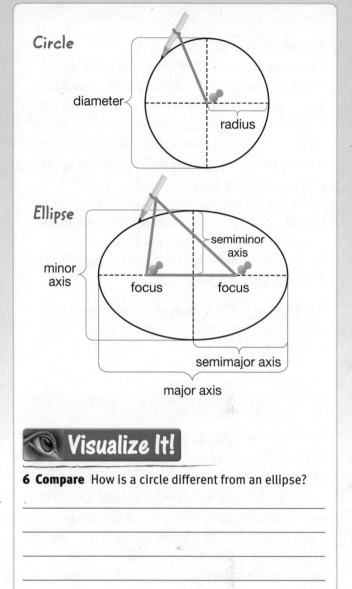

Circle

diameter

radius

Ellipse

semiminor axis

minor axis

focus   focus

semimajor axis

major axis

Visualize It!

6 Compare How is a circle different from an ellipse?

_____

_____

_____

_____

Kepler's First Law

Kepler's careful plotting of the orbit of Mars kept showing Mars's orbit to be a deformed circle. It took Kepler eight years to realize that this shape was an ellipse. This clue led Kepler to propose elliptical orbits for the planets. Kepler placed the sun at one of the foci of the ellipse. This is Kepler's first law.

Active Reading **7 Contrast** What is the difference between Copernicus's and Kepler's description of planetary orbits?

_____

_____

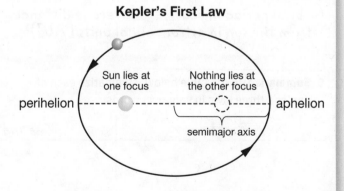

Kepler's First Law

Sun lies at one focus

Nothing lies at the other focus

perihelion

aphelion

semimajor axis

Each planet orbits the sun in an ellipse with the sun at one focus. (For clarity, the ellipse is exaggerated here.)

Kepler's Second Law

Using the shape of an ellipse, Kepler searched for other regularities in Tycho's data. He found that an amazing thing happens when a line is drawn from a planet to the sun's focus on the ellipse. At aphelion, its speed is slower. So, it sweeps out a narrow sector on the ellipse. At perihelion, the planet is moving faster. It sweeps out a thick sector on the ellipse. In the illustration, the areas of both the thin blue sector and the thick blue sector are exactly the same. Kepler found that this relationship is true for all of the planets. This is Kepler's second law.

Active Reading **8 Analyze** At which point does a planet move most slowly in its orbit, at aphelion or perihelion?

As a planet moves around its orbit, it sweeps out equal areas in equal times.

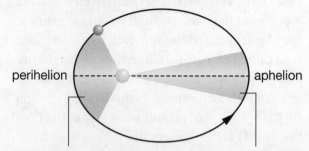

Kepler's Second Law

perihelion --------- aphelion

Near perihelion, a planet sweeps out an area that is short but wide.

Near aphelion, in an equal amount of time, a planet sweeps out an area that is long but narrow.

Kepler's Third Law

When Kepler looked at how long it took for the planets to orbit the sun and at the sizes of their orbits, he found another relationship. Kepler calculated the orbital period and the distance from the sun for the planets using Tycho's data. He discovered that the square of the orbital period was proportional to the cube of the planet's average distance from the sun. This law is true for each planet. This principle is Kepler's third law. When the units are years for the period and AU for the distance, the law can be written:

(orbital period in years)² = (average distance from the sun in astronomical units [AU])³

The square of the orbital period is proportional to the cube of the planet's average distance from the sun.

Kepler's Third Law

p^2 yrs = a^3 AU

perihelion -----a----- aphelion

9 Summarize In the table below, summarize each of Kepler's three laws in your own words.

First law	Second law	Third law

What is the law of universal gravitation?

Using Kepler's laws, Sir Isaac Newton (EYE•zuhk NOOT'n) became the first scientist to mathematically describe how the force of gravity behaved. How could Newton do this in the 1600s before the force could be measured in a laboratory? He reasoned that gravity was the same force that accounted for both the fall of an apple from a tree and the movement of the moon around Earth.

In 1687, Newton formulated the *law of universal gravitation*. The law of universal gravitation states that all objects in the universe attract each other through gravitational force. The strength of this force depends on the product of the masses of the objects. Therefore, the gravity between objects increases as the masses of the objects increase. Gravitational force is also inversely proportional to the square of the distance between the objects. Stated another way this means that as the distance between two objects increases, the force of gravity decreases.

Sir Isaac Newton
(1642–1727)

 Do the Math

Newton's law of universal gravitation says that the force of gravity:
* increases as the masses of the objects increase and
* decreases as the distance between the objects increases

In these examples, M = mass, d = distance, and F = the force of gravity exerted by two bodies.

Sample Problems

A. In the example below, when two balls have masses of M and the distance between them is d, then the force of gravity is F. If the mass of each ball is increased to 2M (to the right) and the distance stays the same, then the force of gravity increases to 4F.

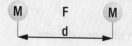

B. In this example, we start out again with a distance of d and masses of M, and the force of gravity is F. If the distance is decreased to ½ d, then the force of gravity increases to 4F.

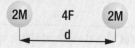

You Try It

Recall that M = mass, d = distance, and F = the force of gravity exerted by two bodies.

10 Calculate Compare the example below to the sample problems. What would the force of gravity be in the example below? Explain your reasoning.

2M   2d   2M

_____

_____

_____

_____

_____

How does gravity affect planetary motion?

The illustrations on this page will help you understand planetary motion. In the illustration at the right, a girl is swinging a ball around her head. The ball is attached to a string. The girl is exerting a force on the string that causes the ball to move in a circular path. The inward force that causes an object to move in a circular path is called **centripetal** (sehn•TRIP•ih•tuhl) **force**.

In the illustration at center, we see that if the string breaks, the ball will move off in a straight line. This is due to the ball's inertia. Inertia is the tendency of an object in motion to continue moving in a straight line unless acted upon by another force.

However, when the string is intact, a force is pulling the ball inward. This force keeps the ball from flying off and moving in a straight line. This force is centripetal force.

In the illustration below, you see that the planets orbit the sun. A force must be preventing the planets from moving out of their orbits and into a straight line. The sun's gravity is the force that keeps the planets moving in orbit around the sun.

As the girl swings the ball, she is exerting a force on the string that causes the ball to move in a circular path.

Just as the string is pulling the ball inward, gravity is keeping the planets in orbit around the sun.

Centripetal force pulls the ball inward, which causes the ball to move in a curved path.

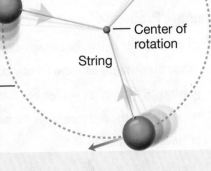

direction centripetal force pulls the ball

direction ball would move if string broke —

Center of rotation

String

path ball takes when — moving around the center of rotation

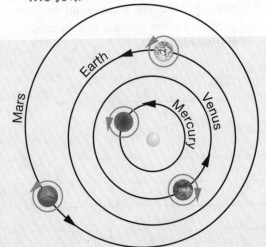

Earth
Mars
Venus
Mercury

11 Model Create a model to explain how gravity and inertia interact in governing the motion of planets in the solar system.

_____

_____

_____

_____

Collapse

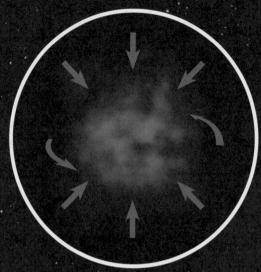

A cloud of dust and gas collapsed 4.6 billion years ago, then began to spin. It may have spun around its axis of rotation once every million years.

How did the solar system form?

The formation of the solar system is thought to have begun 4.6 billion years ago when a cloud of dust and gas collapsed. This cloud, from which the solar system formed, is called the **solar nebula** (SOH•ler NEB•yuh•luh). In a nebula, the inward pull of gravity is balanced by the outward push of gas pressure in the cloud. Scientists think that an outside force, perhaps the explosion of a nearby star, caused the solar nebula to compress and then to contract under its own gravity. It was in a single region of the nebula, which was perhaps several light-years across, that the solar system formed. The sun probably formed from a region that had a mass that was slightly greater than today's mass of the sun and planets.

Active Reading **12 Define** What is the solar nebula?

_____

_____

A Protostellar Disk Formed from the Collapsed Solar Nebula

As a region of the solar nebula collapsed, gravity pulled most of the mass toward the center of the nebula. As the nebula contracted, it began to rotate. As the rotation grew faster, the nebula flattened out into a disk. This disk, which is called a *protostellar disk* (PROH•toh•stehl•er DISK), is where the central star, our sun, formed.

As a region of the solar nebula collapsed, it formed a slowly rotating protostellar disk.

The Sun Formed at the Center of the Protostellar Disk

As the protostellar disk continued to contract, most of the matter ended up in the center of the disk. Friction from matter that fell into the disk heated up its center to millions of degrees, eventually reaching its current temperature of 15,000,000 °C. This intense heat in a densely packed space caused the fusion of hydrogen atoms into helium atoms. The process of fusion released large amounts of energy. This release of energy caused outward pressure that again balanced the inward pull of gravity. As the gas and dust stopped collapsing, a star was born. In the case of the solar system, this star was the sun.

 Active Reading **13 Identify** How did the sun form?

_____

_____

_____

_____

_____

This is an artist's conception of what the protoplanetary disk in which the planets formed might have looked like.

Visualize It!

14 Describe Use the terms *planetesimal* and *protoplanetary disk* to describe the illustration above.

_____

_____

_____

_____

_____

_____

Planetesimals Formed in the Protoplanetary Disk

As the sun was forming, dust grains collided and stuck together. The resulting *dust granules* grew in size and increased in number. Over time, dust granules increased in size until they became roughly meter-sized bodies. Trillions of these bodies occurred in the protostellar disk. Collisions between these bodies formed larger bodies that were kilometers across. These larger bodies, from which planets formed, are called **planetesimals** (plan•ih•TES•uh•muhls). The protostellar disk had become the *protoplanetary disk*. The protoplanetary disk was the disk in which the planets formed.

Dust grains collided and stuck together.

Over time, dust granules grew to become meter-sized bodies.

Planetesimals formed from the collisions of meter-sized bodies.

Visualize It! (Inquiry)

15 Explain How can objects as small as dust grains become the building blocks of planets?

_____

_____

_____

_____

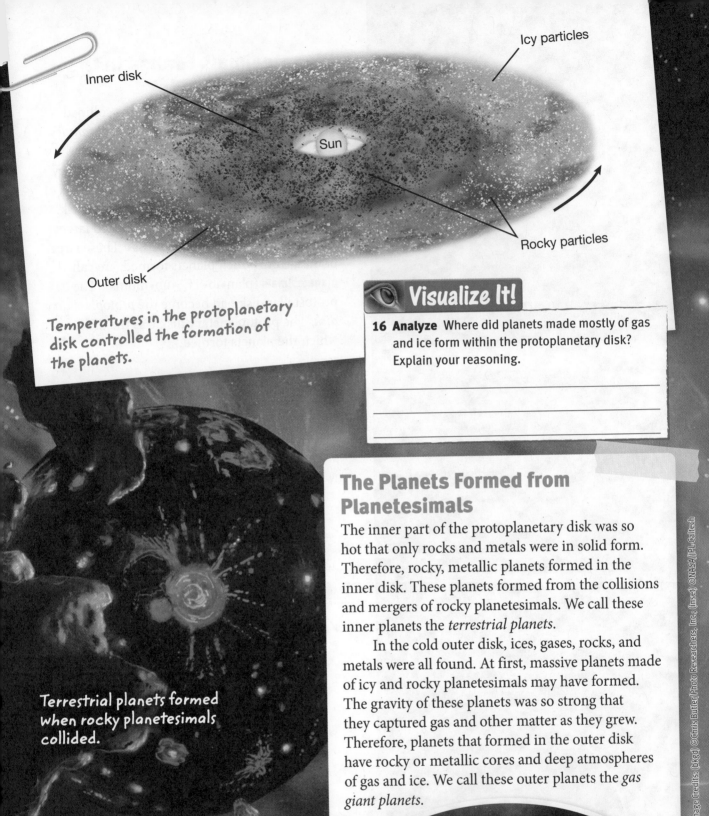

Icy particles

Inner disk

Sun

Rocky particles

Outer disk

Temperatures in the protoplanetary disk controlled the formation of the planets.

Visualize It!

16 Analyze Where did planets made mostly of gas and ice form within the protoplanetary disk? Explain your reasoning.

_____

_____

_____

The Planets Formed from Planetesimals

The inner part of the protoplanetary disk was so hot that only rocks and metals were in solid form. Therefore, rocky, metallic planets formed in the inner disk. These planets formed from the collisions and mergers of rocky planetesimals. We call these inner planets the *terrestrial planets*.

In the cold outer disk, ices, gases, rocks, and metals were all found. At first, massive planets made of icy and rocky planetesimals may have formed. The gravity of these planets was so strong that they captured gas and other matter as they grew. Therefore, planets that formed in the outer disk have rocky or metallic cores and deep atmospheres of gas and ice. We call these outer planets the *gas giant planets*.

Terrestrial planets formed when rocky planetesimals collided.

Gas giant planets captured gas and other matter in the area of their orbits.

17 Describe In the spaces on the left, describe Steps 2 and 4 in the formation of the solar system. In the spaces on the right, draw the last two steps in the formation of the solar system.

Steps in the Formation of the Solar System

Step 1 The Solar Nebula Collapses

A cloud of dust and gas collapses. The balance between the inward pull of gravity and the outward push of pressure in the cloud is upset. The collapsing cloud forms a rotating protostellar disk.

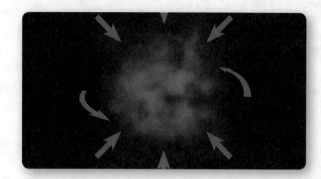

Step 2 The Sun Forms

_____

_____

_____

_____

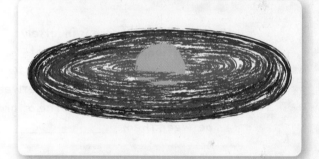

Step 3 Planetesimals Form

Dust grains stick together and form dust granules. Dust granules slowly increase in size until they become meter-sized objects. These meter-sized objects collide to form kilometer-sized objects called *planetesimals*.

Step 4 Planets Form

_____

_____

_____

_____

Visual Summary

To complete this summary, fill in the blank with the correct word or phrase. Then use the key below to check your answers. You can use this page to review the main concepts of the lesson.

The Law of Universal Gravitation

Mass affects the force of gravity.

18 The strength of the force of gravity depends on the product of the _____ of two objects. Therefore, as the masses of two objects increase, the force that the objects exert on one another _____.

Distance affects the force of gravity.

19 Gravitational force is inversely proportional to the square of the _____ between two objects. Therefore, as the distance between two objects increases, the force of gravity between them _____.

Gravity affects planetary motion.

20 The sun exerts a _____, indicated by line B, on a planet so that at point C it is moving around the sun in orbit instead of moving off in a _____ as shown at line A.

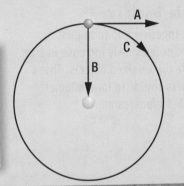

21 Explain In your own words, explain Newton's law of universal gravitation.

Lesson Review

Vocabulary

Fill in the blank with the term that best completes the following sentences.

1 Small bodies from which the planets formed are called _____

2 The path that a body follows as it travels around another body in space is its _____

3 The _____ is the cloud of gas and dust from which our solar system formed.

Key Concepts

4 Define In your own words, define the word *gravity*.

_____
_____
_____

5 Describe How did the sun form?

_____
_____
_____
_____
_____
_____
_____
_____

6 Describe How did planetesimals form?

_____
_____
_____
_____
_____
_____
_____

Critical Thinking

Use the illustration below to answer the following question.

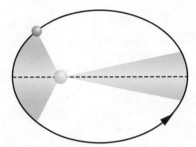

7 Identify What law is illustrated in this diagram?

_____

8 Claims • Evidence • Reasoning Summarize evidence to support the claim that gravity keeps the planets in orbit around the sun. Explain your reasoning.

_____
_____
_____
_____
_____
_____
_____

9 Explain How do temperature differences in the protoplanetary disk explain the arrangement of the planets in the solar system?

_____
_____
_____
_____
_____
_____

My Notes

The Terrestrial Planets

Mars

Earth

Venus

Mercury

ESSENTIAL QUESTION

What is known about the terrestrial planets?

By the end of this lesson, you should be able to describe some of the properties of the terrestrial planets and how the properties of Mercury, Venus, and Mars differ from the properties of Earth.

The terrestrial planets are the four planets that are closest to the sun. Distances between the planets shown here are not to scale.

sun

S6E1.c Planets in the solar system

🧠 Engage Your Brain

1 Define Circle the term that best completes the following sentences.

Venus/Earth/Mars is the largest terrestrial planet.

Mercury/Venus/Mars has clouds that rain sulfuric acid on the planet.

Huge dust storms sweep across the surface of *Mercury/Venus/Mars*.

Venus/Earth/Mars is the most geologically active of the terrestrial planets.

Mercury/Venus/Earth has the thinnest atmosphere of the terrestrial planets.

2 Identify What are properties of Earth that make it a special place in the solar system?

_____

_____

_____

_____

📖 Active Reading

3 Synthesize Many English words have their roots in other languages. Use the Latin words below to make an educated guess about the meaning of the word *astronomy*.

Latin word	Meaning
astrón	star
nomos	law

Example sentence
Some students who are interested in the night sky enter college to study <u>astronomy</u>.

astronomy:

_____

_____

Vocabulary Terms

• terrestrial planet
• astronomical unit

4 Apply As you learn the definition of each vocabulary term in this lesson, create your own definition or sketch to help you remember the meaning of the term.

Extreme to the Core

What are the terrestrial planets?

The **terrestrial planets** are the four small, dense, rocky planets that orbit closest to the sun. In order by distance from the sun, these planets are Mercury, Venus, Earth, and Mars. The terrestrial planets have similar compositions and consist of an outer crust, a central core, and a mantle that lies between the crust and core.

What is known about Mercury?

Mercury (MUR•kyuh•ree) is the planet about which we know the least. Until NASA's *Mariner 10* spacecraft flew by Mercury in 1974, the planet was seen as a blotchy, dark ball of rock. Today, scientists know that the planet's heavily cratered, moon-like surface is composed largely of volcanic rock and hides a massive iron core.

Mercury orbits only 0.39 AU from the sun. The letters *AU* stand for *astronomical unit*, which is the term astronomers use to measure distances in the solar system. One **astronomical unit** equals the average distance between the sun and Earth, or approximately 150 million km. Therefore, Mercury lies nearly halfway between the sun and Earth.

Active Reading

5 Identify As you read the text, underline important characteristics of the planet Mercury.

Statistics Table for Mercury

Distance from the sun	0.39 AU
Period of rotation (length of Mercury day)	58 days 15.5 h
Period of revolution (length of Mercury year)	88 days
Tilt of axis	0°
Diameter	4,879 km
Density	5.44 g/cm³
Surface temperature	-184 °C to 427 °C
Surface gravity	38% of Earth's gravity
Number of satellites	0

Although this may look like the moon, it is actually the heavily cratered surface of the planet Mercury.

Mercury Has the Most Extreme Temperature Range in the Solar System

On Earth, a day lasts 24 h. On Mercury, a day lasts almost 59 Earth days. What does this fact have to do with temperatures on Mercury? It means that temperatures on that part of Mercury's surface that is receiving sunlight can build for more than 29 days. When it is day on Mercury, temperatures can rise to 427 °C, a temperature that is hot enough to melt certain metals. It also means that temperatures on the part of Mercury's surface that is in darkness can fall for more than 29 days. When it is night on Mercury, temperatures can drop to –184 °C. This means that surface temperatures on Mercury can change by as much as 600 °C between day and night. This is the greatest difference between high and low temperatures in the solar system.

Mercury Has a Large Iron Core

Mercury is the smallest planet in the solar system. It has a diameter of only 4,879 km at its equator. Amazingly, Mercury's central core is thought to be around 3,600 km in diameter, which accounts for most of the planet's interior. Scientists originally thought that Mercury had a core of solid iron. However, by observing changes in Mercury's spin as it orbits the sun, astronomers now think that the core is at least partially molten. Why is the core so large? Some scientists think that Mercury may have been struck by another object in the distant past and lost most of the rock that surrounded the core. Other scientists think that long ago the sun vaporized the planet's surface and blasted it away into space.

Think Outside the Book

6 Plan You are an astronaut who will be exploring Mercury. What equipment would you take to Mercury to help you survive?

Mantle

Core

Crust

Visualize It! (Inquiry)

7 Estimate In the figure, you can see that Mercury's core makes up a large percentage of the planet. What percentage of the diameter of Mercury is inside the core?

a 26%

b 50%

c 74%

Harsh Planet

What is known about Venus?

Science-fiction writers once imagined Venus (VEE•nuhs) to be a humid planet with lush, tropical forests. Nothing could be further from the truth. On Venus, sulfuric acid rain falls on a surface that is not much different from the inside of an active volcano.

Venus Is Similar to Earth in Size and Mass

Venus has often been called "Earth's twin." At 12,104 km, the diameter of Venus is 95% the diameter of Earth. Venus's mass is around 80% of Earth's. And the gravity that you would experience on Venus is 89% of the gravity on Earth.

The rotation of Venus is different from the rotation of Earth. Earth has prograde rotation. *Prograde rotation* is the counterclockwise spin of a planet about its axis as seen from above the planet's north pole. Venus, however, has retrograde rotation. *Retrograde rotation* is the clockwise spin of a planet about its axis as seen from above its north pole.

Venus differs from Earth not only in the direction in which it spins on its axis. It takes more time for Venus to rotate once about its axis than it takes for the planet to revolve once around the sun. Venus has the slowest period of rotation in the solar system.

Venus has landforms such as highlands and plains, volcanoes, and impact craters.

Statistics Table for Venus

Distance from the sun	0.72 AU
Period of rotation	243 days (retrograde rotation)
Period of revolution	225 days
Tilt of axis	177.4°
Diameter	12,104 km
Density	5.20 g/cm³
Average surface temperature	465 °C
Surface gravity	89% of Earth's gravity
Number of satellites	0

Gula Mons volcano is approximately 300 km wide and 3 km high.

Impact crater Cunitz, which is 48.5 km wide, was named after Maria Cunitz, a 17th-century European astronomer and mathematician.

Venus Has Craters and Volcanoes

In 1990, the powerful radar beams of NASA's *Magellan* spacecraft pierced the dense atmosphere of Venus. This gave us our most detailed look ever at the planet's surface. There are 168 volcanoes on Venus that are larger than 100 km in diameter. Thousands of volcanoes have smaller diameters. Venus's surface is also cratered. These craters are as much as 280 km in diameter. The sizes and locations of the craters on Venus suggest that around 500 million years ago something happened to erase all of the planet's older craters. Scientists are still puzzled about how this occurred. But volcanic activity could have covered the surface of the planet in one huge outpouring of magma.

The Atmosphere of Venus Is Toxic

Venus may have started out like Earth, with oceans and water running across its surface. However, after billions of years of solar heating, Venus has become a harsh world. Surface temperatures on Venus are hotter than those on Mercury. Temperatures average around 465 °C. Over time, carbon dioxide gas has built up in the atmosphere. Sunlight that strikes Venus's surface warms the ground. However, carbon dioxide in the atmosphere traps this energy, which causes temperatures near the surface to remain high.

Sulfuric acid rains down onto Venus's surface, and the pressure of the atmosphere is at least 90 times that of Earth's atmosphere. No human—or machine—could survive for long under these conditions. Venus is a world that is off limits to human explorers and perhaps all but the hardiest robotic probes.

9 Contrast How is the landscape of Venus different from the landscape of Earth?

_____
_____
_____
_____
_____

Active Reading

10 Identify As you read the text, underline those factors that make Venus an unlikely place for life to exist.

© Houghton Mifflin Harcourt Publishing Company • Image Credits: ©Corbis

No Place Like Home

What is special about Earth?

As far as scientists know, Earth is the only planet in the solar system that has the combination of factors needed to support life. Life as we know it requires liquid water and an energy source. Earth has both. Earth's atmosphere contains the oxygen that animals need to breathe. Matter is continuously cycled between the environment and living things. And a number of ecosystems exist on Earth that different organisms can inhabit.

Earth Has Abundant Water and Life

Earth's vast liquid-water oceans and moderate temperatures provided the ideal conditions for life to emerge and flourish. Around 3.5 billion years ago, organisms that produced food by photosynthesis appeared in Earth's oceans. During the process of making food, these organisms produced oxygen. By 560 million years ago, more complex life forms arose that could use oxygen to release energy from food. Today, the total number of species of organisms that inhabit Earth is thought to be anywhere between 5 million and 30 million.

Active Reading

11 Identify As you read the text, underline characteristics that make Earth special.

Statistics Table for Earth	
Distance from the sun	1.0 AU
Period of rotation	23 h 56 min
Period of revolution	365.3 days
Tilt of axis	23.45°
Diameter	12,756 km
Density	5.52 g/cm³
Temperature	-89 °C to 58 °C
Surface gravity	100% of Earth's gravity
Number of satellites	1

From space, Earth presents an entirely different scene from that of the other terrestrial planets. Clouds in the atmosphere, blue bodies of water, and green landmasses are all clues to the fact that Earth is a special place.

Earth Is Geologically Active

Earth is the only terrestrial planet whose surface is divided into tectonic plates. These plates move around Earth's surface, which causes the continents to change positions over long periods of time. Tectonic plate motion, together with weathering and erosion, has erased most surface features older than 500 million years.

Humans Have Set Foot on the Moon

Between 1969 and 1972, 12 astronauts landed on the moon. They are the only humans to have set foot on another body in the solar system. They encountered a surface gravity that is only about one-sixth that of Earth. Because of the moon's lower gravity, astronauts could not walk normally. If they did, they would fly up in the air and fall over.

Like Mercury, the moon's surface is heavily cratered. It is estimated that about 500,000 craters larger than 1 km dot the moon. There are large dark areas on the moon's surface. These are plains of solidified lava. There are also light-colored areas. These are the lunar highlands.

The moon rotates about its axis in the same time it orbits Earth. Therefore, it keeps the same side facing Earth. During a lunar day, which is a little more than 27 Earth days, the daytime surface temperature can reach 127 °C. The nighttime surface temperature can fall to −173 °C.

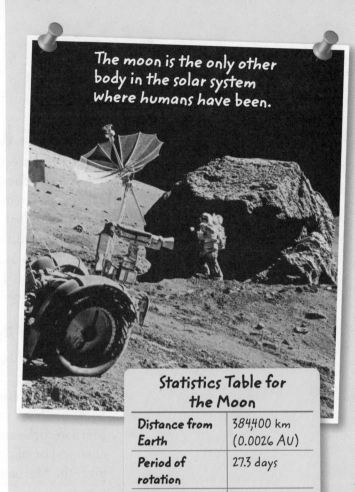

The moon is the only other body in the solar system where humans have been.

Statistics Table for the Moon

Distance from Earth	384,400 km (0.0026 AU)
Period of rotation	27.3 days
Period of revolution	27.3 days
Axial tilt	1.5°
Diameter	3,476 km
Density	3.34 g/cm³
Temperature	−173°C to 127°C
Surface gravity	16.5% of Earth's gravity

12 Identify In the image, circle any signs of life that you see.

Is It Alive?

What is known about Mars?

A fleet of spacecraft is now in orbit around Mars (MARZ) studying the planet. Space rovers have also investigated the surface of Mars. These remote explorers have discovered a planet with an atmosphere that is 100 times thinner than Earth's and temperatures that are little different from the inside of a freezer. They have seen landforms on Mars that are larger than any found on Earth. And these unmanned voyagers have photographed surface features on Mars that are characteristic of erosion and deposition by water.

Mars Is a Rocky, Red Planet

The surface of Mars is better known than that of any other planet in the solar system except Earth. It is composed largely of dark volcanic rock. Rocks and boulders litter the surface of Mars. Some boulders can be as large as a house. A powdery dust covers Martian rocks and boulders. This dust is the product of the chemical breakdown of rocks rich in iron minerals. This is what gives the Martian soil its orange-red color.

Think Outside the Book

13 **Compare** Research the surface and atmospheric features of Mars. Compare these features with those of Earth. How do the two planets compare in terms of the ability to support life? Support your claim with evidence.

Statistics Table for Mars

Distance from the sun	1.52 AU
Period of rotation	24 h 37 min
Period of revolution	1.88 y
Tilt of axis	25.3°
Diameter	6,792 km
Density	3.93 g/cm³
Temperature	−140 °C to 20 °C
Surface gravity	37% of Earth's gravity
Number of satellites	2

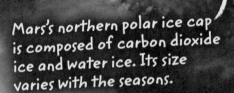

Mars's northern polar ice cap is composed of carbon dioxide ice and water ice. Its size varies with the seasons.

Mars Has Interesting Surface Features

The surface of Mars varies from hemisphere to hemisphere. The northern hemisphere appears to have been covered by lava flows. The southern hemisphere is heavily cratered.

Large volcanoes are found on Mars. At 27 km high and 600 km across, Olympus Mons (uh•LIM•puhs MAHNZ) is the largest volcano and mountain in the solar system. Mars also has very deep valleys and canyons. The canyon system Valles Marineris (VAL•less mar•uh•NAIR•iss) runs from west to east along the Martian equator. It is about 4,000 km long, 500 km wide, and up to 10 km deep. It is the largest canyon in the solar system.

Olympus Mons is the largest volcano in the solar system.

Mars Has a Thin Atmosphere

Mars has a very thin atmosphere that is thought to have been thicker in the past. Mars may have gradually lost its atmosphere to the solar wind. Or a body or bodies that collided with Mars may have caused much of the atmosphere to have been blown away.

Unlike Earth, Mars's atmosphere is composed mostly of carbon dioxide. During the Martian winter, temperatures at the planet's poles grow cold enough for carbon dioxide to freeze into a thin coating. During the summer, when temperatures grow warmer, this coating vanishes.

Winds on Mars can blow with enough force to pick up dust particles from the planet's surface. When this happens, giant dust storms can form. At times, these storms cover the entire planet.

Active Reading **14 Explain** What are two possible reasons why the atmosphere on Mars is so thin? Explain your reasoning.

_____

_____

_____

Hebes Chasma is a 6,000 m–deep depression that is located in the Valles Marineris region.

15 Compare Compare and contrast the physical properties of Mars to the physical properties of Earth.

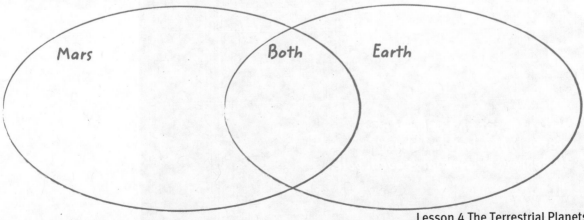

Mars   Both   Earth

Liquid Water Once Flowed on Mars

A number of features on Mars provide evidence that liquid water once flowed on the planet's surface. Many of these features have been struck by asteroids. These asteroid impacts have left behind craters that scientists can use to find the approximate dates of these features. Scientists estimate that many of these features, such as empty river basins, existed on Mars more than 3 billion years ago. Since then, little erosion has taken place that would cause these features to disappear.

In 2000, the *Mars Global Surveyor* took before-and-after images of a valley wall on Mars. Scientists observed the unmistakable trace of a liquid substance that had flowed out of the valley wall and into the valley. Since 2000, many similar features have been seen. The best explanation of these observations is that water is found beneath Mars's surface. At times, this water leaks out onto the Martian surface like spring water on Earth.

This image shows gullies on the wall of a Martian crater. Water that may be stored close to the Martian surface has run downhill into the crater.

16 Describe How do the features in the image at the right indicate that liquid water once flowed on Mars?

_____

_____

_____

_____

Water ice sits on the floor of a crater that is located about 20 degrees below Mars's north pole.

Roving Mars

NEW FRONTIERS

The Mars Exploration Rovers *Spirit* and *Opportunity* landed safely on Mars in January 2004. These robotic geologists were sent to find out if Mars ever had water. They found landforms shaped by past water activity as well as evidence of past groundwater. The last communication from *Spirit* was received in 2010. *Opportunity* was still exploring Mars in 2017.

Curiosity

Curiosity landed on Mars in 2012 to find out if Mars could have once supported life. It has been exploring ever since then and has found the ingredients needed to support life in some of Mars's rocks.

Testing the Rovers on Earth
Before leaving Earth, the rovers were tested under conditions that were similar to those that they would encounter on the Martian surface.

Collecting Data on Mars
The Mars rover **Spirit** took this picture of itself collecting data from the Martian surface.

Extend

Inquiry

17 Infer What advantages would a robotic explorer have over a manned mission to Mars? Explain your reasoning.

18 Hypothesize What kind of evidence would the Mars Exploration Rovers be looking for that indicates water once flowed on Mars?

Visual Summary

To complete this summary, write the answers to the questions on the lines. Then use the key below to check your answers. You can use this page to review the main concepts of the lesson.

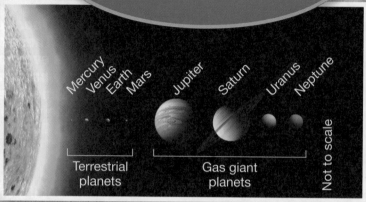

Properties of Terrestrial Planets

Mercury Venus Earth Mars Jupiter Saturn Uranus Neptune

Terrestrial planets

Gas giant planets

Not to scale

Mercury orbits near the sun.

19 Why do temperatures on Mercury vary so much?

_____
_____
_____

Venus is covered with clouds.

20 Why is Venus's surface temperature so high?

_____
_____
_____

Earth has abundant life.

21 What factors support life on Earth?

_____
_____

Mars is a rocky planet.

22 What makes up the surface of Mars?

_____
_____
_____

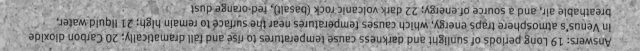

Answers: 19 Long periods of sunlight and darkness cause temperatures to rise and fall dramatically; 20 Carbon dioxide in Venus's atmosphere traps energy, which causes temperatures near the surface to remain high; 21 liquid water, breathable air, and a source of energy; 22 dark volcanic rock (basalt), red-orange dust

23 **Compare** How are important properties of Mercury, Venus, and Mars different from important properties of Earth?

Lesson Review

Vocabulary

Fill in the blanks with the terms that best complete the following sentences.

1 The _____ are the dense planets nearest the sun.

2 An _____ is equal to the distance between the sun and Earth.

Key Concepts

In the following table, write the name of the correct planet next to the property of that planet.

Properties	Planet
3 Identify Which planet has the highest surface temperature in the solar system?	
4 Identify Which planet has very large dust storms?	
5 Identify Which planet is the most heavily cratered of the terrestrial planets?	
6 Identify Which planet has the highest surface gravity of the terrestrial planets?	

7 Explain What is the difference between prograde rotation and retrograde rotation?

_____

_____

_____

8 Describe What characteristics of Venus's atmosphere make the planet so harsh?

_____

_____

_____

Critical Thinking

Use this table to answer the following questions.

Planet	Period of rotation	Period of revolution
Mercury	58 days 15.5 h	88 days
Venus	243 days (retrograde rotation)	225 days
Earth	23 h 56 min	365.3 days
Mars	24 h 37 min	1.88 y

9 Analyze Which planet rotates most slowly about its axis?

_____

10 Analyze Which planet revolves around the sun in less time than it rotates around its axis?

_____

11 Analyze Which planet revolves around the sun in the shortest amount of time?

_____

12 Claims · Evidence · Reasoning Make a claim about the relationship between a planet's temperature and its ability to support life. Support your claim with evidence and explain your reasoning.

_____

_____

_____

_____

_____

_____

_____

_____

My Notes

The Gas Giant Planets

ESSENTIAL QUESTION

What is known about the gas giant planets?

By the end of this lesson, you should be able to describe some of the properties of the gas giant planets and how these properties differ from the physical properties of Earth.

The gas giant planets are the four planets that orbit farthest from the sun. Distances between the planets shown here are not to scale.

Neptune

Uranus

Saturn

Jupiter

S6E1.c Planets in the solar system

Engage Your Brain

1 Predict Circle the term that best completes the following sentences.

Jupiter/Saturn/Uranus is the largest planet in the solar system.

Jupiter/Uranus/Neptune has the strongest winds in the solar system.

Saturn/Uranus/Neptune has the largest ring system of the gas giant planets.

Jupiter/Saturn/Neptune has more moons than any other planet in the solar system.

Jupiter/Uranus/Neptune is tilted on its side as it orbits the sun.

2 Identify What are the objects that circle Saturn? What do you think they are made of?

_____

_____

_____

Active Reading

3 Apply Many scientific words, such as *gas*, also have everyday meanings. Use context clues to write your own definition for each meaning of the word *gas*.

Example sentence
Vehicles, such as cars, trucks, and buses, use gas as a fuel.

gas:

_____

_____

Example sentence
Gas is one of the three common states of matter.

gas:

_____

_____

_____

Vocabulary Terms
- gas giant
- planetary ring

4 Apply This list contains the key terms you'll learn in this section. As you read, circle the definition of each term.

A Giant Among

Jupiter's high winds circle the planet and cause cloud bands to form. Storms, such as the Great Red Spot shown here, form between the cloud bands.

Ganymede

Callisto

Statistics Table for Jupiter	
Distance from the sun	5.20 AU
Period of rotation	9 h 55 min
Period of revolution	11.86 y
Tilt of axis	3.13°
Diameter	142,984 km
Density	1.33 g/cm³
Mean surface temperature	−145 °C
Surface gravity	253% of Earth's gravity
Number of known satellites	62

Active Reading

5 Identify As you read the text, underline important physical properties of the planet Jupiter.

What is a gas giant planet?

Jupiter, Saturn, Uranus, and Neptune are the gas giant planets. They orbit far from the sun. **Gas giants** have deep, massive gas atmospheres, which are made up mostly of hydrogen and helium. These gases become denser the deeper you travel inside. All of the gas giants are large. Neptune, the smallest gas giant planet, is big enough to hold 60 Earths within its volume. The gas giant planets are cold. Mean surface temperatures range from −145 °C on Jupiter to −220 °C on Neptune.

What is known about Jupiter?

Jupiter (JOO•pih•ter) is the largest planet in the solar system. Its volume can contain more than 900 Earths. Jupiter is also the most massive planet. Its mass is twice that of the other seven planets combined. Jupiter has the highest surface gravity in the solar system at 253% that of Earth. And, although all of the gas giant planets rotate rapidly, Jupiter rotates the fastest of all. Its period of rotation is just under 10 h. Wind speeds on Jupiter are high. They can reach 540 km/h. By contrast, Earth's wind speed record is 372 km/h.

Giants!

Europa

Io

Io, Europa, Callisto, and Ganymede are Jupiter's largest moons. All four moons were named for figures in Greek mythology.

Huge Storms Travel Across Jupiter's Surface

Jupiter has some of the strangest weather conditions in the solar system. The winds on Jupiter circle the planet. Clouds are stretched into bands that run from east to west. Storms appear as white or red spots between cloud bands. The best known of these storms is the Great Red Spot. The east–west width of this storm is three times the diameter of Earth. Incredibly, this storm has been observed by astronomers on Earth for the past 350 years.

Jupiter Has the Most Moons

More than 60 moons have been discovered orbiting Jupiter. This is the greatest number of moons to orbit any planet. Jupiter's moons Io (EYE•oh), Europa (yu•ROH•puh), Callisto (kuh•LIS•toh), and Ganymede (GAN•uh•meed) are particularly large. In fact, Ganymede is larger than the planet Mercury.

Jupiter's moon Io is the most volcanically active place in the solar system. There are at least 400 active volcanoes on Io's surface. Jupiter's gravity tugs and pulls on Io. This causes the interior of Io to reach the temperature at which it melts. Lava erupts from Io's volcanoes, which throw tremendous geysers of sulfur compounds into space. Over time, the orbit of Io has become a ring of ejected gases that is visible to the Hubble Space Telescope.

Jupiter's moon Europa has an icy surface. Recent evidence suggests that an ocean of liquid water may lie beneath this surface. Because liquid water is essential for life, some scientists are hopeful that future spacecraft may discover life inside Europa.

6 Apply Io, Europa, Callisto, and Ganymede are known as the *Galilean moons*. The astronomer Galileo discovered these moons using one of the first telescopes. Why do you think that the Galilean moons were the first objects to be discovered with a telescope? Explain your reasoning.

_____

_____

_____

Think Outside the Book

7 Model Select one of the following topics about weather on Jupiter to research: belts and zones; jet streams; storms. Present your findings to the rest of the class in the form of a model. Your model may be handcrafted, or may be an art piece, or may be a computer presentation.

King of the Rings!

What is known about Saturn?

Saturn (SAT•ern) is a near-twin to Jupiter. It is the second-largest gas giant planet and is made mostly of hydrogen and helium. About 800 Earths could fit inside the volume of Saturn. Amazingly, the planet's density is less than that of water.

Saturn Has a Large Ring System

The planetary ring system that circles Saturn's equator is the planet's most spectacular feature. A **planetary ring** is a disk of material that circles a planet and consists of orbiting particles. Saturn's ring system has many individual rings that form complex bands. Between bands are gaps that may be occupied by moons.

Saturn's rings span up to hundreds of kilometers in width, but they are only a few kilometers thick. They consist of trillions of small, icy bodies that are a few millimeters to several hundred meters in size. The rings are mostly pieces left over from the collision of Saturn's moons with comets and asteroids.

Active Reading

8 Identify As you read the text, underline important physical properties about the planet Saturn.

Statistics Table for Saturn

Distance from the sun	9.58 AU
Period of rotation	10 h 39 min
Period of revolution	29.5 y
Tilt of axis	26.73°
Diameter	120,536 km
Density	0.69 g/cm³
Mean surface temperature	−180 °C
Surface gravity	106% of Earth's gravity
Number of known satellites	53

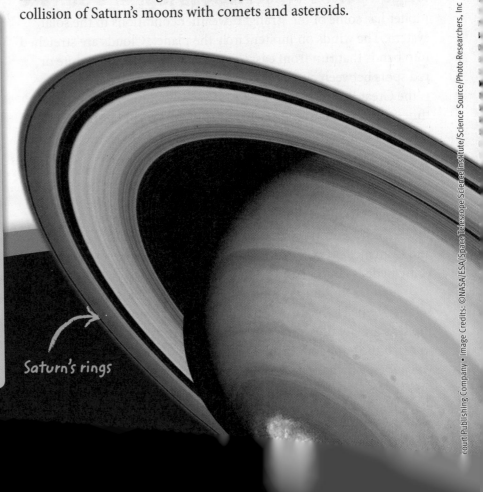

Saturn's rings

court Publishing Company • Image Credits: ©NASA/ESA/Space Telescope Science Institute/Science Source/Photo Researchers, Inc

Saturn's Moon Enceladus Has Water Geysers

In the inner solar system, liquid rock erupts from volcanoes. In some parts of the outer solar system, liquid water erupts from volcanoes. When NASA's *Cassini* spacecraft explored Saturn's moon Enceladus (en•SEL•uh•duhs), it found an icy surface. Scientists believe that Enceladus has a liquid interior beneath this icy surface. Liquid water flows up through cracks in the moon's surface. It either freezes at the surface or forms spectacular water geysers. These geysers are the largest in the solar system.

Saturn's Moon Titan Has a Dense Atmosphere

Titan (TYT'in), the largest moon of Saturn, has an atmosphere that is denser than Earth's. The moon's atmosphere is composed mostly of nitrogen and has traces of compounds such as methane and ethane. Methane clouds form in Titan's atmosphere. From these clouds, methane rain may fall. Unlike Earth, Titan has a crust of ice, which is frozen at a temperature of −180 °C.

In 2005, the *Huygens* (HY•guhnz) Titan probe descended through Titan's atmosphere. It took pictures of a surface with lakes and ponds. The liquid that fills these lakes and ponds is mostly methane.

9 Explain In your own words, write a caption for this illustration of Saturn's moon Enceladus.

_____

_____

_____

Particles that make up Saturn's ring system

Cassini Division in Saturn's ring system

10 Describe Complete this table by writing a description of each structure in Saturn's ring system.

Structure	Description
ring	
gap	
ring particles	

© Houghton Mifflin Harcourt Publishing Company • Image Credits: (bkgd) ©NASA/ESA/Space Telescope Science Institute/Science Source/Photo Researchers, Inc; (t) ©John R. Foster/Photo Researchers, Inc.; (bl) ©NASA/JPL/Space Science Institute; (br) ©Digital Vision/Getty Images

Just Rollin' Along

How is Uranus unique?

11 Identify As you read the text, underline important physical properties of the planet Uranus.

The atmosphere of Uranus (YUR•uh•nuhs) is composed mostly of hydrogen and helium. However, the atmosphere also contains methane. The methane in Uranus's atmosphere absorbs red light, which gives the planet a blue-green color.

Uranus Is a Tilted World

Uranus's axis of rotation is tilted almost 98°. This means that unlike any other planet in the solar system, Uranus is tilted on its side as it orbits the sun. The planet's 27 moons all orbit Uranus's equator, just like the moons of other planets do. The ring system of Uranus also orbits the equator. Scientists are not sure what event caused Uranus's odd axial tilt. But computer models of the four gas giant planets as they were forming may offer an explanation. The huge gravities of Jupiter and Saturn may have caused the orbits of Uranus and Neptune to change. There may also have been many close encounters between Uranus and Neptune that could have tilted the axis of Uranus.

Statistics Table for Uranus

Distance from the sun	19.2 AU
Period of rotation	17 h 24 min (retrograde)
Period of revolution	84 y
Tilt of axis	97.8°
Diameter	51,118 km
Density	1.27 g/cm³
Mean surface temperature	−210 °C
Surface gravity	79% of Earth's gravity
Number of known satellites	27

Visualize It!

12 Predict Earth has an axial tilt of 23.5°, whereas Uranus has an axial tilt of almost 98°. If Earth had the same axial tilt as Uranus, how would the conditions be different at Earth's North and South Poles? Explain your reasoning.

_____

_____

_____

_____

_____

_____

_____

_____

_____

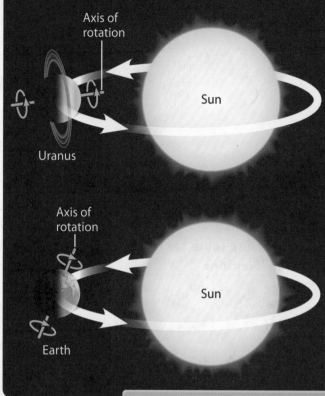

Think Outside the Book

13 Research Astronomers are discovering planets orbiting stars in other solar systems? Find out what kinds of planets astronomers are discovering in these solar systems.

Seasons on Uranus Last 21 Years

It takes Uranus 84 years to make a single revolution around the sun. For about 21 years of that 84-year period, the north pole faces the sun and the south pole is in darkness. About halfway through that 84-year period, the poles are reversed. The south pole faces the sun and the north pole is in darkness for 21 years. So, what are seasons like on Uranus? Except for a small band near the equator, every place on Uranus has winter periods of constant darkness and summer periods of constant daylight. But, during spring and fall, Uranus has periods of both daytime and nighttime just like on Earth.

Uranus's Moon Miranda Is Active

Miranda (muh•RAN•duh) is Uranus's fifth-largest moon. It is about 470 km in diameter. NASA's *Voyager 2* spacecraft visited Miranda in 1989. Data from *Voyager 2* showed that the moon is covered by different types of icy crust. What is the explanation for this patchwork surface? The gravitational forces of Uranus pull on Miranda's interior. This causes material from the moon's interior to rise to its surface. What we see on the surface is evidence of the moon turning itself inside out.

The surface of Uranus's moon Miranda

A Blue, Windy Giant

What is known about Neptune?

Neptune (NEP•toon) is the most distant planet from the sun. It is located 30 times farther from the sun than Earth is. So, sunlight on Neptune is 900 times fainter than sunlight on Earth is. High noon on Neptune may look much like twilight on Earth.

Neptune Is a Blue Ice Giant

Neptune is practically a twin to Uranus. Neptune is almost the same size as Uranus. It also has an atmosphere that is composed of hydrogen and helium, with some methane. The planet's bluish color is caused by the absorption of red light by methane. But because Neptune does not have an atmospheric haze like Uranus does, we can see deeper into the atmosphere. So, Neptune is blue, whereas Uranus is blue-green.

When *Voyager 2* flew by Neptune in 1989, there was a huge, dark area as large as Earth in the planet's atmosphere. This storm, which was located in Neptune's southern hemisphere, was named the *Great Dark Spot*. However, in 1994, the Hubble Space Telescope found no trace of this storm. Meanwhile, other spots that may grow larger with time have been sighted in the atmosphere.

Statistics Table for Neptune

Distance from the sun	30.1 AU
Period of rotation	16 h 7 min
Period of revolution	164.8 y
Tilt of axis	28.5°
Diameter	49,528 km
Density	1.64 g/cm³
Mean surface temperature	−220 °C
Surface Gravity	112% of Earth's gravity
Number of known satellites	13

Great Dark Spot

Visualize It!

14 Predict The wind speeds recorded in Neptune's Great Dark Spot reached 2,000 km/h. Predict what kind of destruction might result on Earth if wind speeds in hurricanes approached 2,000 km/h.

_____

_____

_____

_____

Neptune Has the Strongest Winds

Where does the energy come from that powers winds as fast as 2,000 km/h? Neptune has a warm interior that produces more energy than the planet receives from sunlight. Some scientists believe that Neptune's weather is controlled from inside the planet and not from outside the planet, as is Earth's weather.

Neptune's Moon Triton Has a Different Orbit Than Neptune's Other Moons

Triton (TRYT'in) is the largest moon of Neptune. Unlike the other moons of Neptune, Triton orbits Neptune in the opposite direction from the direction in which Neptune orbits the sun. One explanation for this oddity is that, long ago, there were several large moons that orbited Neptune. These moons came so close together that one moon was ejected. The other moon, Triton, remained behind but began traveling in the opposite direction.

Triton's days are numbered. The moon is slowly spiraling inward toward Neptune. When Triton is a certain distance from Neptune, the planet's gravitational pull will begin pulling Triton apart. Triton will then break into pieces.

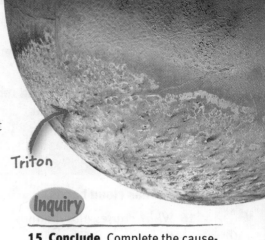

Triton

Inquiry

15 Conclude Complete the cause-and-effect chart by answering the question below.

> Triton spirals inward toward Neptune.

> The gravitational pull of Neptune causes Triton to pull apart.

> Triton breaks into pieces.

What do you think will happen next? Explain your reasoning.

_____

_____

_____

_____

A category 5 hurricane on Earth has sustained wind speeds of 250 km/h. Some effects of the winds of a category 5 hurricane can be seen in this image.

Visual Summary

To complete this summary, write the answers to the questions on the lines. Then use the key below to check your answers. You can use this page to review the main concepts of the lesson.

Properties
of Gas Giant Planets

Mercury Venus Earth Mars Jupiter Saturn Uranus Neptune

Terrestrial planets

Gas giant planets

Not to scale

Jupiter has cloud bands.

16 What causes cloud bands to form on Jupiter?

_____

_____

Saturn has a complex ring system.

17 What are Saturn's rings made up of?

_____

_____

Uranus is tilted on its side.

18 What is the tilt of Uranus's axis of rotation?

_____

_____

Neptune is a blue planet.

19 What gives Neptune its bluish color?

_____

_____

Answers: 16 The high winds on Jupiter circle the planet and cause cloud bands to form; 17 trillions of small, icy bodies; 18 almost 98° (97.8°); 19 the absorption of red light by methane in Neptune's atmosphere

20 Apply Compare the properties of the gas giant planets as a group with properties of Earth. Consider size, surface features, atmospheric features, distance from the sun, and ability to support life.

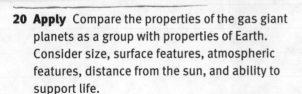

Lesson Review

Vocabulary

Fill in the blank with the term that best completes the following sentences.

1 A large planet that has a deep, massive atmosphere is called a _____.

2 A _____ is a disk of matter that circles a planet and consists of numerous particles in orbit that range in size from a few millimeters to several hundred meters.

Key Concepts

In the following table, write the name of the correct planet next to the property of that planet.

Properties	Planet
3 Identify Which planet has a density that is less than that of water?	
4 Identify Which planet has the strongest winds in the solar system?	
5 Identify Which planet is tilted on its side as it orbits the sun?	
6 Identify Which planet is the largest planet in the solar system?	

7 Compare How does the composition of Earth's atmosphere differ from the composition of the atmospheres of the gas giant planets?

_____

_____

_____

8 Compare How do the periods of rotation and revolution for the gas giant planets differ from those of Earth?

_____

_____

_____

_____

Critical Thinking

Use this diagram to answer the following questions.

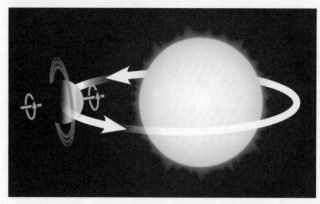

9 Identify Which planet is shown in the diagram? How do you know?

_____

_____

10 Analyze How does the axial tilt of this planet affect its seasons?

_____

_____

_____

_____

11 Claims · Evidence · Reasoning Why do you think the wind speeds on the gas giant planets are so much greater than the wind speeds on Earth? Support your claim with evidence and explain your reasoning.

_____

_____

12 Compare List Earth and the gas giant planets in order from the hottest to the coldest planet. How does the temperature of each planet relate to its distance from the sun?

_____

_____

_____

_____

My Notes

Small Bodies in the Solar System

ESSENTIAL QUESTION

What is found in the solar system besides the sun, planets, and moons?

By the end of this lesson, you should be able to compare and contrast the properties of small bodies in the solar system.

Comet Hale-Bopp was discovered in 1995 and was visible from Earth for 18 months. It is a long-period comet that is thought to take about 2,400 years to orbit the sun.

S6E1.e Comets, asteroids, and meteoroids

Engage Your Brain

1 Predict Check T or F to show whether you think each statement is true or false.

T	F	
☐	☐	Pluto is a planet.
☐	☐	The Kuiper Belt is located beyond the orbit of Neptune.
☐	☐	Comets are made of ice, rock, and dust.
☐	☐	All asteroids have the same composition.
☐	☐	Most meteoroids that enter Earth's atmosphere burn up completely.

2 Identify Can you identify the object that is streaking through the sky in the photograph? What do you think makes this object glow?

_____

_____

_____

_____

_____

Active Reading

3 Apply Many scientific words, such as *belt,* also have everyday meanings. Use context clues to write your own definition for each meaning of the word *belt*.

Example sentence
I found a <u>belt</u> to go with my new pants.

belt:

_____

_____

_____

Example sentence
Short-term comets originate in the Kuiper <u>Belt</u>.

belt:

_____

_____

_____

_____

Vocabulary Terms
• dwarf planet
• Kuiper Belt
• Kuiper Belt object
• comet
• Oort cloud
• asteroid
• meteoroid
• meteor
• meteorite

4 Apply As you learn the definition of each vocabulary term in this lesson, create your own definition or sketch to help you remember the meaning of the term.

Bigger is not better

Where are small bodies in the solar system?

![Active Reading]

5 Identify As you read the text, underline the names of different kinds of small bodies that are found in the solar system.

The sun, planets, and moons are not the only objects in the solar system. Scientists estimate that there are up to a trillion small bodies in the solar system. These bodies lack atmospheres and have weak surface gravity. The largest of the small bodies, the dwarf planets, are found in regions known as the *asteroid belt* and the *Kuiper Belt*. The Kuiper (KAHY•per) Belt is located beyond the orbit of Neptune. Kuiper Belt objects, as you might guess, are located in the Kuiper Belt. Comets, too, are found in the Kuiper Belt. However, comets are also located in the Oort cloud. The Oort (OHRT) cloud is a region that surrounds the solar system and extends almost halfway to the nearest star. Two other types of small bodies, asteroids and meteoroids, are located mostly between the orbits of Venus and Neptune.

Sizes and distances are not to scale.

Mercury   Venus   Earth   Mars   Ceres

Jupiter

What are dwarf planets?

In 2006, astronomers decided that Pluto would no longer be considered a planet. It became the first member of a new group of solar system bodies called *dwarf planets*. Like planets, a **dwarf planet** is a celestial body that orbits the sun and is round because of its own gravity. However, a dwarf planet does not have the mass to have cleared other bodies out of its orbit around the sun.

Five dwarf planets, made of ice and rock, have been identified. Ceres (SIR•eez), located between the orbits of Mars and Jupiter, is about 950 km in diameter and travels at around 18 km/s. Pluto, Eris (IR•is), Haumea (HOW•may•uh), and Makemake (MAH•kay•MAH•kay) are located beyond the orbit of Neptune. They range in size from about 1,500 km (Haumea) to about 2,400 km (Eris). Their orbital periods around the sun range from 250 to 560 years. All travel at speeds of between 3 km/s and 5 km/s.

Active Reading

6 Describe Describe two properties of dwarf planets.

_____
_____
_____
_____
_____
_____

Saturn

Uranus

Neptune

Pluto   Haumea   Makemake   Eris

Visualize It!

7 Analyze Where in the solar system are most of the dwarf planets located?

_____
_____
_____
_____

KBOs

What are Kuiper Belt objects?

The **Kuiper Belt** is a region of the solar system that begins just beyond the orbit of Neptune and contains small bodies made mostly of ice. It extends outward to about twice the orbit of Neptune, a distance of about 55 astronomical units (AU). An AU is a unit of length that is equal to the average distance between Earth and the sun, or about 150,000,000 km. The Kuiper Belt is thought to contain matter that was left over from the formation of the solar system. This matter formed small bodies instead of planets.

A **Kuiper Belt object (KBO)** is any of the minor bodies in the Kuiper Belt outside the orbit of Neptune. Kuiper Belt objects are made of methane ice, ammonia ice, and water ice. They have average orbital speeds of between 1 km/s and 5 km/s. The first Kuiper Belt object was not discovered until 1992. Now, about 1,300 KBOs are known. Scientists estimate that there are at least 70,000 objects in the Kuiper Belt that have diameters larger than 100 km.

Quaoar is a KBO that orbits 43 AU from the sun. It is around 1,260 km in diameter and has one satellite.

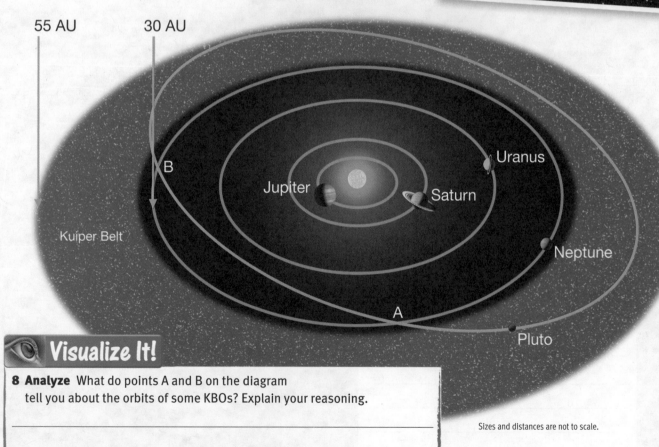

55 AU   30 AU

B

Jupiter

Uranus

Saturn

Kuiper Belt

Neptune

A

Pluto

Visualize It!

8 Analyze What do points A and B on the diagram tell you about the orbits of some KBOs? Explain your reasoning.

_____

_____

Sizes and distances are not to scale.

Pluto: From Planet to KBO

From its discovery in 1930 until 2006, Pluto was considered to be the ninth planet in the solar system. However, beginning in 1992, a new group of small bodies called *Kuiper Belt objects*, or simply KBOs, began to be discovered beyond the orbit of Neptune. Not only are some of the KBOs close to Pluto in size, but some have a similar composition of rock and ice. Astronomers recognized that Pluto was, in fact, a large KBO and not the ninth planet. In 2006, Pluto was redefined as a "dwarf planet" by the International Astronomical Union (IAU).

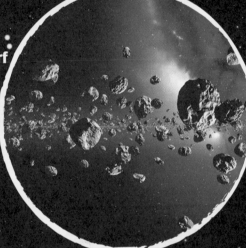

Charon

Pluto

Pluto and Charon
At 2,306 km in diameter, Pluto is the second largest KBO. It is shown in this artist's rendition with Charon (KAIR•uhn), its largest satellite. Many large KBOs have satellites. Some KBOs and their satellites, such as Pluto and Charon, orbit each other.

The Kuiper Belt
The Kuiper Belt is located between 30 AU (the orbit of Neptune) and approximately 55 AU. However, most KBOs have been discovered between 42 and 48 AU, where their orbits are not disturbed by the gravitational attraction of Neptune.

Extend

Inquiry

9 Explain Why is Pluto no longer considered a planet?

10 Research Astronomer Clyde Tombaugh discovered Pluto in 1930. Research why Tombaugh was searching beyond Neptune for "Planet X" and how he discovered Pluto.

11 Claims · Evidence · Reasoning Research the 2006 IAU decision to redefine Pluto as a "dwarf planet." Combine this research with your research on Pluto. Make a claim about whether Pluto should be considered a "dwarf planet" or return to being called the ninth planet in the solar system. Support your claim with evidence and explain your reasoning.

What do we know about comets?

Active Reading 12 **Identify** As you read the text, underline the different parts of a comet and their properties.

A **comet** is a small body of ice, rock, and dust that follows a highly elliptical orbit around the sun. As a comet passes close to the sun, it gives off gas and dust in the form of a coma and a tail.

The speed of a comet will vary depending on how far from or how close to the sun it is. Far from the sun, a comet may travel at speeds as low as 0.32 km/s. Close to the sun, a comet may travel as fast as 445 km/s.

Comets Are Made of a Nucleus and a Tail

All comets have a *nucleus* that is composed of ice and rock. Most comet nuclei are between 1 km and 10 km in diameter. If a comet approaches the sun, solar radiation and heating cause the comet's ice to change to gas. A *coma* is a spherical cloud of gas and dust that comes off of the nucleus. The *ion tail* of a comet is gas that has been ionized, or stripped of electrons, by the sun. The solar wind—electrically charged particles expanding away from the sun—pushes the gas away from the comet's head. So, regardless of the direction a comet is traveling, its ion tail points away from the sun. A second tail made of dust and gas curves backward along the comet's orbit. This *dust tail* can be millions of kilometers long.

Visualize It!

13 **Identify** Use the write-on lines in the diagram to identify the structures of a comet.

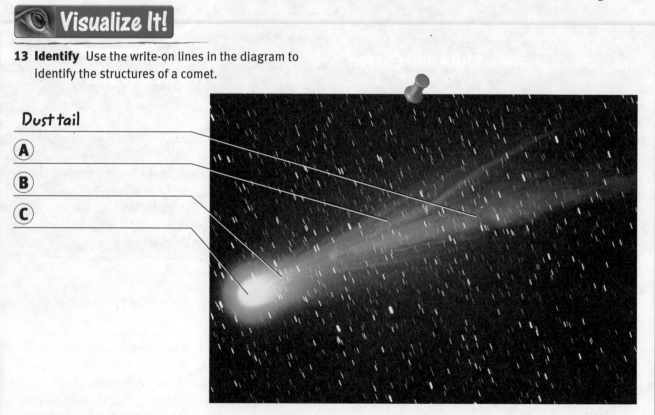

Dust tail

(A)

(B)

(C)

Comets Come from the Kuiper Belt and the Oort Cloud

There are two regions of the solar system where comets come from. The first region is the Kuiper Belt, which is where short-period comets originate. The second region is the Oort cloud, which is where long-period comets originate.

Collisions between objects in the Kuiper Belt produce fragments that become comets. These comets are known as *short-period comets*. Short-period comets take less than 200 years to orbit the sun. Therefore, they return to the inner solar system quite frequently, perhaps every few decades or centuries. Short-period comets also have short life spans. Every time a comet passes the sun, it may lose a layer as much as 1 m thick.

Some comets originate in the Oort cloud. The **Oort cloud** is a spherical region that surrounds the solar system and extends almost halfway to the nearest star. Comets can form in the Oort cloud when two objects collide. Comets can also form when an object in the Oort cloud is disturbed by the gravity of a nearby star and is sent into the inner solar system. Comets that originate in the Oort cloud are called *long-period comets*. Long-period comets may take up to hundreds of thousands of years to orbit the sun.

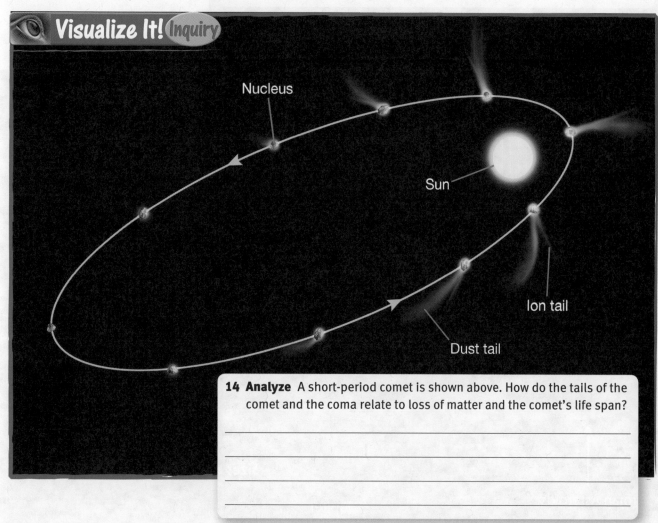

Visualize It! Inquiry

Nucleus

Sun

Ion tail

Dust tail

14 Analyze A short-period comet is shown above. How do the tails of the comet and the coma relate to loss of matter and the comet's life span?

_____

_____

_____

_____

On the rocks

What do we know about asteroids?

📎 **Active Reading** 15 **Identify** As you read the text, underline those places in the solar system where asteroids are located.

An **asteroid** is a small, irregularly shaped, rocky object that orbits the sun. Most asteroids are located between the orbits of Mars and Jupiter. This 300 million–km–wide region is known as the *asteroid belt*. The asteroid belt contains hundreds of thousands of asteroids, called *main-belt asteroids*. The largest main-belt asteroid by diameter is Pallas, which has a diameter of 570 km. The smallest asteroid is 4 m in diameter. Groups of asteroids are also located in the orbits of Jupiter and Neptune (called *Trojan asteroids*) and in the Kuiper Belt. Still other asteroids are called *near-Earth asteroids*. Some of these asteroids cross the orbits of Earth and Venus.

Asteroids in the asteroid belt orbit the sun at about 18 km/s and have orbital periods of 3 to 8 years. Although most asteroids rotate around their axes, some tumble end over end through space.

16 Analyze Where is the asteroid belt located?

_____
_____
_____
_____
_____
_____

Asteroid Belt

Mars

Trojan Asteroids

Trojan Asteroids

Jupiter

Sizes and distances are not to scale.

Asteroids Have Different Compositions

The composition of asteroids varies. Many asteroids have dark surfaces. Scientists think that these asteroids are rich in carbon. Other asteroids are thought to be rocky and to have a core made of iron and nickel. Still other asteroids may have a rocky core surrounded largely by ice. Small, rocky asteroids have perhaps the strangest composition of all. They appear to be piles of rock loosely held together by gravity. Asteroid Itokawa (ee•TOH•kah•wah), shown below, is a rocky asteroid known as a "rubble-pile" asteroid.

Some asteroids contain economic minerals like those mined on Earth. Economic minerals that are found in asteroids include gold, iron, nickel, manganese, cobalt, and platinum. Scientists are now investigating the potential for mining near-Earth asteroids.

Itokawa is a rubble-pile asteroid. Astronomers think that the 500 m-long asteroid may be composed of two asteroids that are joined.

Thin, dusty outer core

Water-ice layer

Rocky inner core

Greetings from Eros!

Think Outside the Book

17 Describe Eros is a near-Earth asteroid that tumbles through space. Imagine that you are the first human to explore Eros. Write a postcard that describes what you found on Eros. Then research the asteroid and find out how close your description came to reality.

Burned Out

What do we know about meteoroids, meteors, and meteorites?

A sand grain- to boulder-sized, rocky body that travels through space is a **meteoroid**. Meteoroids that enter Earth's atmosphere travel at about 52 km/s, as measured by radar on Earth. Friction heats these meteoroids to thousands of degrees Celsius, which causes them to glow. The atmosphere around a meteoroid's path also gets hotter and glows because of friction between the meteoroid and air molecules. A bright streak of light that results when a meteoroid burns up in Earth's atmosphere is called a **meteor**. A **meteorite** is a meteoroid that reaches Earth's surface without burning up.

18 Identify Use the write-on lines below to identify the three objects that are shown.

A A small, rocky body that travels through space is a

_____ .

B The glowing trail of a body that is burning up in Earth's atmosphere is a _____ .

C A body that reaches Earth's surface without burning up is a _____ .

A meteorite 45 m across produced the kilometer-wide Barringer Crater in Arizona about 50,000 years ago.

Meteorites Reach Earth

Meteoroids come from the asteroid belt, Mars, the moon, and comets. Most of the meteoroids that enter Earth's atmosphere do not reach Earth's surface. Many meteoroids explode in the upper atmosphere. These explosions are often recorded by military satellites in orbit around Earth. Other meteoroids skip back into space after briefly crossing the upper atmosphere. However, some large meteoroids that enter Earth's lower atmosphere or strike Earth's surface can be destructive. Scientists estimate that a destructive meteorite impact occurs every 300 to 400 years.

Meteorites Have Different Compositions

Meteorites can be divided into three general groups. The first group of meteorites are the stony meteorites. They are the most common form of meteorite. Stony meteorites are made of silicate minerals, just like rocks on Earth. Some stony meteorites also contain small amounts of organic matter. A much smaller group of meteorites are the iron meteorites. Iron meteorites are composed of iron and nickel. The rarest group of meteorites are stony-iron meteorites. Stony-iron meteorites are composed of both silicate minerals and iron and nickel. All three groups of meteorites can originate from asteroids. However, some stony meteorites come from the moon and Mars.

19 Describe In the boxes below, describe the composition and origin of each group of meteorite. Also, indicate how common each group of meteorite is.

Stony meteorite
_____
_____
_____
_____
_____

Iron meteorite
_____
_____
_____
_____
_____

Stony-iron meteorite
_____
_____
_____
_____

Visual Summary

To complete this summary, answer the questions below. Then use the key below to check your answers. You can use this page to review the main concepts of the lesson.

Small Bodies in the Solar System

Small bodies are found throughout the solar system.

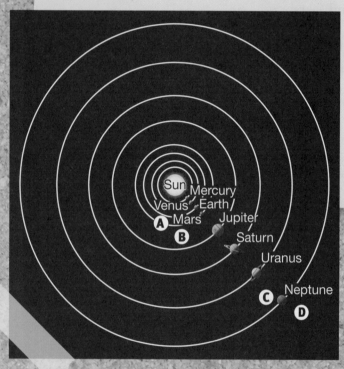

Sun
Mercury
Venus · Earth
Mars · Jupiter
Saturn
Uranus
Neptune
A B C D

Answers: 20 asteroids A, B, C, D; dwarf planets B, D; KBOs C, D; 21 F, F, T

20 Enter the correct letter or letters that indicate a location for each small body in the solar system.

Asteroids	
Dwarf planets	
Kuiper Belt objects	

21 Check true or false to answer the questions below.

T	F	
☐	☐	Comets originate in the asteroid belt and the Kuiper Belt.
☐	☐	Three groups of asteroids are stony, iron, and stony-iron.
☐	☐	Most meteoroids that enter Earth's atmosphere burn up.

22 Compare Make a table in which you compare and contrast comets and asteroids in terms of composition, location in the solar system, and size.

Lesson Review

Vocabulary

Fill in the blank with the term that best completes the following sentences.

1 The _____ is a spherical region that surrounds the solar system and extends almost halfway to the nearest star.

2 A region of the solar system that extends from the orbit of Neptune to about twice the orbit of Neptune is the _____.

3 Most _____ are located between the orbits of Mars and Jupiter.

4 A meteoroid that reaches Earth's surface without burning up is a _____.

Key Concepts

In the following table, write the name of the correct body next to the property of that body.

Property	Body
5 Identify What is a minor body that orbits outside the orbit of Neptune?	
6 Identify What is a small body that follows a highly elliptical orbit around the sun?	
7 Identify What is the largest of the small bodies that are found in the solar system?	
8 Identify What is the glowing trail that results when a meteoroid burns up in Earth's atmosphere?	

Critical Thinking

Use this table to answer the following questions.

Comet	Orbital Period (years)
Borrelly	6.9
Halley	76
Hale-Bopp	2,400
Hyakutake	100,000

9 Apply Which of the comets in the table are short-period comets?

_____

_____

10 Apply Which of the comets in the table most likely originated in the Oort cloud?

_____

_____

11 Infer Why do you think that the speeds of comets increase as they near the sun? Explain your reasoning.

_____

_____

_____

_____

12 Relate Develop questions that scientists might have asked when they discovered both similarities and differences in the characteristics, compositions, and locations of comets, asteroids, and meteoroids.

_____

_____

_____

_____

My Notes

Unit 1 ⟨ Big Idea ⟩ Our solar system is just one of many billions of solar systems in the universe.

Lesson 1
ESSENTIAL QUESTION
What makes up the universe?

Describe the structure of the universe, including the scale of distances in the universe.

Lesson 4
ESSENTIAL QUESTION
What is known about the terrestrial planets?

Describe some of the properties of the terrestrial planets and how the properties of Mercury, Venus, and Mars differ from the properties of Earth.

Lesson 2
ESSENTIAL QUESTION
How did the universe begin?

Summarize the evidence that has led scientists to accept the Big Bang theory to explain the origin of the universe.

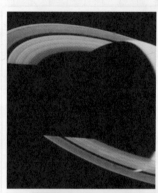

Lesson 5
ESSENTIAL QUESTION
What is known about the gas giant planets?

Describe some of the properties of the gas giant planets and how these properties differ from the physical properties of Earth.

Lesson 3
ESSENTIAL QUESTION
Why is gravity important in the solar system?

Explain the role that gravity played in the formation of the solar system and in determining the motion of the planets.

Lesson 6
ESSENTIAL QUESTION
What is found in the solar system besides the sun, planets, and moons?

Compare and contrast the properties of small bodies in the solar system.

Connect ESSENTIAL QUESTIONS
Lessons 4 and 5

1 Synthesize Explain why the planet Jupiter has more moons than the planet Mars.

_____

_____

_____

_____

Think Outside the Book

2 Synthesize Choose one of these activities to help synthesize what you have learned in this unit.

☐ Using what you learned in lessons 4 and 5, write a short essay explaining where in the solar system besides Earth life could exist.

☐ Using what you learned in lessons 3 and 4, make a poster showing why comets are the fastest-moving bodies in the solar system.

Vocabulary

Fill in each blank with the term that best completes the following sentences.

1 A(n) _____ is a large group of stars, gas, and dust bound together by gravity.

2 The solar system formed from a(n) _____, which is a rotating cloud of gas and dust that formed into the sun and planets.

3 An increase in the wavelength of light as a galaxy moves away from Earth is called a(n) _____ .

4 Earth, Venus, Mars, and Mercury are considered _____, which are highly dense planets nearest the sun.

5 A(n) _____ is a small, rocky object that orbits the sun; many of these objects are located in a band between the orbits of Mars and Jupiter.

Key Concepts

Read each question below, and circle the best answer.

6 This diagram illustrates a historical model of the solar system.

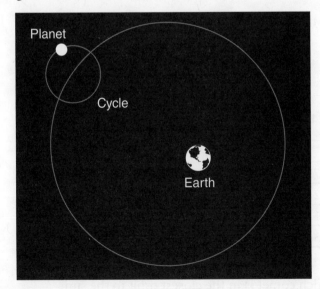

Which type of model is shown?

A geocentric model

C Copernican model

B heliocentric model

D Aristarchan model

7 Which object is farthest away from Earth?

A Barnard's Star, 6 light-years from Earth

B Andromeda galaxy, 2.4 million light-years from Earth

C Triangulum galaxy, 2.6 million light-years from Earth

D Neptune, 4.3 billion kilometers from Earth

8 The Kuiper Belt, pictured below, is generally thought to contain leftover bits from the formation of the solar system.

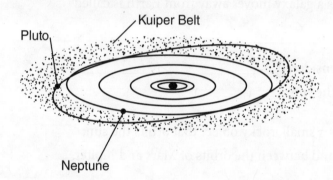

Which of the following describes Kuiper Belt objects?

A often larger than some planets in the solar system

B extremely hot

C minor planet-sized objects that orbit the sun in a flat belt beyond Neptune's orbit

D 100 AU wide

9 Suppose the comets in the table orbited the sun.

Comet Name	Comet Size (km)	Comet Speed (km/h)
Rasmussen	1	750,000
Zigler	10	2
Schier	5	1.5 million
Brant	3	3,700

Using what you know about comets, which comet is in the closest orbit to the sun?

A Rasmussen

C Schier

B Zigler

D Brant

10 Which of the following is a list of the gas giant planets?

   A Jupiter, Saturn, Uranus, and Neptune

   B Earth, Mars, and Venus

   C Pluto, Saturn, and Jupiter

   D Earth, Jupiter, Neptune, and Saturn

11 Below is an illustration of the planet Saturn. Saturn is one of the four gas giant planets.

Saturn

Which of the four statements below is not true about Saturn?

   A It travels around the Sun once every 29.5 years.

   B It is the only planet with a ring system.

   C It is composed mostly of hydrogen and helium gas.

   D It has a large number of moons.

12 Earth, Mercury, and Venus are all classified as terrestrial planets. When compared to Earth, which of the following is true of Mercury and Venus?

   A Mercury and Venus have a higher surface gravity than Earth.

   B Mercury and Venus have a longer period of revolution than Earth.

   C Mercury and Venus have slower periods of rotation (longer days) than Earth.

   D Mercury and Venus are farther away from the sun than Earth.

13 Which of the following lists accurately relates which terrestrial planets have moons and how many moons they have?

   A Mercury and Venus (no moons), Earth (one moon), and Mars (two moons)

   B Mercury, Venus, and Earth (one moon each), and Mars (two moons)

   C Mercury and Venus (no moons), Earth (two moons), and Mars (two moons)

   D Mercury and Venus (no moons), Earth (one moon), and Mars (three moons)

14 The dot in the diagram is a source of light waves. It is moving from right to left across the diagram.

How does the diagram relate to the expanding universe? (Hint: Step 1. Compare the characteristics of the waves in front of the source with those behind the source. Step 2. Think about evidence scientists used to conclude that the universe is expanding. Step 3. Relate the diagram to the evidence.)

   A It shows that light produced during the big bang is still in motion.

   B It shows that objects move faster depending on the type of light they produce.

   C It shows that a source produces light of different wavelengths in different locations.

   D It shows that wavelengths are increased behind an object that is moving away from an observer.

15 Where do stars form?

   A in nebulae

   B on asteroids

   C in a planet's core

   D in sun spots on the surface of the sun

16 Which describes an effect of centripetal force?

   A objects break apart in space

   B objects burn at very high temperatures

   C objects move in a circular path

   D objects move in an elliptical path

17 What does Kepler's first law of planetary motion state?

   A the orbit of a planet around the sun is an ellipse with the sun at one focus

   B the orbit of a planet is dependent on heat

   C the difference between centripetal force and elliptical force

   D the orbital period is infinite

Critical Thinking

Answer the following questions in the space provided.

18 Explain the difference between a meteoroid, a meteor, and a meteorite. Which one would you most likely see on the surface of Earth?

_____

_____

_____

_____

_____

_____

19 Name three characteristics of gas giants that make them different from terrestrial planets.

_____

_____

_____

_____

20 Scientists' understanding of the universe changed over time as new evidence was discovered. How did the work of the following scientists affect the understanding of the universe?

Nicolaus Copernicus

_____

_____

Isaac Newton

_____

_____

Albert Einstein

_____

_____

Edwin Hubble

_____

_____

Connect **ESSENTIAL QUESTIONS**
Lessons 3, 4, 5, and 6

Answer the following question in the space provided.

21 Discuss gravitational force in our universe and how it works. Why is it critical to our universe? Name at least three instances of gravitational forces at work in our solar system.

_____

_____

_____

_____

_____

_____

_____

_____

_____

_____

_____

_____

The Earth-Moon-Sun System

Big Idea

Earth and the moon move in predictable ways and have predictable effects on each other as they orbit the sun.

S6E1., S6E1.a, S6E2., S6E2.a, S6E2.b, S6E2.c, S6E3., S6E3.d

What do you think?

How does the sun provide light and energy? How do tides affect life on Earth? As you explore the unit, gather evidence to help you state and support claims to answer these questions.

Tidal pool exposed by low tide

Unit 2
The Earth-Moon-Sun System

Measuring Shadows

One way to learn more about Earth's rotation and orbit is to study the shadows created by the sun throughout the year. Help students with an ongoing research project, called the Sun Shadows Project. The results are presented at the American Geophysical Union's annual conference every year.

① Think About It

Students at James Monroe Middle School in Albuquerque, New Mexico, asked the following questions: The seasons change, but do the length of shadows? How could this be measured? What do you think?

_____

_____

_____

Scientists in Antarctica measure shadows.

② Ask A Question

What effects do seasons have on the lengths of shadows in your area?

As a class, come up with a prediction. Then, research what students at James Monroe Middle School are doing to gather information.

Things to Consider

Some parts of the world participate in Daylight Savings Time. People move their clocks forward by an hour in the spring and back by an hour in the fall. Daylight Savings Time may affect the way that you will need to collect data in comparison to students at James Monroe Middle School. Make sure to take your measurements when shadows are shortest.

③ Apply Your Knowledge

A List the materials your class will need in order to make and record the measurements to gather the information needed by the students at James Monroe Middle School.

_____

_____

_____

_____

B Decide on a time frame for your class project. Will you participate for an entire season? What factors influence your decision?

_____

_____

_____

_____

_____

_____

C Track the information gathered by your class and draw your own preliminary conclusions.

_____

_____

_____

_____

Take It Home

Who else is participating in the Sun Shadows Project? Research the various national and international groups taking part, such as the U.S. Antarctic Program. See *ScienceSaurus*® for more information about the motions of the Earth and the moon.

Earth's Days, Years, and Seasons

ESSENTIAL QUESTION

How are Earth's days, years, and seasons related to the way Earth moves in space?

By the end of this lesson, you should be able to relate Earth's days, years, and seasons to Earth's movement in space.

S6E2.c Earth's tilt, sunlight, and seasonal changes

In many parts of the world, blooming flowers are one of the first signs that spring has arrived. Spring flowers start blooming with the warmer temperatures of spring, even if there is still snow on the ground.

Lesson Labs

Quick Labs
• Earth's Rotation and Revolution
• Seasons Model

Field Lab
• Sunlight and Temperature

 Engage Your Brain

1 Predict Check T or F to show whether you think each statement is true or false.

T   F

☐   ☐   A day is about 12 hours long.

☐   ☐   A year is about 365 days long.

☐   ☐   When it is summer in the Northern Hemisphere, it is summer all around the world.

2 Apply Write your own caption for this photo of leaves in the space below.

_____

_____

_____

_____

_____

 Active Reading

3 Synthesize The term *rotation* can be tricky to remember because it is used somewhat differently in science than it is in everyday life. In baseball, a pitching *rotation* lists the order of a team's starting pitchers. The order starts over after the last pitcher on the list has played. On the lines below, write down any other examples you can think of that use the term *rotation*.

rotation:

_____

_____

_____

_____

Vocabulary Terms

• rotation   • season
• day   • equinox
• revolution   • solstice
• year

4 Apply As you learn the definition of each vocabulary term in this lesson, create your own definition or sketch to help you remember the meaning of the term.

Spinning in

What determines the length of a day?

Each planet spins on its axis. Earth's axis (ACK•sis) is an imaginary straight line that runs from the North Pole to the South Pole. The spinning of a body, such as a planet, on its axis is called **rotation**. The time it takes a planet to complete one full rotation on its axis is called a **day**.

Active Reading

5 Identify As you read, underline the places on Earth's surface at which the ends of Earth's axis would be.

The Time It Takes for Earth to Rotate Once

Earth rotates in a counterclockwise motion around its axis when viewed from above the North Pole. This means that as a location on Earth's equator rotates from west to east, the sun appears to rise in the east. The sun then appears to cross the sky and set in the west.

As Earth rotates, only one-half of Earth faces the sun at any given time. People on the half of Earth facing the sun experience daylight. This period of time in daylight is called *daytime*. People on the half of Earth that faces away from the sun experience darkness. This period of time in darkness is called *nighttime*.

Earth's rotation is used to measure time. Earth completes one rotation on its axis in 24 hours, or in one day. Most locations on Earth's surface move through daylight and darkness in that time.

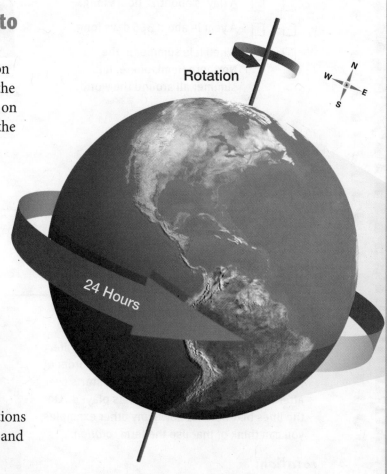

Rotation

24 Hours

Earth's motion is used to measure the length of an Earth day.

Circles

What determines the length of a year?

As Earth rotates on its axis, Earth also revolves around the sun. Although you cannot feel Earth moving, it is traveling around the sun at an average speed of nearly 30 km/s. The motion of a body that travels around another body in space is called **revolution** (reh•vuh•LOO•shun). Earth completes a full revolution around the sun in 365 ¼ days, or about one **year**. We have divided the year into 12 months, each month lasting from 28 to 31 days.

Earth's orbit is not quite a perfect circle. In January, Earth is about 2.5 million kilometers closer to the sun than it is in July. You may be surprised that this distance makes only a tiny difference in temperatures on Earth.

Think Outside the Book

6 Infer How is a leap year, in which a day is added to every fourth year, related to the time it takes Earth to revolve around the sun?

Visualize It!

7 Claims • Evidence • Reasoning Imagine that Earth's current position is at point A. Write the label B to show Earth's position 6 months from now. Explain your reasoning.

This drawing is not to scale.

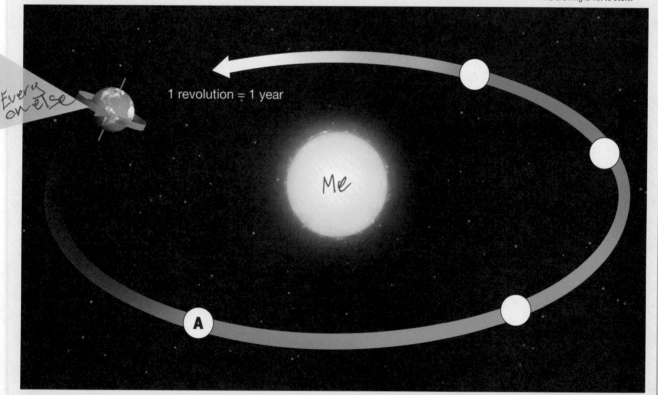

Every one else

1 revolution = 1 year

Me

A

Tilt-a-Whirl

What conditions are affected by the tilt of Earth's axis?

Earth's axis is tilted at 23.5°. Earth's axis always points toward the North Star as Earth revolves around the sun. Thus, during each revolution, the North Pole may be tilted toward the sun or away from the sun, as seen below. When the North Pole is tilted toward the sun, the Northern Hemisphere (HEHM•ih•sfeer) has longer periods of daylight than does the Southern Hemisphere. When the North Pole is tilted away from the sun, the opposite is true.

The direction of tilt of Earth's axis remains the same throughout Earth's orbit around the sun.

23.5°

23.5°

orbit

This drawing is not to scale.

Temperature

The angle at which the sun's rays strike each part of Earth's surface changes as Earth moves in its orbit. When the North Pole is tilted toward the sun, the sun's rays strike the Northern Hemisphere more directly. Thus, the region receives a higher concentration of solar energy and is warmer. When the North Pole is tilted away from the sun, the sun's rays strike the Northern Hemisphere less directly. When the sunlight is less direct, the solar energy is less concentrated and the region is cooler.

The spherical shape of Earth also affects how the sun warms up an area. Temperatures are high at point A in the diagram. This is because the sun's rays hit Earth's surface at a right angle and are focused in a small area. Toward the poles, the sun's rays hit Earth's surface at a lesser angle. Therefore, the rays are spread out over a larger area and the temperatures are cooler.

Visualize It!

8 Apply Which location on the illustration of Earth below receives more direct rays from the sun?
- [ ] A
- [ ] B
- [ ] They receive equal amounts.

9 Claims • Evidence • Reasoning Which location is cooler? Provide evidence for your reasoning.

_____

_____

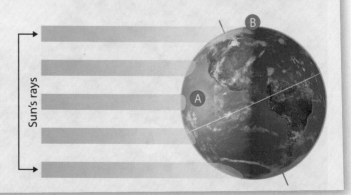

Sun's rays

B

A

Daylight Hours

All locations on Earth experience an *average* of 12 hours of light a day. However, the *actual* number of daylight hours on any given day of the year varies with location. Areas around Earth's equator receive about 12 hours of light a day. Areas on Earth's surface that are tilted toward the sun have more hours of daylight. These areas travel a longer path through the lit part of Earth than areas at the equator. Areas on Earth's surface that are tilted away from the sun have less than 12 hours of light a day. These areas travel a shorter path through the lit part of Earth, as shown below.

This drawing is not to scale.

Sun's Rays

During summer in the Northern Hemisphere, a person has already had many daylight hours by the time a person in the Southern Hemisphere reaches daylight.

About twelve hours later, the person in the Northern Hemisphere is close to daylight again, while the person in the Southern Hemisphere still has many hours of darkness left.

Midnight Sun

When it is summer in the Northern Hemisphere, the time in each day that it is light increases as you move north of the equator. Areas north of the Arctic Circle have 24 hours of daylight, called the "midnight sun," as seen in the photo. At the same time, areas south of the Antarctic Circle receive 24 hours of darkness, or "polar night." When it is winter in the Northern Hemisphere, conditions in the polar areas are reversed.

Visualize It! Inquiry

10 Synthesize Why isn't the area in the photo very warm even though the sun is up all night long? Explain your reasoning.

_____

_____

_____

This composite image shows that the sun never set on this Arctic summer day.

Seasons change...

What causes seasons?

Most locations on Earth experience seasons. Each **season** is characterized by a pattern of temperature and other weather trends. Near the equator, the temperatures are almost the same year-round. Near the poles, there are very large changes in temperatures from winter to summer. We experience seasons due to the changes in the intensity of sunlight and the number of daylight hours as Earth revolves around the sun. So, both the tilt of Earth's axis and Earth's spherical shape play a role in Earth's changing seasons.

As Earth travels around the sun, the area of sunlight in each hemisphere changes. At an **equinox** (EE•kwuh•nahks), sunlight shines equally on the Northern and Southern Hemispheres. Half of each hemisphere is lit, and half is in darkness. As Earth moves along its orbit, the sunlight reaches more of one hemisphere than the other. At a **solstice** (SOHL•stis), the area of sunlight is at a maximum in one hemisphere and at a minimum in the other hemisphere.

- **September Equinox** When Earth is in this position, sunlight shines equally on both poles.
- **December Solstice** About three months later, Earth has traveled a quarter of the way around the sun, but its axis still points in the same direction into space. The North Pole leans away from the sun and is in complete darkness. The South Pole is in complete sunlight.
- **March Equinox** After another quarter of its orbit, Earth reaches another equinox. Half of each hemisphere is lit, and the sunlight is centered on the equator.
- **June Solstice** This position is opposite to the December solstice. Now the North Pole leans toward the sun and is in complete sunlight, and the south pole is in complete darkness.

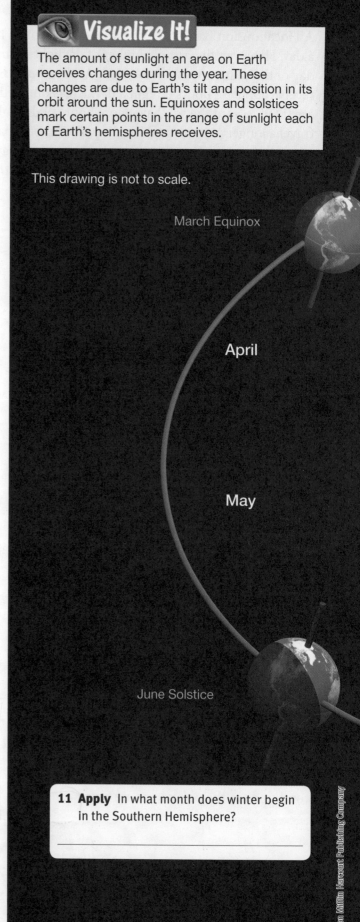

© Houghton Mifflin Harcourt Publishing Company

Visualize It!

The amount of sunlight an area on Earth receives changes during the year. These changes are due to Earth's tilt and position in its orbit around the sun. Equinoxes and solstices mark certain points in the range of sunlight each of Earth's hemispheres receives.

This drawing is not to scale.

March Equinox

April

May

June Solstice

11 Apply In what month does winter begin in the Southern Hemisphere?

_____

12 Infer During which solstice would the sun be at its highest point in the sky in the Northern Hemisphere?

Solstices

The seasons of summer and winter begin on days called *solstices*. Each year on June 21 or 22, the North Pole's tilt toward the sun is greatest. This day is called the *June solstice*. This solstice marks the beginning of summer in the Northern Hemisphere. By December 21 or 22, the North Pole is tilted to the farthest point away from the sun. This day is the December solstice.

February

January

December Solstice

November

October

July

August

September Equinox

Equinoxes

The seasons fall and spring begin on days called *equinoxes*. The hours of daylight and darkness are approximately equal everywhere on Earth on these days. The *September equinox* occurs on September 22 or 23 of each year. This equinox marks the beginning of fall in the Northern Hemisphere. The March equinox on March 20 or 21 of each year marks the beginning of spring.

13 Infer In which parts of the world is an equinox most different from other days of the year?

Visual Summary

To complete this summary, circle the correct word. Then use the key below to check your answers. You can use this page to review the main concepts of the lesson.

The length of a day is determined by Earth's rotation.

14 It takes Earth 24 seconds/(hours) to make one rotation on its axis.

The length of a year is determined by Earth's revolution around the sun.

15 It takes Earth about 365 hours/(days) to revolve around the sun.

Earth's
Days, Years, and Seasons

Earth's tilt affects temperatures and daylight hours at different locations on Earth.

Sun's rays

16 Earth's temperatures and hours of daylight stay the most constant at the (equator)/poles.

This diagram shows how seasons change in the Northern Hemisphere as Earth orbits the sun.

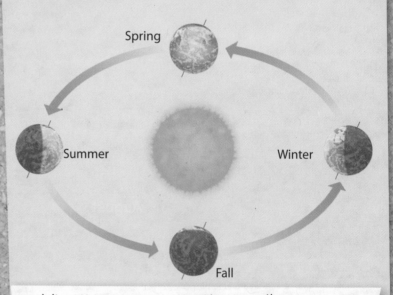

Spring

Summer

Winter

Fall

17 When it is summer in the Northern Hemisphere, it is summer/(winter) in the Southern Hemisphere.

Answers: 14 hours; 15 days; 16 equator; 17 winter

18 **Predict** How would conditions on Earth change if Earth stopped rotating on its axis?

Lesson Review

Vocabulary

In the space provided below, describe how each set of words are related.

1 revolution, year

A revolution around the earth is 1 year

2 rotation, day

It takes 15 days to complete a full rotation

3 season, equinox, solstice

Seasons, equinoxes, and solstices is the temp. changing throughout the year

Key Concepts

4 Identify About how many days are in an Earth year? And how many hours in an Earth day?

24 hours = 1 day. 365 days = 1 year

5 Describe How does the tilt of Earth's axis affect how the sun's rays strike Earth?

6 Synthesize How does the tilt of Earth's axis affect the number of daylight hours and the temperature of a location on Earth?

The tilt causes the sun's radiation to strike the hemispheres at different angles

Critical Thinking

Use this image to answer the questions below.

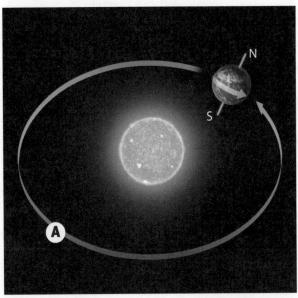

This drawing is not to scale.

7 Identify What season is the Northern Hemisphere experiencing in the image above?

winter

8 Explain How do the tilt of Earth's axis and Earth's movements around the sun cause seasons?

9 Describe If the Earth moves to point A in the image above, what season will the Northern Hemisphere experience?

Summer

My Notes

Analyzing Scientific Explanations

Scientists use different methods to develop scientific explanations in different fields of study. Scientists base their explanations on data collected through observation and measurement. After scientists make observations and collect data, they analyze current explanations for what they observed. If a new observation doesn't fit an existing explanation, scientists might work to revise the explanation or to offer a new one.

Tutorial

The text below illustrates how Ptolemy, a Greek astronomer in the second century CE, would likely have described his work. Consider the following steps as you analyze scientific explanations.

As Aristotle put forth, Earth is at the center of the universe. All other planets and the Sun revolve around Earth, each on its own sphere. The spheres follow this order outward from Earth: Mercury, Venus, the Moon, the Sun, Mars, Jupiter, Saturn, and the Fixed Stars. Each sphere turns at its own steady pace. Bodies do appear to move backward during their wanderings, but that does not mean the spheres do not keep a steady pace. This is explained by the movement of the bodies along smaller spheres that turn along the edge of the larger spheres. My calculations and models agree with and predict the motions of the spheres. The constant turning of the spheres also moves the bodies closer to Earth and farther from Earth, which explains why the bodies appear brighter or darker at different times. Thus, the heavens remain perfect. This perfection leads to music in the heavens, created by the spheres.

Identify the evidence that supports the explanation. At least two different lines of evidence are needed to be considered valid.

Identify any evidence that does not support the explanation. A single line of evidence can disprove an explanation. Often, new evidence makes scientists reevaluate an explanation. By the 1500s, Ptolemy's model was not making accurate predictions. In 1543, Copernicus, a Polish astronomer, proposed a new explanation of how planets move.

Identify any additional lines of evidence that should be considered. They might point to additional investigations to further examine the explanation. The gravitational force between objects was not known in Ptolemy's time. However, it should be considered when explaining the motion of planets.

Decide whether the original explanation is supported by enough evidence. An alternative explanation might better explain the evidence or might explain a wider range of observations.

If possible, propose an alternative explanation that could fit the evidence. Often, a simpler explanation is better if it fits the evidence. Copernicus explained the apparent backward movement and changing brightness of planets by placing the sun at the center of the solar system with the planets revolving around it.

You Try It!

In 2006, an official definition of a planet was determined. Read and analyze the information below concerning the classification of the largest Main Belt asteroid, Ceres.

The members of the International Astronomical Union (IAU) voted for the official definition of a planet to be a celestial body that

1. orbits the sun,
2. has enough mass so that its gravity helps it to maintain a nearly round shape,
3. has cleared the neighborhood around its orbit.

A group suggests that Ceres be considered a planet under the new definition. As the largest Main Belt asteroid, Ceres orbits the sun along with thousands of smaller asteroids. Images of Ceres clearly show its nearly round shape. These points, says the group's leader, should qualify Ceres as a planet.

1 Making Observations Underline lines of evidence that support the explanation.

2 Evaluating Data Circle any lines of evidence that do not support the proposed explanation. Explain why this evidence does not support the classification.

_____
_____
_____
_____

3 Applying Concepts Identify any additional evidence that should be considered when evaluating the explanation.

_____
_____
_____

4 Communicating Ideas If possible, propose an alternative explanation that could fit the evidence.

_____
_____
_____
_____
_____
_____
_____

Take It Home

Pluto was recently reclassified. What was it changed to and why? Identify the evidence that supported the decision. How does this compare to the proposed reclassification of Ceres? List similarities of the two explanations in a chart.

Moon Phases and Eclipses

ESSENTIAL QUESTION

How do Earth, the moon, and the sun affect each other?

By the end of this lesson, you should be able to describe the effects the sun and the moon have on Earth, including gravitational attraction, moon phases, and eclipses.

Why is part of the moon orange? Because Earth is moving between the moon and the sun, casting a shadow on the moon.

S6E2.a Phases of the moon

S6E2.b Solar and lunar eclipses

Lesson Labs

Quick Labs
- Moon Phases
- Lunar Eclipse

S.T.E.M. Lab
- What the Moon Orbits

Engage Your Brain

1 Identify Fill in the blanks with the word or phrase you think correctly completes the following sentences.

We can see the moon because it _____ the light from the sun.

The moon's _____ affects the oceans' tides on Earth.

The impact craters on the moon were created by collisions with _____, meteorites, and asteroids.

2 Describe Write your own caption for this photo in the space below.

_____

_____

_____

_____

_____

Active Reading

3 Synthesize You can often define an unknown word if you know the meaning of its word parts. Use the word parts and sentence below to make an educated guess about the meaning of the word *penumbra*.

Word part	Meaning
umbra	shade or shadow
pen-, from the Latin *paene*	almost

Example sentence
An observer in the <u>penumbra</u> experiences only a partial eclipse.

Vocabulary Terms

- satellite
- gravity
- lunar phases
- eclipse
- umbra
- penumbra

4 Apply As you learn the definition of each vocabulary term in this lesson, create your own definition or sketch to help you remember the meaning of the term.

penumbra: _____

_____

_____

_____

© Houghton Mifflin Harcourt Publishing Company • Image Credits: (bkg) ©Detlev Van Ravenswaay/Photo Researchers, Inc.; (tr) ©Larry Landolfi/Photo Researchers, Inc.

Lesson 2 Moon Phases and Eclipses **129**

'Round and 'Round They Go!

How are Earth, the moon, and the sun related in space?

Earth not only spins on its axis, but like the seven other planets in our solar system, Earth also orbits the sun. A body that orbits a larger body is called a **satellite** (SAT'l•yt). Six of the planets in our solar system have smaller bodies that orbit around each of them. These natural satellites are also called moons. Our moon is Earth's natural satellite.

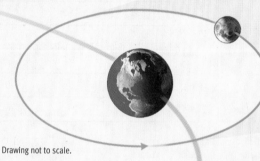

Earth revolves around the sun as the moon revolves around Earth.

Drawing not to scale.

Active Reading

5 Identify As you read, underline the reason that the moon stays in orbit around Earth.

Earth and the Moon Orbit the Sun

All bodies that have mass exert a force that pulls other objects with mass toward themselves. This force is called **gravity.** The mass of Earth is much larger than the mass of the moon, and therefore Earth's gravity exerts a stronger pull on the moon than the moon does on Earth. It is Earth's gravitational pull that keeps the moon in orbit around Earth, forming the Earth–moon system.

The Earth–moon system is itself in orbit around the sun. Even though the sun is relatively far away, the mass of the sun exerts a large gravitational pull on the Earth–moon system. This gravitational pull keeps the Earth–moon system in orbit around the sun.

The Moon Orbits Earth

The pull of Earth's gravity keeps the moon, Earth's natural satellite, in orbit around Earth. Even though the moon is Earth's closest neighbor in space, it is far away compared to the sizes of Earth and the moon themselves.

The distance between Earth and the moon is roughly 383,000 km (238,000 mi)—about a hundred times the distance between New York and Los Angeles. If a jet airliner could travel in space, it would take about 20 days to cover a distance that huge. Astronauts, whose spaceships travel much faster than jets, need about 3 days to reach the moon.

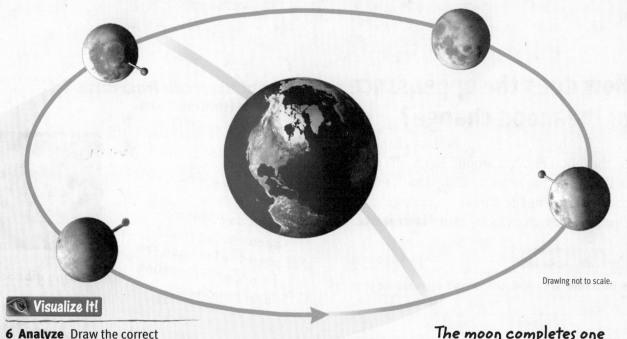

Drawing not to scale.

The moon completes one rotation for every revolution it makes around Earth.

Visualize It!

6 Analyze Draw the correct position of the pin when the moon is in the position shown in the top right corner of this figure.

What does the moon look like from Earth?

The moon is only visible from Earth when it reflects the sunlight that reaches the moon. Although the moon is most easily seen at night, you have probably also seen it during daytime on some days. In the daytime, the moon may only be as bright as a thin cloud and can be easily missed. On some days you can see the moon during both the daytime and at night, whereas on other days, you may not see the moon at all.

When you can look at the moon, you may notice darker and lighter areas. Perhaps you have imagined them as features of a face or some other pattern. People around the world have told stories about the animals, people, and objects they have imagined while looking at the light and dark areas of the moon. The dark and light spots do not change over the course of a month because only one side of the moon faces Earth, often called the near side of the moon. This is because the moon rotates once on its own axis each time it orbits Earth. The moon takes 27.3 days or about a month to orbit Earth once.

Inquiry

7 Analyze How would the moon appear to an observer on Earth if the moon did not rotate?

_____

_____

_____

_____

It's Just a Phase!

How does the appearance of the moon change?

From Earth, the moon's appearance changes. As the moon revolves around Earth, the portion of the moon that reflects sunlight back to Earth changes, causing the moon's appearance to change. These changes are called **lunar phases.**

Active Reading

8 Describe Why does the moon's appearance change?

_____

_____

Lunar Phases Cycle Monthly

The cycle begins with a new moon. At this time, Earth, the moon, and the sun are lined up, such that the near side of the moon is unlit. And so there appears to be no moon in the sky.

As the moon moves along its orbit, you begin to see the sunlight on the near side as a thin crescent shape. The crescent becomes thicker as the moon waxes, or grows. When half of the near side of the moon is in the sunlight, the moon has completed one-quarter of its cycle. This phase is called the *first quarter.*

More of the moon is visible during the second week, or the *gibbous* (GIB•uhs) *phase.* This is when the near side is more than half lit but not fully lit. When the moon is halfway through its cycle, the whole near side of the moon is in sunlight, and we see a full moon.

During the third week, the amount of the moon's near side in the sunlight decreases and it seems to shrink, or wane. When the near side is again only half in sunlight, the moon is three-quarters of the way through its cycle. The phase is called the *third quarter.*

In the fourth week, the area of the near side of the moon in sunlight continues to shrink. The moon is seen as waning crescent shapes. Finally, the near side of the moon is unlit—*new moon.*

Views of the moon from Earth's northern hemisphere

The waxing moon appears to grow each day. This is because the sunlit area that we can see from Earth is getting larger each day.

Waxing gibbous

Full moon

Waning gibbous

Think Outside the Book

9 Claims • Evidence • Reasoning
Look at the night sky and keep a moon journal for a series of nights. Make a claim stating the current phase of the moon. Use your observations as evidence to support your claim and explain your reasoning.

First quarter

Waxing crescent

New moon

Drawing not to scale.

Waning crescent

Third quarter

Visualize It!

10 Analyze What shape does the moon appear to be when it is closer to the sun than Earth is?

The waning moon appears to shrink each day. When the moon is waning, the sunlit area is getting smaller. Notice above that even as the phases of the moon change, the total amount of sunlight that the moon gets remains the same. Half the moon is always in sunlight, just as half of Earth is always in sunlight. The moon phases have a period of 29.5 days.

Exploring Eclipses

How do lunar eclipses occur?

An **eclipse** (ih•KLIPS) is an event during which one object in space casts a shadow onto another. On Earth, a lunar eclipse occurs when the moon moves through Earth's shadow. There are two parts of Earth's shadow, as you can see in the diagram below. The **umbra** (UHM•bruh) is the darkest part of a shadow. Around it is a spreading cone of lighter shadow called the **penumbra** (pih•NUHM•bruh). Just before a lunar eclipse, sunlight streaming past Earth produces a full moon. Then the moon moves into Earth's penumbra and becomes slightly less bright. As the moon moves into the umbra, Earth's dark shadow seems to creep across and cover the moon. The entire moon can be in darkness because the moon is small enough to fit entirely within Earth's umbra. After an hour or more, the moon moves slowly back into the sunlight that is streaming past Earth. A total lunar eclipse occurs when the moon passes completely into Earth's umbra. If the moon misses part or all of the umbra, part of the moon stays light and the eclipse is called a partial lunar eclipse.

You may be wondering why you don't see solar and lunar eclipses every month. The reason is that the moon's orbit around Earth is tilted—by about 5°—relative to the orbit of Earth around the sun. This tilt is enough to place the moon out of Earth's shadow for most full moons and Earth out of the moon's shadow for most new moons.

This composite photo shows the partial and total phases of a lunar eclipse over several hours.

Lunar eclipse

Visualize It!

11 Identify Fill in the boxes with the type of eclipse that would occur if the moon were in the areas being pointed to. Explain your reasoning.

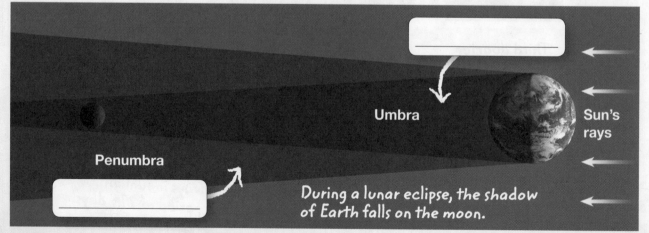

Umbra

Penumbra

Sun's rays

During a lunar eclipse, the shadow of Earth falls on the moon.

Drawing not to scale.

How do solar eclipses occur?

When the moon is directly between the sun and Earth, the shadow of the moon falls on a part of Earth and causes a solar eclipse. During a total solar eclipse, the sun's light is completely blocked by the moon, as seen in this photo. The umbra falls on the area of Earth that lies directly in line with the moon and the sun. Outside the umbra, but within the penumbra, people see a partial solar eclipse. The penumbra falls on the area that immediately surrounds the umbra.

The umbra of the moon is too small to make a large shadow on Earth's surface. The part of the umbra that hits Earth during an eclipse is never more than a few hundred kilometers across, as shown below. So, a total eclipse of the sun covers only a small part of Earth and is seen only by people in particular parts of Earth along a narrow path. A total solar eclipse usually lasts between one to two minutes at any one location. The most recent total eclipse was visible in the United States in 2017, and there is a total eclipse somewhere on Earth about every one to two years.

Solar eclipse

During a solar eclipse, the moon passes between the sun and Earth so that the sun is partially or totally obscured.

📎 **Active Reading**

12 Explain Why is it relatively rare to observe a solar eclipse?

_____

_____

_____

_____

👁 **Visualize It!**

13 Describe Explain what happens during a solar eclipse.

_____

_____

_____

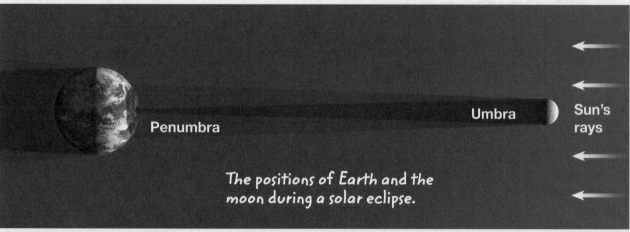

Penumbra   Umbra   Sun's rays

The positions of Earth and the moon during a solar eclipse.

Drawing not to scale.

Visual Summary

To complete this summary, circle the correct word. Then use the key below to check your answers. You can use this page to review the main concepts of the lesson.

Moon Phases and Eclipses

The Earth–moon system orbits the sun.

14 The moon takes about one day/month/year to orbit Earth.

Shadows in space cause eclipses.

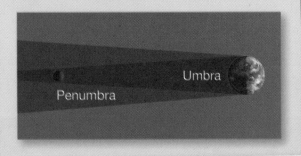

Umbra

Penumbra

15 When the moon is in Earth's umbra, a total solar/lunar eclipse is occurring.

The appearance of the moon depends on the positions of the sun, the moon, and Earth.

16 The fraction of the moon that receives sunlight always/never changes.

Answers: 14 month; 15 lunar; 16 never

17 Describe What causes the lunar phases that we see from Earth?

Lesson Review

Vocabulary

In your own words, define the following terms.

1 gravity

_____

_____

_____

2 satellite

_____

_____

3 umbra

_____

_____

Key Concepts

4 Describe What are two phases of a waxing moon, and how do they appear?

_____

_____

_____

_____

_____

_____

5 Identify Explain why the moon can be seen from Earth.

_____

_____

_____

6 Describe What is the relationship between Earth, the sun, and the moon in space?

_____

_____

_____

_____

_____

_____

Critical Thinking

Use the image below to answer the following question.

7 Identify What type of eclipse is shown in the diagram?

_____

8 Describe Where is the moon in its orbit at the time of a solar eclipse?

_____

9 Infer What phase is the moon in when there is a total solar eclipse?

_____

10 Predict Which shape of the moon will you never see during the daytime, after sunrise and before sunset? *Hint:* Consider the directions of the sun and moon from Earth.

_____

11 Synthesize If you were an astronaut in the middle of the near side of the moon during a full moon, how would the ground around you look? How would Earth, high in your sky look? Describe what is in sunlight and what is in darkness.

_____

_____

_____

_____

_____

My Notes

Earth's Tides

ESSENTIAL QUESTION

What causes tides?

By the end of this lesson, you should be able to explain what tides are and what causes them in Earth's oceans and to describe variations in the tides.

You may wonder why this boat is sitting in such shallow water. This photo was taken at low tide, when the ocean water is below average sea level.

 S6E3.d Waves, currents, and tides in Earth's systems

🧠 Engage Your Brain

1 Describe Fill in the blank with the word that you think correctly completes the following sentences.

The motion of the _____water_____ around Earth is related to tides.

The daily rotation of _____Earth_____ is also related to tides.

During a _____spring_____ tide, the water level is higher than the average sea level.

During a _____neap_____ tide, the water level is lower than the average sea level.

2 Label Draw an arrow to show where you think high tide might be.

→
or
→

Low tide ▶

✏️ Active Reading

3 Synthesize The word *spring* has different meanings. Use the meanings of the word *spring* and the sentence below to make an educated guess about the meaning of the term *spring tides*.

Meanings of *spring*
the season between winter and summer
a source of water from the ground
jump, or rise up
a coiled piece of metal

Example Sentence
During spring tides, the sun, the moon, and Earth are in a straight line, resulting in very high tides.

spring tides:

_____

_____

_____

Vocabulary Terms
• tide
• tidal range
• spring tide
• neap tide

4 Apply As you learn the definition of each vocabulary term in this lesson, create your own definition or sketch to help you remember the meaning of the term.

A Rising Tide of Interest

What causes tides?

The photographs below show the ocean at the same location at two different times. **Tides** are daily changes in the level of ocean water. Tides are caused by the difference in the gravitational force of the sun and the moon across Earth. This difference in gravitational force is called the *tidal force.* The tidal force exerted by the moon is stronger than the tidal force exerted by the sun because the moon is much closer to Earth than the sun is. So, the moon is mainly responsible for tides on Earth.

How often tides occur and how tidal levels vary depend on the position of the moon as it revolves around Earth. The gravity of the moon pulls on every particle of Earth. But because liquids move more easily than solids do, the pull on liquids is much more noticeable than the pull on solids is. The moon's gravitational pull on Earth decreases with the moon's distance from Earth. The part of Earth facing the moon is pulled toward the moon with the greatest force. So, water on that side of Earth bulges toward the moon. The solid Earth is pulled more strongly toward the moon than the ocean water on Earth's far side is. So, there is also a bulge of water on the side of Earth farthest from the moon.

At low tide, the water level is low, and the boats are far below the dock.

At high tide, the water level has risen, and the boats are close to the dock.

What are high tides and low tides?

The bulges that form in Earth's oceans are called high tides. *High tide* is a water level that is higher than the average sea level. Low tides form in the areas between the high tides. *Low tide* is a water level that is lower than the average sea level. At low tide, the water levels are lower because the water is in high-tide areas.

As the moon moves around Earth and Earth rotates, the tidal bulges move around Earth. The tidal bulges follow the motion of the moon. As a result, many places on Earth have two high tides and two low tides each day.

 **Visualize It!**

6 Identify Label the areas where high tides form and the area where the other low tide forms.

Note: Drawing is not to scale.

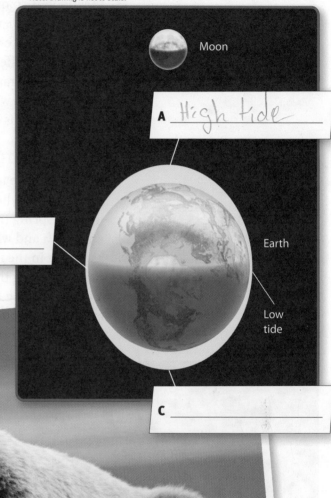

Moon

A __High tide__

Earth

Low tide

B __low tide__

C _____

This grizzly bear in Alaska is taking advantage of low tide by digging for clams.

7 Predict What happens to the bear when high tide comes in? Explain your reasoning.

_____

_____

Tide Me Over

What are two kinds of tidal ranges?

Active Reading

8 Identify As you read, underline the two kinds of tidal range.

Tides are due to the *tidal force,* the difference between the force of gravity on one side of Earth and the other side of Earth. Because the moon is so much closer to Earth than the sun is, the moon's tidal force is greater than the sun's tidal force. The moon's effect on tides is twice as strong as the sun's effect. The combined gravitational effects of the sun and the moon on Earth result in different tidal ranges. A **tidal range** is the difference between the levels of ocean water at high tide and low tide. Tidal range depends on the positions of the sun and the moon relative to Earth.

Spring Tides: The Largest Tidal Range

Tides that have the largest daily tidal range are **spring tides**. Spring tides happen when the sun, the moon, and Earth form a straight line. So, spring tides happen when the moon is between the sun and Earth and when the moon is on the opposite side of Earth, as shown in the illustrations below. In other words, spring tides happen during the new moon and full moon phases, or every 14 days. During these times, the gravitational effects of the sun and moon add together, causing one pair of very large tidal bulges. Spring tides have nothing to do with the season.

Note: Drawings are not to scale.

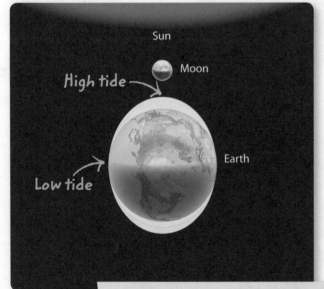

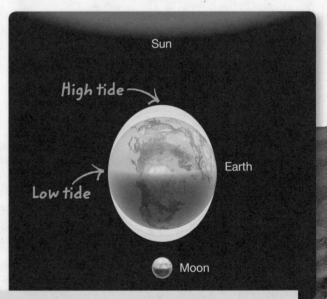

During spring tides, the tidal force of the sun on Earth adds to the tidal force of the moon. The tidal range increases.

Inquiry

9 Inquire Explain why spring tides happen twice a month.

_____

_____

Neap Tides: The Smallest Tidal Range

Tides that have the smallest daily tidal range are **neap tides**. Neap tides happen when the sun, Earth, and the moon form a 90° angle, as shown in the illustrations below. During a neap tide, the gravitational effects of the sun and the moon on Earth do not add together as they do during spring tides. Neap tides occur halfway between spring tides, during the first quarter and third quarter phases of the moon. At these times, the sun and the moon cause two pairs of smaller tidal bulges.

Note: Drawings are not to scale.

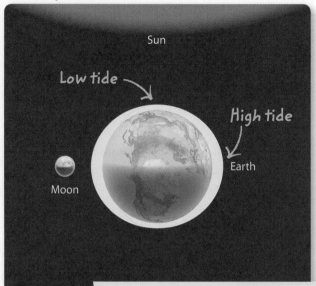

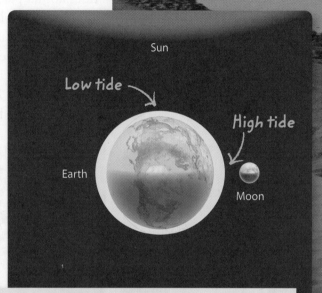

During neap tides, the gravitational effects of the sun and the moon on Earth do not add together. The tidal range decreases.

10 Compare Fill in the Venn diagram to compare and contrast spring tides and neap tides.

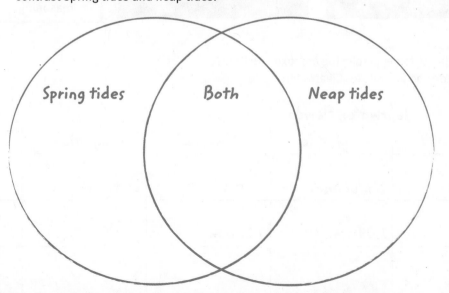

Spring tides   Both   Neap tides

What causes tidal cycles?

The rotation of Earth and the moon's revolution around Earth determine when tides occur. Imagine that Earth rotated at the same speed that the moon revolves around Earth. If this were true, the same side of Earth would always face the moon. And high tide would always be at the same places on Earth. But the moon revolves around Earth much more slowly than Earth rotates. A place on Earth that is facing the moon takes 24 h and 50 min to rotate to face the moon again. So, the cycle of high tides and low tides at that place happens 50 min later each day.

In many places there are two high tides and two low tides each day. Because the tide cycle occurs in 24 h and 50 min intervals, it takes about 6 h and 12.5 min (one-fourth the time of the total cycle) for water in an area to go from high tide to low tide. It takes about 12 h and 25 min (one-half the time of the total cycle) to go from one high tide to the next high tide.

Note: Drawings are not to scale.

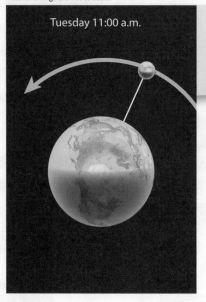

Tuesday 11:00 a.m.

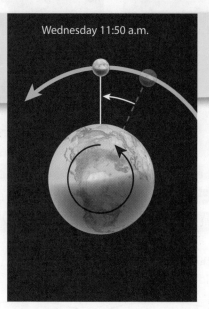

Wednesday 11:50 a.m.

The moon moves only a fraction of its orbit in the time that Earth rotates once.

Think Outside the Book (Inquiry)

11 Inquire Draw a diagram of Earth to show what Earth's tides would be like if the moon revolved around Earth at the same speed that Earth rotates. Summarize the evidence that supports your claim and explain your reasoning.

12 Predict In the table, predict the approximate times of high tide and low tide for Clearwater, Florida.

Tide Data for Clearwater, Florida

Date (2009)	High tide	Low tide	High tide	Low tide
August 19	12:14 a.m.		12:39 p.m.	
August 20	1:04 a.m.	7:17 a.m.		
August 21				

Extreme Living Conditions

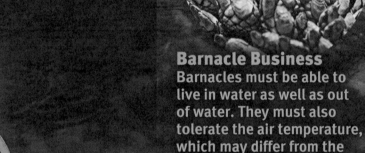

Some organisms living along ocean coastlines must be able to tolerate extreme living conditions. At high tide, much of the coast is under water. At low tide, much of the coast is dry. Some organisms must also survive the constant crashing of waves against the shore.

Barnacle Business

Barnacles must be able to live in water as well as out of water. They must also tolerate the air temperature, which may differ from the temperature of the water.

Ghostly Crabs

Ghost crabs live near the high tide line on sandy shores. They scurry along the sand to avoid being underwater when the tide comes in. Ghost crabs can also find cover between rocks.

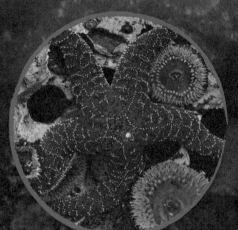

Stunning Starfish

Starfish live in tidal pools, which are areas along the shore where water remains at low tide. Starfish must be able to survive changes in water temperature and salinity.

Extend

Inquiry

13 Identify Describe how living conditions change for two tidal organisms.

14 Research and Record List the names of two organisms that live in the high tide zone or the low tide zone along a coastline of your choice.

15 Describe Imagine a day in the life of an organism you researched in question 14 by doing one of the following:
- make a poster
- write a play
- record an audio story
- make a cartoon

Visual Summary

To complete this summary, fill in the blanks with the correct word. Then use the key below to check your answers. You can use this page to review the main concepts of the lesson.

In many places, two high tides and two low tides occur every day.

16 The type of tide shown here is

_____

The gravitational effects of the moon and the sun cause tides.

17 Tides on Earth are caused mainly by the

_____

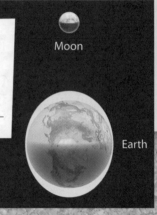

Moon

Earth

Tides on Earth

Note: Drawings are not to scale.

There are two kinds of tidal ranges: spring tides and neap tides.

Sun

Moon

Earth

18 During a spring tide, the sun, moon, and Earth are in a/an

_____

Sun

Moon

Earth

19 During a neap tide, the sun, moon, and Earth form a/an

_____

Answers: 16 low tide; 17 moon; 18 straight line; 19 90° angle

20 **Describe** State how the moon causes tides.

_____

Lesson Review

Vocabulary

Answer the following questions in your own words.

1 Use *tide* and *tidal range* in the same sentence.

_____

_____

2 Write an original definition for *neap tide* and for *spring tide*.

_____

_____

_____

_____

Key Concepts

3 Describe Explain what tides are. Include *high tide* and *low tide* in your answer.

_____

_____

_____

_____

4 Explain State what causes tides on Earth.

_____

_____

_____

5 Identify Write the alignment of the moon, the sun, and Earth that causes a spring tide.

_____

_____

6 Describe Explain why tides happen 50 min later each day.

_____

_____

_____

Critical Thinking

Use this diagram to answer the next question.

Note: Drawing is not to scale.

Last quarter moon

7 Analyze What type of tidal range will Earth have when the moon is in this position?

_____

_____

8 Apply How many days pass between the minimum and the maximum of the tidal range in any given area? Explain your answer.

_____

_____

_____

_____

_____

_____

9 Apply How would the tides on Earth be different if the moon revolved around Earth in 15 days instead of 30 days? Support your claim with evidence.

_____

_____

_____

_____

_____

_____

My Notes

Unit 2 [Big Idea]

Earth and the moon move in predictable ways and have predictable effects on each other as they orbit the sun.

Lesson 1

ESSENTIAL QUESTION
How are Earth's days, years, and seasons related to the way Earth moves in space?

Relate Earth's days, years, and seasons to Earth's movement in space.

Lesson 2

ESSENTIAL QUESTION
How do Earth, the moon, and the sun affect each other?

Describe the effects the sun and the moon have on Earth, including gravitational attraction, moon phases, and eclipses.

Lesson 3

ESSENTIAL QUESTION
What causes tides?

Explain what tides are and what causes them in Earth's oceans, and describe variations in the tides.

Think Outside the Book

2 Synthesize Choose one of these activities to help synthesize what you have learned in this unit.

☐ Using what you learned in lesson 3, analyze the data from a tide table to create a drawing or diagram that explains the causes and effects of tides.

☐ Using what you learned in lessons 1, 2, and 3, describe the hierarchical relationship of gravitational attraction in the Earth-moon-sun system using a poster presentation.

Connect ESSENTIAL QUESTIONS
Lessons 1, 2, and 3

1 Synthesize Name the natural cycles that occur as a result of the Earth-moon-sun system.

_____

_____

_____

_____

Unit 2 Review

Name _____

Vocabulary

Fill in each blank with the term that best completes the following sentences.

1 A _____ is the periodic rise and fall of the water level in the oceans and other large bodies of water.

2 A _____ is the motion of a body that travels around another body in space.

3 The force of _____ keeps Earth and other planets of the solar system in orbit around the sun and keeps the moon in orbit around Earth.

4 A natural or artificial body that revolves around a celestial body that is greater in mass is called a _____.

5 _____ is the counterclockwise spin of a planet or moon as seen from above a planet's north pole.

Key Concepts

Read each question below, and circle the best answer.

6 Look at the table of tide information.

Date	High tide time	High tide height (m)	Low tide time	Low tide height (m)
June 3	6:04 a.m.	6.11	12:01 a.m.	1.76
June 4	6:58 a.m.	5.92	12:54 a.m.	1.87
June 5	7:51 a.m.	5.80	1:47 a.m.	1.90
June 6	8:42 a.m.	5.75	2:38 a.m.	1.87
June 7	9:30 a.m.	5.79	3:27 a.m.	1.75
June 8	10:16 a.m.	5.90	4:13 a.m.	1.56
June 9	11:01 a.m.	6.08	4:59 a.m.	1.32
June 10	11:46 a.m.	6.28	5:44 a.m.	1.05
June 11	12:32 p.m.	6.47	6:30 a.m.	0.78

What was the tidal range on June 9?

A 4.76 m

C 6.08 m

B 7.40 m

D 4.76 ft

7 Aside from Earth's tilt, what other factor contributes to Earth's seasons?

   A the time of the day

   B the energy as heat from the moon

   C the angle of the sun's rays and the number of hours of daylight

   D cold or warm air blowing from the oceans

8 Ann is looking at the night sky. There is a first-quarter moon. What does she see?

   A a moon shaped like a crescent

   B a moon shaped like a half circle

   C a moon shaped like a circle, shining brightly

   D no moon in the sky

9 Which is a similarity between a neap tide and a spring tide?

   A Neap tides occur once a year in fall and spring tides once a year in spring.

   B Each occurs twice a year and relates to the phases of the moon.

   C A neap tide occurs at night, and a spring tide occurs during the day.

   D Each tide occurs twice a month, and is determined by the pull of gravity of the moon.

10 The diagram below shows the relative positions of the sun, the moon, and Earth.

   What does the diagram show?

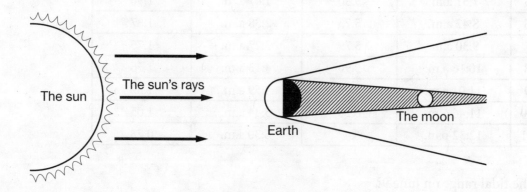

   A a solar eclipse   **C** a first-quarter moon

   B a lunar eclipse   **D** a third-quarter moon

11 During equinox, the sun's rays strike Earth at a 90-degree angle along the equator. What is the result of the equinox?

  A the hours of daylight and the hours of darkness are about the same

  B the hours of daylight are longer than the hours of darkness

  C the hours of darkness are longer than the hours of daylight

  D an unseasonably warm day in the midst of winter

12 Examine the diagram below.

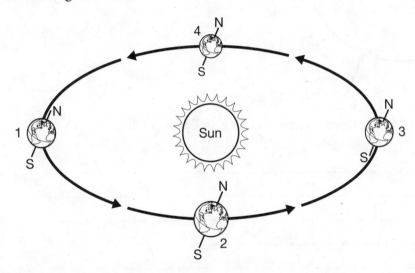

The position labeled "1" represents the season of summer in—

  A the Southern Hemisphere.   **C** the Eastern Hemisphere.

  B Antarctica.   **D** the Northern Hemisphere.

Critical Thinking

Answer the following questions in the space provided.

13 Janais lives near the ocean. How do Earth, the sun, and the moon interact to affect Janais's life?

_____

_____

_____

_____

_____

_____

_____

14 Look at the diagram of Earth.

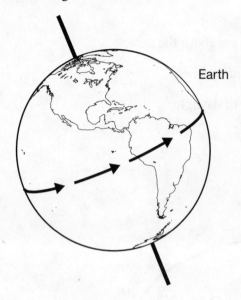

Earth

Describe the rotation of Earth about its axis and why an Earth day is
24 hours long.

_____

_____

_____

_____

_____

_____

_____

Connect **ESSENTIAL QUESTIONS**
Lessons 2 and 3

Answer the following question in the space provided.

15 Explain what causes tides on Earth and why high and low tides occur.

_____

_____

_____

_____

_____

_____

_____

Earth's Water

Waterfalls show the important role gravity plays in moving Earth's water.

Big Idea

Earth's waters cycle through a connected system of atmosphere, land, and oceans, distributing matter and energy around the planet.

S6E3., S6E3.a, S6E3.b, S6E3.c, S6E3.d

What do you think?

Fresh water is found in ponds, lakes, streams, rivers, and underground in aquifers. Where does the water come from? How does water circulate around the planet? As you explore the unit, gather evidence to help you state and support claims to answer these questions.

Humans rely on water to stay healthy.

CITIZEN SCIENCE

Conserving Water

Fresh water evaporates into the air and then condenses to form clouds. It falls from the sky as precipitation and then flows over Earth's surface in streams and rivers. It seeps underground through soil and rocks. Fresh water makes up only a small fraction of Earth's water and is not evenly distributed.

Some watering methods lose a great deal of water to evaporation.

1 Think About It

A Take a quick survey of your classmates. Ask them where the fresh water they use every day at home and at school comes from.

_____

_____

_____

B Ask your classmates to identify different uses of water at your school.

_____

_____

_____

_____

© Houghton Mifflin Harcourt Publishing Company • Image Credits: (t) ©Ken Schulze/Alamy

② Ask a Question

How do you conserve water?

Water is an essential resource for everyone, but it is a limited resource. What are some ways that your school may be wasting water?

_____

_____

_____

_____

_____

_____

_____

_____

Xeriscaping is a method of landscaping by using plants that require less water.

③ Make a Plan

A Make a list of five ways in which the school can conserve water.

_____

_____

_____

_____

_____

B In the space below, sketch out a design for a pamphlet or a poster that you can place in the hallways to promote water conservation at your school.

Take It Home

Take a pamphlet or a poster home. With an adult, talk about ways in which water can be conserved in and around your home. See *ScienceSaurus®* for more information about conservation.

The **Water Cycle**

ESSENTIAL QUESTION

How does water change state and move around on Earth?

By the end of this lesson, you should be able to describe the water cycle and the different processes that are part of the water cycle on Earth.

Water from the ocean evaporates, forms clouds, then falls back into the ocean when it rains. Can you think of other ways water travels between Earth and Earth's atmosphere?

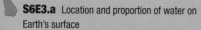

S6E3.a Location and proportion of water on Earth's surface

S6E3.b Sun's role in cycling of water

Quick Labs
• Modeling the Water Cycle
• Can You Make It Rain in a Jar?
• How Does a Cloud Form?
• Out of Thin Air

Exploration Lab
• Changes in Water

Engage Your Brain

1 Predict Circle the word or phrase that best completes the following sentences.

The air inside a glass of ice would feel *warm/cold/room temperature*.

Ice would *melt/evaporate/remain frozen* if it were left outside on a hot day.

Water vapor will *condense on/evaporate from/melt into* the glass of ice from the air.

The ice *absorbs energy from/maintains its energy/releases energy into* the surroundings when it melts.

2 Analyze Using the photo above, solve the word scramble to answer the question: What happens to ice as it warms up?

TI GACNSEH EASTT

_____

Active Reading

3 Synthesize You can often define an unknown word if you know the meaning of the word's origin. Use the meaning of the words' origins and the sentence below to make an educated guess about the meaning of *precipitation* and *evaporation*.

Latin word	Meaning
praecipitare	fall
evaporare	spread out in vapor or steam

Example sentence
Precipitation, in the form of rain, helps replace the water lost by evaporation from the lake.

precipitation:

_____

evaporation:

_____

Vocabulary Terms

• water cycle
• evaporation
• transpiration
• sublimation
• condensation
• precipitation
• cloud
• dew point
• fog

4 Apply As you learn the definition of each vocabulary term in this lesson, write out a sentence using that term to help you remember the meaning of the term.

What goes up...

What is the water cycle?

Movement of water between the atmosphere, land, oceans, and even living things makes up the **water cycle**. Rain, snow, and hail fall on the oceans and land because of gravity. On land, ice and water flow downhill. Water flows in streams, rivers, and waterfalls such as the one in the photo, because of gravity. If the land is flat, water will collect in certain areas forming ponds, lakes, and marshland. Some water will soak through the ground and collect underground as groundwater. Even groundwater flows downhill.

Water and snow can move upward if they turn into water vapor and rise into the air. Plants and animals also release water vapor into the air. In the air, water vapor can travel great distances with the wind. Winds can also move the water in the surface layer of the ocean by creating ocean currents. When ocean currents reach the shore or colder climates, the water will sink if it is cold enough or salty enough. The sinking water creates currents at different depths in the ocean. These are some of the ways in which water travels all over Earth.

Visualize It!

5 Analyze What is the relationship between gravity and water in this image?

_____

_____

_____

_____

How does water change state?

Water is found in three states on Earth: as liquid water, as solid water ice, and as gaseous water vapor. Water is visible as a liquid or a solid, but it is invisible as a gas in the air. Water can change from one state to another as energy is absorbed or released.

Water absorbs energy from its surroundings as it *melts* from solid to liquid. Water also absorbs energy when it *evaporates* from liquid to gas, or when it *sublimates* from solid to gas. Water releases energy into its surroundings when it *condenses* from gas to liquid. Water also releases energy when it *freezes* from liquid to solid, or *deposits* from gas to solid. No water is lost during these changes.

 **Active Reading**

6 Identify As you read, underline each process in which energy is absorbed or released.

Visualize It!

7 Analyze Under each photo, write an example of where you might find water in that state of matter.

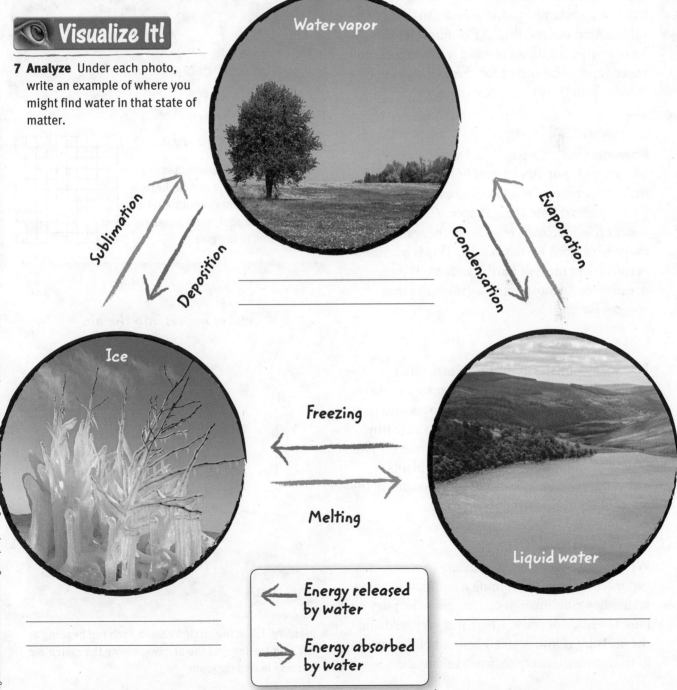

Water vapor

Sublimation

Deposition

Evaporation

Condensation

Ice

Freezing

Melting

Liquid water

← Energy released by water

→ Energy absorbed by water

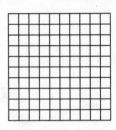

The evaporating water leaves behind a dry, cracked lake bed.

How does water reach the atmosphere?

Water reaches the atmosphere as water vapor in three ways: evaporation (ih•VAP•uh•ray•shuhn), transpiration (tran•spuh•RAY•shuhn), and sublimation (suhb•luh•MAY•shuhn). It takes a lot of energy for liquid or solid water to turn into water vapor. The energy for these changes comes mostly from the sun, as solar energy.

◯ Evaporation

Evaporation occurs when liquid water changes into water vapor. About 90% of the water in the atmosphere comes from the evaporation of Earth's water. Some water evaporates from the water on land. However, most of the water vapor evaporates from Earth's oceans. This is because oceans cover most of Earth's surface. Therefore, oceans receive most of the solar energy that reaches Earth.

◯ Transpiration

Like many organisms, plants release water into the environment. Liquid water turns into water vapor inside the plant and moves into the atmosphere through stomata. Stomata are tiny holes that are found on some plant surfaces. This release of water vapor into the air by plants is called **transpiration**. About 10% of the water in the atmosphere comes from transpiration.

◯ Sublimation

When solid water changes directly to water vapor without first becoming a liquid, it is called **sublimation**. Sublimation can happen when dry air blows over ice or snow, where it is very cold and the pressure is low. A small amount of the water in the atmosphere comes from sublimation.

Do the Math **You Try It**

8 Graph Show the percentage of water vapor in the atmosphere that comes from evaporation by coloring the equivalent number of squares in the grid.

Water moves into the air.

A   B   C

Visualize It!

9 Identify Fill in the circles beside each red heading at left with the label of the arrow showing the matching process in this diagram.

What happens to water in the atmosphere?

Water reaches the atmosphere as water vapor. In the atmosphere, water vapor mixes with other gases. To leave the atmosphere, water vapor must change into liquid or solid water. Then the liquid or solid water can fall to Earth's surface.

◯ Condensation

Remember, **condensation** (kahn•den•SAY•shuhn) is the change of state from a gas to a liquid. If air that contains water vapor is cooled enough, condensation occurs. Some of the water vapor condenses on small particles, such as dust, forming little balls or tiny droplets of water. These water droplets float in the air as clouds, fog, or mist. At the ground level, water vapor may condense on cool surfaces as dew.

◯ Precipitation

In clouds, water droplets may collide and "stick" together to become larger. If a droplet becomes large enough, it falls to Earth's surface as precipitation (prih•sip•ih•TAY•shuhn). **Precipitation** is any form of water that falls to Earth from clouds. Three common kinds of precipitation shown in the photos are rain, snow, and hail. Snow and hail form if the water droplets freeze. Most rain falls into the oceans because most water evaporates from ocean surfaces and oceans cover most of Earth's surface. But winds carry clouds from the ocean over land, increasing the amount of precipitation that falls on land.

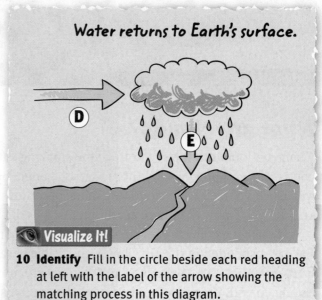

Water returns to Earth's surface.

👁 **Visualize It!**

10 Identify Fill in the circle beside each red heading at left with the label of the arrow showing the matching process in this diagram.

11 Summarize Fill in the boxes to describe how precipitation forms.

Hail

Snow

Rain

```
┌─────────────────┐
│ _____   │ ──▶ Small droplet
│ _____   │           │
└─────────────────┘           ▼
        ┌─────────────────┐
        │ _____   │ ──▶ Large droplet
        │ _____   │     falls to Earth.
        └─────────────────┘
```

Head in the Clouds

What are clouds?

When you look into the sky, you see the amazing shapes that clouds take and how quickly those shapes change. But, have you ever asked yourself what clouds are made of or how they form? And did you know that there are different types of clouds?

A **cloud** is a collection of small water droplets or ice crystals that are suspended in the air. Clouds are visible because water droplets and ice crystals reflect light. Clouds are most often associated with precipitation. However, the reality is that most cloud types do not produce precipitation.

How do clouds affect climate?

The precipitation that falls from clouds has a significant effect on local climate. In particular, the pattern of precipitation of an area will determine the climate of that area. For instance, a desert is an area that receives less than 25 cm of precipitation a year. But, a tropical rainforest may average 250 cm of precipitation a year.

Clouds also affect temperatures on Earth. About 25% of the sun's energy that reaches Earth is reflected back into space by clouds. Low-altitude clouds, which are thick and reflect more sunlight, help to cool Earth. On the other hand, thin, high-altitude clouds absorb some of the energy that radiates from Earth. Part of this energy is reradiated back to Earth's surface. This warms Earth, because this energy is not directly lost to space.

Active Reading 12 **Describe** What are two ways in which clouds affect Earth's climate?

_____

_____

_____

13 **Apply** Sketch a cloud, and write a caption that relates the drawing to the content on this page.

_____

_____

_____

_____

How do clouds form?

Clouds form when water vapor condenses, or changes from a gas to a liquid. For water vapor to condense, two things must happen. Air must be cooled to its dew point, and there must be a solid surface on which water molecules can condense.

Air Cools to the Dew Point

As warm air rises in Earth's atmosphere, it expands and cools. If air rises high enough into the atmosphere, it cools to its dew point. **Dew point** is the temperature at which the rate of condensation equals the rate of evaporation. *Evaporation* is the change of state from a liquid to a gas that usually occurs at the surface of a liquid. Evaporation takes place at the surface of an ocean, lake, stream, or other body of water. Water vapor in the air can condense and form water droplets or ice crystals when the temperature is at or below the dew point.

Water Droplets or Ice Crystals Form on Nuclei

Water molecules condense much more rapidly when there is a solid surface on which to condense. In clouds, tiny solid particles called *cloud condensation nuclei* are the surfaces on which water droplets condense. Examples of cloud condensation nuclei include dust, salt, soil, and smoke.

Clouds are most commonly made of very large numbers of very small water droplets. However, at high altitudes, where temperatures are very cold, clouds are composed of ice crystals.

D Cloud formation takes place.

C Condensation takes place on nuclei.

condensation nucleus
0.0002 millimeter diameter

cloud droplet
0.05 millimeter diameter

B

_____

_____

A Warm air rises, expands, and cools.

14 Conclude Complete the flow chart by filling in the missing information.

What is the role of solar energy in cloud formation?

The water cycle is the movement of water between the atmosphere, land, and ocean. Solar energy drives the water cycle and, therefore, provides the energy for cloud formation.

About 50 percent of the sun's incoming energy is absorbed by land, by water on the land's surface, and by surface waters in the oceans. This absorbed energy causes liquid water at the water's surface to become water vapor, a gas. This process is called evaporation. The water vapor rises into the atmosphere with air that has been warmed near Earth's surface.

Solar energy does not warm the surface of Earth evenly. Unequal heating of Earth's surface causes areas of high pressure and low pressure to form in the atmosphere. Air flows horizontally from areas of high pressure to areas of low pressure. This horizontal movement of air is called *wind*. Wind causes clouds to move around Earth's surface. However, for air to be cooled to its dew point so that clouds can form, the air is pushed up, or is lifted, into the atmosphere.

What processes cool air enough to form clouds?

 **Active Reading** **15 Identify** As you read, underline the processes that can cool air enough to form clouds.

There are several ways in which air can be cooled to its dew point. These include frontal and orographic lifting (ohr•uh•GRAF•ik LIFT•ing). Frontal lifting can occur when a warm air mass rises over a cold air mass. Once the rising air cools to its dew point, condensation occurs and clouds form.

Frontal lifting can also occur when a mass of cold air slides under a mass of warm air, pushing the warm air upward. The rising air cools to the dew point. Clouds form that often develop into thunderstorms.

Orographic lifting occurs when an obstacle, such as a mountain range, forces a mass of air upward. Water vapor in the air cools to its dew point and condenses. The clouds that form release large amounts of precipitation as rain or snow as they rise up the mountain. The other side of the mountain receives little precipitation.

Visualize It!

16 Compare The images below show two processes by which clouds form when an air mass is lifted. In what ways are these two processes similar? In what ways are these two processes different?

_____

_____

_____

Frontal Lifting

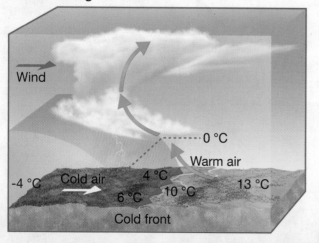

Orographic Lifting

How does fog form?

Water vapor that condenses very near Earth's surface is called **fog**. Fog forms when moist air at or near Earth's surface cools to its dew point. Fog is simply a cloud that forms at ground level.

Ground fog, which is also called *radiation fog*, generally forms in low-lying areas on clear, calm nights. As Earth's surface cools, moist air near the ground cools to its dew point. Water vapor in the air condenses into water droplets, which form fog.

Fog also forms when warm, moist air moves across cold water and is cooled to its dew point. This is how sea fog, or advection fog, forms. Unlike ground fog, sea fog occurs at all times of day.

Another type of fog forms when evaporation takes place into cold air that is lying over warmer water. Called *steam fog*, this fog appears as steam directly above bodies of water. It occurs most commonly on cold fall mornings.

Fog is a hazard because it reduces visibility. Very dense fog can reduce visibility to a few meters. Water droplets in fog scatter light. This makes objects difficult for people to see clearly. Without visible landmarks, it is also hard to judge distance and speed.

Active Reading

17 Identify As you read the text, underline ways in which fog forms.

Visualize It!

18 Describe Which type of fog is shown below, and why does it form above cold water?

Ground fog forms at night when Earth's surface cools. Moist air near the ground cools to its dew point, which causes water vapor to condense.

How does water move on land and in the oceans?

After water falls to Earth, it flows and circulates all over Earth. On land, water flows downhill, both on the surface and underground. However, most of Earth's precipitation falls into the oceans. Ocean currents move water around the oceans.

Runoff and Infiltration

All of the water on land flows downhill because of gravity. Streams, rivers, and the water that flows over land are types of *runoff*. Runoff flows downhill toward oceans, lakes, and marshlands.

Some of the water on land seeps into the ground. This process is called *infiltration* (in•fil•TRAY•shuhn). Once undergound, the water is called *groundwater*. Groundwater also flows downhill through soil and rock.

Active Reading

19 Compare How do runoff and groundwater differ?

_____

_____

_____

Visualize It!

20 Summarize Write a caption describing how water is moving in the diagram above.

_____

_____

_____

Icebergs can be carried over long distances by ocean currents.

Ice Flow

Much of Earth's ice is stored in large ice caps in Antarctica and Greenland. Some ice is stored in glaciers at high altitudes all over Earth. Glaciers cover about 10% of Earth's surface. Glaciers can be called "rivers of ice" because gravity also causes glaciers to flow slowly downhill. Many glaciers never leave land. However, some glaciers flow to the ocean, where pieces may break off, as seen in the photo, and float far out to sea as icebergs.

Ocean Circulation

Winds move ocean water on the surface in great currents, sometimes for thousands of miles. At some shores, or if the water is very cold or salty, it will sink deep into the ocean. This movement helps create deep ocean currents. Both surface currents and deep ocean currents transport large amounts of water from ocean to ocean.

Water Works

What does the water cycle transport?

In the water cycle, each state of water has some energy in it. This energy is released into or absorbed from its surroundings as water changes state. The energy in each state of water is then transported as the water moves from place to place. Matter is also transported as water and the materials in the water move all over Earth. Therefore, the water cycle moves energy and matter through Earth's atmosphere, land, oceans, and living things.

Energy

Energy is transported in the water cycle through changes of state and by the movement of water from place to place. For example, water that evaporates from the ocean carries energy into the atmosphere. This movement of energy can generate hurricanes. Also, cold ocean currents can cool the air along a coastline by absorbing the energy from the air and leaving the air cooler. This energy is carried away quickly as the current continues on its path. Such processes affect the weather and climate of an area.

Matter

Earth's ocean currents move vast amounts of water all over the world. These currents also transport the solids in the water and the dissolved salts and gases. Rivers transfer water from land into the ocean. Rivers also carry large amounts of sand, mud, and gravel as shown below. Rivers form deltas and floodplains, where some of the materials from upstream collect in areas downstream. Rivers also carve valleys and canyons, and carry the excess materials downstream. Glaciers also grind away rock and carry the ground rock with them as they flow.

Visualize It!

22 **Compare** Are the two rivers shown here transporting the same kinds of matter? Use evidence from the photo to support your claim.

_____

_____

Visualize It! The Water Cycle

Water is continuously changing state and moving from place to place in the water cycle. This diagram shows these processes and movements.

23 Identify Label each arrow to show which process the arrow represents.

24 Identify Shade in the arrows that indicate where water is changing state.

Condensation

Evaporation

Precipitation

Sublimation

_____

_____

_____

Think Outside the Book Inquiry

25 Apply Write about an interview with a water molecule. Write a story, or design a pamphlet describing one possible trip that a water molecule could take through the water cycle. Share your project with classmates.

Visual Summary

To complete this summary, write a term that describes the process happening in each of the images. Then use the key below to check your answers. You can use this page to review the main concepts of the lesson.

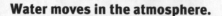

Water moves in the atmosphere.

26 _____

The Water Cycle

Water moves into the atmosphere.

28 _____

Water moves on land and in oceans.

27 _____

Answers: 26 condensation or precipitation; 27 iceflow, runoff, infiltration, or ocean current; 28 evaporation, transpiration, or sublimation

29 Predict Describe what might happen to the water cycle if less solar energy reached Earth and how Earth's climate would be affected.

_____

Lesson Review

Vocabulary

Write the correct label A, B, C, or D under each term to indicate the definition of that term.

1 water cycle

_____

2 evaporation

_____

3 precipitation

_____

4 condensation

_____

A the change of state from a liquid to a gas

B the change of state from a gas to a liquid

C the movement of water between the atmosphere, land, oceans, and living things

D any form of water that falls to Earth's surface from the clouds

Key Concepts

5 Identify List the three ways in which water reaches the atmosphere and tell which way accounts for most of the water in the atmosphere.

_____

_____

_____

_____

6 Classify Which of the processes of the water cycle occur by releasing energy? Use evidence to support your claim and explain your reasoning.

_____

_____

_____

7 Identify What happens to water once it reaches Earth's surface?

_____

_____

_____

8 Summarize Describe how three common types of precipitation form.

_____

_____

_____

_____

Critical Thinking

Use this diagram to answer the following questions.

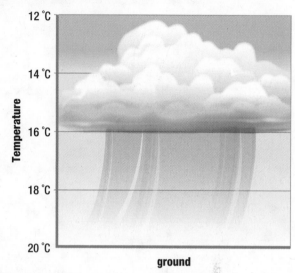

9 Analyze What is the dew-point temperature at which cloud formation began?

_____

_____

10 Explain Why doesn't cloud formation take place until the dew-point temperature is reached?

_____

_____

_____

_____

11 Infer Why does the amount of water that flows in a river change during the year?

_____

_____

12 Evaluate Warm ocean currents cool as they flow along a coastline, away from the equator. Explain what is transported and how.

_____

_____

_____

My Notes

Surface Water and Groundwater

ESSENTIAL QUESTION

How does fresh water flow on Earth?

By the end of this lesson, you should be able to explain the processes involved in the flow of water, both above and below the ground.

S6E3.a Location and proportion of water on Earth's surface

Fresh water flows on Earth's surface, sometimes tumbling over waterfalls like these.

Lesson Labs

Quick Labs
- Modeling Groundwater
- Model a Stream

Exploration Lab
- Aquifers and Development

Engage Your Brain

1 Identify Read over the following vocabulary terms. In the spaces provided, place a + if you know the term well, a ~ if you have heard of the term but are not sure what it means, and a ? if you are unfamiliar with the term. Then write a sentence that includes one of the words you are most familiar with.

_____ tributary
_____ surface water
_____ aquifer

Sentence using known word:

_____

_____

_____

2 Describe Write your own caption for this photo.

_____

_____

_____

_____

Active Reading

3 Apply Many scientific words, such as *channel*, also have everyday meanings. Use context clues to write your own definition for each meaning of the word *channel*.

Example sentence:
She didn't like the TV show, so she changed the channel.

channel:

_____

_____

Example sentence:
The channel of the river was broad and deep.

channel:

_____

_____

Vocabulary Terms

- surface water
- groundwater
- water table
- channel
- tributary
- watershed
- divide
- aquifer

4 Identify As you read, create a reference card for each vocabulary term. On one side of the card, write the term and its meaning. On the other side, draw an image that illustrates or makes a connection to the term. These cards can be used as bookmarks in the text so that you can refer to them while studying.

Getting Your Feet Wet

Where on Earth is fresh water found?

About 97% of Earth's water is salty, which leaves only 3% as fresh water. Most of that small amount of fresh water is frozen as ice and snow, so only about 1% of Earth's water is fresh liquid water. This fresh liquid water is found both on and below Earth's surface.

This tiny percentage of Earth's water must meet the large demand that all living things have for fresh, clean water. In addition to providing drinking water, fresh water is used for agriculture, industry, transportation, and recreation. It also provides a place to live for many plants and animals.

On Earth's Surface

 **6 Identify** As you read, underline three examples of surface water.

Water above Earth's surface is called **surface water**. Surface water is found in streams, rivers, and lakes. It either comes from precipitation, such as rain, or from water that comes up from the ground to Earth's surface. Springs are an example of underground water coming up to the surface. Surface water flows from higher ground to lower ground. Water that flows across Earth's surface is called *runoff*. Eventually, runoff can enter bodies of water.

Beneath Earth's Surface

Active Reading **7 Identify** As you read, underline how surface water becomes groundwater.

Not all runoff becomes surface water. Some runoff and surface water seep down into the ground. Water drains through the soil and filters down into underground rock, collecting in spaces between rock particles. The water found in the spaces between rock particles below Earth's surface is called **groundwater**.

Most drinking water in the United States comes from groundwater supplies. To use these supplies, people drill down to the water table to reach reservoirs of groundwater. The **water table** is the upper boundary, or surface, of groundwater.

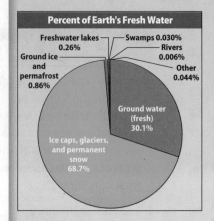

Percent of Earth's Fresh Water

Freshwater lakes 0.26%
Swamps 0.030%
Ground ice and permafrost 0.86%
Rivers 0.006%
Other 0.044%
Ground water (fresh) 30.1%
Ice caps, glaciers, and permanent snow 68.7%

Visualize It!

5 Analyze Write two questions this graph could help you answer. Then explain how the graph answers your questions.

_____

_____

_____

_____

Visualize It!

8 List Water is marked with the letters A–E on the illustration. Which letters mark surface water and which mark groundwater?

Surface water: _____

Groundwater: _____

Precipitation is fresh water that falls to Earth's surface from clouds.

Precipitation can flow downhill on Earth's surface as runoff.

Precipitation and runoff can collect in bodies of water, forming surface water.

The water table marks the upper surface of underground water.

Water that seeps underground and into spaces in rocks and soil becomes groundwater.

Cry Me a River

How does water move on Earth's surface?

As precipitation falls on Earth's surface, it flows from higher to lower areas. The water that does not seep below the surface flows together and forms streams. The water erodes rocks and soil, eventually forming channels. A **channel** is the path that a stream follows. Over time, a channel gets wider and deeper, as the stream continues to erode rock and soil.

A **tributary** is a smaller stream that feeds into a river and eventually into a river system. A river system is a network of streams and rivers that drains an area of its runoff.

B

A

Visualize It!

9 Identify Label *tributary*, *river*, *divide*, and *stream load* in the spaces provided on the illustration.

C

Within Watersheds

A **watershed** is the area of land that is drained by a river system. Streams, rivers, flood plains, lakes, ponds, wetlands, and groundwater all contribute water to a watershed. Watersheds are separated from one other by a ridge or an area of higher ground called a **divide**. Precipitation that falls on one side of a divide enters one watershed while the precipitation that falls on the other side of a divide enters another watershed.

The largest watershed in the United States is the Mississippi River watershed. It has hundreds of tributaries. It extends from the Rocky Mountains, in the west, to the Appalachian Mountains, in the east, and down the length of the United States, from north to south.

Many factors affect the flow of water in a watershed. For example, plants slow runoff and reduce erosion. The porosity and permeability of rocks and sediment determine how much water can seep down into the ground. The steepness of land affects how fast water flows over a watershed.

Active Reading 10 **State** Which land feature separates watersheds?

In Rivers and Streams

Gradient is a measure of the change in elevation over a certain distance. In other words, gradient describes the steepness, or slope, of the land. The higher the gradient of a river or stream, the faster the water moves. The faster the water moves, the more energy it has to erode rock and soil.

A river's *flow* is the amount of water that moves through the river channel in a given amount of time. Flow increases during a major storm or when warm weather rapidly melts snow. An increase in flow causes an increase in a river's speed.

Materials carried by a stream are called *stream load*. Streams with a high flow carry a larger stream load. The size of the particles depends on water speed. Faster streams can carry larger particles. Streams eventually deposit their stream loads where the speed of the water decreases. This commonly happens as streams enter lakes and oceans.

Active Reading 11 **Summarize** How would an increase in gradient affect the speed of water?

D

How does groundwater flow?

Although you can see some of Earth's fresh water in streams and lakes, you cannot see the large amount of water that flows underground as groundwater. Earth has much more fresh groundwater than fresh surface water.

It Trickles Down from Earth's Surface

Water from precipitation or streams may seep below the surface and become groundwater. Groundwater is either stored or it flows underground. It can enter back into streams and lakes, becoming surface water again. An **aquifer** is a body of rock or sediment that stores groundwater and allows it to flow.

Recall that the water table is the upper surface of underground water. The water table can rise or fall depending on the amount of water in the aquifer. In wet regions, the water table can be at or just beneath the soil's surface. In wetland areas, the water table is above the soil's surface.

It Fills Tiny Spaces Underground

An aquifer stores water in open spaces, or *pores,* between particles of rock or sediment. The storage space in an aquifer is measured by *porosity,* the percentage of the rock that is composed of pore space. The greater the pore space is, the higher the porosity is. A cup of gravel, for example, has higher porosity than a cup of sand does.

Permeability is a measure of how easily water can flow through an aquifer. High permeability means that many pores in the aquifer are connected, so water can flow easily. Aquifers with both high porosity and high permeability are useful as a water resource.

Visualize It!

12 Label Draw an arrow, ↑ (high) or ↓ (low), to indicate the porosity and permeability of each rock sample. One is already completed as an example.

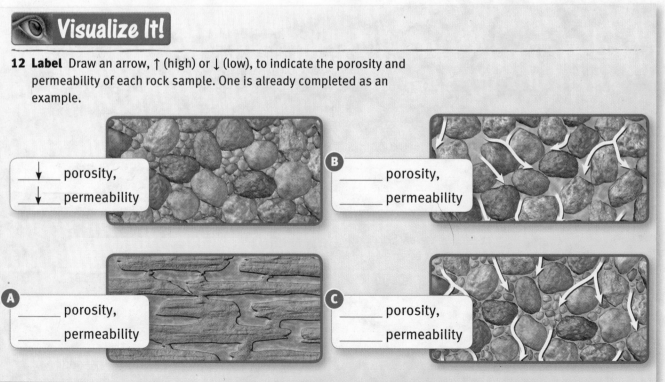

____↓____ porosity,
____↓____ permeability

B _____ porosity,
_____ permeability

A _____ porosity,
_____ permeability

C _____ porosity,
_____ permeability

It Is Recharged and Discharged

Surface water that trickles down into the ground can reach the water table and enter an aquifer. This process is called *recharge,* and occurs in an area called the *recharge zone.*

Where the water table meets the surface, water may pool to form a wetland or may flow out as a spring. The process by which groundwater becomes surface water is called *discharge* and happens in *discharge zones.* Discharge can feed rivers, streams, and lakes. Groundwater is also discharged where water is extracted from wells that are drilled down into the water table. Through discharge and recharge, the same water circulates between surface water and groundwater.

Think Outside the Book Inquiry

14 Claims • Evidence • Reasoning
During times of little or no rainfall, many communities have regulations limiting water use. Imagine that you live in a community with a depleted aquifer. Develop and defend a set of regulations that you think residents should follow. Clearly state evidence to support your claim and explain your reasoning.

Visualize It!

13 Label On the illustration below, write a caption for *discharge zone* and for *aquifer.*

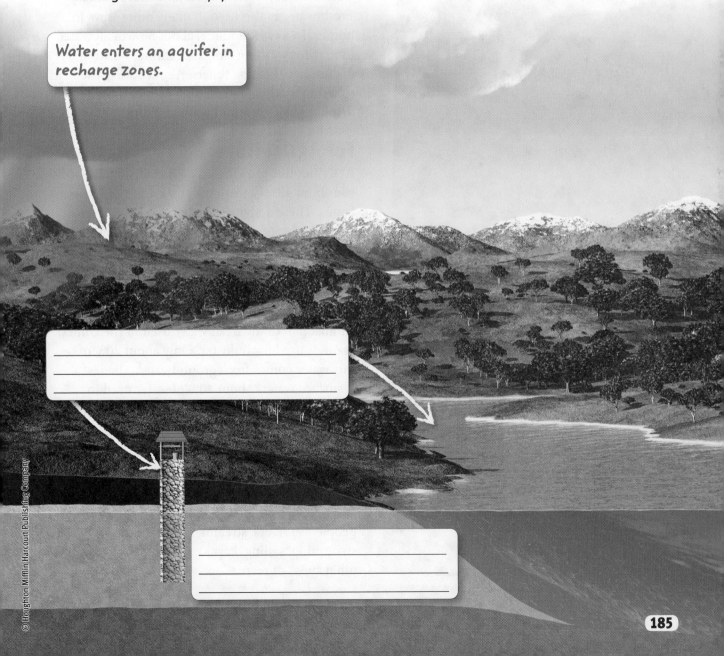

Water enters an aquifer in recharge zones.

Making a Splash

Active Reading

15 Identify As you read this page, underline how water is used in a typical home.

How do people use surface water and groundwater?

About 75% of all the fresh water used in the United States comes from surface water. The other 25% comes from groundwater. But surface water and groundwater are connected. In human terms, they are one resource. People use this freshwater resource in many different ways.

For Drinking and Use at Home

Groundwater is an important source of drinking water. Surface water is used for drinking, too. Fresh water is also used in many other ways in homes. In a typical home, about 50% of all water used is for washing clothes, bathing, washing dishes, and flushing toilets. About 33% is used to water lawns and gardens. The rest is used for drinking, cooking, and washing hands.

For Agriculture

Activities like growing crops and raising livestock use about 40% of fresh water used in the United States. These activities account for about 70% of all groundwater use. A little over half the water used in agriculture comes from surface water. A little less than half comes from groundwater.

For Industry

Almost half of the fresh water used in the United States is used for industry. Only about 20% of this water comes from groundwater. The rest is surface water. About 40% of water used in industry helps cool elements in power plants.

For Transportation and Recreation

Surface water is also used to transport products and people from place to place. In addition, people use rivers, streams, and lakes for swimming, sailing, kayaking, water skiing, and other types of recreation.

These rafters enjoy the exhilaration of river rapids.

Troubled Waters

Each hour, about 15,114 babies are born around the world. The human population has skyrocketed over the last few hundred years. But the amount of fresh water on Earth has remained roughly the same. The limited supply of fresh water is an important resource that must be managed so that it can meet the demands of a growing population.

Scientists are developing technologies for obtaining clean, fresh water to meet global needs. Here, a boy uses a water purifier straw that filters disease-causing microbes and certain other contaminants from surface water. The straw is inexpensive and can filter 700 L of water before it needs to be replaced—that's about how much water the average person drinks in one year.

Like many places on Earth, Zimbabwe is experiencing severe water shortages. The country has been plagued by droughts since the 1980s. Scientists estimate that about 1 billion people around the world do not have an adequate supply of clean, fresh water.

Extend

Inquiry

16 Infer Most of Earth is covered by water. How can we be experiencing shortages of drinking water?

17 Research Find out which diseases are caused by microbes found in untreated surface water. How might the water purifier straw reduce the number of people getting these diseases?

18 Recommend Conserving water is one way to ensure adequate supplies of drinking water. Work with a group to develop a plan to reduce water use at school. Present your plan to the class. As a class, select the best aspects of each group's plan. Combine the best suggestions into a document to present to the school administration.

Visual Summary

To complete this summary, fill in the blank with the correct word or phrase. Then, use the key below to check your answers. You can use this page to review the main concepts of the lesson.

Surface Water and Groundwater

Fresh surface water is found in streams, rivers, and lakes.

19 Smaller streams, or _____, flow into the main river channel.

Groundwater is found in pore spaces in rocks and sediment below Earth's surface.

20 The surface area where water enters an aquifer is called the _____ zone.

People use fresh water in homes, agriculture, and industry, for transportation, and for recreation.

21 Most industrial fresh water comes from rivers and other sources of _____

Answers: 19 tributaries; 20 recharge; 21 surface water

22 Claims • Evidence • Reasoning Could a raindrop become surface water, then groundwater, and then end up back on Earth's surface again? Use evidence to support your claim and explain your reasoning.

Lesson Review

Vocabulary

In your own words, define the following terms.

1 surface water

_____

_____

2 watershed

_____

_____

3 groundwater

_____

_____

4 water table

_____

_____

5 aquifer

_____

_____

Key Concepts

6 Identify What three factors describe the movement of surface water in streams and rivers?

_____

_____

_____

7 Explain How does the gradient of a river affect its flow?

_____

_____

_____

8 Describe How quickly would groundwater flow through rock with high porosity and high permeability? Explain your answer.

_____

_____

_____

Critical Thinking

9 Conclude An area's rate of groundwater recharge exceeds its rate of groundwater discharge. What can you conclude about the area's groundwater supply? Explain your reasoning.

_____

_____

_____

_____

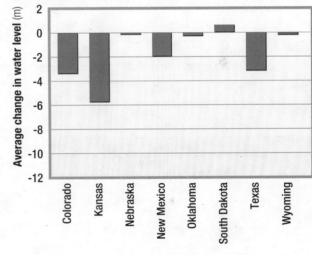

Use this graph to answer the following questions.

Average Water-Level Changes in the High Plains Aquifer by State (1980–2013)

State *Source:* USGS, 2013

10 Analyze What has happened to the amount of water in the High Plains Aquifer over time?

_____

_____

11 Infer What might account for the changes described in question 10?

_____

_____

_____

_____

_____

_____

My Notes

Lesson 3

Earth's Oceans
and the
Ocean Floor

ESSENTIAL QUESTION

What lies within and beneath Earth's oceans?

By the end of this lesson, you should be able to describe the properties and physical features of Earth's oceans.

S6E3.a Location and proportion of water on Earth's surface

S6E3.c The world's oceans

Scientists use technology such as robot submersibles to explore the deepest depths of the ocean.

© Houghton Mifflin Harcourt Publishing Company • Image Credits; (tr) ©Randy Olson/National Geographic/Getty Images; ©HMH

Lesson Labs

Quick Labs
- Evaporation Rates
- Ocean Density

Exploration Lab
- Measuring Salinity

Engage Your Brain

1 Predict Look at this photo. How much of Earth do you think is covered by oceans?

_____

_____

2 Describe Write a word or phrase beginning with each letter of the word OCEAN that describes oceans.

O _____

C _____

E _____

A _____

N _____

Active Reading

3 Apply Use context clues to write your own definitions for the words *salinity* and *ocean trench*.

Example sentence
Adding salt to a solution increases the solution's <u>salinity</u>.

salinity:

_____

_____

_____

Example sentence
The deepest parts of the ocean are the <u>ocean trenches</u>.

ocean trench:

_____

_____

Vocabulary Terms

- salinity
- thermocline
- continental margin
- deep-ocean basin
- mid-ocean ridge
- ocean trench

4 Apply As you learn the definition of each vocabulary term in this lesson, make your own definition or sketch to help you remember the meaning of the term.

Feelin' Blue

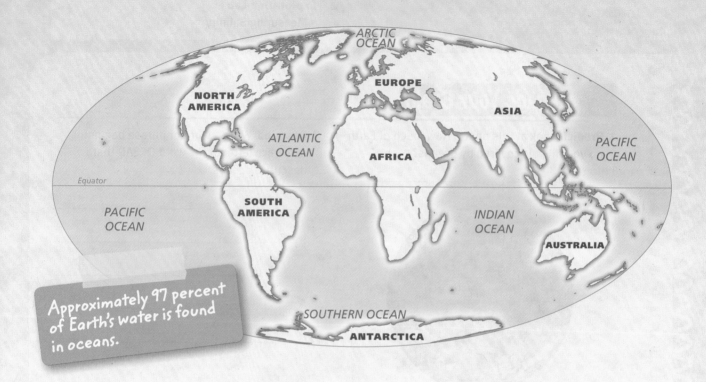

Approximately 97 percent of Earth's water is found in oceans.

What are Earth's five main oceans?

You can see on the map above that the continents are like huge islands surrounded by one vast, interconnected global ocean. Almost three-fourths of Earth is covered by ocean water. In places, the global ocean is more than 11 km deep.

Earth's global ocean is divided into five main oceans. The largest is the Pacific Ocean. It contains about half of Earth's water. The Atlantic Ocean is next in size. It stretches in a north-south direction. The third-largest ocean, the Indian Ocean, is found mainly in the Southern Hemisphere. The Southern Ocean is located near Antarctica. The smallest ocean, the Arctic Ocean, is nearly covered by ice much of the year.

What are some characteristics of ocean water?

 **Active Reading**

5 Identify As you read, underline characteristics of ocean water.

Like all matter, ocean water has both chemical and physical properties. Its chemical characteristics include **salinity**, or the amount and type of dissolved salts, and the amount and type of gases in the seawater. Its physical characteristics include temperature and density.

Salinity

On average, one kilogram of seawater contains about 35 g of dissolved salts. Thus, the overall salinity of seawater is about 3.5 percent.

Dissolved salts come from different sources. Water flowing on or under Earth's surface weathers rocks and carries calcium, magnesium, and sodium ions into the ocean. Underwater volcanoes and vents release solutions that are the source of chloride ions.

Over time, the salinity of seawater has remained relatively steady. However, it does vary from place to place. The salinity of water near the ocean's surface can be lower than average in areas where freshwater streams enter the ocean or where abundant precipitation falls into the ocean. Conversely, salinity can be higher than average in areas where rates of evaporation are high.

The white substance isn't snow. Above, a woman breaks apart salt that is left behind as water evaporates from these shallow, salty pools in Sri Lanka.

Temperature

Ocean water temperature varies by latitude, by depth, and by season. There are three distinct temperature layers by depth. The top layer, or surface zone, is the warmest layer. This layer is heated by the sun. The thermocline is the next zone. In the **thermocline**, water temperature drops with increased depth faster than it does in other layers. The deep zone is the deepest layer, and the coldest.

By latitude, the warmest surface water is near the equator. The coldest is near the poles. But the surface zone is generally warmer than deeper water regardless of latitude. Surface water is warmest in summer and coldest in winter. Driven by winds and density differences, both surface currents and deep currents travel through the global ocean, distributing energy in the form of heat.

Visualize It!

Ocean water temperature varies by latitude (above) and depth (right).

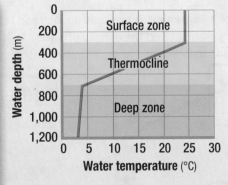

6 Identify At what latitude and depth is ocean water warmest?

_____

_____

Density

Recall that *density* is a measure of the mass of a substance divided by its volume. The density of ocean water depends on temperature and salinity. Salt water is denser than fresh water because salt water contains a large amount of dissolved solids.

Temperature also affects water density. As liquid ocean water becomes colder, its molecules move around less and pack closer together. Thus, cold ocean water is denser than warm ocean water.

Temperature affects the density of ocean water more than salinity does. So the densest ocean water is found near the poles, where the ocean surface is coldest. In the global ocean, differences in density drive the circulation of deep ocean currents, which distribute energy in the form of heat throughout the ocean.

Visualize It!

The yellow cups contain water that is dyed blue. The blue water is trickling out of holes poked in the bottoms of the yellow cups and into the beakers. The beakers contain fresh water at room temperature.

7 Infer One of the yellow cups contains water that is colder and saltier than the other. Which cup is it? Explain your answer.

_____

_____

_____

_____

 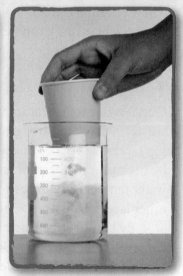

Can you tell what the difference is between these two trials?

8 Claims • Evidence • Reasoning How would an increase in salinity and a decrease in temperature affect the density of water? In the diagram, state your claim and use evidence to explain your reasoning.

Increase in salinity		Effect on density
Decrease in temperature		

Seeing the Sea

How is the ocean floor studied?

As you learned earlier in this lesson, the ocean is 11 km deep in some places. People cannot safely dive down to such extreme depths. So what lies at the deepest, darkest part of the ocean? How do scientists learn about the ocean floor? They use technology such as sonar, drills, underwater exploration vessels, and satellites.

Visualize It!

Differences in the times that sound waves take to return to the ship allow scientists to calculate the depth and shapes of ocean floor features.

9 Describe Draw arrows in the boxes to show the directions in which the sound waves are moving.

With Sonar

Sonar stands for *sound navigation and ranging*. This technology uses sound waves to measure distances. Scientists use sonar to determine the ocean's depth by sending sound pulses from a ship down into the ocean. The sound moves through the water, bounces off the ocean floor, and returns to the ship, where the sound waves are picked up by receivers. Computers on the ship calculate the time the sound takes to travel from the ship to the ocean floor and back again. The deeper the water is, the longer the round trip takes. Sonar data can be used to make maps of the ocean floor.

Features on the ocean floor can be mapped by using sonar.

10 Justify Which technologies would you use to explore the underwater landscape shown in this illustration? Explain why you chose these technologies.

_____

_____

_____

_____

_____

_____

_____

_____

With Satellites

Satellites can measure variations in the height of the ocean's surface. The features of the ocean floor can affect the height of the water above them. Scientists can use satellite data to make maps of the sea floor. Satellites can gather data from much larger areas than sonar can. Satellites can also measure other features, such as the ocean's surface temperature, with a high degree of accuracy.

In Underwater Vessels

Just as astronauts explore space by using rockets, scientists use underwater vessels to explore the oceans. Some vessels have pilots and can carry researchers. Other vessels are remotely operated. Remotely operated vehicles, or ROVs, are "flown" from the surface by remote control. ROVs can be used to explore the ocean at depths that are too dangerous for piloted vessels to explore.

With Deep-Sea Drilling

Scientists can collect cores, or long tubes of rock and sediment, from the sea floor. Cores are drilled using equipment on large ships. By studying the layers of rock and sediment in the cores, scientists learn about the history of Earth. For example, through drilling, scientists have found evidence of sea-floor spreading, which occurs where tectonic plates move apart.

In Deep Water

What are the two main regions of the ocean floor?

Picture yourself in a piloted research vessel deep below the ocean surface. What would you see on the ocean floor? The ocean floor is not all flat. It has features that include the world's longest mountain chain and deep canyons. The two main regions of the ocean floor are the continental margin and the deep-ocean basin.

The Continental Margin

The **continental margin** is the edge of the continent that is covered by the ocean. The continental margin is divided into the continental shelf, the continental slope, and the continental rise. These divisions are based on depth and changes in slope.

The continental shelf is a relatively flat underwater extension of the continent, which is the land that is above water. The shelf ends at a steeply sloping region, the continental slope. The ocean floor eventually becomes a more gently sloping terrain. This gently sloping area is the continental rise.

The Deep-Ocean Basin

The **deep-ocean basin** begins at the end of the continental margin. It extends under the deepest parts of the ocean. The deep-ocean basin includes narrow depressions and flat, smooth plains.

Active Reading 11 **Apply** Imagine the ocean is a giant swimming pool. Which region would be the shallow end, and which region would be the deep end?

_____

_____

_____

The continental margin has three parts.

Boston
New York
Washington, D.C.
Savannah

Continental Shelf
Continental Slope
Continental Rise
Continental Margin
Deep-Ocean Basin

ATLANTIC OCEAN

What are the features of the ocean floor?

You may know that the movement of tectonic plates forms features, such as mountains and volcanoes, on continents. These movements also form features on the ocean floor. As Earth's tectonic plates move, the plates slide past each other, collide with each other, or move away from each other. As a result, mid-ocean ridges, trenches, and seamounts form.

Visualize It!

12 Label On the drawing, label the continental shelf and slope.

A Continental _____

B Continental _____

Active Reading

13 Identify As you read, underline how mid-ocean ridges form.

Mid-Ocean Ridge: Diverging Plates

A long, undersea mountain chain that forms along the floor of the ocean is called a **mid-ocean ridge**. Mid-ocean ridges occur at the boundaries of Earth's tectonic plates, where plates move apart from each other. This motion creates a crack in the ocean floor called a rift, and allows hot magma to move upward. The magma rises through the rift and cools to form new rock. The ridges, like the ocean crust, are made of this rock. The world's longest mountain chain is a mid-ocean ridge that stretches about 65,000 km along the global ocean floor.

Abyssal Plains: Very Flat Regions of Earth

The large, flat, almost level area of the deep-ocean basin is called the *abyssal plain*. This area is covered with layers of fine sediment. Some of these sediments are carried here by wind and ocean currents. Other sediment is made of the remains of organisms that settle to the ocean floor when the organisms die.

Think Outside the Book Inquiry

14 Hypothesize Select a feature of the ocean floor. Write a research question about this feature. Then write two possible hypotheses.

Ocean Trenches: Subducting Plates

A long, narrow depression in the deep-ocean basin is called an **ocean trench**. The Mariana Trench, in the Pacific Ocean, is the deepest place in Earth's crust. Ocean trenches form where one tectonic plate subducts, or moves under, another plate.

As the plates move, the subducting plate releases fluids into surrounding rock. The surrounding rock melts, forming magma, which may rise to the surface to form volcanoes. Earthquakes are also common in and along subduction zones.

Volcanic islands like this one can form over a tectonic plate boundary or a hot spot.

Seamounts and Volcanic Islands: Where Magma Rises

Submerged volcanic mountains on the ocean floor are called seamounts. They may form at tectonic plate boundaries. Seamounts can also form far from plate boundaries over places called hot spots. At a hot spot, magma breaks through the overlying plate. The resulting volcano may grow into a seamount.

If a seamount grows above sea level, it becomes a *volcanic island*. The Hawaiian Islands are volcanic islands that formed over a hot spot.

© Houghton Mifflin Harcourt Publishing Company • Image Credits: ©Dana Stephenson/Getty Images

Visual Summary

To complete this summary, circle the correct word. Then, use the key below to check your answers. You can use this page to review the main concepts of the lesson.

Earth's Oceans and the Ocean Floor

About three-fourths of Earth is covered by oceans.

15 The Pacific Ocean is the smallest / largest ocean.

16 Sonar uses sound / light waves to measure distance to the ocean floor.

The properties of ocean water include salinity, temperature, and density.

17 The temperature of ocean water varies with depth, usually forming two / three distinct layers.

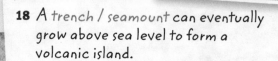

The two main regions of the ocean floor are the continental margin and the deep-ocean basin.

18 A trench / seamount can eventually grow above sea level to form a volcanic island.

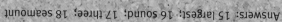

Answers: 15 largest; 16 sound; 17 three; 18 seamount

19 **Model** Design a way to model the features of the ocean floor.

Lesson Review

Vocabulary

Draw a line to connect the following terms to their definitions.

1 continental margin

2 deep-ocean basin

3 mid-ocean ridge

4 ocean trench

5 salinity

6 thermocline

A a water layer with great temperature changes

B a long, narrow underwater depression

C the measure of the amount of dissolved salts in a given amount of liquid

D a long, underwater mountain chain

E the edge of the continent covered by ocean water

F the part of the ocean that begins at the end of the continental margin

Key Concepts

7 Sequence In order from largest to smallest, what are Earth's five main oceans?

_____

_____

_____

_____

8 List What are the three main temperature layers in the ocean?

_____

_____

_____

9 Identify What two properties affect the density of ocean water?

_____

_____

_____

_____

_____

Critical Thinking

Use the graph to answer the questions that follow.

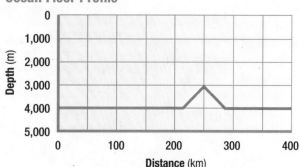

Ocean Floor Profile

10 Infer What major region does this profile most likely represent?

_____

_____

11 Analyze What types of features are evident on the profile?

_____

_____

_____

12 Infer Suppose the salinity of surface ocean water is high in a particular place. What might you infer about the area's rates of evaporation? Use evidence to support your claim and explain your reasoning.

_____

_____

_____

_____

_____

_____

13 Assess How is exploring oceans similar to exploring space?

_____

_____

_____

_____

_____

_____

My Notes

S6E3.c The world's oceans

Understanding a Bathymetric Map

Topographic maps are contour maps that illustrate the mountains, valleys, and hills on land. Bathymetric maps are contour maps that illustrate similar features on the ocean floor.

Tutorial

A bathymetric map uses curved contour lines that each represent a specific depth. Colors are also often used to show different depths. Because sea level is at 0 meters, increasing depths are shown by negative numbers. The bathymetric map below shows a part of the Mariana Trench, the deepest known part of the world's ocean.

Bathymetric Map

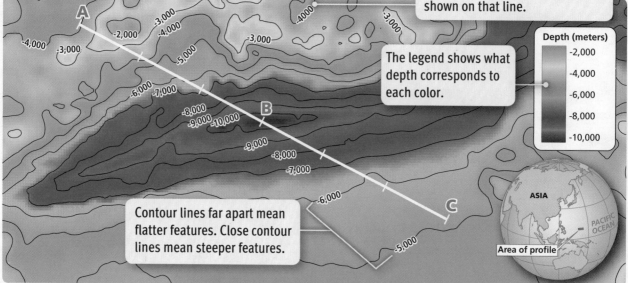

Every point along a contour line is at the same depth, the number shown on that line.

The legend shows what depth corresponds to each color.

Contour lines far apart mean flatter features. Close contour lines mean steeper features.

Bathymetric Profile

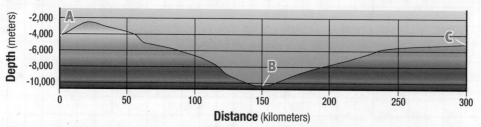

Distance (kilometers)

A bathymetric profile shows the change in depth across any chosen reference line on a bathymetric map. This profile details the change in depth across the line ABC shown on the map above. To see how the profile was made, move your finger along the line ABC on the map. Every time you cross a contour line, check that the profile crosses the same depth line on the grid.

You Try It!

Now follow the steps below to draw the profile for this bathymetric map of a region near Monterey Bay, California.

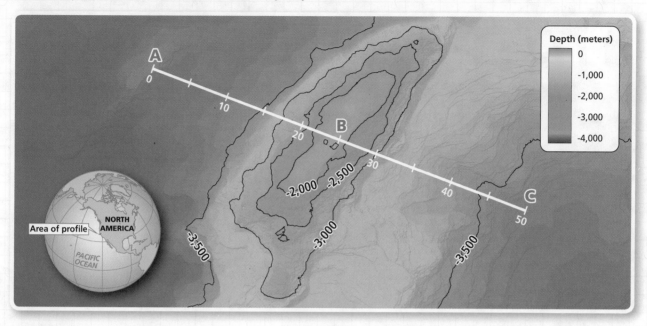

Profile Grid

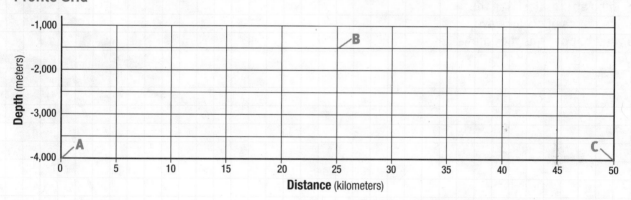

1 List Use the color legend to estimate the depths at points A, B, and C. Record this data in the table below.

Point	Color	Depth
A		
B		
C		

2 Distinguish For each tick mark on the line ABC, place a dot on the corresponding profile grid line at the correct depth.

3 Graph Move your finger along the ABC line on the map and place a dot on the profile grid at the correct depth for each contour line you cross.

4 Draw To complete the profile, connect the dots you plotted.

5 Evaluate Describe the ocean floor feature that you just plotted. From your observations, what questions could you ask about physical characteristics and geological history of this area of the ocean floor?

_____

_____

_____

_____

_____

_____

Ocean Waves

ESSENTIAL QUESTION

How does an ocean wave form and move?

By the end of this lesson, you should be able to describe the characteristics of ocean waves and what happens as they move through the ocean.

You've probably seen an ocean wave before, but did you know not all ocean waves are the same? In this lesson, you'll find out how ocean waves form and how they move.

S6E3.d Waves, currents, and tides in Earth's systems

Lesson Labs

Quick Labs
- Making Waves
- Factors in Wave Formation

Exploration Lab
- Wave Movement

Engage Your Brain

1 Identify Read the following vocabulary terms. In the spaces provided, place a + if you know the term well, a ~ if you have heard the term but are not sure what it means, and a ? if you are unfamiliar with the term. Then write a sentence that includes one of the words you are most familiar with.

_____ **wave**

_____ **crest**

_____ **tsunami**

Sentence using known word:

_____

_____

2 Describe Imagine you are a photographer who is taking a set of photos for a lesson about ocean waves. Describe the photos you will take. Be specific.

_____

_____

_____

_____

_____

_____

_____

Active Reading

3 Synthesize You can often define an unknown word if you know the meaning of its word parts. Use the word parts and sentences below to make an educated guess about the meaning of the term *wave period*.

Word part	Meaning
wave	a periodic disturbance
period	an interval of time

Example sentence
Edward watched waves travel under his boat. It took about two seconds for each wave to pass, so he knew the <u>wave period</u> was two seconds.

wave period:

_____

_____

_____

Vocabulary Terms
- wave
- ocean wave
- crest
- trough
- wavelength
- wave period
- mechanical wave
- tsunami

4 Apply As you learn the definition of each vocabulary term in this lesson, create your own definition or sketch to help you remember the meaning of the term.

© Houghton Mifflin Harcourt Publishing Company • Image Credits: (bg) ©Douglas Peebles/Corbis

Catch the Wave

What are some properties of a wave?

Have you ever seen a surfer riding waves? Or have you jumped in a pool and made waves? A **wave** is any disturbance that transfers energy through matter or empty space. An **ocean wave** is a disturbance that transfers energy through ocean water.

Size

Waves are made up of two main parts—crests and troughs. A **crest** is the highest point of a wave. A **trough** is the lowest point of a wave. The top of a rise on a roller-coaster track is similar to the crest of a wave. The bottom of a dip in the track resembles the trough of a wave. The distance between two adjacent wave crests or wave troughs is a **wavelength**. Wave *amplitude* is half the distance between the crest and the trough. The diagram below shows the parts of a wave.

👁 **Visualize It!**

5 Describe Use a ruler to find the amplitude of this wave.

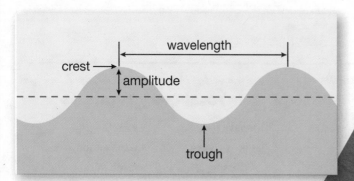

6 Apply Use a ruler to draw a wave with a wavelength of 3 cm.

This wave is transferring energy.

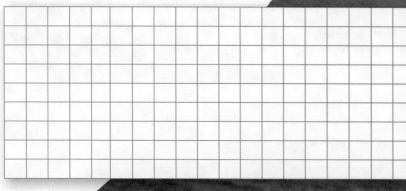

Frequency and Wave Period

Wavelength and amplitude are not the only properties used to describe a wave. Waves also vary in frequency and wave period. These two properties are related, but different.

Frequency is the number of waves produced in a given amount of time. You can measure the frequency of an ocean wave by counting how many waves pass a fixed point in a certain amount of time. If you see five waves pass the point in ten seconds, then the frequency is 5 waves per 10 seconds, or 0.5 waves/second.

Wave period, in contrast, is a measurement of how much time it takes for a wave to pass the fixed point. In other words, it is the inverse of frequency. Frequency is measured in waves/time while wave period is measured in time/wave.

Wave Speed

Waves come in many different sizes and travel at different speeds. *Wave speed* is how fast a wave travels. To calculate wave speed, you can multiply the wave's wavelength by its frequency, as shown below. For any given wave, an increase in either the frequency of the wave or the wavelength will cause an increase in wave speed.

wave speed (v) = wavelength (λ) × frequency (f)

Wave speed is measured in distance/time.

Do the Math

Imagine you are in a boat on the open ocean. You count 5 waves passing under your boat in 10 seconds. You estimate the wavelength to be 2 m.

Sample Problem

A What do you know?

wave frequency and wavelength

B What do you want to find out?

wave speed

C Write the formula:

wave speed (v) = wavelength (λ) × frequency (f)

D Substitute into the formula:

$v = 2 \ m/wave \times 0.5 \ waves/s$

E Calculate and check your units:

$2 \ m/wave \times 0.5 \ waves/s = 1 \ m/s$

Answer: 1 m/s

You Try It!

7 Calculate You count 2 waves traveling right under your boat in 10 seconds. You estimate the wavelength to be 3 m. What is the wave speed?

Identify

A What do you know?

B What do you want to find out?

Plan

C Write the formula:

D Substitute into the formula:

Solve

E Calculate and check your units:

Answer:

Surf's UP!

What causes ocean waves?

Waves carry energy. Ocean waves are a type of wave known as a **mechanical wave**. Mechanical waves carry energy through matter, such as water. Ocean waves form when energy is transferred from a source such as wind to the ocean water.

Active Reading **8 Identify** As you read, underline the source of energy that causes each wave to form.

Wind

Most ocean waves form when energy in the atmosphere is transferred to the ocean's surface. Wind blows across the water's surface and transfers energy to the water. The energy is then carried by the wave, usually all the way to the ocean shore.

Have you ever wondered why ocean waves are different sizes? When wind begins to blow over water, small waves, or ripples, form. If the wind keeps blowing, more energy is transferred to the ripples. They grow into larger waves. The longer the wind blows in the same direction across the water, the more energy is transferred from the wind to the water, and the larger the waves become.

These waves were caused by wind blowing across the water.

Visualize It!

9 Claims • Evidence • Reasoning Look at the boats in the photo. Which direction is the wind blowing? What evidence supports your claim? Explain your reasoning.

_____

_____

_____

Earthquakes

Waves can also form from other sources of energy. For example, underwater earthquakes can cause waves to form in the ocean. You could model this process by using a thin aluminum pan filled with water. Pushing up on the bottom of the pan will cause water in the tray to move.

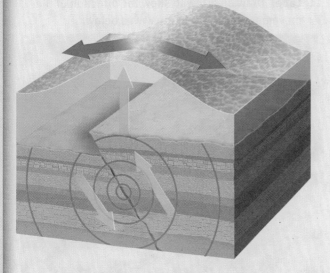

Volcanoes

Underwater volcanoes are another source of energy that can cause waves to form. Underwater volcanoes cause waves in a very similar way to how underwater earthquakes form waves. As the volcano erupts, the surrounding water is displaced, sending out a wave in all directions.

Landslides

Underwater landslides can also displace water and cause waves. The ocean floor is made up of many features, including towering cliffs and the world's longest mountain chains. Landslides along these landforms push the surrounding water. The energy is then transferred outward, lifting the sea surface above the landslide.

Meteorites and Asteroids

Meteorites and asteroids are rocky bodies from space that can collide with Earth. If a meteorite or asteroid lands in the ocean, it can displace enough water to cause large waves. If a large asteroid landed in the Atlantic Ocean, for example, the resulting wave could flood much of the east coast of the United States.

Doing the Wave

What happens when a wave moves through the water?

If you have watched ocean waves, you may have noticed that water seems to move across the ocean's surface. But this movement is only an illusion. Actually, waves don't move water. Instead, they transfer energy through the water.

Energy Travels

As you learned on the previous pages, most waves form when winds blow. Wind transfers energy to the water. As the energy moves through the water, so do the waves. But the water itself does not travel with the energy.

Water Rises and Falls But Stays in the Same Place

Notice in the illustration that the floating seagull remains in approximately the same spot as the wave travels from left to right. The water and the seagull do not move with the wave, but only rise and fall in circular movements. This circular movement of water is generally the greatest at the ocean surface. Wave energy affects surface water to a depth of about half a wavelength. Deeper water is not affected by the energy of surface waves.

Active Reading **10 Compare** How does the movement of water compare to the movement of energy in a wave?

_____

_____

_____

11 Label Draw an arrow to show the direction of the movement of energy in the waves below.

Like the bird in this illustration, water remains in the same place as waves travel through it.

Watts from Waves

Every minute of every day, waves are crashing against the coastline of the United States. That's a lot of energy being delivered directly to our doorstep! In fact, the Department of Energy estimates that about 7% of our electrical energy needs could be met by capturing the wave energy along our coastlines.

This is the Pelamis Wave Energy Converter

Anchor

Power cable

The up-and-down motion of Pelamis is converted by a generator into electrical energy.

Electrical energy is transferred to the power cable.

The power cable carries energy back to shore.

Extend

Inquiry

12 Explain What are some advantages to using wave energy instead of fossil fuels to generate electricity?

13 Identify Research some disadvantages, such as the impact on marine life, to installing wave power generators along a coastline.

14 Model Build a model of a wave power generator. Include labels to show how the wave energy is transformed into electrical energy.

Totally Turbulent

What happens when a wave reaches the shore?

Ocean waves can transfer energy over very long distances. In fact, waves can travel thousands of miles across the ocean's surface. The energy is carried all the way to the shore.

Energy Decreases with Depth

Why do waves crash on shore? The figure below shows how changes in the depth of water cause waves to crash. When waves reach water shallower than one-half their wavelength, they begin to interact with the ocean floor. As waves touch the ocean floor, the waves transfer energy to the ocean floor. As a result, the water at the bottom of the wave slows down.

It Breaks in Shallow Water

As water depth decreases, wave height increases, because more water is forced between wave crests. The top of the wave travels faster than the bottom of the wave, which is dragging on the ocean floor. Eventually, gravity pulls the wave crests down, and they crash onto the shore. These waves that crash onto shore are called breakers.

Wavelengths are constant

Wavelengths shorten

Breakers form

It Transfers Energy to the Shore

Most ocean waves reach the shore and transfer their energy to the beach environment. The energy of the wave and the angle at which the wave hits the shore determine how much energy is transferred. High-energy waves can quickly erode beaches. Strong waves can even throw boulders and other debris up on the beach, particularly during storms.

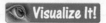 Visualize It!

15 Explain Why do waves break as they reach the shore?

_____

_____

_____

© Houghton Mifflin Harcourt Publishing Company • Image Credits: ©Witold Skrypczak/Alamy

What is a tsunami?

Surfers can go to Hawaii to catch some of the highest waves in the world. But even the best surfers would not be able to handle a tsunami. A **tsunami** [tsoo•NAH•mee] is a series of waves that form when a large volume of ocean water is suddenly moved up or down. This movement can be caused by earthquakes, volcanic eruptions, landslides, or the impact of a meteorite or asteroid. The illustration below shows how an underwater earthquake can cause a tsunami.

Most tsunamis occur in the Pacific Ocean, because many earthquakes occur in that region. When a tsunami approaches land, the waves slow down and get taller as they interact with the ocean floor. Tsunamis can reach more than 30 m in height as they slam into the coast, destroying almost everything in their path. The huge volume of water that crashes onto shore then rushes back into the ocean. This powerful flow of water, called an undertow, can be as destructive as the tsunami itself.

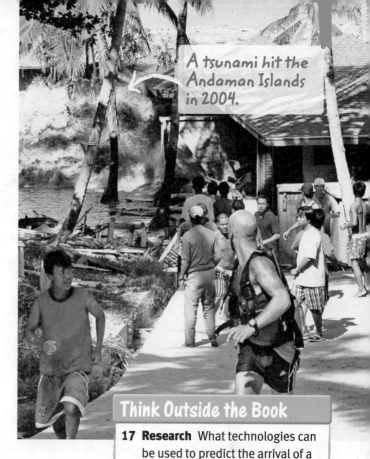

A tsunami hit the Andaman Islands in 2004.

Think Outside the Book

17 Research What technologies can be used to predict the arrival of a tsunami? Select two, and describe the advantages and drawbacks of each. Support your claims with evidence from your research.

Visualize It!

16 Explain Review the illustration. Then describe the sequence of events in the illustration by writing a caption for each event.

A This tsunami was caused by

_____

_____

_____

B As the waves reach shore,

_____

_____

_____

_____

C The undertow from a tsunami can

_____

_____

Visual Summary

To complete this summary, fill in the blanks and circle the correct term. Then use the key below to check your answers. You can use this page to review the main concepts of the lesson.

Ocean Waves

Waves vary in size, frequency, wave period, and speed.

18 A wave's speed is equal to its _____ multiplied by its _____

Ocean waves form as energy is transferred to the water.

19 Waves form when energy is transferred to ocean water by:

- _____
- earthquakes and volcanoes
- _____
- meteorite and asteroid impacts

Wave energy is carried all the way to shore.

20 Waves transfer _____, not matter.

21 When a wave approaches the shoreline, it slows down/speeds up.

22 Claims • Evidence • Reasoning How does energy play a role in the formation of ocean waves? Use evidence to support your claim and explain your reasoning.

© Houghton Mifflin Harcourt Publishing Company • Image Credits: (tr) ©Neil Rabinowitz/Corbis

Lesson Review

Vocabulary

Define Fill in the blank with the correct term.

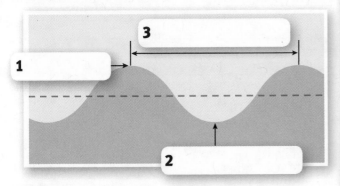

Define For each pair of terms, explain how the meanings of the terms differ.

4 *wave* and *tsunami*

_____

_____

_____

5 *wave period* and *wave speed*

_____

_____

_____

_____

Key Concepts

6 Summarize How do most ocean waves form?

_____

_____

7 Describe What happens to the energy in an ocean wave as the wave reaches the shore?

_____

_____

_____

_____

8 Calculate A scientist determines that an ocean wave has a wavelength of 4.3 m and a frequency of 0.2 waves/second. What is the wave's speed?

_____

_____

Critical Thinking

Use the table to answer the following question.

Wave	Time wave passes Buoy 1	Time wave passes Buoy 2
A	8:15 a.m.	8:21 a.m.
B	1:24 p.m.	1:36 p.m.
C	6:58 p.m.	7:02 p.m.

9 Calculate Which wave has the smallest wave period? What is its period?

_____

_____

_____

10 Synthesize Which property of a wave do you think changes the most as the wave approaches the shore? Explain your reasoning.

_____

_____

_____

_____

_____

_____

11 Claims • Evidence • Reasoning Suppose a person sailing a ship saw breaking waves 1 kilometer offshore. Should the person try to sail the ship through the area or steer around it? Use evidence to support your claim and explain your reasoning.

_____

_____

_____

_____

_____

_____

_____

My Notes

Ocean Currents

ESSENTIAL QUESTION

How does water move in the ocean?

By the end of this lesson, you should be able to describe the movement of ocean water, explain what factors influence this movement, and explain why ocean circulation is important in the Earth system.

This iceberg off the coast of Newfoundland broke off an Arctic ice sheet and drifted south on ocean surface currents.

S6E3.d Waves, currents, and tides in Earth's systems

✋ Lesson Labs

Quick Labs
- Modeling the Coriolis Effect
- The Formation of Deep Currents
- Can Messages Travel on Ocean Water?

Engage Your Brain

1 Predict Check T or F to show whether you think each statement is true or false.

T	F	
☐	☐	Ocean currents are always cold.
☐	☐	Continents affect the directions of currents.
☐	☐	Currents only flow near the surface of the ocean.
☐	☐	Wind affects currents.
☐	☐	The sun affects currents near the surface of the ocean.

2 Analyze What can you learn about ocean currents from this image?

_____

_____

_____

_____

This image shows sea ice caught in ocean currents.

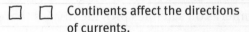

Active Reading

3 Synthesize You can often define an unknown word if you know the meaning of its word parts. Use the word parts and sentence below to make an educated guess about the meaning of the word *upwelling*.

Word part	Meaning
up-	from beneath the ground or water
well	to rise

Example Sentence
In areas where <u>upwelling</u> occurs, plankton feed on nutrients from deep in the ocean.

upwelling:

_____

_____

Vocabulary Terms
- ocean current
- surface current
- Coriolis effect
- deep current
- convection current
- upwelling

4 Apply As you learn the definition of each vocabulary term in this lesson, create your own definition or sketch to help you remember the meaning of the term.

Going with the Flow

What are ocean currents?

The oceans contain streamlike movements of water called **ocean currents**. Ocean currents that occur at or near the surface of the ocean, caused by wind, are called **surface currents**. Most surface currents reach depths of about 100 m, but some go deeper. Surface currents also reach lengths of several thousand kilometers and can stretch across oceans. An example of a surface current is the Gulf Stream. The Gulf Stream is one of the strongest surface currents on Earth. The Gulf Stream transports, or moves, more water each year than is transported by all the rivers in the world combined.

Infrared cameras on satellites provide images that show differences in temperature. Scientists add color to the images afterward to highlight the different temperatures, as shown below.

What affects surface currents?

Surface currents are affected by three factors: continental deflections, the Coriolis effect, and global winds. These factors keep surface currents flowing in distinct patterns around Earth.

Active Reading

5 Identify As you read, underline three factors that affect surface currents.

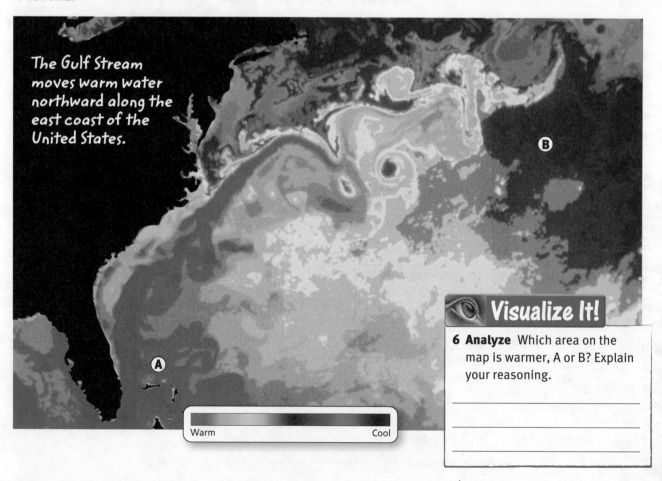

The Gulf Stream moves warm water northward along the east coast of the United States.

Ⓐ Ⓑ

Warm   Cool

Visualize It!

6 Analyze Which area on the map is warmer, A or B? Explain your reasoning.

_____
_____
_____

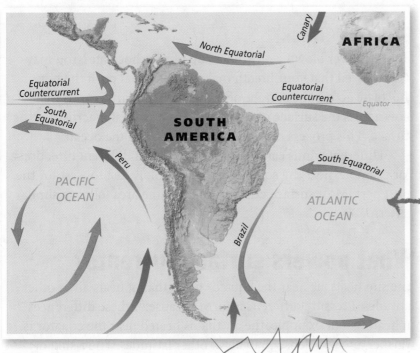

7 Identify Circle areas on the map where ocean currents have been deflected by a land mass.

Currents change direction when they meet continents.

Continental Deflections

If Earth's surface were covered only with water, surface currents would simply travel continually in one direction. However, water does not cover the entire surface of Earth. Continents rise above sea level over about one-third of Earth's surface. When surface currents meet continents, the currents are deflected and change direction. For example, the South Equatorial Current turns southward as it meets the coast of South America.

The Coriolis Effect

Earth's rotation causes all wind and ocean currents, except on the equator, to be deflected from the paths they would take if Earth did not rotate. The deflection of moving objects from a straight path due to Earth's rotation is called the **Coriolis effect** (kawr•ee•OH•lis ih•FEKT). Earth is spherical, so Earth's circumference at latitudes above and below the equator is shorter than the circumference at the equator. But the period of rotation is always 24 hours. Therefore, points on Earth near the equator travel faster than points closer to the poles.

The difference in speed of rotation causes the Coriolis effect. For example, wind and water traveling south from the North Pole actually go toward the southwest instead of straight south. Wind and water deflect to the right because the wind and water move east more slowly than Earth rotates beneath them. In the Northern Hemisphere, currents are deflected to the right. In the Southern Hemisphere, currents are deflected to the left.

The Coriolis effect is most noticeable for objects that travel over long distances, without any interruptions. Over short distances, the difference in Earth's rotational speed from one point to another point is not great enough to cause noticeable deflection.

In the Northern Hemisphere, currents are deflected to the right.

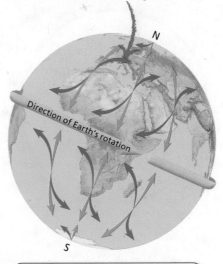

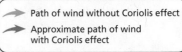

Path of wind without Coriolis effect

Approximate path of wind with Coriolis effect

Global Winds

Have you ever blown gently on a cup of hot chocolate? You may have noticed that your breath makes ripples that push the hot chocolate across the surface of the liquid. Similarly, winds that blow across the surface of Earth's oceans push water across Earth's surface. This process causes surface currents in the ocean.

Different winds cause currents to flow in different directions. For example, near the equator, the winds blow east to west for the most part. Most surface currents in the same area follow a similar pattern.

What powers surface currents?

The sun heats air near the equator more than it heats air at other latitudes. Pressure differences form because of these differences in heating. For example, the air that is heated near the equator is warmer and less dense than air at other latitudes. The rising of warm air creates an area of low pressure near the equator. Pressure differences in the atmosphere cause the wind to form. So, the sun causes winds to form, and winds cause surface currents to form. Therefore, the major source of the energy that powers surface currents is the sun.

8 Analyze Fill in the cause-and-effect chart to show how the sun's energy powers surface ocean currents.

The sun heats the atmosphere.

Global Surface Winds

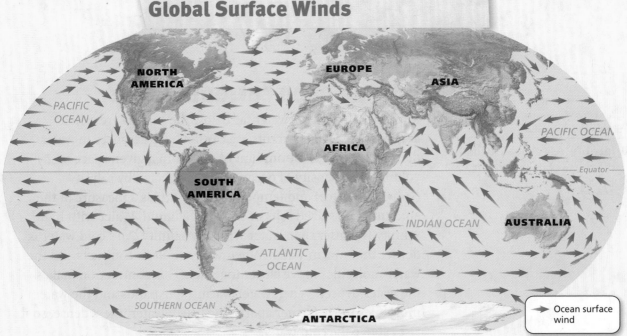

North America, Europe, Asia, Pacific Ocean, Africa, South America, Atlantic Ocean, Indian Ocean, Australia, Southern Ocean, Antarctica

Equator

→ Ocean surface wind

Global Surface Currents

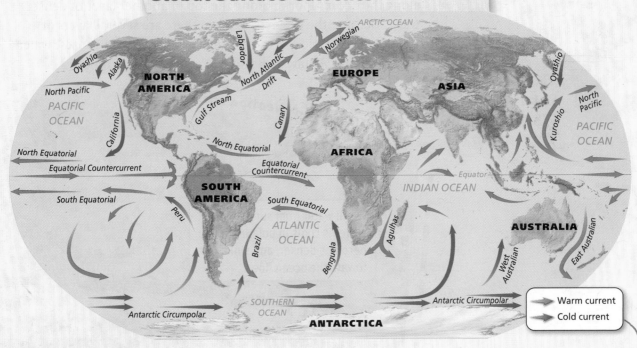

Oyashio, Alaska, North Pacific, Labrador, North Atlantic Drift, Norwegian, ARCTIC OCEAN, EUROPE, ASIA, Oyashio, North Pacific, PACIFIC OCEAN, California, Gulf Stream, Canary, Kuroshio, PACIFIC OCEAN, North Equatorial, North Equatorial, AFRICA, Equatorial Countercurrent, Equator, Equatorial Countercurrent, INDIAN OCEAN, South Equatorial, SOUTH AMERICA, South Equatorial, Peru, ATLANTIC OCEAN, Brazil, Benguela, Agulhas, AUSTRALIA, West Australian, East Australian, Antarctic Circumpolar, SOUTHERN OCEAN, ANTARCTICA, Antarctic Circumpolar

→ Warm current
→ Cold current

Visualize It!

9 Analyze Circle the same area on each map. Describe what you observe about these two areas.

_____

_____

_____

Current Events

How do deep currents form?

10 Identify As you read, underline the cause of deep currents.

Movements of ocean water far below the surface are called **deep currents**. Deep currents are caused by differences in water density. *Density* is the amount of matter in a given space or volume. The density of ocean water is affected by salinity (suh•LIN•ih•tee) and temperature. *Salinity* is a measure of the amount of dissolved salts or solids in a liquid. Water with high salinity is denser than water with low salinity. And cold water is denser than warm water. When water cools, it contracts and the water molecules move closer together. This contraction makes the water denser. When water warms, it expands and the water molecules move farther apart. The warm water is less dense, so it rises above the cold water.

When ocean water at the surface becomes denser than water below it, the denser water sinks. The water moves from the surface to the deep ocean, forming deep currents. Deep currents flow along the ocean floor or along the top of another layer of denser water. Because the ocean is so deep, there are several layers of water at any location in the ocean. The deepest and densest water in the ocean is Antarctic Bottom Water, near Antarctica.

Polar region

Convection current

B Warm water from surface currents cools in polar regions, becomes denser, and sinks toward the ocean floor.

C Deep currents carry colder, denser water in the deep ocean from polar regions to other parts of Earth.

11 Illustrate Complete the drawing at part B on the diagram.

What are convection currents?

As you read about convection currents, refer to the illustration below. Surface currents and deep currents are linked in the ocean. Together they form convection currents. In the ocean, a **convection current** is a movement of water that results from density differences. Convection currents can be vertical, circular, or cyclical. Think of convection currents in the ocean as a conveyor belt. Surface currents make up the top part of the belt. Deep currents make up the bottom part of the belt. Water from a surface current may become a deep current in areas where water density increases. Deep current water then rises up to the surface in areas where the surface current is carrying low-density water away.

How do convection currents transfer energy?

Convection currents transfer energy. Water at the ocean's surface absorbs energy from the sun. Surface currents carry this energy to colder regions. The warm water loses energy to its surroundings and cools. As the water cools, it becomes denser and it sinks. The cold water travels along the ocean bottom. Then, the cold water rises to the surface as warm surface water moves away. The cold water absorbs energy from the sun, and the cycle continues.

Think Outside the Book Inquiry

12 **Apply** Would water following a convection current undergo temperature changes? Use evidence to support your claim and explain your reasoning.

Surface currents carry warmer, less dense water from warm equatorial regions to polar areas.

A

D

Earth

Equatorial region

Water from deep currents rises to replace water that leaves in surface currents.

Inquiry

13 **Inquire** How are convection currents important in the Earth system? Use evidence to support your reasoning.

_____

_____

Note: Drawing is not to scale.

That's Swell!

What is upwelling?

At times, winds blow toward the equator along the northwest coast of South America and the west coast of North America. These winds cause surface currents to move away from the shore. The warm surface water is then replaced by cold, nutrient-rich water from the deep ocean in a process called **upwelling**. The deep water contains nutrients, such as iron and nitrate.

Upwelling is extremely important to ocean life. The nutrients that are brought to the surface of the ocean support the growth of phytoplankton (fy•toh•PLANGK•tuhn) and zooplankton. These tiny plants and animals are food for other organisms, such as fish and seabirds. Many fisheries are located in areas of upwelling because ocean animals thrive there. Some weather conditions can interrupt the process of upwelling. When upwelling is reduced, the richness of the ocean life at the surface is also reduced.

14 Identify As you read, underline the steps that occur in upwelling.

The livelihood of these Peruvian fishermen depends on upwelling.

15 Predict What might happen to the fisheries if upwelling stopped? Explain your reasoning.

_____

_____

_____

_____

_____

_____

_____

On the coast of California, upwelling sustains large kelp forests.

Wind

Warm surface water

During upwelling, cold, nutrient-rich water from the deep ocean rises to the surface.

Why It Matters

Hitching a Ride!

A CHANGING WORLD

What do coconuts, plankton, and sea turtles have in common? They get free rides on ocean currents.

World Travel

When baby sea turtles are hatched on a beach, they head for the ocean. They can then pick up ocean currents to travel. Some travel from Australia to South America on currents.

Sprouting Coconuts!

This sprouting coconut may be transported by ocean currents to a beach. This transport explains why coconut trees can grow in several areas.

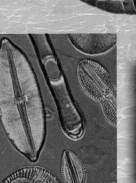

Fast Food

Diatoms are a kind of phytoplankton. They are tiny, one-celled plants that form the basis of the food chain. Diatoms ride surface currents throughout the world.

Extend

Inquiry

16 Identify List three organisms transported by ocean currents.

17 Research Investigate the Sargasso Sea. State why a lot of plastic collects in this sea. Find out whether any plastic collects on the shoreline nearest you.

18 Explain Describe how plastic and other debris can collect in the ocean by doing one of the following:
- make a poster
- write a poem
- write a song
- write a short story

Traveling the World

What do ocean currents transport?

Active Reading

19 Identify As you read, underline the description of how energy reaches the poles.

Ocean water circulates through all of Earth's ocean basins. The paths are like the main highway on which ocean water flows. If you could follow a water molecule on this path, you would find that the molecule takes more than 1,000 years to return to its starting point! Along with water, ocean currents also transport dissolved solids, dissolved gases, and energy around Earth.

20 Describe Choose a location on the map. Using your finger, follow the route you would take if you could ride a current. Describe your route. Include the direction you go and the landmasses you pass.

_____

_____

_____

_____

_____

Antarctica is not shown on this map, but the currents at the bottom of the map circulate around Antarctica.

Ocean Currents Transport Energy

Global ocean circulation is very important in the transport of energy in the form of heat. Remember that ocean currents flow in huge convection currents that can be thousands of kilometers long. These convection currents carry about 40% of the energy that is transported around Earth's surface.

Near the equator, the ocean absorbs a large amount of solar energy. The ocean also absorbs energy from the atmosphere. Ocean currents carry this energy from the equator toward the poles. When the warm water travels to cooler areas, the energy is released back into the atmosphere. Therefore, ocean circulation has an important influence on Earth's climate.

In the Pacific Ocean, surface currents transport energy from the tropics to latitudes above and below the equator.

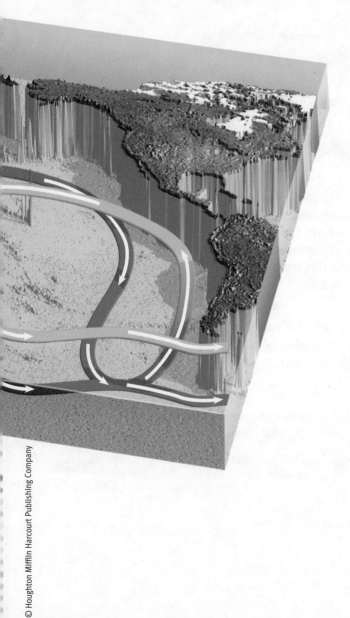

Ocean Currents Transport Matter

Besides water, ocean currents transport whatever is in the water. The most familiar dissolved solid in ocean water is sodium chloride, or table salt. Other dissolved solids are important to marine life. Ocean water contains many nutrients—such as nitrogen and phosphorus—that are important for plant and animal growth.

Ocean water also transports gases. Gases in the atmosphere are absorbed by ocean water at the ocean surface. As a result, the most abundant gases in the atmosphere—nitrogen, oxygen, argon, and carbon dioxide—are also abundant in the ocean. Dissolved oxygen and carbon dioxide are necessary for the survival of many marine organisms.

21 List Write three examples of matter besides water that are transported by ocean currents.

_____

_____

_____

_____

_____

Visual Summary

To complete this summary, draw an arrow to show each type of ocean current. Fill in the blanks with the correct word. Then use the key below to check your answers. You can use this page to review the main concepts of the lesson.

Surface currents are streamlike movements of water at or near the surface of the ocean.

22 The direction of a surface current is affected by

_____ ,

_____ ,

and _____

Deep currents are streamlike movements of ocean water located far below the surface.

23 Deep currents form where the

_____

of ocean water increases.

Ocean Currents

A convection current in the ocean is any movement of matter that results from differences in density.

24 A convection current in the ocean transports matter and

_____

Upwelling is the process in which warm surface water is replaced by cold water from the deep ocean.

25 The cold water from deep in the ocean contains

_____

Answers: 22 continental deflections, the Coriolis effect, global winds; 23 density; 24 energy; 25 nutrients

26 **Describe** State the two general patterns of global ocean circulation.

_____

Lesson Review

Vocabulary

Fill in the blanks with the terms that best complete the following sentences.

1 _____ are streamlike movements of water in the ocean.

2 The _____ causes currents in open water to move in a curved path rather than a straight path.

3 _____ causes cold, nutrient-rich waters to move up to the ocean's surface.

Key Concepts

4 Explain List the steps that show how the sun provides the energy for surface ocean currents.

_____

_____

_____

_____

_____

5 Explain State how a deep current forms.

_____

_____

_____

_____

_____

6 Describe Explain how a convection current transports energy around the globe.

_____

_____

_____

_____

7 List Write the three factors that affect surface ocean currents.

_____

_____

_____

Critical Thinking

Use this diagram to answer the following questions.

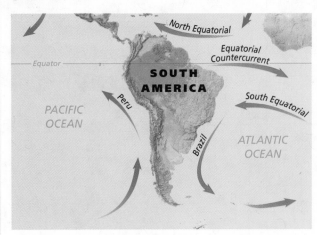

8 Apply Explain why the direction of the South Equatorial current changes. Provide evidence to support your reasoning.

_____

_____

_____

_____

9 Apply If South America were not there, explain how the direction of the South Equatorial current would be different.

_____

_____

_____

_____

_____

10 Apply Describe how surface currents would be affected if Earth did not rotate.

_____

_____

_____

_____

_____

_____

_____

My Notes

Unit 3 [Big Idea]

Earth's waters cycle through a connected system of atmosphere, land and oceans, distributing matter and energy around the planet.

Lesson 1
ESSENTIAL QUESTION
How does water change state and move around on Earth?

Describe the water cycle and the different processes that are part of the water cycle on Earth.

Lesson 4
ESSENTIAL QUESTION
How does an ocean wave form and move?

Describe the characteristics of ocean waves and what happens as they move through the ocean.

Lesson 2
ESSENTIAL QUESTION
How does fresh water flow on Earth?

Explain the processes involved in the flow of water, both above and below the ground.

Lesson 5
ESSENTIAL QUESTION
How does water move in the ocean?

Describe the movement of ocean water, explain what factors influence this movement, and explain why ocean circulation is important in the Earth system.

Lesson 3
ESSENTIAL QUESTION
What lies within and beneath Earth's oceans?

Describe the properties and physical features of Earth's oceans.

[Connect] ESSENTIAL QUESTIONS
Lessons 1, 2 and 3

1 Synthesize Explain why precipitation on Earth's surface is less common on land than it is over the oceans. Base your answer on the water cycle.

_____

_____

_____

_____

Think Outside the Book

2 Synthesize Choose one of these activities to help synthesize what you have learned in this unit.

☐ Using what you learned in lessons 3 and 4, make a flipbook that shows how an earthquake along a fault near a subducting plate might affect the ocean water above it.

☐ Using what you learned in lessons 3 and 5, make a poster presentation describing how the temperature of ocean water is important to distributing energy as heat around the global ocean.

Unit 3 Review

Name _____

Vocabulary

Fill in each blank with the term that best completes the following sentences.

1 An ocean layer in which the temperature drops with depth faster than in other layers is called a _____ .

2 A wave that requires a medium such as air or water through which to travel is called a _____ wave.

3 The continuous movement of water between the atmosphere, the land, the oceans, and living things is called the _____.

4 A _____ is any movement of matter that results from differences in density.

5 A _____ is the area of land that is drained by a river system.

Key Concepts

Read each question below, and circle the best answer.

6 A glass of ice water is shown below before and after it reaches room temperature.

Which of the following correctly explains something that occurred in the time between these two images?

A The ice cubes expanded in volume as they melted into liquid water.

B As water vapor condensed on the glass, it absorbed energy.

C The water droplets outside the glass absorbed energy as they evaporated.

D Some liquid water inside the glass sublimated into water vapor in the air.

7 Which of these circle graphs most correctly shows the approximate proportions of fresh water and salt water on the surface of the earth?

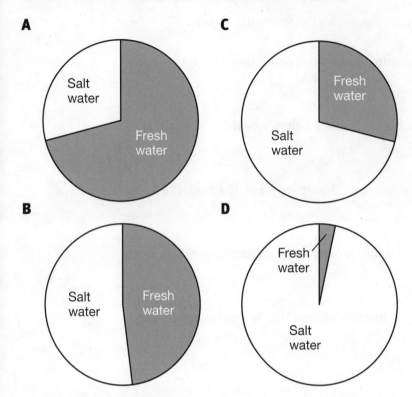

A

Salt water

Fresh water

C

Fresh water

Salt water

B

Salt water

Fresh water

D

Fresh water

Salt water

8 Which of the following is not a way that water reaches Earth's atmosphere?

A condensation

C sublimation

B evaporation

D transpiration

9 Which of the following correctly shows the chain of energy transfers that create surface currents on the ocean?

A solar energy → wind energy → surface currents

B wind energy → solar energy → surface currents

C tidal energy → wind energy → surface currents

D geothermal energy → wind energy → surface currents

10 A certain percentage of water that falls to Earth's surface as precipitation does not become surface water or groundwater and does not evaporate back into the atmosphere. Which of the following most likely explains what happens to this water?

   A The water falls into the ocean, where it evaporates back into the atmosphere.

   B The water is stored as snow and ice on Earth's surface.

   C The water molecules are broken down into hydrogen and oxygen atoms.

   D The water is absorbed and used by plants.

11 Which of the following is an incorrect statement about the flow of water through watersheds?

   A A watershed can be fed by groundwater.

   B The boundary separating two watersheds is called a divide.

   C Plant life often alters the flow of water in a watershed by causing erosion.

   D The gradient of the land can affect the flow of water through a watershed.

12 Which of the following is the name for all the materials carried by a stream other than the water itself?

   A discharge

   B flow

   C gradient

   D stream load

13 Looking at a pole at the end of a pier, Maria counted 20 wave crests pass the pole in 10 seconds. She also estimated that the wavelength was 8 pole widths. If the pole is 0.5 meters wide, what was the approximate wave speed?

   A 2 m/s

   B 4 m/s

   C 8 m/s

   D 16 m/s

14 The picture below shows a method of studying the ocean.

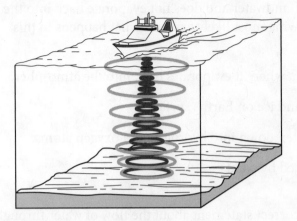

Which of the following best explains this method of studying the ocean?

A A bright beam of white light is being shone down through the ocean to illuminate the ocean floor.

B Sound waves are being sent down through the ocean, and the variation in time taken for the sound waves to return tells how the depth varies.

C A satellite is being used to measure variations in the gravitational field of the Earth, which tells the variation in the depth of the ocean.

D A remotely operated vehicle is being piloted from the ship to take pictures of the ocean floor.

15 A scientist measured the salinity of the ocean water at the surface every 100 meters along a coastline. The measurements are displayed in the line graph below.

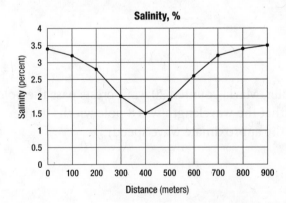

What best describes the dip in salinity centered at 400 meters along the shore?

A A factory dumps wastewater with 10% salinity into that area of the ocean.

B More sunlight reaches that area of the coastline causing more evaporation.

C The instruments must be faulty, since ocean water does not vary in salinity.

D A river's mouth at around 400 meters carries freshwater into the ocean.

16 The dashed lines on this map indicate the path of a 2004 tsunami.

December 2004 Tsunami

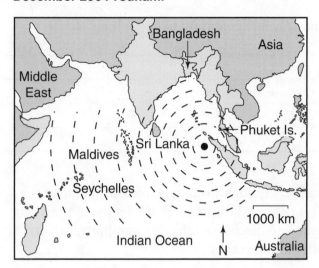

Would an observer standing on a beach on the southeast shore of Sri Lanka have known that a tsunami was coming?

A Yes, because the water would have rushed away from shore.

B No, because the observer was not in the path of the tsunami.

C Yes, because storm clouds would have formed offshore to the southeast.

D No, because the winds that caused the tsunami were from the northeast.

17 Which type of current occurs when the ocean's surface water becomes denser than the water below it and sinks?

A Coriolis current   **C** surface current

B deep current   **D** upwelling

18 The drawing below shows a snapshot of a wave.

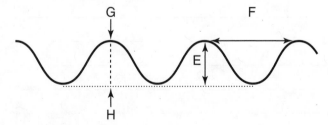

What does the measurement labeled E equal?

A The wave's period   **C** The wave's amplitude

B The wave's wavelength   **D** Twice the wave's amplitude

Critical Thinking

Answer the following questions in the space provided.

19 Explain what an upwelling is and why it is important to ocean life.

_____

_____

_____

_____

20 Suppose a massive amount of salt was suddenly dumped into one region of the ocean. How would the movement of water be affected in the region of the ocean where the salt was dumped? Be sure to discuss the changes in salinity, density, and the type of ocean current that would result.

_____

_____

_____

_____

_____

Connect **ESSENTIAL QUESTIONS**
Lessons 3, 4, and 5

Answer the following question in the space provided.

21 Most of the energy that powers ocean waves and ocean currents ultimately comes from the sun. Using what you learned in Lessons 3, 4, and 5, describe how ocean waves and ocean currents transfer solar energy around the globe.

_____

_____

_____

_____

_____

_____

Earth's Atmosphere, Weather, and Climate

Earth's atmosphere is divided into different layers. These clouds have formed in the troposphere, the lowest layer of the atmosphere where most weather occurs.

Big Idea

The sun's energy drives atmospheric changes that create Earth's weather and climate systems.

S6E4., S6E4.a, S6E4.b, S6E4.c, S6E4.d, S6E4.e, S6E5., S6E5.g, S6E6., S6E6.c

Wind is the movement of air caused by differences in air pressure.

What do you think?

Like other parts of the Earth system, energy is transferred through Earth's atmosphere. What are the three processes by which energy is transferred through the atmosphere? As you explore the unit, gather evidence to help you state and support claims to answer this question.

Unit 4
Earth's Atmosphere, Weather, and Climate

CITIZEN SCIENCE
Clearing the Air

In some areas, there are many vehicles on the roads every day. Some of the gases from vehicle exhausts react with sunlight to form ozone. There are days when the concentration of ozone is so high that it becomes a health hazard. Those days are especially difficult for people who have problems breathing. What can you do to reduce gas emissions?

1 Think About It

A How do you get to school every day?

_____

_____

_____

B How many of the students in your class come to school by car?

_____

Gas emissions are high during rush-hour traffic.

© Houghton Mifflin Harcourt Publishing Company • Image Credits: ©Luis Castaneda Inc./The Image Bank/Getty Images

② Ask A Question

How can you reduce the number of vehicles students use to get to school one day each month?

With your teacher and classmates, brainstorm different ways in which you can reduce the number of vehicles students use to get to school.

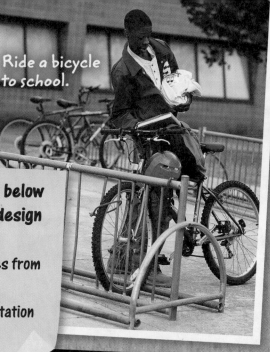

Ride a bicycle to school.

Check off the points below as you use them to design your plan.

☐ how far a student lives from school

☐ the kinds of transportation students may have available to them

③ Make A Plan

A Write down different ways that you can reduce the number of vehicles that bring students to school.

_____
_____
_____
_____
_____
_____
_____

B Create a short presentation for your principal that outlines how the whole school could become involved in your vehicle-reduction plan. Write down the points of your presentation in the space below.

_____
_____
_____
_____
_____
_____
_____
_____
_____

C In the space below, design a sign-up sheet that your classmates will use to choose how they will come to school on the designated day.

Take It Home

Give your presentation to an adult. Then, have the adult brainstorm ways to reduce their daily gas emissions.

The Atmosphere

ESSENTIAL QUESTION

What is the atmosphere?

By the end of this lesson, you should be able to describe the composition and structure of the atmosphere and explain how the atmosphere protects life and insulates Earth.

The atmosphere is a very thin layer compared to the whole Earth. However, it is essential for life on our planet.

S6E4.a Atmospheric layers and greenhouse gases

Lesson Labs

Quick Labs
- Modeling Air Pressure
- Modeling Air Pressure Changes with Altitude

Field Lab
- Measuring Oxygen in the Air

Engage Your Brain

1 Predict Check T or F to show whether you think each statement is true or false.

T F

☐ ☐ Oxygen is in the air we breathe.

☐ ☐ Pressure is not a property of air.

☐ ☐ The air around you is part of the atmosphere.

☐ ☐ As you climb up a mountain, the temperature usually gets warmer.

2 Explain Does the air in this balloon have mass? Why or why not?

_____

_____

_____

_____

_____

Active Reading

3 Synthesize Many English words have their roots in other languages. Use the ancient Greek words below to make an educated guess about the meanings of the words *atmosphere* and *mesosphere*.

Greek word	Meaning
atmos	vapor
mesos	middle
sphaira	ball

Vocabulary Terms

- atmosphere
- air pressure
- thermosphere
- mesosphere
- stratosphere
- troposphere
- ozone layer
- greenhouse effect

4 Apply As you learn the definition of each vocabulary term in this lesson, create your own definition or sketch to help you remember the meaning of the term.

atmosphere:

_____

_____

mesosphere:

_____

_____

Up and Away!

What is Earth's atmosphere?

The mixture of gases that surrounds Earth is the **atmosphere**. This mixture is most often referred to as air. The atmosphere has many important functions. It protects you from the sun's damaging rays and also helps to maintain the right temperature range for life on Earth. For example, the temperature range on Earth allows us to have an abundant amount of liquid water. Many of the components of the atmosphere are essential for life, such as the oxygen you breathe.

A Mixture of Gases and Small Particles

As shown below, the atmosphere is made mostly of nitrogen gas (78%) and oxygen gas (21%). The other 1% is other gases. The atmosphere also contains small particles such as dust, volcanic ash, sea salt, and smoke. There are even small pieces of skin, bacteria, and pollen floating in the atmosphere!

Water is also found in the atmosphere. Liquid water, as water droplets, and solid water, as snow and ice crystals, are found in clouds. But most water in the atmosphere exists as an invisible gas called water vapor. Under certain conditions, water vapor can change into solid or liquid water. Then, snow or rain might fall from the sky.

 **Visualize It!**

5 Identify Fill in the missing percentage for oxygen.

Nitrogen is the most abundant gas in the atmosphere.

Oxygen is the second most abundant gas in the atmosphere.

The remaining 1% of the atmosphere is made up of argon, carbon dioxide, water vapor, and other gases.

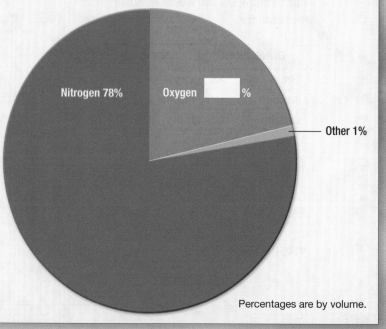

Composition of the Atmosphere

Nitrogen 78%

Oxygen ___ %

Other 1%

Percentages are by volume.

How do pressure and temperature change in the atmosphere?

Active Reading

6 Identify As you read, underline what happens to temperature and to pressure as altitude increases.

The atmosphere is held around Earth by gravity. Gravity pulls gas molecules in the atmosphere toward Earth's surface, causing air pressure. **Air pressure** is the measure of the force with which air molecules push on an area of a surface. At sea level, air pressure is over 1 lb for every square centimeter of your body. That is like carrying a 1-liter bottle of water on the tip of your finger!

However, air pressure is not the same throughout the atmosphere. Although there are many gas molecules that surround you on Earth, there are fewer and fewer gas molecules in the air as you move away from Earth's surface. So, as altitude increases, air pressure decreases.

As altitude increases, air temperature also changes. These changes are mainly due to the way solar energy is absorbed in the atmosphere. Some parts of the atmosphere are warmer because they contain a high percentage of gases that absorb solar energy. Other parts of the atmosphere contain less of these gases and are cooler.

Inquiry

7 Explain Why does a mountain climber need an oxygen supply at very high altitudes, even though the air still contains 21% oxygen?

_____

_____

_____

At high altitudes such as the top of Mount Everest, air pressure and temperature are lower than they are at sea level.

Look Way Up

What are the layers of the atmosphere?

Earth's atmosphere is divided into four layers, based on temperature and other properties. As shown at the right, these layers are the troposphere (TROH•puh•sfir), stratosphere (STRAT•uh•sfir), mesosphere (MEZ•uh•sfir), and thermosphere (THER•muh•sfir). Although these names sound complicated, they give you clues about the layers' features. *Tropo-* means "turning" or "change," and the troposphere is the layer where gases turn and mix. *Strato-* means "layer," and the stratosphere is where gases are layered and do not mix very much. *Meso-* means "middle," and the mesosphere is the middle layer. Finally, *thermo-* means "heat," and the thermosphere is the layer where temperatures are highest.

Think Outside the Book

8 Describe Research the part of the thermosphere called the ionosphere. Describe what the aurora borealis is.

The aurora borealis occurs in the thermosphere.

Thermosphere

The **thermosphere** is the uppermost layer of the atmosphere. The temperature increases as altitude increases because gases in the thermosphere absorb high-energy solar radiation. Temperatures in the thermosphere can be 1,500 °C or higher. However, the thermosphere feels cold. The density of particles in the thermosphere is very low. Too few gas particles collide with your body to transfer heat energy to your skin.

Mesosphere

The **mesosphere** is between the thermosphere and stratosphere. In this layer, the temperature decreases as altitude increases. Temperatures can be as low as −120 °C at the top of the mesosphere. Meteoroids begin to burn up in the mesosphere.

Stratosphere

The **stratosphere** is between the mesosphere and troposphere. In this layer, temperatures generally increase as altitude increases. Ozone in the stratosphere absorbs ultraviolet radiation from the sun, which warms the air. An ozone molecule is made of three atoms of oxygen. Gases in the stratosphere are layered and do not mix very much.

Troposphere

The **troposphere** is the lowest layer of the atmosphere. Although temperatures near Earth's surface vary greatly, generally, temperature decreases as altitude increases. This layer contains almost 80% of the atmosphere's total mass, making it the densest layer. Almost all of Earth's carbon dioxide, water vapor, clouds, air pollution, weather, and life forms are in the troposphere.

© Houghton Mifflin Harcourt Publishing Company • Image Credits: ©Carol Falcetta/Flickr/Getty Images

In the graph, the green line shows pressure change with altitude.
The red line shows temperature change with altitude.

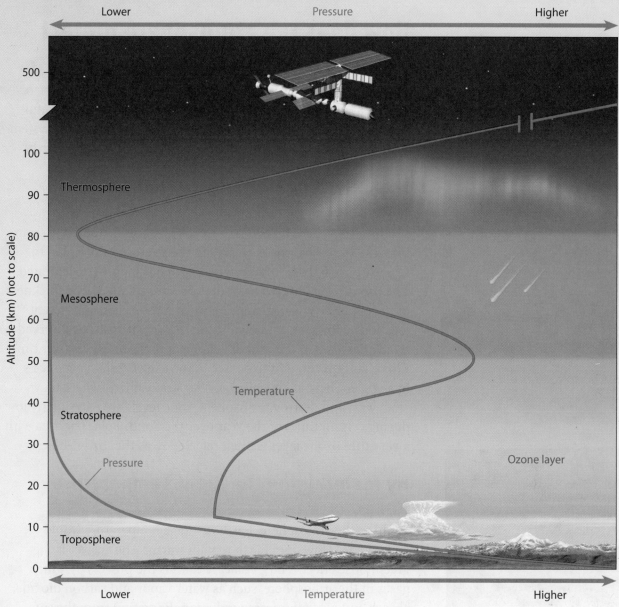

The layers of the atmosphere are
defined by changes in temperature.

9 Analyze Interpret the data
provided to indicate how air
pressure and temperature
change with increased altitude in
each layer. One answer has been
provided for you. Explain how the
gas composition and density of
each layer relates to these data
trends.

Layer	Air pressure	Temperature
Thermosphere	decreases	
Mesosphere		
Stratosphere		
Troposphere		

Visualize It!

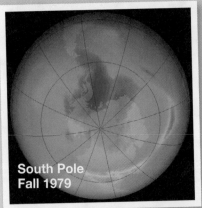

South Pole
Fall 1979

Less ozone   More ozone

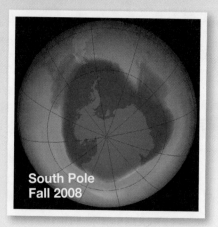

South Pole
Fall 2008

10 Compare How did the ozone layer over the South Pole change between 1979 and 2008? Explain the evidence that supports your claim.

_____

_____

_____

How does the atmosphere protect life on Earth?

The atmosphere surrounds and protects Earth. The atmosphere provides the air we breathe. It also protects Earth from harmful solar radiation and from space debris that enters the Earth system. In addition, the atmosphere controls the temperature on Earth.

By Absorbing or Reflecting Harmful Radiation

Earth's atmosphere reflects or absorbs most of the radiation from the sun. The **ozone layer** is an area in the stratosphere, 15 km to 40 km above Earth's surface, where ozone is highly concentrated. The ozone layer absorbs most of the solar radiation. The thickness of the ozone layer can change between seasons and at different locations. However, as shown at the left, scientists have observed a steady decrease in the overall volume of the ozone layer over time. This change is thought to be due to the use of certain chemicals by people. These chemicals enter the stratosphere, where they react with and destroy the ozone. Ozone levels are particularly low during certain times of the year over the South Pole. The area with a very thin ozone layer is often referred to as the "ozone hole."

By Maintaining the Right Temperature Range

Without the atmosphere, Earth's average temperature would be very low. How does Earth remain warm? The answer is the greenhouse effect. The **greenhouse effect** is the process by which gases in the atmosphere, such as water vapor and carbon dioxide, absorb and give off infrared radiation. Radiation from the sun warms Earth's surface, and Earth's surface gives off infrared radiation. Greenhouse gases in the atmosphere absorb some of this infrared radiation and then reradiate it. Some of this energy is absorbed again by Earth's surface, while some energy goes out into space. Because greenhouse gases keep energy in the Earth system longer, Earth's average surface temperature is kept at around 15°C (59°F). In time, all the energy ends up back in outer space.

Active Reading **11 List** Name two examples of greenhouse gases.

_____

_____

© Houghton Mifflin Harcourt Publishing Company • Image Credits: (tl) ©NASA; (bl) ©NASA

the Sun ...

The Greenhouse Effect

Greenhouse gas molecules absorb and emit infrared radiation.

Atmosphere without Greenhouse Gases

Without greenhouse gases in Earth's atmosphere, radiation from Earth's surface is lost directly to space.

Average Temperature: -18°C

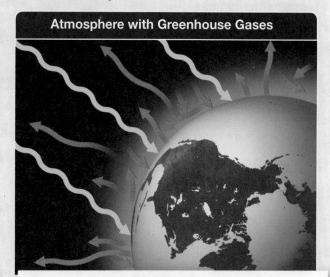

Atmosphere with Greenhouse Gases

With greenhouse gases in Earth's atmosphere, radiation from Earth's surface is lost to space more slowly, which makes Earth's surface warmer.

Average Temperature: 15°C

sunlight   infrared radiation

The atmosphere is much thinner than shown here.

Visualize It!

12 Illustrate Draw your own version of how greenhouse gases keep Earth warm.

Visual Summary

To complete this summary, fill in the blanks with the correct word or phrase. Then, use the key below to check your answers. You can use this page to review the main concepts of the lesson.

Both air pressure and temperature change within the atmosphere.

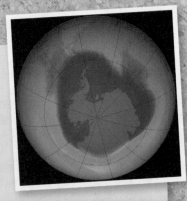

The atmosphere protects Earth from harmful radiation and helps to maintain a temperature range that supports life.

13 As altitude increases, air pressure

_____

14 Earth is protected from harmful solar radiation by the

_____

The Atmosphere

The atmosphere is divided into four layers, according to temperature and other properties.

15 The four layers of the atmosphere are the

_____

_____

_____

_____

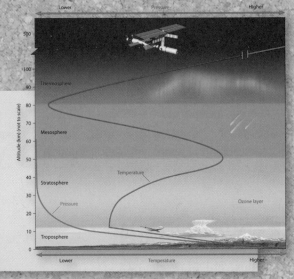

stratosphere, mesosphere, thermosphere.
Answers: 13 decreases. 14 ozone layer; 15 troposphere,

16 **Hypothesize** What do you think Earth's surface would be like if Earth did not have an atmosphere? Explain your reasoning.

Lesson Review

Vocabulary

Fill in the blanks with the terms that best complete the following sentences.

1 The _____ is a mixture of gases that surrounds Earth.

2 The measure of the force with which air molecules push on a surface is called _____ .

3 The _____ is the process by which gases in the atmosphere absorb and reradiate heat.

Key Concepts

4 List Name three gases in the atmosphere.

_____

_____

5 Identify What layer of the atmosphere contains the ozone layer?

_____

6 Identify What layer of the atmosphere contains almost 80% of the atmosphere's total mass?

_____

7 Describe How and why does air pressure change with altitude in the atmosphere?

_____

_____

_____

_____

8 Explain What is the name of the uppermost layer of the atmosphere? Why does it feel cold there, even though the temperature can be very high?

_____

_____

_____

_____

Critical Thinking

9 Hypothesize What would happen to life on Earth if the ozone layer was not present? Explain your reasoning.

_____

_____

10 Claims · Evidence · Reasoning A friend says that temperature increases as altitude increases because you're moving closer to the sun. Is this true? Explain the evidence that supports your claim.

_____

_____

11 Predict Why would increased levels of greenhouse gases contribute to higher temperatures on Earth?

_____

_____

_____

Use this graph to answer the following questions.

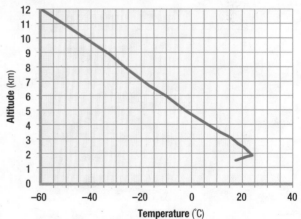

Changes in Temperature with Altitude

Source: National Weather Service. Data taken at Riverton, Wyoming, 2001

12 Analyze The top of Mount Everest is at about 8,850 m. What would the approximate air temperature be at that altitude? _____

13 Analyze What is the total temperature change between 3 km and 7 km above Earth's surface? _____

My Notes

Energy Transfer

ESSENTIAL QUESTION

How does energy move through Earth's system?

By the end of this lesson, you should be able to summarize the three mechanisms by which energy is transferred through Earth's system.

These icicles are absorbing energy from the sun, causing them to melt.

 S6E4.b Solar energy transfer

Lesson Labs

Quick Labs
• The Sun's Angle and Temperature
• How Does Color Affect Temperature?
• Modeling Convection

S.T.E.M. Lab
• Heat from the Sun

Engage Your Brain

1 Describe Fill in the blank with the word or phrase that you think correctly completes the following sentences.

An example of something hot is

_____

An example of something cold is

_____

The sun provides us with

_____

A thermometer is used to measure

_____

2 Explain If you placed your hands around this mug of hot chocolate, what would happen to the temperature of your hands? Why do you think this would happen?

_____

_____

_____

_____

_____

_____

Active Reading

3 Apply Many scientific words, such as *heat*, are used to convey different meanings. Use context clues to write your own definition for each meaning of the word *heat*.

The student won the first <u>heat</u> of the race.

heat:

_____

_____

The man wondered if his rent included <u>heat</u>.

heat:

_____

_____

Energy in the form of <u>heat</u> was transferred from the hot pan to the cold counter.

heat:

_____

_____

Vocabulary Terms

• temperature   • radiation
• thermal energy   • convection
• thermal expansion   • conduction
• heat

4 Identify This list contains the vocabulary terms you'll learn in this lesson. As you read, circle the definition of each term.

Hot and Cold

How are energy and temperature related?

All matter is made up of moving particles, such as atoms or molecules. When particles are in motion, they have kinetic energy. Because particles move at different speeds, each has a different amount of kinetic energy.

Temperature (TEM•per•uh•chur) is a measure of the average kinetic energy of particles. The faster a particle moves, the more kinetic energy it has. As shown below, the more kinetic energy the particles of an object have, the higher the temperature of the object. As an object's temperature increases, the particles move faster and move apart. As the space between particles increases, the substance expands. The increase in volume that results from an increase in temperature is called **thermal expansion**.

Thermal energy is the total kinetic energy of particles. A teapot full of tea at a high temperature has more thermal energy than a teapot full of tea at a lower temperature. Thermal energy, but not temperature, depends on the number of particles. The more particles there are in an object, the greater the object's thermal energy. The tea in a teapot and a cup may be at the same temperature, but the tea in the pot has more thermal energy because there is more of it.

Visualize It!

5 Analyze Which container holds particles with the higher average kinetic energy?

_____

_____

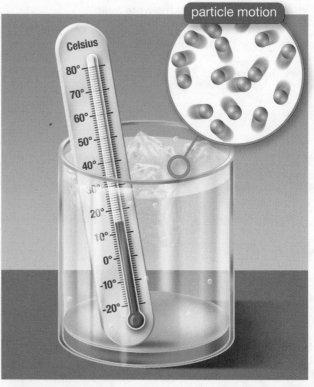

Getting Warm

What is heat?

You might think of the word *heat* when you imagine something that feels hot. But heat also has to do with things that feel cold. In fact, heat is what causes objects to feel hot or cold. You may often use the word *heat* to mean different things. However, in this lesson, the word *heat* has only one meaning. **Heat** is the energy that is transferred between objects that are at different temperatures.

Energy Transferred Between Objects

When objects that have different temperatures come into contact, energy will be transferred between them until both objects reach the same temperature. The direction of this energy transfer is always from the object with the higher temperature to the object with the lower temperature. When you touch something cold, energy is transferred from your body to that object. When you touch something hot, like the pan shown below, energy is transferred from that object to your body.

Active Reading

6 Identify As you read, underline the direction of energy transfer between objects that are at different temperatures.

 **Visualize It!**

7 Predict Draw an arrow to show the direction in which energy is transferred between the pan and the oven mitts. Explain your reasoning.

This pan is being removed from the oven and is very hot.

Heat

How is energy transferred by radiation?

On a summer day, you can feel warmth from the sun on your skin. But how did that energy reach you from the sun? The sun transfers energy to Earth by radiation. **Radiation** is the transfer of energy as electromagnetic (ee•LEK•troh•mag•NEH•tik) waves. Radiation can transfer energy between objects that are not in direct contact with each other. Many objects other than the sun also radiate energy as light and heat. These include a hot burner on a stove and a campfire, shown below.

Electromagnetic Waves

Energy from the sun is called *electromagnetic radiation*. This energy travels in waves. You are probably familiar with one form of radiation called *visible light*. You can see the visible light that comes from the sun. Electromagnetic radiation includes other forms of energy, which you cannot see. Most of the warmth that you feel from the sun is infrared radiation. This energy has a longer wavelength and lower energy than visible light. Higher-energy radiation includes x-rays and ultraviolet light.

Visualize It!

8 Analyze Write a caption for the campfire photo on the right. Make sure the caption relates the image to radiation.

_____

_____

_____

Energy from this hot burner is being transferred by radiation.

Energy from the sun is transferred through space.

Where does radiation occur on Earth?

We live almost 150 million km from the sun. Yet almost all of the energy on Earth is transmitted from the sun by radiation. The sun is the major source of energy for processes at Earth's surface. Receiving that energy is absolutely vital for life on Earth. The electromagnetic waves from the sun also provide energy that drives the water cycle.

When solar radiation reaches Earth, some of the energy is reflected and scattered by Earth's atmosphere. But much of the energy passes through Earth's atmosphere and reaches Earth's surface. Some of the energy that Earth receives from the sun is absorbed by the atmosphere, geosphere, and hydrosphere. Then, the energy is changed into thermal energy. This thermal energy may be reradiated into the Earth system or into space. Much of the energy is transferred through Earth's systems by the two other ways—convection and conduction.

9 Summarize Give two examples of what happens when energy from the sun reaches Earth.

_____

_____

_____

_____

Heating Up

How is energy transferred by convection?

Have you ever watched a pot of boiling water, such as the one below? If so, you have seen convection. **Convection** (kuhn•VECK•shuhn) is the transfer of energy due to the movement of matter. As water warms up at the bottom of the pot, some of the hot water rises. At the same time, cooler water from other parts of the pot sink and replace the rising water. This water is then warmed and the cycle continues.

Convection Currents

Convection involves the movement of matter due to differences in density. Convection occurs because most matter becomes less dense when it gets warmer. When most matter becomes warmer, it undergoes thermal expansion and a decrease in density. This less-dense matter is forced upward by the surrounding colder, denser matter that is sinking. As the hot matter rises, it cools and becomes more dense. This causes it to sink back down. This cycling of matter is called a *convection current*. Convection most often occurs in fluids, such as water and air. But convection can also happen in solids.

wax

energy sources

convection current

Visualize It! Inquiry

11 Apply How is convection related to the rise and fall of wax in lava lamps?

_____

_____

_____

_____

Where does convection occur on Earth?

If Earth's surface is warmer than the air, energy will be transferred from the ground to the air. As the air becomes warmer, it becomes less dense. This air is pushed upward and out of the way by cooler, denser air that is sinking. As the warm air rises, it cools and becomes denser and begins to sink back toward Earth's surface. This cycle moves energy through the atmosphere.

Convection currents also occur in the ocean because of differences in the density of ocean water. Denser water sinks to the ocean floor, and less dense water moves toward the surface. The density of ocean water is influenced by temperature and the amount of salt in the water. Cold water is denser than warmer water. Water that contains a lot of salt is denser than less-salty water.

Energy produced deep inside Earth heats rock in the mantle. The heated rock becomes less dense and is pushed up toward Earth's surface by the cooler, denser surrounding rock. Once cooled near the surface, the rock sinks. These convection currents transfer energy from Earth's core toward Earth's surface. These currents also cause the movement of tectonic plates.

Active Reading **12 Name** What are three of Earth's spheres in which energy is transferred by convection?

_____

_____

Visualize It!

13 Apply Draw the convection current that could occur in the body of water in this image.

Convection currents occur throughout the Earth system.

Ouch!

How is energy transferred by conduction?

Have you ever touched an ice cube and wondered why it feels cold? An ice cube has only a small amount of energy, compared to your hand. Energy is transferred to the ice cube from your hand through the process of conduction. **Conduction** (kuhn•DUHK•shuhn) is the transfer of energy from one object to another object through direct contact.

Direct Contact

Remember that the atoms or molecules in a substance are constantly moving. Even a solid block of ice has particles in constant motion. When objects at different temperatures touch, their particles interact. Conduction involves the faster-moving particles of the warmer object transferring energy to the slower-moving particles in the cooler object. The greater the difference in energy of the particles, the faster the transfer of energy by conduction occurs.

Active Reading **14 Apply** Name two examples of conduction that you experience every day.

_____

_____

_____

_____

These desert sands would feel hot because of conduction.

Where does conduction occur on Earth?

Energy can be transferred between the geosphere and the atmosphere by conduction. When cooler air molecules come into direct contact with the warm ground, energy is passed to the air by conduction. Conduction between the ground and the air happens only within a few centimeters of Earth's surface.

Conduction also happens between particles of air and particles of water. For example, if air transfers enough energy to liquid water, the water may evaporate. If water vapor transfers energy to the air, the kinetic energy of the water decreases. As a result, the water vapor may condense to form liquid water droplets.

Inside Earth, energy transfers between rock particles by conduction. However, rock is a poor conductor of heat, so this process happens very slowly.

Visualize It!

15 Compare Does conduction also occur in a city like the one shown below? Explain.

_____
_____
_____
_____
_____
_____

16 Summarize Complete the following spider map by describing the three types of energy transfer. One answer has been started for you.

Radiation
Transfer of energy as
_____
_____

_____
_____
_____

Types of Energy Transfer

_____
_____
_____

Visual Summary

To complete this summary, fill in the blanks with the correct word or phrase. Then, use the key below to check your answers. You can use this page to review the main concepts of the lesson.

Energy Transfer

Heat is the energy that is transferred between objects that are at different temperatures.

17 The particles in a hot pan have _____ kinetic energy than the particles in a cool oven mitt.

Energy can be transferred in different ways.

18 The three ways that energy can be transferred are labeled in the image as

A: _____

B: _____

C: _____

Answers: 17 more; 18 A: radiation, B: conduction, C: convection

19 Apply What type of energy transfer is responsible for making you feel cold when you are swimming in cool water? Explain your reasoning.

Lesson Review

Vocabulary

In your own words, define the following terms.

1 radiation

_____

_____

2 convection

_____

_____

3 conduction

_____

_____

Key Concepts

4 Compare What is the difference between temperature, thermal energy, and heat?

_____

_____

_____

_____

_____

_____

5 Describe What is happening to a substance undergoing thermal expansion?

_____

_____

_____

_____

6 Explain What is the main source of energy for most processes at Earth's surface?

_____

7 Summarize What happens when two objects at different temperatures touch? Name one place where it occurs in Earth's system.

_____

_____

_____

8 Identify What is an example of convection in Earth's system?

_____

Critical Thinking

9 Apply Why can metal utensils get too hot to touch when you are cooking with them?

_____

_____

_____

10 Predict A plastic spoon that has a temperature of 78°F is placed into a bowl of soup that has a temperature of 84°F. What do you predict will happen? Explain your reasoning.

_____

_____

_____

_____

_____

Use this image to answer the following questions.

11 Analyze Name one example of where energy transfer by radiation is occurring.

_____

12 Analyze Name one example of where energy transfer by conduction is occurring.

_____

13 Analyze Name one example of where energy transfer by convection is occurring.

_____

My Notes

Lesson 3

Wind in the Atmosphere

ESSENTIAL QUESTION

What is wind?

By the end of this lesson, you should be able to explain how energy provided by the sun causes atmospheric movement, called wind.

 S6E4.b Solar energy transfer

 S6E4.c Interaction between unequal heating and Earth's rotation

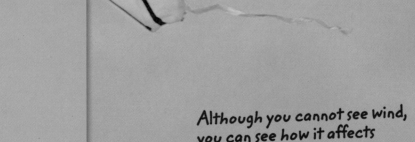

Although you cannot see wind, you can see how it affects things like these kites.

Engage Your Brain

1 Predict Check T or F to show whether you think each statement is true or false.

T	F	
☐	☐	The atmosphere is often referred to as air.
☐	☐	Wind does not have direction.
☐	☐	During the day, there is often a wind blowing toward shore from the ocean or a large lake.
☐	☐	Cold air rises and warm air sinks.

2 Explain If you opened the valve on this bicycle tire, what would happen to the air inside of the tire? Why do you think that would happen?

_____

_____

_____

Active Reading

3 Synthesize You can often define an unknown phrase if you know the meaning of its word parts. Use the word parts below to make an educated guess about the meanings of the phrases *local wind* and *global wind*.

Word part	Meaning
wind	movement of air due to differences in air pressure
local	involving a particular area
global	involving the entire Earth

Vocabulary Terms
- wind
- Coriolis effect
- global wind
- jet stream
- local wind

4 Identify This list contains the vocabulary terms you'll learn in this lesson. As you read, circle the definition of each term.

local wind:

_____

_____

global wind:

_____

_____

Blow It Out!

What causes wind?

The next time you feel the wind blowing, you can thank the sun! The sun does not warm the whole surface of the Earth in a uniform manner. This uneven heating causes the air above Earth's surface to be at different temperatures. Cold air is more dense than warmer air is. Colder, denser air sinks. When denser air sinks, it places greater pressure on the surface of Earth than warmer, less-dense air does. This results in areas of higher air pressure. Air moves from areas of higher pressure toward areas of lower pressure. The movement of air caused by differences in air pressure is called **wind**. The greater the differences in air pressure, the faster the air moves.

Areas of High and Low Pressure

Cold, dense air at the poles creates areas of high pressure at the poles. Warm, less-dense air at the equator forms an area of lower pressure. This pressure gradient results in global movement of air. However, instead of moving in one circle between the equator and the poles, air moves in smaller circular patterns called *convection cells,* shown below. As air moves from the equator, it cools and becomes more dense. At about 30°N and 30°S latitudes, a high-pressure belt results from the sinking of air. Near the poles, cold air warms as it moves away from the poles. At around 60°N and 60°S latitudes, a low-pressure belt forms as the warmed air is pushed upward.

Visualize It!

5 Identify In the white oval area on the map, draw the convection cell that was left out. Use a pencil to indicate warm air and a pen to indicate cool air.

The warming and cooling of air produces pressure belts every 30° of latitude.

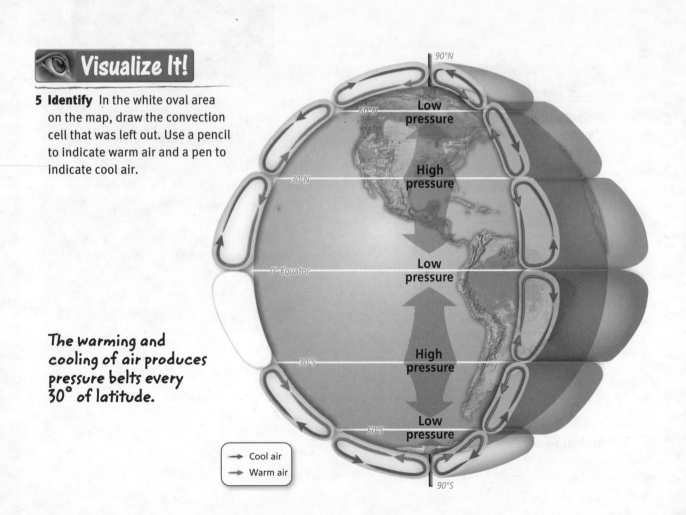

How does Earth's rotation affect wind?

Pressure differences cause air to move between the equator and the poles. If Earth was not rotating, winds would blow in a straight line. However, winds are deflected, or curved, due to Earth's rotation, as shown below. The apparent curving of the path of a moving object from an otherwise straight path due to Earth's rotation is called the **Coriolis effect** (kohr•ee•OH•lis ih•FEKT). This effect is most noticeable over long distances.

Because each point on Earth makes one complete rotation every day, points closer to the equator must travel farther and, therefore, faster than points closer to the poles do. When air moves from the equator toward the North Pole, it maintains its initial speed and direction. If the air travels far enough north, it will have traveled farther east than a point on the ground beneath it. As a result, the air appears to follow a curved path toward the east. Air moving from the North Pole to the equator appears to curve to the west because the air moves east more slowly than a point on the ground beneath it does. Therefore, in the Northern Hemisphere, air moving to the north curves to the east and air moving to the south curves to the west.

Active Reading

6 Identify As you read, underline how air movement in the Northern Hemisphere is influenced by the Coriolis effect.

Visualize It!

7 Label In the white ovals on the map, draw the direction and path of the winds that would occur at those locations on Earth.

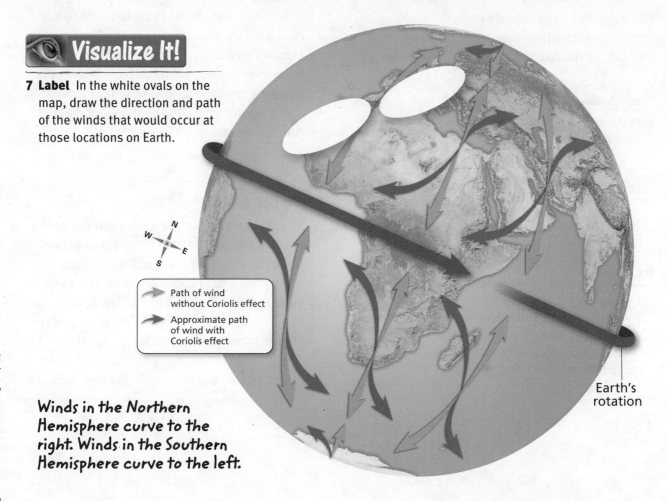

Path of wind without Coriolis effect

Approximate path of wind with Coriolis effect

Earth's rotation

Winds in the Northern Hemisphere curve to the right. Winds in the Southern Hemisphere curve to the left.

Blowin' Around

What are examples of global winds?

Recall that air travels in circular patterns called convection cells that cover approximately 30° of latitude. Pressure belts at every 30° of latitude and the Coriolis effect produce patterns of calm areas and wind systems. These wind systems occur at or near Earth's surface and are called **global winds**. As shown at the right, the major global wind systems are the *polar easterlies* (EE•ster•leez), the *westerlies* (WES•ter•leez), and the *trade winds*. Winds such as polar easterlies and westerlies are named for the direction from which they blow. Calm areas include the doldrums and the horse latitudes.

Active Reading

8 Explain If something is being carried by westerlies, what direction is it moving toward?

_____

_____

Think Outside the Book Inquiry

9 Model Winds are described according to their direction and speed. Research wind vanes and what they are used for. Design and build your own wind vane.

Trade Winds

The trade winds blow between 30° latitude and the equator in both hemispheres. The rotation of Earth causes the trade winds to curve to the west. Therefore, trade winds in the Northern Hemisphere come from the northeast, and trade winds in the Southern Hemisphere come from the southeast. These winds became known as the trade winds because sailors relied on them to sail from Europe to the Americas.

Westerlies

The westerlies blow between 30° and 60° latitudes in both hemispheres. The rotation of Earth causes these winds to curve to the east. Therefore, westerlies in the Northern Hemisphere come from the southwest, and westerlies in the Southern Hemisphere come from the northwest. The westerlies can carry moist air over the continental United States, producing rain and snow.

Polar Easterlies

The polar easterlies blow between the poles and 60° latitude in both hemispheres. The polar easterlies form as cold, sinking air moves from the poles toward 60°N and 60°S latitudes. The rotation of Earth causes these winds to curve to the west. In the Northern Hemisphere, polar easterlies can carry cold Arctic air over the majority of the United States, producing snow and freezing weather.

The major global wind systems

10 Identify Label the polar easterlies, the westerlies, and the trade winds in the white boxes on the map.

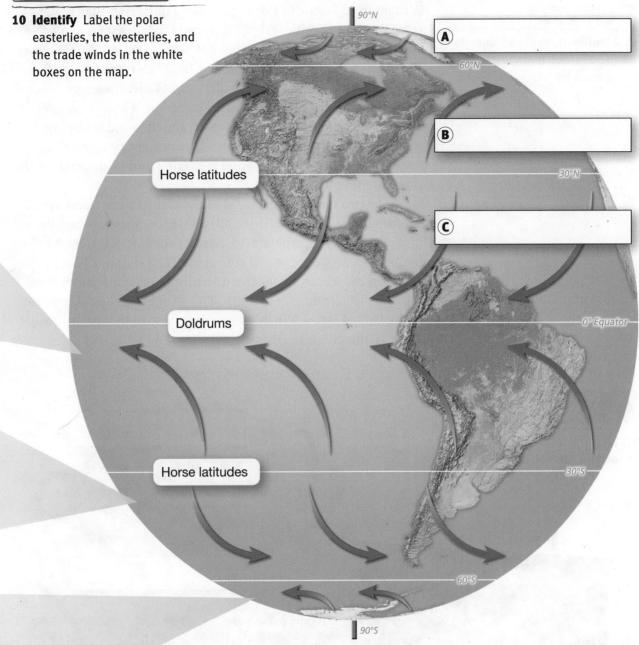

The Doldrums and Horse Latitudes

The trade winds of both hemispheres meet in a calm area around the equator called the *doldrums* (DOHL•druhmz). Very little wind blows in the doldrums because the warm, less-dense air results in an area of low pressure. The name doldrums means "dull" or "sluggish." At about 30° latitude in both hemispheres, air stops moving and sinks. This forms calm areas called the *horse latitudes*. This name was given to these areas when sailing ships carried horses from Europe to the Americas. When ships were stalled in these areas, horses were sometimes thrown overboard to save water.

The Jet Streams

A flight from Seattle to Boston can be 30 min faster than a flight from Boston to Seattle. Why? Pilots can take advantage of a jet stream. **Jet streams** are narrow belts of high-speed winds that blow from west to east, between 7 km and 16 km above Earth's surface. Airplanes traveling in the same direction as a jet stream go faster than those traveling in the opposite direction of a jet stream. When an airplane is traveling "with" a jet stream, the wind is helping the airplane move forward. However, when an airplane is traveling "against" the jet stream, the wind is making it more difficult for the plane to move forward.

The two main jet streams are the polar jet stream and the subtropical (suhb•TRAHP•i•kuhl) jet stream, shown below. Each of the hemispheres experiences these jet streams. Jet streams follow boundaries between hot and cold air and can shift north and south. In the winter, as Northern Hemisphere temperatures cool, the polar jet stream moves south. This shift brings cold Arctic air to the United States. When temperatures rise in the spring, this jet stream shifts to the north.

Active Reading

11 Identify As you read, underline the direction that the jet streams travel.

Visualize It!

12 Identify Label the polar jet stream and the subtropical jet stream in the Northern Hemisphere.

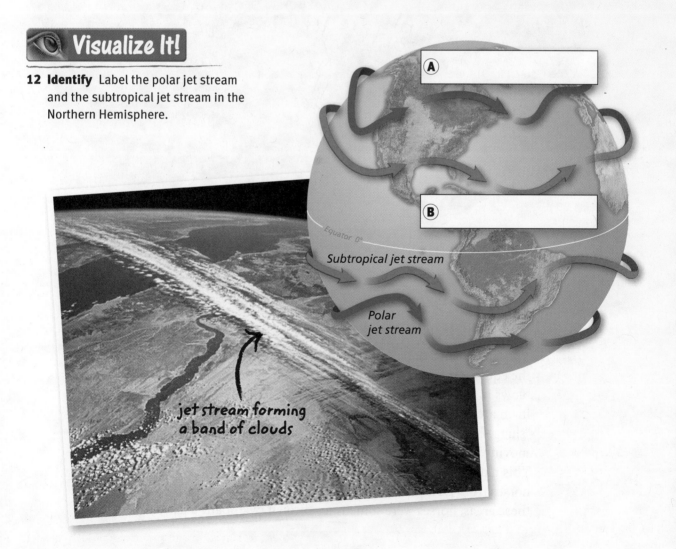

A

B

Equator 0°

Subtropical jet stream

Polar jet stream

jet stream forming a band of clouds

Desert Trades

How does some of the Sahara end up in the Americas? Global winds carry it.

Trade Wind Carriers
Trade winds can carry Saharan dust across the Atlantic Ocean to Florida and the Caribbean.

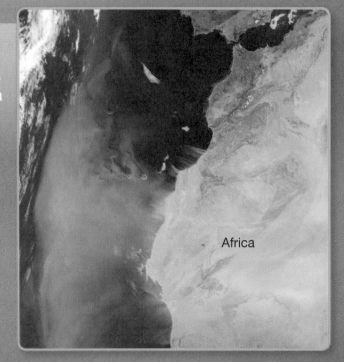

Africa

Florida Meets the Sahara
This hazy skyline in Miami is the result of a dust storm. Where did the dust come from? It all started in the Sahara.

The Sahara
The Sahara is the world's largest hot desert. Sand and dust storms that produce skies like this are very common in this desert.

Extend

Inquiry

13 Explain Look at a map and explain how trade winds carry dust from the Sahara to the Caribbean.

14 Relate Investigate the winds that blow in your community. Where do they usually come from? Identify the wind system that could be involved. Explain how the evidence supports your claim.

15 Claims · Evidence · Reasoning Investigate how winds played a role in distributing radioactive waste that was released after an explosion at the Chernobyl Nuclear Power Plant in Ukraine. Make a claim based on evidence that you find. Present your findings as a map illustration or in a poster.

Feelin' Breezy

What are examples of local winds?

Local geographic features, such as a body of water or a mountain, can produce temperature and pressure differences that cause local winds. Unlike global winds, **local winds** are the movement of air over short distances. They can blow from any direction, depending on the features of the area.

Sea and Land Breezes

Have you ever felt a cool breeze coming off the ocean or a lake? If so, you were experiencing a sea breeze. Large bodies of water take longer to warm up than land does. During the day, air above land becomes warmer than air above water. The colder, denser air over water flows toward the land and pushes the warm air on the land upward. While water takes longer to warm than land does, land cools faster than water does. At night, cooler air on land causes a higher-pressure zone over the land. So, a wind blows from the land toward the water. This type of local wind is called a land breeze.

Active Reading

16 Identify As you read, underline two examples of geographic features that contribute to the formation of local winds.

Visualize It!

17 Analyze Label the areas of high pressure and low pressure.

sea breeze

Ⓑ _____ pressure

Ⓐ _____ pressure

land breeze

Ⓓ _____ pressure

Ⓒ _____ pressure

Valley and Mountain Breezes

Areas that have mountains and valleys experience local winds called mountain and valley breezes. During the day, the sun warms the air along the mountain slopes faster than the air in the valleys. This uneven heating results in areas of lower pressure near the mountain tops. This pressure difference causes a valley breeze, which flows from the valley up the slopes of the mountains. Many birds float on valley breezes to conserve energy. At nightfall, the air along the mountain slopes cools and moves down into the valley. This local wind is called a mountain breeze.

valley breeze

Ⓑ _____ pressure

Ⓐ _____ pressure

mountain breeze

Ⓓ _____ pressure

Ⓒ _____ pressure

Visual Summary

To complete this summary, circle the correct word or phrases. Then use the key below to check your answers. You can use this page to review the main concepts of the lesson.

Wind is the movement of air from areas of higher pressure to areas of lower pressure.

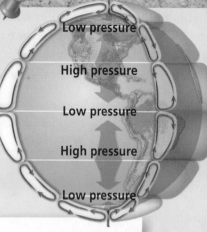

Low pressure

High pressure

Low pressure

High pressure

Low pressure

19 Cool air sinks, causing an area of high / low air pressure.

Global wind systems occur on Earth.

20 High-speed wind between 7 km and 16 km above Earth's surface is a jet stream / mountain breeze.

Wind in the Atmosphere

Geographic features can produce local winds.

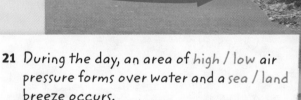

21 During the day, an area of high / low air pressure forms over water and a sea / land breeze occurs.

22 Explain Sketch a model to explain how differences in air temperatures and the rotation of the Earth causes local winds and global winds.

Lesson Review

Vocabulary

Fill in the blanks with the term that best completes the following sentences.

1 Another term for air movement caused by differences in air pressure is

_____

2 Pilots often take advantage of the

_____ , which are high-speed winds between 7 km and 16 km above Earth's surface.

3 The apparent curving of winds due to Earth's rotation is the _____

Key Concepts

4 Explain How does the sun cause wind?

_____

_____

_____

_____

5 Predict If Earth did not rotate, what would happen to the global winds? Why?

_____

_____

_____

6 Explain How do convection cells in Earth's atmosphere cause high- and low-pressure belts?

_____

_____

_____

_____

7 Describe What factors contribute to global winds? Identify areas where winds are weak.

_____

_____

_____

_____

8 Identify Name a latitude where each of the following occurs: polar easterlies, westerlies, and trade winds.

_____

_____

Critical Thinking

9 Predict How would local winds be affected if water and land absorbed and released heat at the same rate? Explain your reasoning.

_____

_____

_____

10 Compare How is a land breeze similar to a sea breeze? How do they differ?

_____

_____

_____

_____

Use this image to answer the following questions.

11 Analyze What type of local wind would you experience if you were standing in the valley? Explain your reasoning.

_____

_____

12 Infer Would the local wind change if it was nighttime? Explain.

_____

_____

_____

My Notes

What Influences Weather?

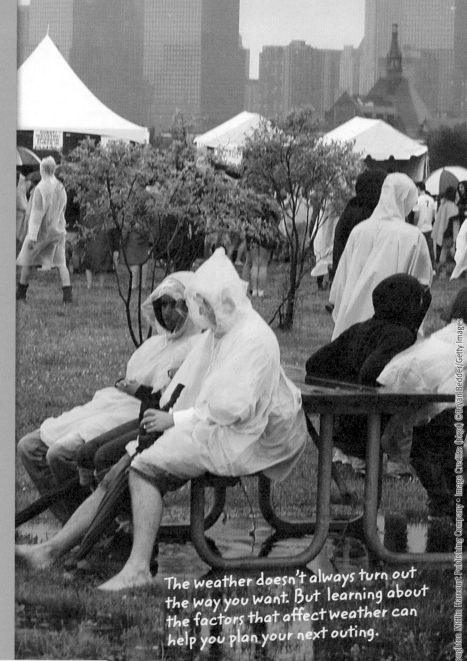

ESSENTIAL QUESTION

How do the water cycle and other global patterns affect local weather?

By the end of this lesson, you should be able to explain how global patterns in Earth's system influence weather.

> **S6E4.c** Interaction between unequal heating and Earth's rotation

> **S6E4.d** Air pressure, weather fronts, air masses, and weather events

> **S6E4.e** Effects of moisture on weather patterns and events

The weather doesn't always turn out the way you want. But learning about the factors that affect weather can help you plan your next outing.

✋ **Lesson Labs**

Quick Labs
• Analyze Weather Patterns
• Coastal Climate Model

Exploration Lab
• Modeling El Niño

🧠 Engage Your Brain

1 Predict Check T or F to show whether you think each statement is true or false.

T	F	
☐	☐	The water cycle affects weather.
☐	☐	Air can be warmed or cooled by the surface below it.
☐	☐	Warm air sinks, cool air rises.
☐	☐	Winds can bring different weather to a region.

2 Explain How can air temperatures along this coastline be affected by the large body of water that is nearby?

_____

_____

_____

✏️ Active Reading

3 Infer A military front is a contested armed frontier between opposing forces. A *weather front* occurs between two air masses, or bodies of air. What kind of weather do you think usually happens at a weather front?

_____

_____

_____

_____

_____

Vocabulary Terms

• air mass	• weather
• front	• humidity
• jet stream	• relative humidity
• air pressure	• dew point
• wind	• precipitation
• visibility	• cloud
	• fog

4 Apply As you learn the definition of each vocabulary term in this lesson, create your own definition or sketch to help you remember the meaning of the term.

Wonder about Weather?

What is weather?

Weather is the condition of Earth's atmosphere at a certain time and place. Different observations give you clues to the weather. If you see plants moving from side to side, you might infer that it is windy. If you see a gray sky and wet, shiny streets, you might decide to wear a raincoat. People talk about weather by describing factors such as temperature, air pressure, wind, humidity, precipitation, and *visibility* (viz•uh•BIL•i•tee).

What are temperature, air pressure, and wind?

Temperature is a measure of how hot or cold something is. An instrument called a *thermometer* is used to measure temperature. Air temperature is one of the most commonly reported factors of weather.

Air pressure is another factor used in weather reporting. Air pressure is the force of air molecules pushing on an area. Changes in air pressure are often used in predicting weather conditions. Air pressure is measured using an instrument called a *barometer* (buh•RAHM•i•ter).

Wind is air that moves horizontally, or parallel to the ground. Wind moves from areas of high air pressure to areas of low air pressure. Wind speed is measured with an anemometer (an•uh•MAHM•i•ter). Wind direction is measured by using a wind vane or a windsock.

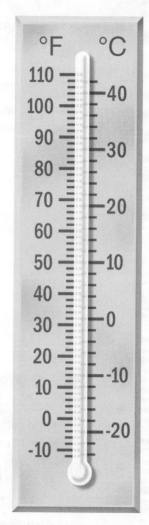

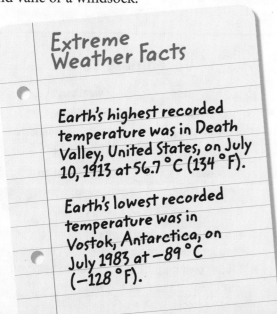

Extreme Weather Facts

Earth's highest recorded temperature was in Death Valley, United States, on July 10, 1913 at 56.7 °C (134 °F).

Earth's lowest recorded temperature was in Vostok, Antarctica, on July 1983 at −89 °C (−128 °F).

Visualize It!

5 Identify Color in the liquid in the thermometer above to show Earth's average temperature in 2009 (58 °F). Write the Celsius temperature that equals 58 °F on the line below.

_____

What is humidity and how does it affect weather?

As water evaporates from oceans, lakes, and ponds, it becomes water vapor, or a gas that is in the air. The amount of water vapor in the air is called **humidity**. As more water evaporates and becomes water vapor, the humidity of the air increases.

Humidity is often described through relative humidity. **Relative humidity** is the amount of water vapor in the air compared to the amount of water vapor needed to reach saturation. As shown below, when air is saturated, the rates of evaporation and condensation are equal. Saturated air has a relative humidity of 100%. A psychrometer (sy•KRAHM•i•ter) is an instrument that is used to measure relative humidity.

Air can become saturated when evaporation adds water vapor to the air. Air can also become saturated when it cools to its dew point. The **dew point** is the temperature at which more condensation than evaporation occurs. When air temperature drops below the dew point, condensation forms. This can cause dew on surfaces cooler than the dew point. It also can form fog and clouds.

📖 **Active Reading**

6 Identify Underline the name of the instrument used to measure relative humidity.

👁 **Visualize It!**

7 Sketch In the space provided, draw what happens in air that is below the dew point.

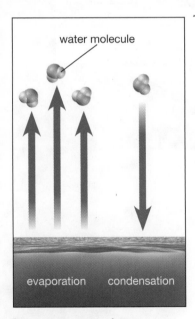

In unsaturated air, more water evaporates into the air than condenses back into the water.

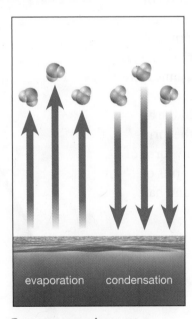

In saturated air, the amount of water that evaporates equals the amount that condenses.

When air cools below its dew point, more water vapor condenses into water than evaporates.

8 Explain Why does dew form on grass overnight?

_____

_____

Water, Water

How does the water cycle affect weather?

The *water cycle* is the continuous movement of water between the atmosphere, the land, the oceans, and living things. In the water cycle, shown to the right, water is constantly being recycled between liquid, solid, and gaseous states. The water cycle involves the processes of evaporation, condensation, and precipitation.

Evaporation occurs when liquid water changes into water vapor, which is a gas. Condensation occurs when water vapor cools and changes from a gas to a liquid. A change in the amount of water vapor in the air affects humidity. Clouds and fog form through condensation of water vapor. A **cloud** is condensed water vapor that is suspended in air. **Fog** is water vapor that has condensed very close to Earth's surface. Fog is often responsible for reducing **visibility,** a measure of the transparency of the atmosphere.

Water vapor that has condensed in the air to form clouds can return to Earth in the form of precipitation. **Precipitation** refers to any form of water that falls to Earth from clouds. Forms of precipitation include rain, snow, sleet, and hail.

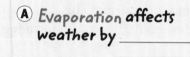
Active Reading

9 List Name at least 5 forms that water can take throughout the water cycle.

_____

_____

Visualize It!

10 Summarize Describe how the water cycle influences weather by completing the sentences on the picture.

Ⓐ *Evaporation* **affects weather by** _____

_____

_____

Everywhere . . .

How do air masses affect weather?

Ⓑ Condensation affects weather by _____
_____
_____

Ⓒ Precipitation affects weather by _____
_____
_____

Runoff

👁 **Visualize It!** (Inquiry)

11 Identify What elements of weather are different on the two mountaintops? Explain why.

_____
_____
_____
_____
_____

Putting Up a **Front**

How do air masses affect weather?

12 Identify As you read, underline how air masses form.

You have probably experienced the effects of air masses—one day is hot and humid, and the next day is cool and pleasant. The weather changes when a new air mass moves into your area. An **air mass** is a large volume of air in which temperature and moisture content are nearly the same throughout. An air mass forms when the air over a large region of Earth stays in one area for many days. The air gradually takes on the temperature and humidity of the land or water below it. When an air mass moves, it can bring these characteristics to new locations. Air masses can change temperature and humidity as they move to a new area.

Where do fronts form?

When two air masses meet, density differences usually keep them from mixing. A cool air mass is more dense than a warm air mass. A boundary, called a **front**, forms between the air masses. For a front to form, one air mass must run into another air mass. The kind of front that forms depends on how these air masses move relative to each other, and on their relative temperature and moisture content. Fronts result in a change in weather as they pass. They usually affect weather in the middle latitudes of Earth. Fronts do not often occur near the equator because air masses there do not have big temperature differences.

The boundary between air masses, or front, cannot be seen, but is shown here to illustrate how air masses can take on the characteristics of the surface below them.

Air masses that form above water are moist.

Air masses that form above land are dry.

Cold Fronts Form Where Cold Air Moves under Warm Air

Warm air is less dense than cold air is. So, a cold air mass that is moving can quickly push up a warm air mass. If the warm air is moist, clouds will form. Storms that form along a cold front are usually short-lived but can move quickly and bring heavy rain or snow. Cooler weather follows a cold front.

13 Apply If you hear that a cold front is headed for your area, what type of weather might you expect? Explain your reasoning.

_____

_____

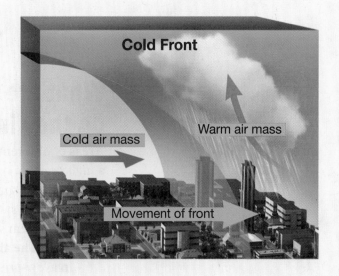

Cold Front

Warm air mass

Cold air mass

Movement of front

Warm Fronts Form Where Warm Air Moves over Cold Air

A warm front forms when a warm air mass follows a retreating cold air mass. The warm air rises over the cold air, and its moisture condenses into clouds. Warm fronts often bring drizzly rain and are followed by warm, clear weather.

14 Identify The rainy weather at the edge of a warm front is a result of

☐ the cold air mass that is leaving.

☐ the warm air rising over the cold air.

☐ the warm air mass following the front.

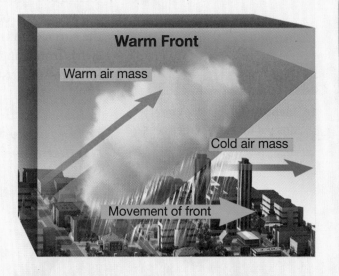

Warm Front

Warm air mass

Cold air mass

Movement of front

Stationary Fronts Form Where Cold and Warm Air Stop Moving

In a stationary front, there is not enough wind for either the cold air mass or the warm air mass to keep moving. So, the two air masses remain in one place. A stationary front can cause many days of unchanging weather, usually clear.

15 Infer When could a stationary front become a warm or cold front? Explain your reasoning.

_____

_____

Inquiry

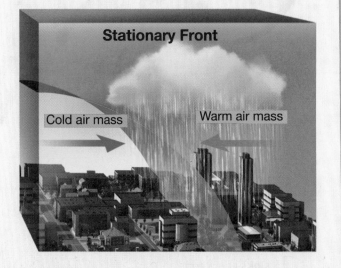

Stationary Front

Cold air mass

Warm air mass

Feeling the Pressure!

What are pressure systems, and how do they interact?

Areas of different air pressure cause changes in the weather. In a *high-pressure system*, air sinks slowly down. As the air nears the ground, it spreads out toward areas of lower pressure. Most high-pressure systems are large and change slowly. When a high-pressure system stays in one location for a long time, an air mass may form. The air mass can be warm or cold, humid or dry.

In a *low-pressure system*, air rises and so has a lower air pressure than the areas around it. As the air in the center of a low-pressure system rises, the air cools.

The diagram below shows how a high-pressure system can form a low-pressure system. Surface air, shown by the black arrows, moves out and away from high-pressure centers. Air above the surface sinks and warms. The green arrows show how air swirls from a high-pressure system into a low-pressure system. In a low-pressure system, the air rises and cools.

16 Identify Choose the correct answer for each of the pressure systems shown below.

A high-pressure system can spiral into a low-pressure system, as illustrated by the green arrows below. In the Northern Hemisphere, air circles in the directions shown.

A In a high-pressure system, air

☐ rises and cools.

☐ sinks and warms.

B in a low-pressure system, air

☐ rises and cools.

☐ sinks and warms.

How do different pressure systems affect us?

When air pressure differences are small, air doesn't move very much. If the air remains in one place or moves slowly, the air takes on the temperature and humidity of the land or water beneath it. Each type of pressure system has it own unique weather pattern. By keeping track of high- and low-pressure systems, scientists can predict the weather.

High-Pressure Systems Produce Clear Weather

High-pressure systems are areas where air sinks and moves outward. The sinking air is denser than the surrounding air, and the pressure is higher. Cooler, denser air moves out of the center of these high-pressure areas toward areas of lower pressure. As the air sinks, it gets warmer and absorbs moisture. Water droplets evaporate, relative humidity decreases, and clouds often disappear. A high-pressure system generally brings clear skies and calm air or gentle breezes.

Low-Pressure Systems Produce Rainy Weather

Low-pressure systems have lower pressure than the surrounding areas. Air in a low-pressure system comes together, or converges, and rises. As the air in the center of a low-pressure system rises, it cools and forms clouds and rain. The rising air in a low-pressure system causes stormy weather.

A low-pressure system can develop wherever there is a center of low pressure. One place this often happens is along a boundary between a warm air mass and a cold air mass. Rain often occurs at these boundaries, or fronts.

 **Visualize It!**

17 Match Label each picture as a result of a high- or low-pressure system. Then, draw a line from each photo to its matching air-pressure diagram.

(A)

(B)

Warm air rises

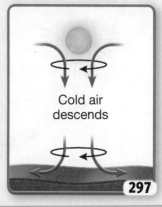

Cold air descends

Windy Weather

How do global wind patterns affect local weather?

Winds are caused by unequal heating of Earth's surface—which causes air pressure differences—and can occur on a global or on a local scale. On a local scale, air-pressure differences affect both wind speed and wind direction at a location. On a global level, there is an overall movement of surface air from the poles toward the equator. The heated air at the equator rises and forms a low-pressure belt. Cold air near the poles sinks and creates high-pressure centers. Because air moves from areas of high pressure to areas of low pressure, it moves from the poles to the equator. At high altitudes, the warmed air circles back toward the poles.

Temperature and pressure differences on Earth's surface also create regional wind belts. Winds in these belts curve to the east or the west as they blow, due to Earth's rotation. This curving of winds is called the *Coriolis effect* (kohr•ee•OH•lis eff•EKT). Winds would flow in straight lines if Earth did not rotate. Winds bring air masses of different temperatures and moisture content to a region.

Visualize It!

18 Apply Trade winds bring

☐ cool air to the warmer equatorial regions.

☐ warm air to the cooler, higher latitudes.

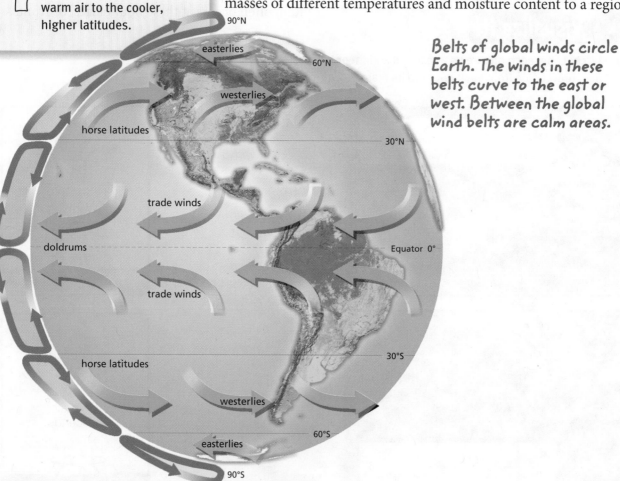

Belts of global winds circle Earth. The winds in these belts curve to the east or west. Between the global wind belts are calm areas.

90°N
easterlies
60°N
westerlies
horse latitudes
30°N
trade winds
doldrums
Equator 0°
trade winds
horse latitudes
30°S
westerlies
60°S
easterlies
90°S

How do jet streams affect weather?

Long-distance winds that travel above global winds for thousands of kilometers are called **jet streams**. Air moves in jet streams with speeds that are at least 92 kilometers per hour and are often greater than 180 kilometers per hour. Like global and local winds, jet streams form because Earth's surface is heated unevenly. They flow in a wavy pattern from west to east.

Each hemisphere usually has two main jet streams, a polar jet stream and a subtropical jet stream. The polar jet streams flow closer to the poles in summer than in winter. Jet streams can affect temperatures. For example, a polar jet stream can pull cold air down from Canada into the United States and pull warm air up toward Canada. Jet streams also affect precipitation patterns. Strong storms tend to form along jet streams. Scientists must know where a jet stream is flowing to make accurate weather predictions.

Active Reading **19 Identify** What are two ways jet streams affect weather?

_____

_____

_____

_____

In winter months, the polar jet stream flows across much of the United States.

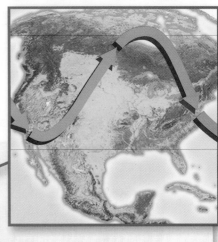

Polar jet stream

Subtropical jet streams

Polar jet stream

Visualize It!

20 Infer How does the polar jet stream influence the weather on the southern tip of South America?

_____

_____

_____

_____

Ocean Effects

How do ocean currents influence weather?

The same global winds that blow across the surface of Earth also push water across Earth's oceans, causing surface currents. Different winds cause currents to flow in different directions. The flow of surface currents moves energy as heat from one part of Earth to another. As the map below shows, both warm-water and cold-water currents flow from one ocean to another. Water near the equator carries energy from the sun to other parts of the ocean. The energy from the warm currents is transferred to colder water or to the atmosphere, changing local temperatures and humidity.

Oceans also have an effect on weather in the form of hurricanes and monsoons. Warm ocean water fuels hurricanes. Monsoons are winds that change direction with the seasons. During summer, the land becomes much warmer than the sea in some areas of the world. Moist wind flows inland, often bringing heavy rains.

Warm current

Cold current

Surface currents are caused by winds. They distribute energy across Earth's surface, changing local temperature and humidity.

Cool Ocean Currents Lower Coastal Air Temperatures

As currents flow, they warm or cool the atmosphere above, affecting local temperatures. The California current is a cold-water current that keeps the average summer high temperatures of coastal cities such as San Diego around 26 °C (78 °F). Cities that lie inland at the same latitude have warmer averages. The graph below shows average monthly temperatures for San Diego and El Centro, California.

Visualize It!

22 Claims · Evidence · Reasoning Do the data shown provide evidence to support the claim made above? Explain your reasoning.

_____

_____

_____

Average Monthly Temperatures

Source: weather.com

Warm Ocean Currents Raise Coastal Air Temperatures

In areas where warm ocean currents flow, coastal cities have warmer winter temperatures than inland cities at similar latitudes. For example, temperatures vary considerably from the coastal regions to the inland areas of Norway due to the warmth of the North Atlantic Current. Coastal cities such as Bergen have relatively mild winters. Inland cities such as Lillehammer have colder winters but temperatures similar to the coastal cities in summer.

Visualize It!

23 Identify Circle the city that is represented by each color in the graph.

■ Lillehammer/Bergen

■ Lillehammer/Bergen

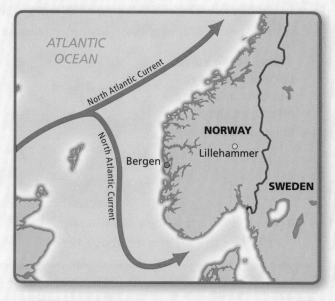

Average Monthly High Temperatures

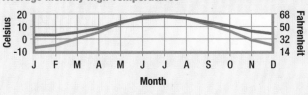

Source: worldweather.org

Visual Summary

To complete this summary, circle the correct word. Then, use the key below to check your answers. You can use this page to review the main concepts of the lesson.

Influences of Weather

Understanding the water cycle is key to understanding weather.

24 Weather is affected by the amount of oxygen / water in the air.

A front forms where two air masses meet.

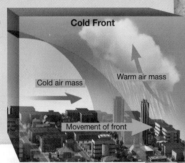

Cold Front

Cold air mass

Warm air mass

Movement of front

25 When a warm air mass and a cool air mass meet, the warm / cool air mass usually moves upward.

Low-pressure systems bring stormy weather, and high-pressure systems bring dry, clear weather.

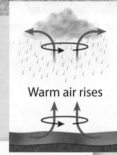

Warm air rises

26 In a low-pressure system, air moves upward / downward.

Pressure differences from the uneven heating of Earth's surface cause predictable patterns of wind.

27 Global wind patterns occur as, due to temperature differences, air rises / sinks at the poles and rises / sinks at the equator.

Global ocean surface currents can have warming or cooling effects on the air masses above them.

28 Warm currents have a warming / cooling effect on the air masses above them.

Answers: 24 water; 25 warm; 26 upward; 27 sinks; rises; 28 warming

29 **Synthesize** How do air masses cause weather changes?

_____

Lesson Review

Vocabulary

For each pair of terms, explain how the meanings of the terms differ.

1 *front* and *air mass*

_____

_____

_____

2 *high-pressure system* and *low-pressure system*

_____

_____

_____

3 *jet streams* and *global wind belts*

_____

_____

_____

Key Concepts

4 Apply If the weather becomes stormy for a short time and then becomes colder, which type of front has most likely passed? Explain your reasoning.

_____

_____

_____

5 Describe Explain how an ocean current can affect the temperature and the amount of moisture of the air mass above the current and above nearby coastlines.

_____

_____

_____

6 Synthesize How does the water cycle affect weather?

_____

_____

_____

Critical Thinking

Use the diagram below to answer the following question.

Cool air descends   Warm air rises

7 Interpret How does the movement of air affect the type of weather that forms from high-pressure and low-pressure systems?

_____

_____

_____

_____

_____

8 Explain How does the polar jet stream affect temperature and precipitation in North America?

_____

_____

_____

_____

_____

9 Describe Explain how changes in weather are caused by the interaction of air masses.

_____

_____

_____

_____

_____

_____

My Notes

Severe Weather and Weather Safety

ESSENTIAL QUESTION

How can humans protect themselves from hazardous weather?

By the end of this lesson, you should be able to describe the major types of hazardous weather and the ways human beings can protect themselves from hazardous weather and from sun exposure.

S6E4.d Air pressure, weather fronts, air masses, and weather events

S6E4.e Effects of moisture on weather patterns and events

Lightning is often the most dangerous part of a thunderstorm. Thunderstorms are one type of severe weather that can cause a lot of damage.

© Houghton Mifflin Harcourt Publishing Company • Image Credits: ©A. T. Willett/The Image Bank/Getty Images

Lesson Labs

Quick Labs
• Create your Own Lightning
• Sun Protection

Exploration Lab
• Preparing for Severe Weather

Engage Your Brain

1 Describe Fill in the blanks with the word or phrase that you think correctly complete the following sentences.

A _____ forms a funnel cloud and has high winds.

A flash or bolt of light across the sky during a storm is called _____,

_____ is the sound that follows lightning during a storm.

One way to protect yourself from the sun's rays is to wear _____.

2 Identify Name the weather event that is occurring in the photo. What conditions can occur when this event happens in an area?

_____

_____

_____

_____

Active Reading

3 Synthesize Use the sentence below to help you make an educated guess about what the term *storm surge* means. Write the meaning below.

Example sentence
Flooding causes tremendous damage to property and lives when a <u>storm surge</u> moves onto shore.

storm surge: _____

_____

_____

_____

Vocabulary Terms

• thunderstorm   • hurricane
• lightning   • storm surge
• thunder   • tornado

4 Apply As you learn the definition of each vocabulary term in this lesson, create your own definition or sketch to help you remember the meaning of the term.

☑ Take Cover!

What do we know about thunderstorms?

SPLAAAAAT! BOOOOM! The loud, sharp noise of thunder might surprise you, and maybe even make you jump. The thunder may have been joined by lightning, wind, and rain. A **thunderstorm** is an intense local storm that forms strong winds, heavy rain, lightning, thunder, and sometimes hail. A thunderstorm is an example of severe weather. Severe weather is weather that can cause property damage and sometimes death.

Thunderstorms Form from Rising Air

Thunderstorms get their energy from humid air. When warm, humid air near the ground mixes with cooler air above, the warm air creates an updraft that can build a thunderstorm quickly. Cold downdrafts bring precipitation and eventually end the storm by preventing more warm air from rising.

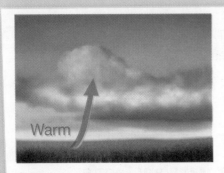

Step 1
In the first stage, warm air rises and forms a cloud. The water vapor releases energy when it condenses into cloud droplets. This energy increases the air motion. The cloud continues building up.

Step 2
Ice particles may form in the low temperatures near the top of the cloud. As the ice particles grow large, they begin to fall and pull cold air down with them. This strong downdraft brings heavy rain or hail.

Step 3
During the final stage, the downdraft can spread out and block more warm air from moving upward into the cloud. The storm slows down and ends.

5 Describe What role do air masses, fronts, and air pressure play in the formation of a thunderstorm?

_____

_____

_____

Lightning is a Discharge of Electrical Energy

If you have ever shuffled your feet on a carpet, you may have felt a small shock when you touched a doorknob. If so, you have experienced how lightning forms. **Lightning** is an electric discharge that happens between a positively charged area and a negatively charged area. While you walk around, electrical charges can collect on your body. When you touch someone or something else, the charges jump to that person or object in a spark of electricity. In a similar way, electrical charges build up near the tops and bottoms of clouds as pellets of ice move up and down through the clouds. Suddenly, a flash of lightning will spark from one place to another.

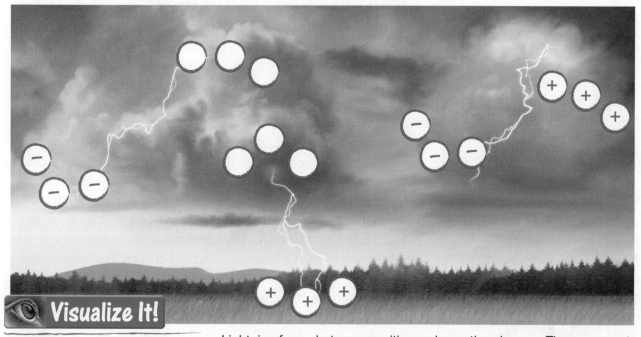

Visualize It!

6 Label Fill in the positive and negative charges in the appropriate spaces provided.

Lightning forms between positive and negative charges. The upper part of a cloud usually carries a positive electric charge. The lower part of the cloud carries mainly negative charges. Lightning is a big spark that jumps between parts of clouds, or between a cloud and Earth's surface.

Active Reading

7 Identify As you read, underline the explanation of what causes thunder during a storm.

Thunder Is a Result of Rapidly Expanding Air

When lightning strikes, the air along its path is heated to a high temperature. The superheated air quickly expands. The rapidly moving air causes the air to vibrate and release sound waves. The result is **thunder**, the sound created by the rapid expansion of air along a lightning strike.

You usually hear thunder a few seconds after you see a lightning strike, because light travels faster than sound. You can count the seconds between a lightning flash and the sound of thunder to figure out about how far away the lightning is. For every 3 seconds between lightning and its thunder, add about 1 km to the lightning strike's distance from you.

☑ Plan Ahead!

What do we know about hurricanes?

A **hurricane** is a tropical low-pressure system with winds blowing at speeds of 119 km/h (74 mi/h) or more—strong enough to uproot trees. Hurricanes are called typhoons when they form over the western Pacific Ocean and cyclones when they form over the Indian Ocean.

Active Reading

8 Identify As you read, underline the definition of *hurricane*.

Hurricanes Need Water to Form and Grow

A hurricane begins as a group of thunderstorms moving over tropical ocean waters. Thunderstorms form in areas of low pressure. Near the equator, warm ocean water provides the energy that can turn a low-pressure center into a violent storm. As water evaporates from the ocean, energy is transferred from the ocean water into the air. This energy makes warm air rise faster. Tall clouds and strong winds develop. As winds blow across the water from different directions into the low-pressure center, the paths bend into a spiral. The winds blow faster and faster around the low-pressure center, which becomes the center of the hurricane.

As long as a hurricane stays above warm water, it can grow bigger and more powerful. As soon as a hurricane moves over land or over cooler water, it loses its source of energy. The winds lose strength and the storm dies out. If a hurricane moves over land, the rough surface of the land reduces the winds even more.

Hurricanes in the Northern Hemisphere usually move westward with the trade winds. Near land, however, they will often move north or even back out to sea.

Hurricane Ike moves into the Gulf of Mexico on September 10, 2008.

Atlantic Ocean

Path of Hurricane Ike

Gulf of Mexico

Caribbean Sea

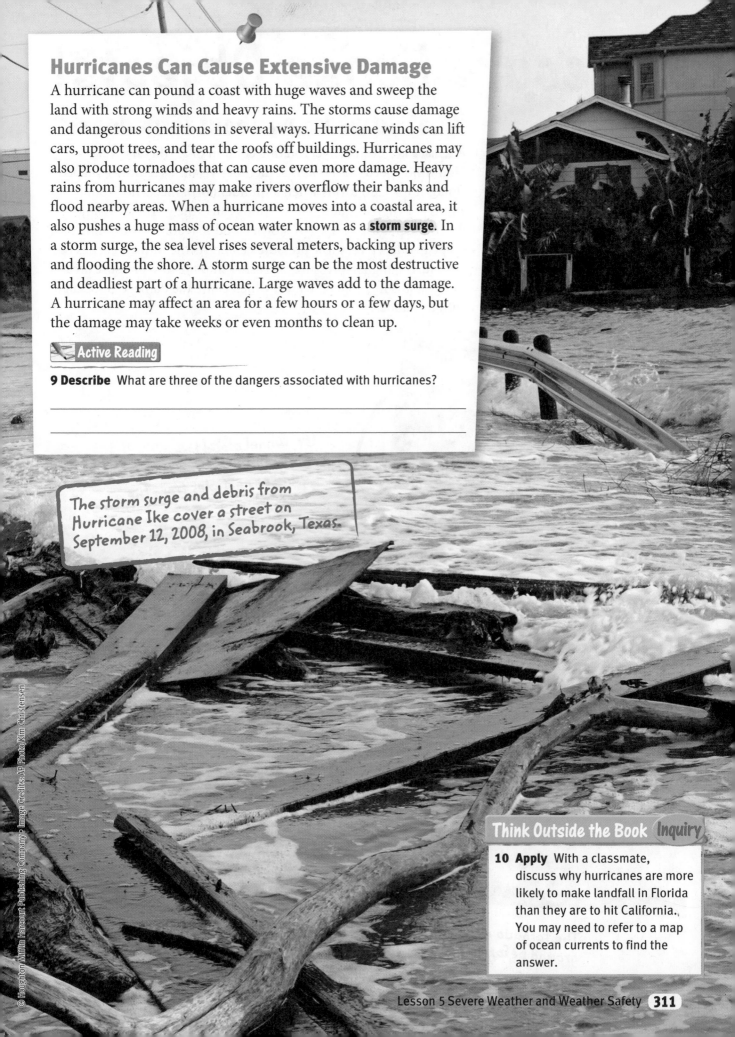

Hurricanes Can Cause Extensive Damage

A hurricane can pound a coast with huge waves and sweep the land with strong winds and heavy rains. The storms cause damage and dangerous conditions in several ways. Hurricane winds can lift cars, uproot trees, and tear the roofs off buildings. Hurricanes may also produce tornadoes that can cause even more damage. Heavy rains from hurricanes may make rivers overflow their banks and flood nearby areas. When a hurricane moves into a coastal area, it also pushes a huge mass of ocean water known as a **storm surge**. In a storm surge, the sea level rises several meters, backing up rivers and flooding the shore. A storm surge can be the most destructive and deadliest part of a hurricane. Large waves add to the damage. A hurricane may affect an area for a few hours or a few days, but the damage may take weeks or even months to clean up.

Active Reading

9 Describe What are three of the dangers associated with hurricanes?

_____

_____

The storm surge and debris from Hurricane Ike cover a street on September 12, 2008, in Seabrook, Texas.

Think Outside the Book Inquiry

10 Apply With a classmate, discuss why hurricanes are more likely to make landfall in Florida than they are to hit California. You may need to refer to a map of ocean currents to find the answer.

☑ Secure Loose Objects!

What do we know about tornadoes?

A **tornado** is a destructive, rotating column of air that has very high wind speeds and that is sometimes visible as a funnel-shaped cloud. A tornado forms when a thunderstorm meets horizontal winds at a high altitude. These winds cause the warm air rising in the thunderstorm to spin. A storm cloud may form a thin funnel shape that has a very low pressure center. As the funnel reaches the ground, the higher-pressure air rushes into the low-pressure area. The result is high-speed winds, which cause the damage associated with tornadoes.

Clouds begin to rotate, signaling that a tornado may form.

The funnel cloud becomes visible as the tornado picks up dust from the ground or particles from the air.

The tornado moves along the ground before it dies out.

© Houghton Mifflin Harcourt Publishing Company • Image Credits: (t) ©Jim Edds/Photo Researchers, Inc.; (c) ©Digital Vision/Getty Images; (b) ©Reed Timmer/SPL/Photo Researchers, Inc.

Think Outside the Book

11 Illustrate Read the description of the weather conditions that cause tornadoes and draw a sketch of what those conditions might look like.

Most Tornadoes Happen in the Midwest

Tornadoes happen in many places, but they are most common in the United States in *Tornado Alley*. Tornado Alley reaches from Texas up through the midwestern United States, including Iowa, Kansas, Nebraska, and Ohio. Many tornadoes form in the spring and early summer, typically along a front between cool, dry air and warm, humid air.

Tornadoes Can Cause Extensive Damage

The danger of a tornado is mainly due to the high speed of its winds. Winds in a tornado's funnel may have speeds of more than 400 km/h. Most injuries and deaths caused by tornadoes happen when people are struck by objects blown by the winds or when they are trapped in buildings that collapse.

Active Reading

12 Identify As you read, underline what makes a tornado so destructive.

13 Summarize In the overlapping sections of the Venn diagram, list the characteristics that are shared by the different types of storms. In the outer sections, list the characteristics that are specific to each type of storm.

Thunderstorms

Hurricanes

Tornadoes

14 Conclude Write a summary that describes the information in the Venn diagram.

_____

_____

_____

_____

☑ Be Prepared!

What can people do to prepare for severe weather?

Severe weather is weather that can cause property damage, injury, and sometimes death. Hail, lightning, high winds, tornadoes, hurricanes, and floods are all part of severe weather. Hailstorms can damage crops and cars and can break windows. Lightning starts many forest fires and kills or injures hundreds of people and animals each year. Winds and tornadoes can uproot trees and destroy homes. Flooding is also a leading cause of weather-related deaths. Most destruction from hurricanes results from flooding due to storm surges.

Think Outside the Book Inquiry

15 Apply Research severe weather in your area and come up with a plan for safety.

Plan Ahead

Have a storm supply kit that contains a battery-operated radio, batteries, flashlights, candles, rain jackets, tarps, blankets, bottled water, canned food, and medicines. Listen to weather announcements. Plan and practice a safety route. A safety route is a planned path to a safe place.

Listen for Storm Updates

During severe weather, it is important to listen to local radio or TV stations. Severe weather updates will let you know the location of a storm. They will also let you know if the storm is getting worse. A *watch* is given when the conditions are ideal for severe weather. A *warning* is given when severe weather has been spotted or is expected within 24 h. During most kinds of severe weather, it is best to stay indoors and away from windows. However, in some situations, you may need to evacuate.

Follow Flood Safety Rules

Sometimes, a place can get so much rain that it floods, especially if it is a low-lying area. So, like storms, floods have watches and warnings. However, little advance notice can usually be given that a flood is coming. A flash flood is a flood that rises and falls very quickly. The best thing to do during a flood is to find a high place to stay until it is over. You should always stay out of floodwaters. Even shallow water can be dangerous because it can move fast.

What can people do to stay safe during thunderstorms?

Stay alert when thunderstorms are predicted or when dark, tall clouds are visible. If you are outside and hear thunder, seek shelter immediately and stay there for 30 min after the thunder ends. Heavy rains can cause sudden, or flash, flooding, and hailstones can damage property and harm living things.

Lightning is one of the most dangerous parts of a thunderstorm. Because lightning is attracted to tall objects, it is important to stay away from trees if you are outside. If you are in an open area, stay close to the ground so that you are not the tallest object in the area. If you can, get into a car. Stay away from ponds, lakes, or other bodies of water. If lightning hits water while you are swimming or wading in it, you could be hurt or killed. If you are indoors during a thunderstorm, avoid using electrical appliances, running water, and phone lines.

How can people stay safe during a tornado?

Tornadoes are too fast and unpredictable for you to attempt to outrun, even if you are in a car. If you see or hear a tornado, go to a place without windows, such as a basement, a storm cellar, or a closet or hallway. Stay away from areas that are likely to have flying objects or other dangers. If you are outside, lie in a ditch or low-lying area. Protect your head and neck by covering them with your arms and hands.

How can people stay safe during a hurricane?

If your family lives where hurricanes may strike, have a plan to leave the area, and gather emergency supplies. If a hurricane is approaching your area, listen to weather reports for storm updates. Secure loose objects outside, and cover windows with storm shutters or boards. During a storm, stay indoors and away from windows. If ordered to evacuate the area, do so immediately. After a storm, be aware of downed power lines, hanging branches, and flooded areas.

16 Apply What would you do in each of these scenarios? Explain your reasoning.

Scenario	What would you do?
You are swimming at an outdoor pool when you hear thunder in the distance.	
You and your family are watching TV when you hear a tornado warning that says a tornado has been spotted in the area.	
You are listening to the radio when the announcer says that a hurricane is headed your way and may make landfall in 3 days.	

☑ Use Sun Sense!

How can people protect their skin from the sun?

![Active Reading]

17 Identify As you read, underline when the sun's ray's are strongest during the day.

Human skin contains melanin, which is the body's natural protection against ultraviolet (UV) radiation from the sun. The skin produces more melanin when it is exposed to the sun, but UV rays will still cause sunburn when you spend too much time outside. It is particularly important to protect your skin when the sun's rays are strongest, usually between 10 A.M and 4 P.M.

Know the Sun's Hazards

It's easy to notice the effects of a sunburn. Sunburn usually appears within a few hours after sun exposure. It causes red, painful skin that feels hot to the touch. Prolonged exposure to the sun will lead to sunburn in even the darkest-skinned people. Sunburn can lead to skin cancer and premature aging of the skin. The best way to prevent sunburn is to protect your skin from the sun, even on cloudy days. UV rays pass right through clouds and can give you a false feeling of protection from the sun.

Wear Sunscreen and Protective Clothing

Even if you tan easily, you should still use sunscreen. For most people, a sun protection factor (SPF) of 30 or more will prevent burning for about 1.5 h. Babies and people who have pale skin should use an SPF of 45 or more. In addition, you can protect your skin and eyes in different ways. Seek the shade, and wear hats, sunglasses, and perhaps even UV light-protective clothing.

Have fun in the sun! Just be sure to protect your skin from harmful rays.

How can people protect themselves from summer heat?

Heat exhaustion is a condition in which the body has been exposed to high temperatures for an extended period of time. Symptoms include cold, moist skin, normal or near-normal body temperature, headache, nausea, and extreme fatigue. *Heat stroke* is a condition in which the body loses its ability to cool itself by sweating because the victim has become dehydrated.

Limit Outdoor Activities

When outdoor temperatures are high, be cautious about exercising outdoors for long periods of time. Pay attention to how your body is feeling, and go inside or to a shady spot if you are starting to feel light-headed or too warm.

Drink Water

Heat exhaustion and heat stroke can best be prevented by drinking 6 to 8 oz of water at least 10 times a day when you are active in warm weather. If you are feeling overheated, dizzy, nauseous, or are sweating heavily, drink something cool (not cold). Drink about half a glass of cool water every 15 min until you feel like your normal self.

Drinking water is one of the best things you can do to keep yourself healthy in hot weather.

Visualize It!

18 Claims • Evidence • Reasoning Analyze the photo of the people at the beach. Are they protecting themselves from overexposure to the sun? State a claim and support it with evidence from the photo.

_____

_____

_____

_____

_____

_____

_____

_____

Know the Signs of Heat Stroke

Active Reading 19 Identify Underline signs of heat stroke in the paragraph below.

Heat stroke is life threatening, so it is important to know the signs and treatment for it. Symptoms of heat stroke include hot, dry skin; higher than normal body temperature; rapid pulse; rapid, shallow breathing; disorientation; and possible loss of consciousness.

What to Do In Case of Heat Stroke

☐ Seek emergency help immediately.

☐ If there are no emergency facilities nearby, move the person to a cool place.

☐ Cool the person's body by immersing it in a cool (not cold) bath or using wet towels.

☐ Do not give the person food or water if he or she is vomiting.

☐ Place ice packs under the person's armpits.

Visual Summary

To complete this summary, circle the correct word or phrase. Then use the key below to check your answers. You can use this page to review the main concepts of the lesson.

Severe Weather

Thunderstorms are intense weather systems that produce strong winds, heavy rain, lightning, and thunder.

20 One of the most dangerous parts of a thunderstorm is lightning / thunder.

A hurricane is a large, rotating tropical weather system with strong winds that can cause severe property damage.

21 An important step to plan for a hurricane is to buy raingear / stock a supply kit.

Tornadoes are rotating columns of air that touch the ground and can cause severe damage.

22 The damage from a tornado is mostly caused by associated thunderstorms / high-speed winds.

It is important to plan ahead and listen for weather updates in the event of severe weather.

23 One of the biggest dangers of storms that produce heavy rains or storm surges is flooding / low temperatures.

Prolonged exposure to the sun can cause sunburn, skin cancer, and heat-related health effects.

24 One of the best ways to avoid heat-related illnesses while in the sun is to stay active / drink water.

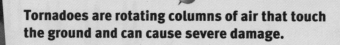

Answers: 20 lightning; 21 stock a supply kit; 22 high-speed winds; 23 flooding; 24 drink water

---

25 **Synthesize** What are three ways in which severe weather can be dangerous?

Lesson Review

Vocabulary

Draw a line that matches the term with the correct definition.

1 hurricane

2 tornado

3 severe weather

4 thunderstorm

5 storm surge

A a huge mass of ocean water that floods the shore

B a storm with lightning and thunder

C a violently rotating column of air stretching to the ground

D weather that can potentially destroy property or cause loss of life

E a tropical low-pressure system with winds of 119 km/h or more

Key Concepts

6 Thunder is caused by _____

7 An electrical discharge between parts of clouds or a cloud and the ground is called _____

8 The sun's ultraviolet rays can cause skin damage including sunburn and even skin _____

9 Explain How can a person prepare for hazardous weather well in advance?

_____
_____
_____

10 Describe What can people do to stay safe before and during a storm with high winds and heavy rains?

_____
_____
_____

Critical Thinking

Use the map below to answer the following question.

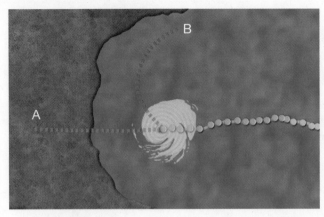

11 Interpret Would a hurricane be more likely to remain a hurricane if it reached point A or point B? Explain your reasoning.

_____
_____
_____

12 Explain Why do hurricanes form in tropical latitudes?

_____
_____
_____

13 Describe How can you use the terms air pressure, air masses, and fronts to describe the formation of a tornado?

_____
_____
_____

14 Explain Why is hail sometimes dangerous?

_____
_____
_____

15 Summarize What can you do to avoid overexposure to the sun's rays?

_____
_____
_____

My Notes

Lesson 6

Weather Maps and Weather Prediction

ESSENTIAL QUESTION

What tools do we use to predict weather?

By the end of this lesson, you should understand how meteorologists forecast the weather using weather maps and other data.

Weather forecasters use radar and satellite images to warn people of the approach of severe weather.

 S6E4.d Air pressure, weather fronts, air masses, and weather events

 S6E4.e Effects of moisture on weather patterns and events

 **Engage Your Brain**

1 Describe Fill in the blank with the word or phrase that you think correctly completes the following sentences.

The job of a _____ is to analyze scientific data to predict future weather conditions.

The location, movement, and intensity of precipitation can be found by using

_____

The elements of weather that are measured and analyzed to make accurate forecasts include

_____

2 Assess What industry is represented in the photo below? What other industries rely on accurate weather forecasts?

_____

_____

Active Reading

3 Synthesize You can often define an unknown word if you know the meaning of its word parts. Use the word parts and sentence below to make an educated guess about the meaning of the word *meteorology*.

Word part	Meaning
meteoron	phenomenon in the sky
-ology	the study of, science of

Example sentence
Studying <u>meteorology</u> helps you to understand weather events.

meteorology:

_____

_____

Vocabulary Terms
• weather forecasting
• meteorology
• station model

4 Identify This list contains the vocabulary terms you'll learn in this lesson. As you read, circle the definition of each term.

Cloudy with a chance of ...

What is weather forecasting?

Looking at the weather outdoors in the morning helps you to decide what clothes to wear that day. Different observations give clues to the current weather. The leaves in the trees may be moving if it is windy. If the sky is gray and the streets are shiny, it may be raining.

Checking the weather forecast also helps determine how the weather might change. **Weather forecasting** is the analysis of scientific data to predict future weather conditions.

What elements of weather are forecast?

Weather forecasters study the elements of weather to make detailed predictions. The study of weather and Earth's atmosphere is called **meteorology** [mee•tee•uh•RAHL•uh•jee]. Scientists who study meteorology are called *meteorologists*.

Eight elements of weather are observed around the clock. These elements are air temperature, humidity, wind direction, wind speed, clouds, precipitation, atmospheric pressure, and visibility. Using these eight elements to make accurate weather forecasts helps people stay safe and comfortable. To make the best predictions, meteorologists need accurate data.

5 Infer Forest firefighters need accurate and detailed weather forecasts. What weather elements would these firefighters be most interested in? Explain your reasoning.

_____
_____
_____
_____
_____
_____

Visualize It!

6 Apply Identify three elements of weather that appear in this beach scene.

A _____

B _____

C _____

The Hurricane Hunters

Flying in stormy weather can be an uncomfortable and frightening experience. Yet, some pilots are trained to fly into the most intense storms. The Hurricane Hunters of the National Oceanic and Atmospheric Administration (NOAA) fly right into the eye of tropical storms and hurricanes to collect valuable data. Weather forecasters use the data to predict a storm's path and intensity.

Hurricane Hunter Planes

The weather-sensing equipment aboard NOAA's WP-3D Orion is quite advanced. The planes are equipped with radar in the nose, in the tail, and on the underside of the fuselage. Radiometers on the wings measure wind speed once every second. These and other data are sent immediately to the airplane's computer system.

UNITED STATES DEPT. OF COMM

Wind gust probe

Weather radar for 360-degree view

Sensors are released from the plane's belly.

Falling Dropsonde

A lightweight instrument package called a *dropsonde* [DRAHP•sahnd] is launched from the aircraft. As the dropsonde descends through the storm, it collects data twice every second. Data about temperature, humidity, wind speed, and air pressure are sent back to the plane.

Extend

Inquiry

7 Explain How do airplanes help weather forecasters make predictions about the movement and intensity of storms?

8 Research Find out about another technology that is used to gather weather data by sea or by air.

9 Assess Explain how this technology is used in an oral report, poster presentation, or slide show.

What's Going on *up There?*

How are weather data collected?

To predict the weather, meteorologists must look at data that come from different sources. Meteorologists use many kinds of advanced technologies to gather this data. These technologies are found at ground stations and in balloons, aircraft, and satellites.

By Ground Stations

Land-based ground stations, also called *automated surface stations*, collect weather data from the lower atmosphere 24 hours a day. A variety of weather-sensing instruments are found at these ground stations. These instruments measure pressure, temperature, humidity, precipitation, wind speed, visibility, and cloud cover. Many ground stations are located near airports and transmit computer-generated voice observations to aircraft regularly.

By Radar

Weather radar is useful for finding the location, movement, and intensity of storms. Radar works by bouncing radio waves off precipitation. The stronger the signal that is returned to the radar, the heavier the precipitation is. Also, the longer it takes for the signal to return to the radar, the farther away the precipitation is.

Doppler radar, a type of weather radar, can detect precipitation and air motion within a storm. This technology is important for detecting and tracking severe storms and tornadoes.

Satellites, balloons, and aircraft can provide wide views of Earth's weather systems.

Visualize It!

10 Apply Which town is experiencing the most severe weather? What evidence supports your claim?

_____

_____

_____

11 Apply In which town is it raining lightly? Explain the evidence supporting your claim.

_____

_____

_____

Colors represent the intensity of precipitation.

Radar Map of a Strong Storm

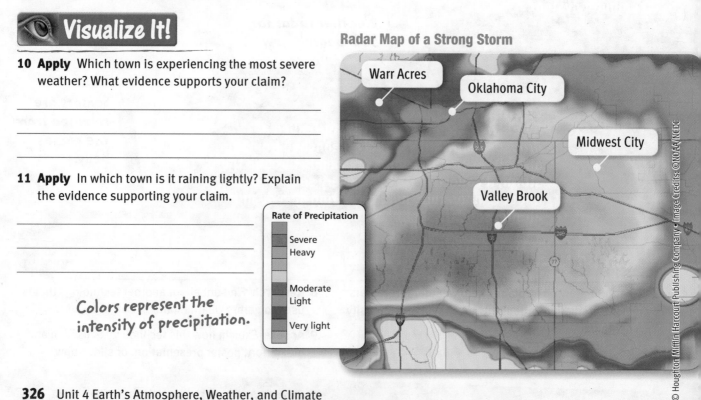

Warr Acres

Oklahoma City

Midwest City

Valley Brook

Rate of Precipitation

Severe
Heavy

Moderate
Light

Very light

By Balloons and Aircraft

Weather-sensing instruments carried by aircraft and balloons measure weather conditions in the middle to upper atmosphere. Aircraft can carry a variety of weather-sensing instruments and collect data in places far from ground stations, such as over oceans.

Weather balloons are released twice daily from stations around the world. These balloons collect weather information at different altitudes. Weather balloons carry a small instrument package called a radiosonde [RAY•dee•oh•sahnd]. Radiosondes measure atmospheric pressure, air temperature, and humidity up to about 32 km. They also measure wind speed and direction. Radiosondes send data by radio signal to ground stations.

Balloons such this one can gather weather data from high up in the atmosphere.

By Satellites

Orbiting weather satellites at high altitudes provide data on water vapor, cloud-top temperatures, and the movement of weather systems. Geostationary satellites and polar-orbiting satellites monitor Earth's weather. Geostationary weather satellites monitor Earth from a fixed position thousands of kilometers above Earth. Polar-orbiting satellites circle Earth and provide global information from hundreds of kilometers above Earth's surface. Cameras on satellites take images at regular intervals to track weather conditions on Earth. Digital images are sent back to ground stations. These images can be animated to show changes in weather over time.

Active Reading **12 Compare** What is the difference between geostationary and polar-orbiting satellites?

_____

_____

Think Outside the Book **Inquiry**

13 Describe Research ways that weather predictions were made before the use of aircraft, balloons, and satellites.

What kinds of symbols and maps are used to analyze the weather?

In the United States, meteorologists with the National Weather Service (NWS) collect and analyze weather data. The NWS prepares weather maps and station models to make weather data easy to use and understand.

Station Models

A **station model** is a set of meteorological symbols that represent the weather at a particular observing station. Station models are often shown on weather maps. Placing many station models on a map makes it possible to see large weather patterns, such as fronts.

A station model is a small circle that is surrounded by a set of symbols and numbers that represent current weather data at a specific location. Key weather elements shown on a station model are temperature, wind speed and direction, cloud cover, air pressure, and dew point. Note that the pointer, or wind barb, for wind direction points *into* the wind.

 Active Reading

14 Identify What are the key weather elements shown by a station model?

_____

_____

_____

_____

Visualize It!

15 Observe Where are the temperature and dew point recorded on a station model?

_____

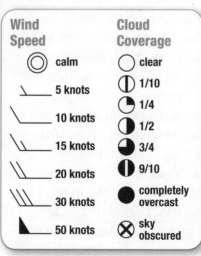

Wind Speed

- ◎ calm
- ╲ 5 knots
- ╲ 10 knots
- ╲ 15 knots
- ╲ 20 knots
- ╲ 30 knots
- ◣ 50 knots

Cloud Coverage

- ○ clear
- ◐ 1/10
- ◔ 1/4
- ◑ 1/2
- ◕ 3/4
- ◑ 9/10
- ● completely overcast
- ⊗ sky obscured

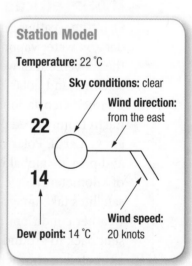

Station Model

Temperature: 22 °C

Sky conditions: clear

Wind direction: from the east

22

14

Dew point: 14 °C

Wind speed: 20 knots

16 Apply Draw a station model below to represent the following conditions: air temperature 8 °C; dew point 6 °C; sky 1/2 overcast; wind 15 knots from the south.

Surface Weather Maps

Meteorologists commonly use surface weather maps to show forecasts on television. A surface weather map displays air pressure and the locations of fronts. Precipitation may also be shown.

Air pressure is shown by using isobars. Isobars are lines that connect points of equal air pressure and are marked in units called *millibars*. Isobars form closed loops. The center of these loops is marked with either a capital H (high) or L (low). A capital H represents a center of high pressure, and a capital L represents a center of low pressure.

Fronts are also shown on surface weather maps. Blue lines with blue triangles are cold fronts. Red lines with red half circles are warm fronts. Stationary fronts alternate between blue and red.

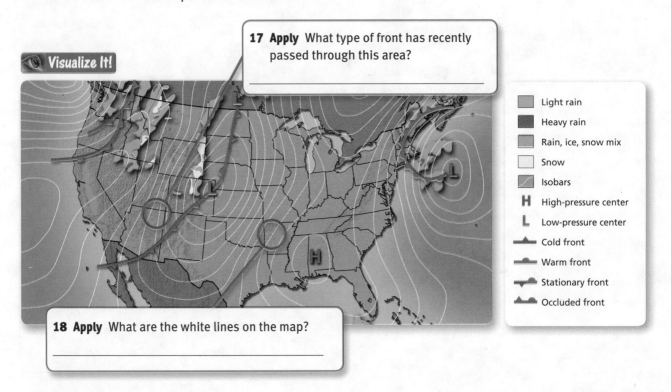

Visualize It!

17 Apply What type of front has recently passed through this area?

_____

18 Apply What are the white lines on the map?

_____

Light rain
Heavy rain
Rain, ice, snow mix
Snow
Isobars
H High-pressure center
L Low-pressure center
Cold front
Warm front
Stationary front
Occluded front

Upper-Air Charts

Another type of weather map used to analyze weather is the upper-air chart. Upper-air charts are based on data collected by instruments carried into the atmosphere by weather balloons.

Upper-air charts show wind and air pressure at middle and upper levels of Earth's atmosphere. Information from upper air charts indicates if and where weather systems will form, and if these systems will move, remain stationary, or fall apart. In addition, these charts are used to determine the position of jet streams. Airlines and airplane pilots use upper-air charts to determine flight paths and possible areas of turbulence.

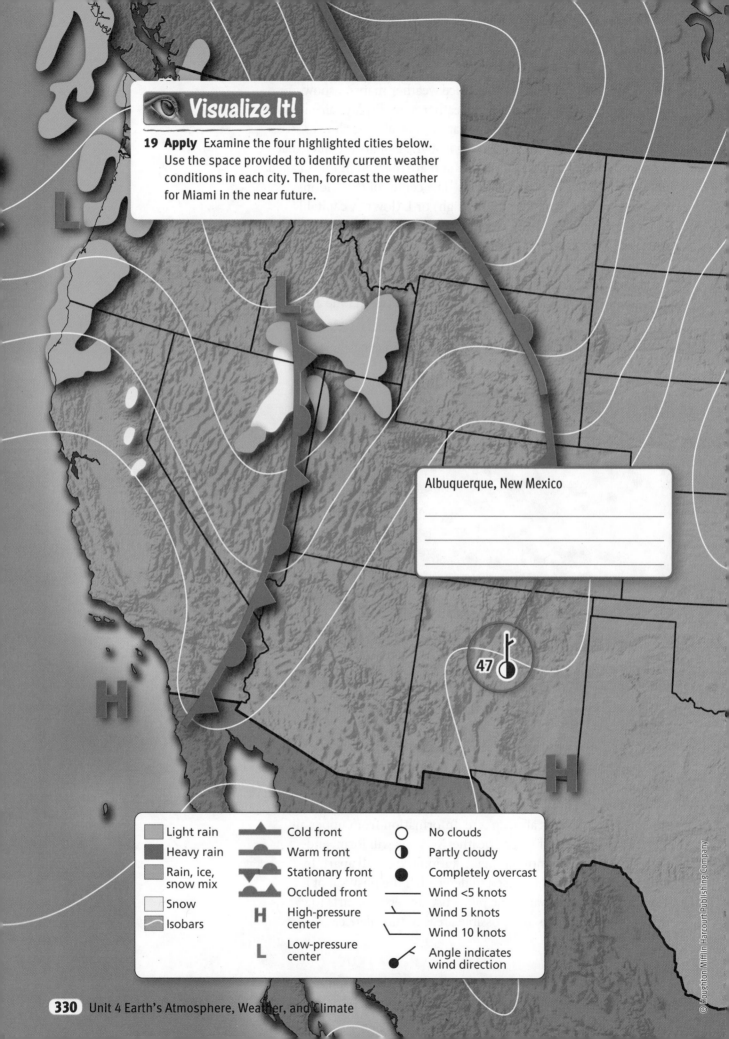

Visualize It!

19 Apply Examine the four highlighted cities below. Use the space provided to identify current weather conditions in each city. Then, forecast the weather for Miami in the near future.

Albuquerque, New Mexico

_____

_____

_____

Light rain	Cold front	○ No clouds	
Heavy rain	Warm front	◑ Partly cloudy	
Rain, ice, snow mix	Stationary front	● Completely overcast	
Snow	Occluded front	— Wind <5 knots	
Isobars	**H** High-pressure center	Wind 5 knots	
	L Low-pressure center	Wind 10 knots	
		Angle indicates wind direction	

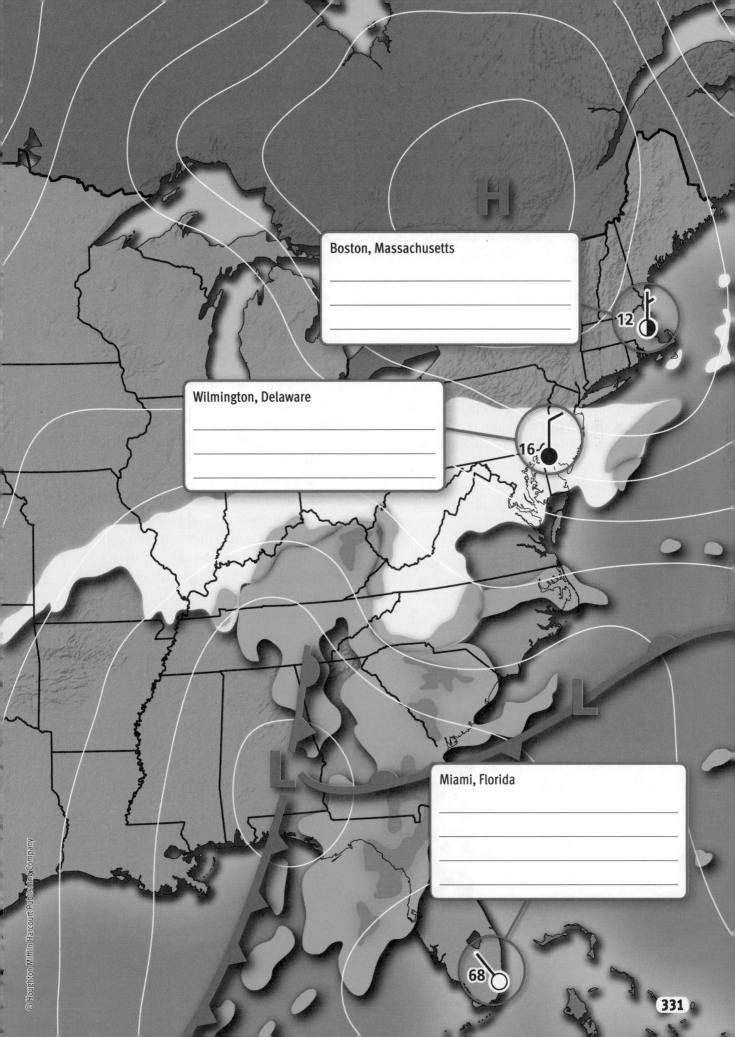

Boston, Massachusetts
_____
_____
_____

12

Wilmington, Delaware
_____
_____
_____

16

Miami, Florida
_____
_____
_____
_____

68

H

L

L

What are some types of weather forecasts?

As supercomputers have become faster in recent years, forecasts have also improved. Increasing amounts of weather data can be combined to create more accurate forecasts. The NWS, NOAA, and local meteorologists use computer models to develop short-range, medium-range, and long-range forecasts. These forecasts are made available to the public by radio, television, newspaper, and the Internet.

Short-Range and Medium-Range Weather Forecasts

Short-range weather forecasts make predictions about the weather 0 to 3 days into the future. Medium-range weather forecasts predict weather conditions between 3 days and 7 days into the future. Temperature, wind, cloud cover, and precipitation are predicted with different degrees of accuracy.

Weather forecasting is an imperfect science. Many variables affect weather, and all of these variables are changing constantly. In general, short-term forecasts are more accurate than forecasts made for longer periods of time. Yet, given the continuous changes that occur in the atmosphere, even short-range forecasts cannot always be accurate.

Long-Range Weather Forecasts

Most people want to know what the weather will be like in the near future. However, some people need to know what the weather will be like over a longer time period. The NWS issues long-range forecasts for periods of time that range from weeks to months into the future. Using sea surface temperatures and high-level winds, forecasters can make general predictions about the future. For example, they can predict if the weather will be warmer or colder or wetter or drier than average for a certain region. However, they cannot predict the temperature or if it will rain on a particular day.

20 Infer Why is it important for the farmer to know the long-range forecast?

_____

_____

_____

Some meteorologists prepare specialized forecasts for farmers.

Hazardous Weather Forecasts

An important job of meteorologists is to warn the public about severe weather. This information is shown as a weather "crawl" at the bottom of a television screen. The NWS issues three types of hazardous weather forecasts: weather advisories, weather watches, and weather warnings.

A weather advisory is issued when the expected weather conditions will not be a serious hazard but may cause inconvenience if caution is not used. When severe weather conditions are possible over a large geographic area, a weather watch is issued. People should prepare and have a plan of action in place in case a storm threatens. A weather warning is issued when weather conditions that pose a threat to life and property are happening or are about to happen. People who live in the path of the storm need to take immediate action.

Active Reading **21 Compare** What is the difference between a weather watch and a weather warning?

_____
_____
_____
_____
_____
_____
_____
_____

The National Weather Service issues weather advisories, weather watches, and weather warnings to inform the public about hazardous weather.

Visualize It!

22 Compose Write a caption for the photo based on a hazardous weather forecast.

_____

Visual Summary

To complete this summary, check the box that indicates true or false. Then use the key below to check your answers. You can use this page to review the main concepts of the lesson.

Weather Maps and Weather Prediction

Weather forecasting is the analysis of scientific data to predict likely future weather conditions.

T   F
23 ☐ ☐ In order to forecast the weather, meteorologists gather weather data for five important weather elements.

Different kinds of weather data can be shown together on station models and weather maps.

T   F
24 ☐ ☐ Two types of weather maps that meteorologists use to show the weather are surface weather maps and upper-air charts.

Weather data come from many sources on land and in the air.

T   F
25 ☐ ☐ Weather balloons and aircraft allow for surface weather observations.

Meteorologists use computer models to make short-range, medium-range, and long-range weather forecasts.

T   F
26 ☐ ☐ Three types of hazardous weather forecasts are weather advisories, weather watches, and weather warnings.

Answers: 23 F; 24 T; 25 F; 26 T

---

27 Synthesis Describe the technologies used to gather data, prepare a forecast, and broadcast a forecast for a town in the path of a hurricane.

Lesson Review

Vocabulary

Fill in the blank with the term that best completes the following sentences.

1 A _____ is a group of meteorological symbols that represents the weather at a particular observing station.

2 _____ is the analysis of scientific data to predict likely future weather conditions.

3 The scientific study of Earth's atmosphere and weather is called _____

Key Concepts

4 **List** What are the eight elements of weather that are observed for making weather forecasts?

_____

_____

_____

_____

5 **Identify** What kinds of data do surface weather maps provide?

_____

_____

_____

6 **Summarize** Describe each of the three types of hazardous weather forecasts.

_____

_____

_____

_____

_____

_____

_____

_____

_____

_____

_____

Critical Thinking

Use the diagram to answer the following questions.

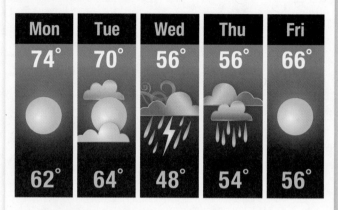

Mon	Tue	Wed	Thu	Fri
74°	70°	56°	56°	66°
62°	64°	48°	54°	56°

7 **Analyze** On what day will there likely be severe weather?

_____

8 **Claims · Evidence · Reasoning** Between which two days will a cold front arrive? Explain the evidence and reasoning to support your claim.

_____

_____

_____

9 **Diagram** Draw a station model based on the Thursday forecast, if winds are 15 knots from the northwest.

10 **Assess** Why do you think weather observations are made frequently at airports around the world?

_____

_____

_____

_____

_____

My Notes

J. Marshall Shepherd

METEOROLOGIST AND CLIMATOLOGIST

J. Marshall Shepherd

Dr. Marshall Shepherd, who works at the University of Georgia, has been interested in weather since he made his own weather-collecting instruments for a school science project. Although the instruments he uses today, like computers and satellites, are much larger and much more powerful than the ones he made in school, they give him some of the same information.

In his work, Dr. Shepherd tries to understand weather events, such as hurricanes and thunderstorms, and relate them to current weather and climate change. He once led a team that used space-based radar to measure rainfall over urban areas. The measurements confirmed that the areas downwind of major cities experience more rainfall in summer than other areas in the same region. He explained that the excess heat retained by buildings and roads changes the way the air circulates, and this causes rain clouds to form.

While the most familiar field of meteorology is weather forecasting, research meteorology is also used in air pollution control, weather control, agricultural planning, climate change studies, and even criminal and civil investigations.

Social Studies Connection

An almanac is a type of calendar that contains various types of information, including weather forecasts and astronomical data, for every day of the year. Many people used almanacs before meteorologists started to forecast the weather. Use an almanac from the library or the Internet to find out what the weather was on the day that you were born.

JOB BOARD

Atmospheric Scientist

What You'll Do: Collect and analyze data on Earth's air pressure, humidity, and winds to make short-range and long-range weather forecasts. Work around the clock during weather emergencies like hurricanes and tornadoes.

Where You Might Work: Weather data collecting stations, radio and television stations, or private consulting firms.

Education: A bachelor's degree in meteorology, or in a closely related field with courses in meteorology, is required. A master's degree is necessary for some jobs.

Snow Plow Operator

What You'll Do: In areas that receive snowfall, prepare the roads by spreading a mixture of sand and salt on the roads when snow is forecast. After a snowfall, drive snow plows to clear snow from roads and walkways.

Where You Might Work: For public organizations or private companies in cities and towns that receive snowfall.

Education: In most states, there is no special license needed, other than a driver's license.

Airplane Pilot

What You'll Do: Fly airplanes containing passengers or cargo, or for crop dusting, search and rescue, or fire-fighting. Before flights, check the plane's control equipment and weather conditions. Plan a safe route. Pilots communicate with air traffic control during flight to ensure a safe flight and fill out paperwork after the flight.

Where You Might Work: Flying planes for airlines, the military, radio and tv stations, freight companies, flight schools, farms, national parks, or other businesses that use airplanes.

Education: Most pilots will complete a four-year college degree before entering a pilot program. Before pilots become certified and take to the skies, they need a pilot license and many hours of flight time and training.

Climate

Earth has a wide variety of climates, including polar climates like the one shown here. What kind of climate do you live in?

ESSENTIAL QUESTION

How is climate affected by energy from the sun and variations on Earth's surface?

By the end of this lesson, you should be able to describe the main factors that affect climate and explain how scientists classify climates.

 S6E4.c Interaction between unequal heating and Earth's rotation

 S6E5.g Earth's changing surface and climate

✋ **Lesson Labs**

Quick Labs
• Determining Climate
• Factors That Affect Climate
• The Angles of the Sun's Rays
Field Lab
• How Land Features Affect Climate

🧠 Engage Your Brain

1 Predict Check T or F to show whether you think each statement is true or false.

T F

☐ ☐ Locations in Florida and Oregon receive the same amount of sunlight on any given day.

☐ ☐ Temperature is an important part of determining the climate of an area.

☐ ☐ The climate on even the tallest mountains near the equator is too warm for glaciers to form.

☐ ☐ Winds can move rain clouds from one location to another.

2 Infer Volcanic eruptions can send huge clouds of gas and dust into the air. These dust particles can block sunlight. How might the eruption of a large volcano affect weather for years to come?

_____

_____

_____

_____

_____

✏️ Active Reading

3 Synthesize You can often define an unknown word if you know the meaning of its word parts. Use the word parts and sentence below to make an educated guess about the meaning of the word *topography*.

Word part	Meaning
topos-	place
-graphy	writing

Example sentence
The <u>topography</u> of the area is varied, because there are hills, valleys, and flat plains all within a few square miles.

topography:

_____

_____

Vocabulary Terms

• **weather**   • **topography**
• **climate**   • **elevation**
• **latitude**   • **surface currents**

4 Apply As you learn the definition of each vocabulary term in this lesson, create your own definition or sketch to help you remember the meaning of the term.

How's the **Climate?**

What determines climate?

Weather conditions change from day to day. **Weather** is the condition of Earth's atmosphere at a particular time and place. **Climate**, on the other hand, describes the weather conditions in an area over a long period of time. For the most part, climate is determined by temperature and precipitation (prih•SIP•ih•tay•shuhn). But what factors affect the temperature and precipitation rates of an area? Those factors include latitude, wind patterns, elevation, locations of mountains and large bodies of water, and nearness to ocean currents.

Temperature

Temperature patterns are an important feature of climate. Although the average temperature of an area over a period of time is useful information, using only average temperatures to describe climate can be misleading. Areas that have similar average temperatures may have very different temperature ranges.

A temperature range includes all of the temperatures in an area, from the coldest temperature extreme to the warmest temperature extreme. Organisms that thrive in a region are those that can survive the temperature extremes in that region. Temperature ranges provide more information about an area and are unique to the area. Therefore, temperature ranges are a better indicator of climate than are temperature averages.

Desert region

Polar region

Precipitation

Precipitation, such as rain, snow, or hail, is also an important part of climate. As with temperature, the average yearly precipitation alone is not the best way to describe a climate. Two places that have the same average yearly precipitation may receive that precipitation in different patterns during the year. For example, one location may receive small amounts of precipitation throughout the year. This pattern would support plant life all year long. Another location may receive all of its precipitation in a few months of the year. These months may be the only time in which plants can grow. So, the pattern of precipitation in a region can determine the types of plants that grow there and the length of the growing season. Therefore, the pattern of precipitation is a better indicator of the local climate than the average precipitation alone.

Think Outside the Book Inquiry

8 **Apply** With a classmate, discuss what condition, other than precipitation, is likely related to better plant growth in the temperate area shown directly below than in the desert on the bottom right.

Visualize It!

7 **Interpret** Match the climates represented in the bar graph below to the photos by writing *A*, *B*, or *C* in the blank circles.

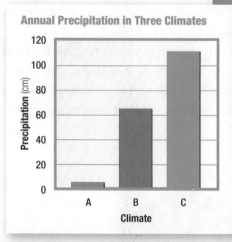

Annual Precipitation in Three Climates

(bar graph: y-axis "Precipitation (cm)" from 0 to 120; x-axis "Climate" with bars A, B, C. A ≈ 5, B ≈ 65, C ≈ 110)

There are enough resources in the area for plants to thickly cover the ground.

Some plants that grow in deserts have long roots to reach the water deep underground.

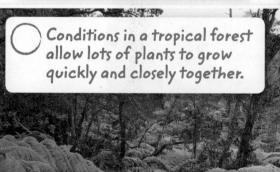

Conditions in a tropical forest allow lots of plants to grow quickly and closely together.

Here Comes the Sun!

How is the sun's energy related to Earth's climate?

The climate of an area is directly related to the amount of energy from the sun, or *solar energy*, that the area receives. This amount depends on the latitude (LAT•ih•tood) of the area. **Latitude** is the angular distance in degrees north and south from the equator. Different latitudes receive different amounts of solar energy. The available solar energy powers the water cycle and winds, which affect the temperature, precipitation, and other factors that determine the local climate.

Latitude Affects the Amount of Solar Energy an Area Receives and that Area's Climate

Latitude helps determine the temperature of an area, because latitude affects the amount of solar energy an area receives. The figure below shows how the amount of solar energy reaching Earth's surface varies with latitude. Notice that the sun's rays travel in lines parallel to one another. Near the equator, the sun's rays hit Earth directly, at almost a 90° angle. At this angle, the solar energy is concentrated in a small area of Earth's surface. As a result, that area has high temperatures. At the poles, the sun's rays hit Earth at a lesser angle than they do at the equator. At this angle, the same amount of solar energy is spread over a larger area. Because the energy is less concentrated, the poles have lower temperatures than areas near the equator do.

Active Reading

9 Identify As you read, underline how solar energy affects the climate of an area.

Visualize It!

10 Analyze What is the difference between the sun's rays that strike at the equator and the sun's rays that strike at the poles?

_____

_____

_____

_____

The amount of solar energy an area receives depends on latitude.

Drawing is not to scale.

The Sun Powers the Water Cycle

It is easy to see how the water cycle affects weather and climate. For example, when it rains or snows, you see precipitation. In the water cycle, energy from the sun warms the surface of the ocean or other body of water. Some of the liquid water evaporates, becoming invisible water vapor, a gas. When cooled, some of the vapor condenses, turning into droplets of liquid water and forming clouds. Some water droplets collide, becoming larger. Once large enough, they fall to Earth's surface as precipitation.

11 **Apply** Using the figure below, explain how the water cycle affects the climate of an area.

_____

_____

_____

_____

_____

Clouds

Condensation

Precipitation

Water vapor

Water storage in ice and snow

Surface runoff

Evaporation

The Sun Powers Wind

The sun warms Earth's surface unevenly, creating areas of different air pressure. As air moves from areas of higher pressure to areas of lower pressure, it is felt as wind, as shown below. Global and local wind patterns transfer energy around Earth's surface, affecting global and local temperatures. Winds also carry water vapor from place to place. If the air cools enough, the water vapor will condense and fall as precipitation. The speed, direction, temperature, and moisture content of winds affect the climate and weather of the areas they move through.

Warm, less dense air rises, creating areas of low pressure.

Cold, more dense air sinks, creating areas of high pressure.

Wind forms when air moves from a high-pressure area to a low-pressure area.

Warm surface

Cool surface

Latitude Isn't Everything

How do Earth's features affect climate?

Active Reading

12 Identify As you read, underline how topography affects the climate of a region.

On land, winds have to flow around or over features on Earth's surface, such as mountains. The surface features of an area combine to form its **topography** (tuh•PAHG•ruh•fee). Topography influences the wind patterns and the transfer of energy in an area. An important aspect of topography is elevation. **Elevation** refers to the height of an area above sea level. Temperature changes as elevation changes. Thus, topography and elevation affect the climate of a region.

Topography Can Affect Winds

Even the broad, generally flat topography of the Great Plains gives rise to unique weather patterns. On the plains, winds can flow steadily over large distances before they merge. This mixing of winds produces thunderstorms and even tornadoes.

Mountains can also affect the climate of an area, as shown below. When moist air hits a mountain, it is forced to rise up the side of the mountain. The rising air cools and often releases rain, which supports plants on the mountainside. The air that moves over the top of the mountain is dry. The air warms as it descends, creating a dry climate, which supports desert formation. Such areas are said to be in a *rain shadow,* because the air has already released all of its water by the time it reaches this side of the mountain.

Visualize It!

13 Apply Circle the rain gauge in each set that corresponds to how much rain each side of the mountain is likely to receive.

The Rain Shadow Effect

The Wet Side Air rises up the mountainside. The rising air cools and releases precipitation. The precipitation supports a lush plant community in this area.

The Dry Side Dry air flows over the mountain and warms as it sinks. The warm air absorbs moisture and creates conditions under which deserts may develop.

Elevation Influences Temperature

Elevation has a very strong effect on the temperature of an area. If you rode a cable car up a mountain, the temperature would decrease by about 6.5 °C (11.7 °F) for every kilometer you rose in elevation. Why does it get colder as you move higher up? Because the lower atmosphere is mainly warmed by Earth's surface that is directly below it. The warmed air lifts to higher elevations, where it expands and cools. Even close to the equator, temperatures at high elevations can be very cold. For example, Mount Kilimanjaro in Tanzania is close to the equator, but it is still cold enough at the peak to support a permanent glacier. The example below shows how one mountain can have several types of climates.

14 Apply Circle the thermometer that shows the most likely temperature for each photo at different elevations.

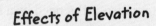

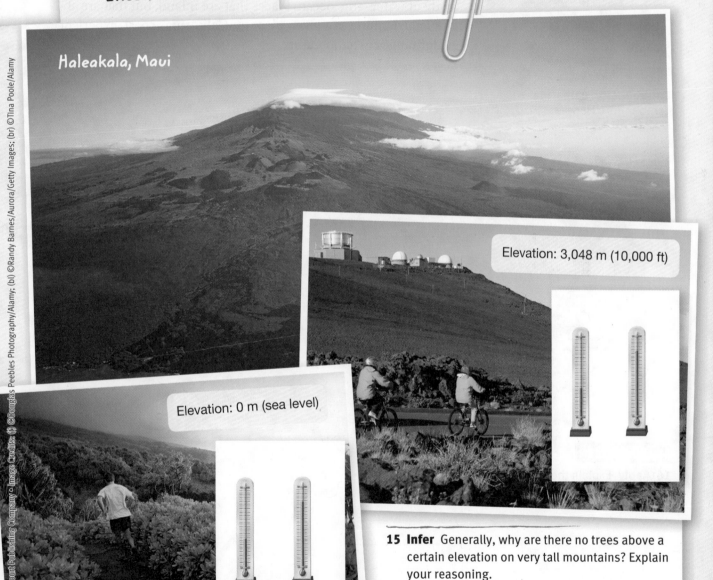

Haleakala, Maui

Elevation: 3,048 m (10,000 ft)

Elevation: 0 m (sea level)

15 Infer Generally, why are there no trees above a certain elevation on very tall mountains? Explain your reasoning.

_____

_____

Waterfront Property

How do large bodies of water affect climate?

Large bodies of water, such as the ocean, can influence an area's climate. Water absorbs and releases energy as heat more slowly than land does. So, water helps moderate the temperature of nearby land. Sudden or extreme temperature changes rarely take place on land near large bodies of water. The state of Michigan, which is nearly surrounded by the Great Lakes, has more moderate temperatures than places far from large bodies of water at the same latitude. California's coastal climate is also influenced by a large body of water—the ocean. Places that are inland, but that are at the same latitude as a given place on California's coast, experience wider ranges of temperature.

Crescent City, California
Temperature Range:
4 °C to 19 °C
Latitude 41.8°N

Council Bluffs, Iowa
Temperature Range:
-11 °C to 30.5 °C
Latitude 41.3°N

Cleveland, Ohio
Temperature Range:
-4 °C to 28 °C
Latitude 41.4°N

GULF STREAM

ANTILLES CURRENT

CARIBBEAN CURRENT

Visualize It!

16 Apply Explain the difference in temperature ranges between Crescent City, Council Bluffs, and Cleveland.

_____

_____

_____

_____

_____

_____

How do ocean currents affect climate?

An *ocean current* is the movement of water in a certain direction. There are many different currents in the oceans. Ocean currents move water and distribute energy and nutrients around the globe. The currents on the surface of the ocean are called **surface currents.** Surface currents are driven by winds and carry warm water away from the equator and carry cool water away from the poles.

Cold currents cool the air in coastal areas, while warm currents warm the air in coastal areas. Thus, currents moderate global temperatures. For example, the Gulf Stream is a surface current that moves warm water from the Gulf of Mexico northeastward, toward Great Britain and Europe. The British climate is mild because of the warm Gulf Stream waters. Polar bears do not wander the streets of Great Britain, as they might in Natashquan, Canada, which is at a similar latitude.

NORWAY CURRENT

Natashquan, Canada
Temperature Range:
-18 °C to 14 °C
Latitude: 50.2°N

London, England
Temperature Range:
2 °C to 22 °C
Latitude 51.5°N

LABRADOR CURRENT

NORTH ATLANTIC CURRENT

GULF STREAM

ATLANTIC OCEAN

CANARY CURRENT

17 Summarize How do currents distribute heat around the globe?

_____

_____

_____

👁 **Visualize It!**

18 Infer How do you think that the Canary current affects the temperature in the Canary Islands? Explain your reasoning.

_____

_____

_____

Canary Islands, Spain
Temperature Range:
12 °C to 26 °C
Latitude 28°N

NORTH EQUATORIAL CURRENT

Zoning Out

What are the three major climate zones?

Earth has three major types of climate zones: tropical, temperate, and polar. These zones are shown below. Each zone has a distinct temperature range that relates to its latitude. Each of these zones has several types of climates. These different climates result from differences in topography, winds, ocean currents, and geography.

Active Reading

19 Identify Underline the factor that determines the temperature ranges in each zone.

Temperate

Temperate climates have an average temperature below 18 °C (64 °F) in the coldest month and an average temperature above 10 °C (50 °F) in the warmest month. There are five temperate zone subclimates: marine west coast climates, steppe climates, humid continental climate, humid subtropical climate, and Mediterranean climate. The temperate zone is characterized by lower temperatures than the tropical zone. It is located between the tropical zone and the polar zone.

Visualize It!

20 Label What climate zone is this?

_____

Polar

The polar zone, at latitudes of 66.5° and higher, is the coldest climate zone. Temperatures rarely rise above 10 °C (50 °F) in the warmest month. The climates of the polar regions are referred to as the *polar climates*. There are three types of polar zone subclimates: subarctic climates, tundra climates, and polar ice cap climates.

ARCTIC OCEAN

NORTH AMERICA

ATLANTIC OCEAN

23.5°N

0°–Equator

PACIFIC OCEAN

SOUTH AMERICA

23.5°S

66.5°S

SOUTH

21 Summarize Fill in the table for either the factor that affects climate or the effect on climate the given factor has.

Factor	Effect on climate
Latitude	
	Cooler temperatures as you travel up a tall mountain
Winds	
	Moderates weather so that highs and lows are less extreme
Surface ocean currents	
	Impacts wind patterns and the transfer of energy in an area

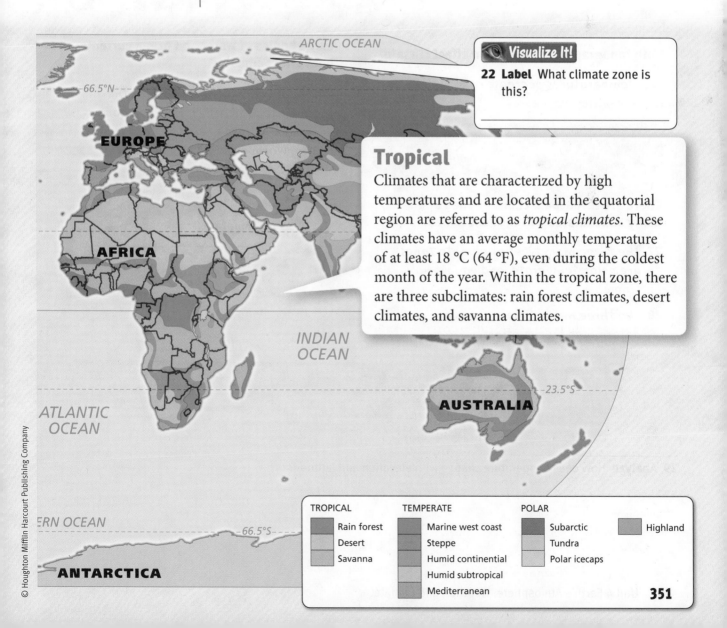

ARCTIC OCEAN

66.5°N

EUROPE

AFRICA

INDIAN OCEAN

ATLANTIC OCEAN

AUSTRALIA

23.5°S

ERN OCEAN

66.5°S

ANTARCTICA

Visualize It!

22 Label What climate zone is this?

Tropical

Climates that are characterized by high temperatures and are located in the equatorial region are referred to as *tropical climates*. These climates have an average monthly temperature of at least 18 °C (64 °F), even during the coldest month of the year. Within the tropical zone, there are three subclimates: rain forest climates, desert climates, and savanna climates.

TROPICAL	TEMPERATE	POLAR	
Rain forest	Marine west coast	Subarctic	Highland
Desert	Steppe	Tundra	
Savanna	Humid continential	Polar icecaps	
	Humid subtropical		
	Mediterranean		

Visual Summary

To complete this summary, circle the correct word or phrase. Then, use the key below to check your answers. You can use this page to review the main concepts of the lesson.

Climate

Temperature and precipitation are used to describe climate.

23 Climate is the characteristic weather conditions in a place over a short/long period.

Winds transfer energy and moisture to new places.

24 Winds can affect the amount of precipitation in/elevation of an area.

Both topography and elevation affect climate.

25 Temperatures decrease as elevation increases/decreases.

Large bodies of water and ocean currents both affect climate.

26 Large bodies of water affect the climate of nearby land when cool waters absorb energy as heat from the warm air/cold land.

There are three main climate zones and many subclimates within those zones.

27 The three main types of climate zones are polar, temperate, and equatorial/tropical.

28 The three main climate zones are determined by elevation/latitude.

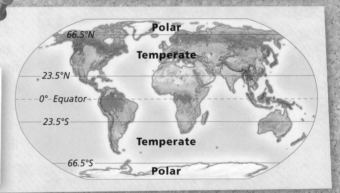

29 **Analyze** How does temperature change with elevation and latitude?

Lesson Review

Vocabulary

In your own words, define the following terms.

1 topography

_____

_____

2 climate

_____

_____

Key Concepts

Fill in the table below.

Factor	Effect on Climate
3 Identify Latitude	
4 Identify Elevation	
5 Identify Large bodies of water	
6 Identify Wind	

7 Explain What provides Great Britain with a moderate climate? How?

_____

_____

_____

8 Identify What are two characteristics used to describe the climate of an area?

_____

Critical Thinking

Use the image below to answer the following question.

9 Claims · Evidence · Reasoning Location A receives nearly 200 cm of rain each year, while Location B receives only 30 cm. Explain why Location A gets so much more rain. Use the words *rain shadow* and *precipitation* in your answer and explain your reasoning.

_____

_____

_____

_____

_____

_____

10 Analyze What climate zone are you in if the temperatures are always very warm? Where is this zone located on Earth?

_____

11 Analyze How does the sun's energy affect the climate of an area?

_____

_____

_____

_____

My Notes

Climate Change

ESSENTIAL QUESTION

What are the causes and effects of climate change?

By the end of this lesson, you should be able to describe climate change and the causes and effects of climate change.

Temperatures are rising in the Arctic. Warmer temperatures cause the ice sheets to freeze later and melt sooner. With less time on the ice to hunt for seals, polar bears are struggling to survive.

S6E5.g Earth's changing surface and climate

S6E6.c Rise in global temperatures

🧠 Engage Your Brain

1 Predict Check T or F to show whether you think each statement is true or false.

T   F

☐ ☐ There have been periods on Earth when the climate was colder than the climate is today.

☐ ☐ The ocean does not play a role in climate.

☐ ☐ Earth's climate is currently warming.

☐ ☐ Humans are contributing to changes in climate.

2 Describe Write your own caption relating this photo to climate change.

_____

_____

_____

✏️ Active Reading

3 Apply Many scientific terms, such as *greenhouse effect,* also have everyday meanings. Use context clues to write your own definition for the words *greenhouse* and *effect*.

Example sentence
The <u>greenhouse</u> is filled with tropical plants that are found in Central America.

greenhouse:

_____

_____

_____

Example sentence
What are some of the <u>effects</u> of staying up too late?

effect:

_____

_____

_____

Vocabulary Terms

• ice age
• greenhouse effect
• global warming

4 Identify As you read, create a reference card for each vocabulary term. On one side of the card, write the term and its meaning. On the other side, draw an image that illustrates or makes a connection to the term. These cards can be used as bookmarks in the text so that you can refer to them while studying.

The Temps are a–Changin'

What are some natural causes of climate change?

The weather conditions in an area over a long period of time are called *climate*. While climate tends to be stable, there is much evidence to show that Earth's climate has changed significantly during its history. For example, scientists have discovered fossils in many places where the climate is now too cold to support those life forms. A number of natural causes can lead to changes in an area's climate. Natural changes in climate can be long-term or short-term.

Movement of Tectonic Plates

Tectonic plate motion has contributed to long-term climate change over billions of years. And Earth's plates are still moving!

The present continents once fit together as a single landmass called *Pangaea* (pan•JEE•uh). Pangaea began to break up about 200 million years ago. By 20 million years ago, the continents had moved close to their current positions.

The eruption of Mt. Pinatubo sent ash and gases as high as 34 km into the atmosphere.

Visualize It!

5 Infer Today, Antarctica is the coldest desert on Earth. But fossils of trees and dinosaurs have been found on this harsh continent. Explain how life could thrive on ancient Antarctica.

_____

_____

_____

Antarctica was part of the supercontinent Pangaea about 250 million years ago. Antarctica is located at the South Pole today.

Some continents grew warmer as they moved closer to the equator. Other continents, such as Antarctica, moved to colder, higher latitudes.

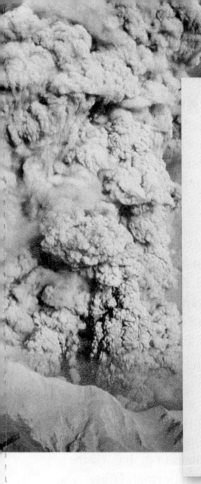

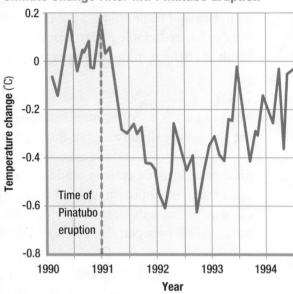

Climate Change After Mt. Pinatubo Eruption

This graph shows the *change* in average global temperature, not the actual temperature.

Source: Goddard Institute for Space Studies, NASA, 1997

Particles in the Atmosphere

Short-term changes in climate can be due to natural events that send *particulates* into the atmosphere. Particulates are tiny, solid particles that are suspended in air or water. They absorb some of the sun's energy and reflect some of the sun's energy back into space. This process temporarily lowers temperatures on Earth.

Where do particulates come from? Asteroid impacts throw large amounts of dust into the atmosphere. Dust from the asteroid that struck near Mexico around 65 million years ago would have blocked the sun's rays. This reduction in sunlight may have limited photosynthesis in plants. The loss of plant life may have caused the food chain to collapse and led to dinosaur extinction.

Volcanic eruptions also release enormous clouds of ash and gases into the atmosphere. Particulates from large eruptions can circle Earth. The average global surface temperature fell by about 0.5 °C for several years after the 1991 eruption of Mt. Pinatubo in the Philippines. Twenty million tons of sulfur dioxide and 5 km³ of ash were blasted into the atmosphere. The sulfur-rich gases combined with water to form an Earth-cooling haze.

Active Reading **7 Describe** Give one example of a long-term and one example of a short-term change in climate caused by natural factors.

_____

_____

Visualize It!

6 Analyze What happened to global temperatures after the eruption of Mt. Pinatubo? How long did this effect last?

_____

_____

_____

During El Niño years, heavy rains fall in the usually dry southwestern United States. This rain can cause floods that wash out roads.

What are some causes of repeating patterns of climate change?

From day to day, or even year to year, the weather can change quite a lot. Some of these changes are relatively unpredictable, but others are due to predictable patterns or cycles. These patterns are the result of changes in the way energy is distributed around Earth.

Sun Cycles

Most of Earth's energy comes from the sun. And the output from the sun is very slightly higher during times of higher sunspot activity. Sunspots are dark areas on the sun that appear and disappear. Sunspot activity tends to increase and decrease in a cycle that lasts approximately 11 years. The effect of this sunspot cycle on global temperatures is not dramatic. But studies show a possible link between the sunspot cycle and global rain patterns.

El Niño and La Niña

Changes in ocean temperature also affect climate. During El Niño years, ocean temperatures are higher than usual in the tropical Pacific Ocean. The warmer water causes changes in global weather patterns. Some areas are cooler and wetter than normal. Other areas are warmer and dryer than normal.

The opposite effect occurs during La Niña years. Ocean temperatures are cooler than normal in the equatorial eastern Pacific Ocean. El Niño and La Niña conditions usually alternate, and both can lead to conditions such as droughts and flooding.

Do the Math

8 Calculate About what percentage of years are El Niño years, with warmer than average ocean temperatures? About what percentage are La Niña years? About what percentage are neither El Niño or La Niña years?

_____

_____

Cycles of El Niño and La Niña

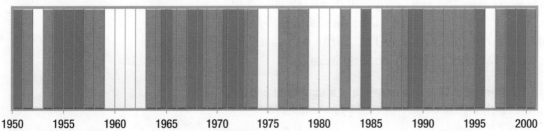

1950   1955   1960   1965   1970   1975   1980   1985   1990   1995   2000

■ La Niña years
■ El Niño years

Source: International Research Institute for Climate and Society, Columbia University, 2007

Visualize It!

During the last 2 million years, continental ice sheets have expanded far beyond the polar regions. There have been multiple advances of ice sheets (glacial periods) and retreats of ice sheets (interglacial periods). The timeline shows recent glacial and interglacial periods.

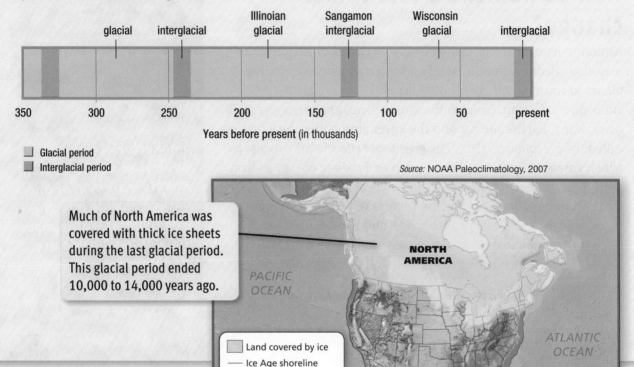

Cycles of the Recent Ice Age

glacial | interglacial | Illinoian glacial | Sangamon interglacial | Wisconsin glacial | interglacial

350   300   250   200   150   100   50   present

Years before present (in thousands)

☐ Glacial period
■ Interglacial period

Source: NOAA Paleoclimatology, 2007

Much of North America was covered with thick ice sheets during the last glacial period. This glacial period ended 10,000 to 14,000 years ago.

PACIFIC OCEAN

NORTH AMERICA

ATLANTIC OCEAN

☐ Land covered by ice
— Ice Age shoreline
— Present-day shoreline
— Present-day border

Ice Ages

The geological record shows that at different times Earth's climate has been both cooler *and* warmer than it is today. Earth's history contains multiple extremely cold periods when thick sheets of ice covered much of the continents. These periods are called *ice ages*. An **ice age** is a long period of cooling during which ice sheets spread beyond the polar regions. The exact cause of ice ages is not fully understood. Some hypotheses propose that ice ages include changes in Earth's orbit, shifts in the balance of incoming and outgoing solar radiation, and changes in heat exchange rates between the equator and the poles.

Geologic evidence indicates that ice ages occur over widely spaced intervals of time—approximately every 200 million years. Each ice age lasts for millions of years. The most recent ice age began about 2 million years ago, with its peak about 20,000 years ago. Large ice sheets still cover Greenland and Antarctica.

9 Infer Locate your home state on the map. Then, describe the climate your state likely experienced during the last glacial period.

_____

_____

_____

Active Reading **10 List** What are some possible causes of ice ages?

_____

Is It Getting HOTTER?

How do humans affect climate change?

Although natural events cause climate change, human activities may also affect Earth's climate. Human activities can cause the planet to warm when greenhouse gases are released into the atmosphere. Certain gases in the atmosphere, known as *greenhouse gases*, warm Earth's surface and the lower atmosphere by a process called the *greenhouse effect*. The **greenhouse effect** is the process by which gases in the atmosphere absorb and radiate energy as heat back to Earth. Greenhouse gases include carbon dioxide (CO_2), water vapor, methane, and nitrous oxide. Without greenhouse gases, energy would escape into space, and Earth would be colder. Two ways that humans release greenhouse gases into the atmosphere are by burning fossil fuels and by deforestation.

Active Reading **11 List** What are four greenhouse gases?

Smokestacks from a coal-burning power plant release water vapor and carbon dioxide into the atmosphere. Water vapor and carbon dioxide are greenhouse gases.

By Burning Fossil Fuels

There is now evidence to support the idea that humans are causing a rise in global CO_2 levels. Burning fossil fuels, such as gasoline and coal, adds greenhouse gases to the atmosphere. Since the 1950s, scientists have measured increasing levels of CO_2 and other greenhouse gases in the atmosphere. During this same period, the average global surface temperature has also been rising.

Correlation is when two sets of data show patterns that can be related. Both CO_2 level and average global surface temperature have been increasing over the same period of time, as shown by the graphs on the following page. So, there is a correlation between CO_2 levels in Earth's atmosphere and rising temperature. However, even though the two trends can be correlated, this does not show causation, or that one causes the other. In order to show causation, an explanation for how one change causes another has to be accepted. The explanation lies in the greenhouse effect. CO_2 is a greenhouse gas. An increase in greenhouse gases will warm Earth's surface and lower atmosphere. As greenhouse gas levels in the atmosphere have been rising, Earth's surface temperatures have been increasing, and so have temperatures in Earth's lower atmosphere. This shows that it is likely that rising CO_2 levels are causing global warming.

By Deforestation

Some processes, such as burning fossil fuels, add CO_2 and other carbon-based gases to the atmosphere. Processes that emit carbon into the atmosphere are called *carbon sources*. Processes such as the growth of plants and trees remove carbon from the atmosphere. Processes that remove carbon from the atmosphere are called *carbon sinks*. Deforestation is the mass removal of trees for farming, timber, and land development. The loss of trees represents the loss of an important carbon sink. Deforestation often includes the burning of trees, which is another source of carbon dioxide. So deforestation affects the amount of carbon in the atmosphere by converting a carbon sink into a carbon source.

Scientists think that the deforestation of rain forests plays a large role in greenhouse gas emissions. Tropical deforestation is thought to release 1.5 billion tons of carbon each year.

Active Reading **12 Describe** How does deforestation affect the amount of carbon dioxide that is in the atmosphere?

_____

_____

Deforestation is one of the leading sources of greenhouse gases.

Visualize It!

13 Apply Based on the trend shown in the graph, how do you expect CO_2 levels to change over the next 20 years? How does the evidence support your prediction?

_____

_____

14 Explain Describe the changes in average global temperature during the years represented by the CO_2 graph.

_____

_____

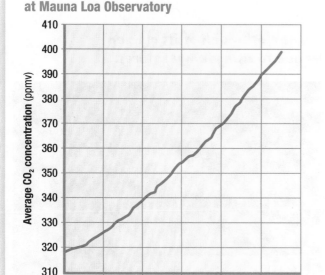

Atmospheric Carbon Dioxide (CO_2) at Mauna Loa Observatory

Average CO_2 concentration (ppmv) vs. Year (1960–2020)

Source: NOAA, 2015

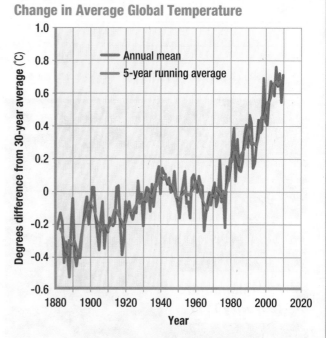

Change in Average Global Temperature

Degrees difference from 30-year average (°C) vs. Year (1880–2020)

— Annual mean
— 5-year running average

Source: Goddard Institute for Space Studies, NASA, 2010

What are some predicted effects of climate change?

Data show that the world's climate has been warming in recent years. **Global warming** is a gradual increase in average global temperature. Global warming will affect global weather patterns, global sea level, and life on Earth.

Effects on the Atmosphere

Studies show that the average global surface temperature has increased by about 0.3 °C to 0.8 °C over the last 100 years. Even small changes in temperature can greatly affect weather and precipitation. Scientists predict that warming will generate more severe weather. Predictions suggest that storms will be more powerful and occur more frequently. It has also been predicted that as much as half of Earth's surface may be affected by drought.

Effects on the Hydrosphere and Cryosphere

Much of the ice on Earth occurs in glaciers in mountains, arctic sea ice, and ice sheets that cover Greenland and Antarctica. As temperatures increase, some of this ice will melt. A 2010 report observed record-setting hot temperatures, which resulted in record ice melt of the Greenland ice sheet.

When ice on land melts, global sea level rises because water flows into the ocean. Global sea level rose by 10 to 20 cm during the 1900s. Scientists project that sea level may rise 60 cm by 2100. Higher sea level is expected to increase flooding in coastal areas, some of which are highly populated. New York City; Shanghai, China; and Mumbai, India; are some cities that could be affected.

15 Infer How do melting ice caps and glaciers affect sea level?

_____

_____

_____

Mt. Kilimanjaro has lost much of its glacier in recent years due to rising temperatures.

Mt. Kilimanjaro
February 1993

Mt. Kilimanjaro
February 2000

© Houghton Mifflin Harcourt Publishing Company • Image Credits: (bg) ©Paul Souders/Corbis; (bl) ©Jim Williams, NASA GSFC Scientific Visualization Studio, and the Landsat 7 Science Team; (br) ©Jim Williams, NASA GSFC Scientific Visualization Studio, and the Landsat 7 Science Team

A warmer climate may force some species northward, including sugar maples.

Legend:
- Current sugar maple distribution
- Possible future sugar maple distribution

Hudson Bay

CANADA

Winnipeg · Montreal · Halifax · Ottawa ⊛ · Toronto · Detroit · Chicago · Boston · New York · Washington, D.C. · St. Louis · Louisville

ATLANTIC OCEAN

Effects on the Biosphere

Active Reading **17 Summarize** Underline some of the effects of predicted climate change on the biosphere.

Scientists predict that global warming will change ecosystems. These changes may threaten the survival of many plant and animal species. Some species may move to cooler areas or even go extinct. Some butterflies, foxes, and alpine plants have already moved north to cooler climates. In Antarctica, emperor penguin populations could be reduced by as much as 95 percent by the end of this century if sea ice loss continues at its current rate. On the other hand, some species may benefit from expanded habitats in a warmer world.

Changes in temperature and precipitation will affect crops and livestock. If Earth warms more than a few degrees Celsius, many of the world's farms could suffer. Higher temperatures, reduced rainfall, and severe flooding can reduce crop production. Changes in weather will especially affect developing countries with large rural areas, such as countries in South Asia.

Warmer temperatures could increase the number of heat-related deaths and deaths from certain diseases, such as malaria. However, deaths associated with extreme cold could decrease.

16 Infer Some plant home ranges are shifting northward due to regional warming. What might happen to plant populations that are unable to spread northward? Explain your reasoning.

_____

_____

_____

_____

How are climate predictions made?

Instruments have been placed in the atmosphere, in the oceans, on land, and in space to collect climate data. NASA now has more than a dozen spacecraft in orbit that are providing continuous data on Earth's climate. These data are added to historical climate data that are made available to researchers at centers worldwide. The data are used to create climate models. *Climate models* use mathematical formulas to describe how different variables affect Earth's climate. Today, there are about a dozen climate models that can be used to simulate different parts of the Earth system and the interactions that take place between them.

When designing a model to predict future climate change, scientists first model Earth's current climate system. If the model does a good job describing current conditions, then the variables are changed to reflect future conditions. Scientists usually run the model multiple times using different variables.

Climate models are the means by which scientists predict the effects of an increase in greenhouse gases on future global climate. These models use the best data available about the ways in which Earth's systems interact. No climate model can perfectly reproduce the system that is being modeled. However, as our understanding of Earth's systems improves, models of climate change are becoming more accurate.

Visualize It!

18 Predict As Earth is warming, the oceans are rising. This is due to both melting ice and the expansion of water as it warms. Predict what the change in sea level will be by the year 2020 if the current trend continues. You may draw on the graph to extend the current trend.

_____

_____

Sea level has been rising steadily since the late 1800s. By the year 2000, global average sea level had risen 50 mm above mean sea level, represented by 0 on the graph.

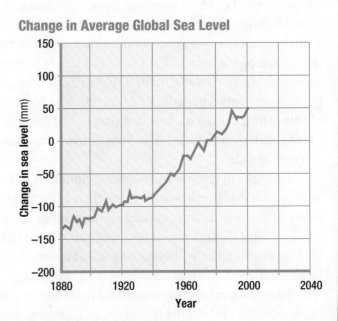

Change in Average Global Sea Level

Source: National Climatic Data Center, NOAA, 2007

Think Clean and Green

How can people reduce their impact on climate change?

People can take action to reduce climate change and its effects. Countries are working together to reduce their impact on Earth's climate. Communities and individuals are also doing their part to reduce greenhouse gas emissions.

Reduce Greenhouse Gas Emissions

The Kyoto Protocol, an international environmental agreement to reduce greenhouse gas emissions, was adopted in 1997. The Kyoto Protocol is the only existing international treaty in which nations have agreed to reduce CO_2 emissions. As of 2010, 191 countries had signed the protocol. At present, the Kyoto Protocol faces many complex challenges. One of the greatest challenges is that developing nations, which will be the largest future sources of CO_2 emissions, did not sign the protocol.

Individuals can reduce their impact on climate by conserving energy, increasing energy efficiency, and reducing the use of fossil fuels. Greenhouse gas emissions can be reduced by driving less and by switching to nonpolluting energy sources. Simple energy conservation solutions include turning off lights and replacing light bulbs. Recycling and reusing products also reduce energy use.

For most materials, recycling uses less energy than making products from scratch. That means less greenhouse gases are emitted.

Do the Math You Try It

19 Calculate How much energy is saved by using recycled aluminum to make new aluminum cans instead of making aluminum cans from raw materials?

_____

_____

20 Calculate By what percentage does recycling aluminum reduce energy use?

_____

_____

_____

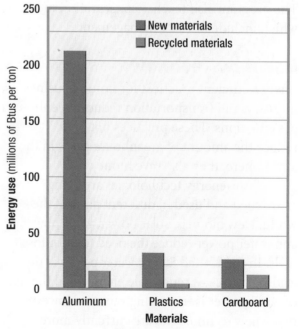

Energy Use for New vs. Recycled Materials

Source: US EPA Solid Waste Management and Greenhouse Gases, 2002

- Reduce use of automobiles.
- Use new, cleaner technologies.
- Plant a tree.

Reduce the Rate of Deforestation

Deforestation contributes up to 20 percent of greenhouse gases globally. Planting trees and supporting reforestation programs are ways that carbon sources can be balanced by carbon sinks. Another solution is to educate people about the importance of the carbon that is stored in forests for stabilizing climate. In 2008, the United Nations began a program called REDD, or *Reducing Emissions from Deforestation and Forest Degradation*. REDD offers incentives to developing countries to reduce deforestation. The program also teaches conservation methods, which include forestry management.

Use New Technologies

Energy-efficient practices for homes, businesses, industry, and transportation reduce greenhouse gas emissions. These practices not only reduce the amount of greenhouse gases in the atmosphere, they also save money.

Clean-energy technologies are being researched and used in different parts of the world. New biofuels, solar power, wind power, and water power reduce the need to burn fossil fuels. In the United States, water power is the leading source of renewable energy, and the use of wind power is increasing rapidly. However, many new technologies are currently more expensive than fossil fuels.

21 Summarize Use the table to summarize ways in which sources of greenhouse gases in the atmosphere can be reduced.

Sources of greenhouse gases	Ways to reduce greenhouse gases
cars	Walk or use bikes more often.

© Houghton Mifflin Harcourt Publishing Company • Image Credits: ©Richard Hutchings/Photo Researchers, Inc.

What are some economic and political issues related to climate change?

Active Reading **22 Identify** Underline some of the economic and political issues that are related to climate change.

Climate change affects the entire Earth, no matter where greenhouse gases are produced. This makes climate change a global issue. The scientific concerns that climate change poses are not the only issues that have to be taken into account. There are economic and political issues involving climate change that are equally important.

Climate change is an economic issue. The cost of climate change includes the costs of crop failure, storm damage, and human disease. However, developing countries may not be able to afford technologies needed to reduce human impact on climate.

Climate change is also a political issue. Political action can lead to regulations that reduce greenhouse gas emissions. However, these laws may be challenged by groups who disagree with the need for change or disagree about what needs to change. No matter what choices are made to handle the challenges of climate change, it will take groups of people working together to make a difference.

Think Outside the Book Inquiry

23 Apply Research a recent extreme weather event from anywhere in the world. How might this event be related to climate change? Present your findings to the class as a news report or poster.

Climate change may make unusual weather the new norm. Rome, Italy, was brought to a standstill by unusually cold and snowy weather in 2010.

In Australia, years of unusually dry and hot weather led to devastating forest fires in 2009. Australia also suffered damaging floods in 2010.

24 Predict What are the possible economic and social consequences of unusually warm weather in a cold climate or unusually cool weather in a warm climate? Explain your reasoning.

_____

_____

_____

Visual Summary

To complete this summary, fill in the blanks with the missing word or phrase. Then, use the key below to check your answers. You can use this page to review the main concepts of the lesson.

Natural factors have changed Earth's climate many times during Earth's history.

25 _____ have moved across Earth's surface over time and once formed a supercontinent called Pangaea.

Global warming affects many of Earth's systems.

27 If average global surface temperature continues to rise, then severe storms may become more _____

Climate Change

Greenhouse gases have a warming effect on the surface of Earth.

26 Scientists think that there is a connection between rising levels of _____ and rising _____

There are steps that people can take to reduce their impact on climate change.

28 People can reduce their impact on climate change by reducing greenhouse emissions and deforestation, and by _____

Sample answers: 25 Tectonic plates; 26 CO$_2$ (carbon dioxide); global temperatures; 27 frequent; 28 using new technologies

29 **Synthesize** How can burning fossil fuels cause global warming?

Lesson Review

Vocabulary

Fill in the blank with the term that best completes the following sentences.

1 _____ is a gradual increase in average global surface temperature.

2 A long period of climate cooling during which ice sheets spread beyond the polar regions is called a(n) _____

3 The warming of Earth's surface and lower atmosphere that occurs when greenhouse gases absorb and reradiate energy is called the _____

Key Concepts

4 Claims · Evidence · Reasoning Greenland is an island located northeast of Canada. It lies partly above the Arctic Circle. Fossils of tropical breadfruit trees more than 65 million years old have been found on Greenland. Construct an argument using this finding to support the claim that Earth's climate has undergone natural changes during its history.

_____

_____

_____

_____

5 Identify What are some predicted effects of climate change linked to global warming?

_____

_____

_____

6 Summarize List ways in which humans can reduce the rate of climate change.

_____

_____

_____

_____

_____

Critical Thinking

Use the graph to answer the following questions.

Change in Average Global Temperature

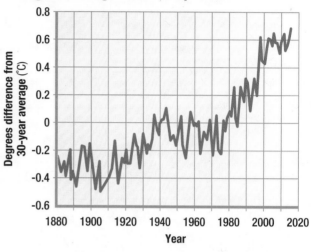

Source: Goddard Institute for Space Studies, NASA, 2015

7 Analyze Describe the trend shown in this graph. Why is it helpful to have many decades of data to make a graph such as this?

_____

_____

_____

8 Infer What might cause average global surface temperature to rise and fall from year to year?

_____

_____

_____

9 Infer Why might some countries be more reluctant than others to take steps to reduce levels of greenhouse gases?

_____

_____

_____

_____

_____

My Notes

Unit 4 ▸ Big Idea ◂ The sun's energy drives atmospheric changes that create Earth's weather and climate systems.

Lesson 1
ESSENTIAL QUESTION
What is the atmosphere?

Describe the composition and structure of the atmosphere and explain how the atmosphere protects life and insulates Earth.

Lesson 2
ESSENTIAL QUESTION
How does energy move through Earth's system?

Summarize the three mechanisms by which energy is transferred through Earth's system.

Lesson 3
ESSENTIAL QUESTION
What is wind?

Explain how energy provided by the sun causes atmospheric movement, called wind.

Lesson 4
ESSENTIAL QUESTION
How do the water cycle and other global patterns affect local weather?

Explain how global patterns in Earth's system influence weather.

Lesson 5
ESSENTIAL QUESTION
How can humans protect themselves from hazardous weather?

Describe the major types of hazardous weather and the ways human beings can protect themselves from hazardous weather and from sun exposure.

Lesson 6
ESSENTIAL QUESTION
What tools do we use to predict weather?

Understand how meteorologists forecast the weather using weather maps and other data.

Lesson 7
ESSENTIAL QUESTION
How is climate affected by energy from the sun and variations on Earth's surface?

Describe the main factors that affect climate and explain how scientists classify climates.

Lesson 8
ESSENTIAL QUESTION
What are the causes and effects of climate change?

Describe climate change and the causes and effects of climate change.

Think Outside the Book

2 Synthesize Choose one of these activities to help synthesize what you have learned in this unit.

☐ Using what you learned in lessons 1 and 2, explain how solar radiation contributes to the greenhouse effect. Include the terms *radiation* and *reradiation* in your explanation.

☐ Using what you learned in lessons 4 and 5, make a poster presentation about water vapor and the formation of severe weather.

Connect ESSENTIAL QUESTIONS
Lessons 4 and 6

1 Synthesize Explain how a change in air pressure can signal a change in weather.

_____

_____

Vocabulary

Check the box to show whether each statement is true or false.

T	F	
☐	☐	**1** <u>Radiation</u> is a measure of the average kinetic energy of the particles in an object.
☐	☐	**2** A <u>jet stream</u> is a violently rotating column of air stretching from a cloud to the ground.
☐	☐	**3** The <u>stratosphere</u> is the top layer of Earth's atmosphere.
☐	☐	**4** <u>Weather</u> is the characteristic pattern of temperature, humidity, and precipitation in an area over a long period of time.
☐	☐	**5** The curving of the path of a moving object as a result of Earth's rotation is called the <u>Coriolis effect</u>.

Key Concepts

Read each question below, and circle the best answer.

6 The picture below shows all three methods of energy transfer.

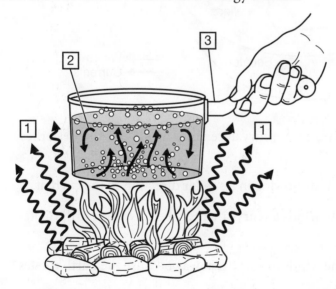

Which of these correctly identifies the three methods of energy transfer?

A 1: convection   2: radiation   3: conduction

B 1: radiation   2: conduction   3: convection

C 1: conduction   2: convection   3: radiation

D 1: radiation   2: convection   3: conduction

7 If it rained all day but stopped and then cooled down considerably at night, what weather phenomenon would you likely observe that night?

A fog

C sleet

B hail

D thunder

8 What results when air surrounding a bolt of lightning experiences a rapid increase in temperature and pressure?

A A tornado forms.

C Thunder is created.

B Hail forms.

D Rain condenses.

9 Refer to the diagram of winds and currents below to answer the question.

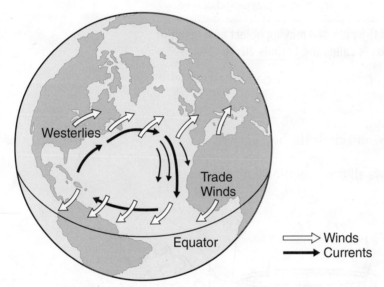

Which of the following best explains the curvature of the arrows for the westerlies and the trade winds?

A The ocean currents create winds flowing in a similar direction to the current.

B The Coriolis effect causes the winds to curve that way because the Earth rotates from left to right.

C The Coriolis effect causes the winds to curve that way because the Earth rotates from right to left.

D The sun is shining and warming the air from the right side of this diagram.

10 An astronomer studying planets outside our solar system has analyzed the atmospheres of four planets. Which of these planets' atmospheres would be most able to support a colony of humans?

A Planet A: 76% Nitrogen, 23% Oxygen, 1% Other

B Planet B: 82% Nitrogen, 11% Oxygen, 7% Other

C Planet C: 78% Nitrogen, 1% Oxygen, 21% Other

D Planet D: 27% Nitrogen, 3% Oxygen, 70% Other

11 Refer to the picture below to answer the question.

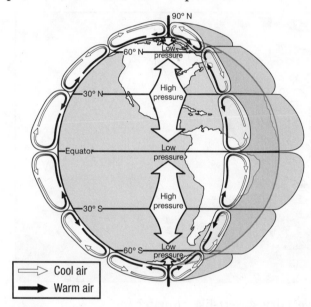

Which of the following is most responsible for the moving bands of air around Earth that are shown in the picture above?

A conduction   **C** Coriolis effect

B convection   **D** greenhouse effect

12 Which of the following describes the general pattern of winds near the equator?

A Winds are generally weak because the equator is a region where low and high air pressure atmospheric bands come together.

B Winds are generally strong because the equator is a region where low and high air pressure atmospheric bands come together.

C Winds are generally strong because the equator is a region of mostly high air pressure.

D Winds are generally weak because the equator is a region of mostly low air pressure.

13 What do the curved concentric lines on weather forecast maps show?

   A The lines show the direction in which the wind will blow.

   B The lines show where rain will fall.

   C The lines connect points of equal temperature.

   D The lines connect points of equal air pressure.

14 The picture below shows an exaggerated side view of an ocean on the left and a mountain range on the right. The arrows indicate the movement of air and moisture from the ocean.

Which region is most likely to have a dry, desert-like climate?

A region R   **C** region T

B region S   **D** region W

15 Which of these is not a currently predicted effect of global climate change?

   A rising sea levels

   B increased precipitation everywhere on the globe

   C reduction in Arctic sea ice

   D more severe storms

16 The graph below shows the amount of carbon dioxide measured in the atmosphere between about 1960 and 2005.

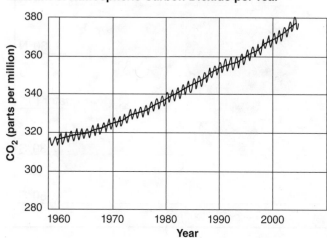

Amount of Atmospheric Carbon Dioxide per Year

What conclusion can you make from the data displayed in the graph?

A The amount of carbon dioxide in the atmosphere more than doubled between 1960 and 2000.

B An increasing number of cars on the road between 1960 and 2000 caused an increase in carbon dioxide levels in the atmosphere.

C There was an overall increase in the level of carbon dioxide in the atmosphere between 1960 and 2000.

D Average global temperatures increased between 1960 and 2000 as a result of the increase in carbon dioxide in the atmosphere.

Critical Thinking

Answer the following questions in the space provided.

17 Suppose you were a superhero who could fly up through the atmosphere while feeling the temperature and air pressure change around you. Describe your trip in a paragraph, naming the four main atmospheric layers and telling how the temperature and air pressure change as you pass through each.

_____

_____

_____

_____

18 Explain two ways in which forecasters collect weather data.

_____

_____

19 The map below shows the three different climate zones on Earth.

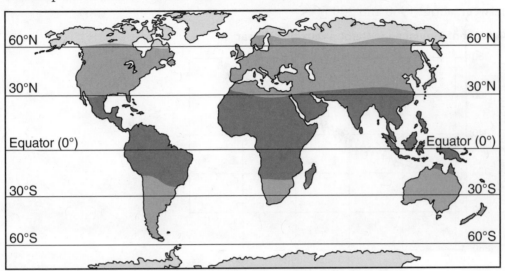

Label each climate zone on the map. Then describe the temperature and precipitation typical of each zone.

_____

_____

_____

Explain how latitude affects the climate of each zone.

_____

_____

_____

Connect **ESSENTIAL QUESTIONS**
Lessons 1, 2, 4, 5, and 7

Answer the following question in the space provided.

20 Even if you do not live on a coast, the movement of water in the oceans and water vapor in the atmosphere over the oceans does affect your weather. Using what you learned in lessons 1, 2, 4, 5, and 7, describe how the water cycle and the global movement of water through ocean currents and winds affect the climate of your local region.

_____

_____

_____

_____

_____

Earth's Surface

Big Idea

Continuous processes on Earth form and change minerals and rocks, as well as landforms and soil.

S6E5., S6E5.b, S6E5.c, S6E5.d, S6E5.e, S6E5.h

Most of Florida's underground caves are also under water, which makes them ideal for diving.

What do you think?

Florida has many caves underground. How might these caves have formed? What type of minerals or rocks make up these caves? As you explore the unit, gather evidence to help you state and support claims to answer these questions.

Sinkholes often form suddenly.

CITIZEN SCIENCE

Save a Beach

Like many other features on land, beaches can also change over time. But what could be powerful enough to wash away a beach? Waves and currents.

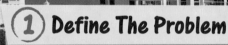

① Define The Problem

People love to visit the beach. Many businesses along the beach survive because of the tourists that visit the area. But in many places, the beach is being washed away by ocean waves and currents.

Beaches draw lots of tourists.

© Houghton Mifflin Harcourt Publishing Company • Image Credits: (bkgd) ©Franz Marc Frei/Photolibrary; (b) ©Katja Kreder/Photolibrary

(2) Think About It

When waves from the ocean hit the beach at an angle, the waves will often pull some of the sand back into the ocean with them. This sand may then be carried away by the current. In this way, a beach can be washed away. What could you do to prevent a sandy beach from washing away? Looking at the photo below, design a way to prevent the beach from washing away. Then, conduct an experiment to test your design.

Check off the questions below as you use them to design your experiment.

✔ How will you create waves?

✔ At what angle should the waves hit the beach?

✔ Will people still be able to use the beach if your method were used?

Waves carry the sand back into the ocean with them.

(3) Make A Plan

A Make a list of the materials you will need for your experiment in the space below.

_____

_____

_____

B Draw a sketch of the setup of your experiment in the space below.

C Conduct your experiment. Briefly state your findings.

_____

_____

_____

Take It Home

Find an area, such as the banks of a pond or a road, which may be eroding in your neighborhood. Study the area. Then, prepare a short presentation for your class on how to prevent erosion in this area. See *ScienceSaurus*® **for more information about erosion.**

Weathering

ESSENTIAL QUESTION

How does weathering change Earth's surface?

By the end of this lesson, you should be able to analyze the effects of physical and chemical weathering on Earth's surface, including examples of each kind of weathering.

S6E5.d Weathering, erosion, and deposition

S6E5.e Effect of natural processes and human activity on Earth's surface

Wave Rock in Australia may look like an ocean wave, but it was actually formed when the rock in the middle of this formation weathered faster than the rock at the top.

Lesson Labs

Quick Labs
- Mechanical Weathering
- Weathering Chalk
- How Can Materials on Earth's Surface Change?

Engage Your Brain

1 Predict Check T or F to show whether you think each statement is true or false.

T	F	
☑	☐	Rocks can change shape and composition over time.
☐	☑	Rocks cannot be weathered by wind and chemicals in the air.
☑	☐	A rusty car is an example of weathering.
☑	☐	Plants and animals can cause weathering of rocks.

2 Describe Your class has taken a field trip to a local stream. You notice that the rocks in the water are rounded and smooth. Write a brief description of how you think the rocks changed over time.

_____

_____

_____

_____

_____

_____

_____

_____

Active Reading

3 Synthesize You can often find clues to the meaning of a word by examining the use of that word in a sentence. Read the following sentences and write your own definition for the word *abrasion*.

Example sentences
Bobby fell on the sidewalk and scraped his knee. The <u>abrasion</u> on his knee was painful because of the loss of several layers of skin.

Vocabulary Terms
- weathering
- physical weathering
- abrasion
- chemical weathering
- oxidation
- acid precipitation

4 Apply As you learn the definition of each vocabulary term in this lesson, create your own definition or sketch to help you remember the meaning of the term.

abrasion:

_____

_____

_____

_____

BreakIt Down

What is weathering?

Did you know that sand on a beach may have once been a part of a large boulder? Over millions of years, a boulder can break down into many smaller pieces. The breakdown of rock material by physical and chemical processes is called **weathering**. Two kinds of weathering are *physical weathering* and *chemical weathering*.

What causes physical weathering?

Rocks can get smaller and smaller without a change in the composition of the rock. This is an example of a physical change. The process by which rock is broken down into smaller pieces by physical changes is **physical weathering**. Temperature changes, pressure changes, plant and animal actions, water, wind, and gravity are all agents of physical weathering.

As materials break apart, they can become even more exposed to physical changes. For instance, a large boulder can be broken apart by ice and water over time. Eventually, the boulder can split in two. Now there are two rocks exposed to the agents of physical weathering. In other words, the amount of surface area exposed to the agents of physical weathering increases. The large boulder can become thousands of tiny rocks over time as each new rock increases the amount of surface area able to be weathered.

Active Reading

5 Identify As you read, place the names of some common agents of physical weathering in the graphic organizer below.

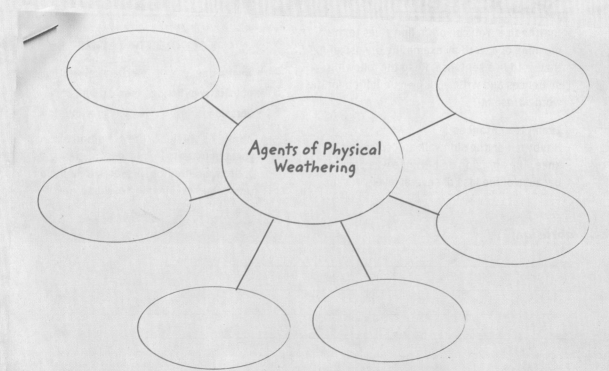

Agents of Physical Weathering

6 Describe Write a caption for each of the images to describe the process of ice wedging

Ice Wedging

Water

Ice

Water

Ice

Temperature Change

Changes in temperatures can cause a rock to break apart. A rise in temperature will cause a rock to expand. A decrease in temperature will cause a rock to contract. Repeated temperature changes can weaken the structure of a rock, causing the rock to crumble. Even changes in temperature between day and night can cause rocks to expand and contract. In desert regions differences in day and night temperatures can be significant. Rocks can weaken and crumble from the stress caused by these temperature changes.

Ice wedging, sometimes known as *frost wedging*, can also cause rocks to physically break apart, as shown in the image below. Ice wedging causes cracks in rocks to expand as water seeps in and freezes. When water collects in cracks in rock and the temperature drops, the water may freeze. Water expands as it freezes to become ice. As the ice expands, the crack will widen. As more water enters the crack, it can expand to an even larger size. Eventually, a small crack in a rock can cause even the largest of rocks to split apart.

7 Hypothesize Where on Earth would physical weathering from temperature changes be most common? Least common? Explain.

_____

_____

_____

These cracks, which were caused by ice wedging, will continue to expand over time.

Enchanted Rock was once buried deep inside Earth.

Pressure Change

Physical weathering can be caused by pressure changes. Rocks formed under pressure deep within Earth can become exposed at the surface. As overlying materials are removed above the rock, the pressure decreases. As a result, the rock expands, causing the outermost layers of rock to separate from the underlying layers, as shown to the left. *Exfoliation* (ex•foh•lee•AY•shun) is the process by which the outer layers of rock slowly peel away due to pressure changes. Enchanted Rock in Texas is a 130 m–high dome of granite that is slowly losing the outermost layers of rock due to exfoliation and other processes.

Animal Action

Animals can cause physical weathering. Many animals dig burrows into the ground, allowing more rock to be exposed. Common burrowing animals include ground squirrels, prairie dogs, ants, and earthworms. These animals move soils and allow new rocks, soils, and other materials to be exposed at the surface, as shown below. Materials can undergo weathering below the surface, but are more likely to be weathered once exposed at the surface.

👁 **Visualize It!**

8 Describe Write a caption for each animal describing how it might cause physical weathering.

Prairie dog

A _____

Earthworm

B _____

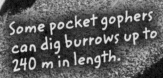
Some pocket gophers can dig burrows up to 240 m in length.

C _____

Wind, Water, and Gravity

Rock can be broken down by the action of other rocks over time. **Abrasion** (uh•BRAY•zhuhn) is the breaking down and wearing away of rock material by the mechanical action of other rock. Three agents of physical weathering that can cause abrasion are moving water, wind, and gravity. Also, rocks suspended in the ice of a glacier can cause abrasion of other rocks on Earth's surface.

In moving water, rock can become rounded and smooth. Abrasion occurs as rocks are tumbled in water, hitting other rocks. Wind abrasion occurs when wind lifts and carries small particles in the air. The small particles can blast away at surfaces and slowly wear them away. During a landslide, large rocks can fall from higher up a slope and break more rocks below, causing abrasion.

9 Identify As you read, underline the agents of weathering that cause abrasion.

Rocks are tumbled in water, causing abrasion.

Wind-blown sand can blast small particles away.

Rocks can be broken down in a landslide.

Plant Growth

You have probably noticed that just one crack in a sidewalk can be the opening for a tiny bit of grass to grow. Over time, a neglected sidewalk can become crumbly from a combination of several agents of physical weathering, including plant growth. Why?

Roots of plants do not start out large. Roots start as tiny strands of plant matter that can grow inside small cracks in rocks. As the plant gets bigger, so do the roots. The larger a root grows, the more pressure it puts on rock. More pressure causes the rock to expand, as seen to the right. Eventually, the rock can break apart.

Think Outside the Book Inquiry

10 Summarize Imagine you are a rock. Write a short biography of your life as a rock, describing the changes you have gone through over time.

This tree started as a tiny seedling and eventually grew to split the rock in half.

Reaction

What causes chemical weathering?

Chemical weathering changes both the composition and appearance of rocks. **Chemical weathering** is the breakdown of rocks by chemical reactions. Agents of chemical weathering include oxygen in the air and acids.

Reactions with Oxygen

Oxygen in the air or in water can cause chemical weathering. Oxygen reacts with the compounds that make up rock, causing chemical reactions. The process by which other chemicals combine with oxygen is called **oxidation** (ahk•sih•DAY•shuhn).

Rock surfaces sometimes change color. A color change can mean that a chemical reaction has taken place. Rocks containing iron can easily undergo chemical weathering. Iron in rocks and soils combines quickly with oxygen that is dissolved in water. The result is a rock that turns reddish orange. This is rust! The red color of much of the soil in the southeastern United States and of rock formations in the southwestern United States is due to the presence of rust, as seen in the image below.

Reactions with Acid Precipitation

Acids break down most minerals faster than water alone. Increased amounts of acid from various sources can cause chemical weathering of rock. Acids in the atmosphere are created when chemicals combine with water in the air. Rain is normally slightly acidic. When fossil fuels are burned, other chemicals combine with water in the atmosphere to produce even stronger acids. When these stronger acids fall to Earth, they are called **acid precipitation** (AS•id prih•sip•ih•TAY•shuhn). Acid precipitation is recognized as a problem all around the world and causes rocks to break down and change composition.

 **Active Reading 12 Describe** How does acid precipitation cause rocks to weather faster?

_____

_____

 **Active Reading**

11 Identify As you read, underline examples of chemical weathering.

These rocks in Arizona are red because of oxidation.

Reactions with Acids in Groundwater

Water in the ground, or groundwater, can cause chemical weathering. As groundwater moves through spaces or cracks in rock, acids in the water can cause rocks to dissolve. A small crack in a rock can result in the formation of extensive cave systems that are carved out over time under Earth's surface, as shown to the right. The dissolved rock material is carried in water until it is later deposited. Stalactites (stuh•LAHK•tyt) and stalagmites (stuh•LAHG•myt) are common features in cave systems as dissolved chemicals are deposited by dripping water underground.

Reactions with Acids in Living Things

Acids are produced naturally by certain living organisms. For instance, lichens (LY•kuhns) and mosses often grow on rocks and trees. As they grow on rocks, they produce weak acids that can weather the rock's surface. As the acids move through tiny spaces in the rocks, chemical reactions can occur. The acids will eventually break down the rocks. As the acids seep deeper into the rocks, cracks can form. The rock can eventually break apart when the cracks get too large.

Stalactites

Stalagmites

The dissolved rock from acidic groundwater can later be deposited in different locations.

This gear is rusted, which indicates that a chemical reaction has taken place.

Think Outside the Book

13 **Apply** Think of an item made by humans that could be broken down by the agents of physical and chemical weathering. Give evidence that supports your claim for how the item was weathered.

Visual Summary

To complete this summary, fill in the blanks with the correct word or phrase. Then use the answer key to check your answers. You can use this page to review the main concepts of the lesson.

Weathering

Physical weathering breaks rock into smaller pieces by physical means.

Chemical weathering breaks down rock by chemical reactions.

14 Label the images with the type of physical weathering shown.

A _____

B _____

C _____

15 Label the images with the type of chemical weathering shown.

A _____

B _____

16 Claims • Evidence • Reasoning State why some rocks are more easily weathered than other rocks. Summarize evidence to support your claim and explain your reasoning.

© Houghton Mifflin Harcourt Publishing Company • Image Credits: (tree) ©geogphotos/Alamy; (mountains) ©Nathan Chor/iStock/Getty Images Plus/Getty Images; (cave) ©Peter Mc Cabe/Alamy; (worm) ©Dr. Jeremy Burgess/Photo Researchers, Inc.; (rocks) ©Hans Strand/Stone/Getty Images

Lesson Review

Vocabulary

Fill in the blank with the term that best completes the following sentences.

1 Acid precipitation is an agent of _____ weathering.

2 The gradual wearing away or breaking down of rocks by abrasion is a type of _____ weathering.

3 The process of _____ causes rocks to change composition when reacting with oxygen.

4 The mechanical breakdown of rocks by the action of other rocks and sand particles is called _____

Key Concepts

5 Compare What are some similarities and differences between physical and chemical weathering?

_____

_____

_____

_____

6 List Provide examples of physical weathering and chemical weathering in the chart below.

Physical Weathering	Chemical Weathering

7 Compare What are some similarities between ice wedging and plant root growth in a rock?

_____

_____

_____

Critical Thinking

Use the graph to answer the following questions.

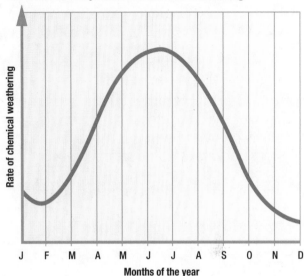

The Effect of Temperature on Rates of Weathering

8 Analyze Which two months had the highest rates of chemical weathering?

_____

_____

9 Apply Why do you think those two months had the highest rates of chemical weathering?

_____

_____

_____

_____

_____

_____

10 Infer Coastal regions are often affected by abrasion. What processes would cause increased abrasion along a coastal region? Explain.

_____

_____

_____

_____

My Notes

Erosion and Deposition by Water

ESSENTIAL QUESTION

How does water change Earth's surface?

By the end of this lesson, you should be able to relate the processes of erosion and deposition by water to the landforms that result from these processes.

Rivers aren't only found on Earth's surface. They also flow underground! Underground rivers can carve out caves full of channels, waterfalls, and even lakes.

 S6E5.d Weathering, erosion, and deposition

S6E5.e Effect of natural processes and human activity on Earth's surface

Lesson Labs

Quick Labs
• Wave Action on the Shoreline
• Moving Sediment
• Modeling Stalactites and Stalagmites

Exploration Lab
• Exploring Stream Erosion and Deposition

 **Engage Your Brain**

1 Predict Check T or F to show whether you think each statement is true or false.

T   F

☐   ☐   Water is able to move rocks as big as boulders.

☐   ☐   Rivers can help to break down mountains.

☐   ☐   Water cannot change rock underneath Earth's surface.

☐   ☐   Waves and currents help to form beaches.

2 Explain Write a caption that explains how you think this canyon formed.

_____

_____

_____

Active Reading

3 Synthesize Several of the vocabulary terms in this lesson are compound words, or two separate words combined to form a new word that has a new meaning. Use the meanings of the two separate words to make an educated guess about the meaning of the compound terms shown below.

flood + plain = floodplain

_____

_____

ground + water = groundwater

_____

_____

shore + line = shoreline

_____

_____

sand + bar = sandbar

_____

_____

Vocabulary Terms

• erosion
• deposition
• floodplain
• marsh
• delta
• alluvial fan
• groundwater
• shoreline
• beach
• sandbar
• barrier island

4 Apply As you learn the definition of each vocabulary term in this lesson, create your own definition or sketch to help you remember the meaning of the term.

Go with the Flow

How does flowing water change Earth's surface?

If your job was to carry millions of tons of rock and soil across the United States, how would you do it? You might use a bulldozer or a dump truck, but your job would still take a long time. Did you know that rivers and other bodies of flowing water do this job every day? Flowing water, as well as wind and ice, can move large amounts of material, such as soil and rock. Gravity also has a role to play. Gravity causes water to flow and rocks to fall downhill.

By Erosion

Acting as liquid conveyor belts, rivers and streams erode soil, rock, and sediment. *Sediment* is tiny grains of broken-down rock. **Erosion** is the process by which sediment and other materials are moved from one place to another. Eroded materials in streams may come from the stream's own bed and banks or from materials carried to the stream by rainwater runoff. Over time, erosion causes streams to widen and deepen.

By Deposition

After streams erode rock and soil, they eventually drop, or deposit, their load downstream. **Deposition** is the process by which eroded material is dropped. Deposition occurs when gravity's downward pull on sediment is greater than the push of flowing water or wind. This usually happens when the water or wind slows down. A stream deposits materials along its bed, banks, and mouth, which can form different landforms.

---

5 Compare Fill in the Venn diagram to compare and contrast erosion and deposition.

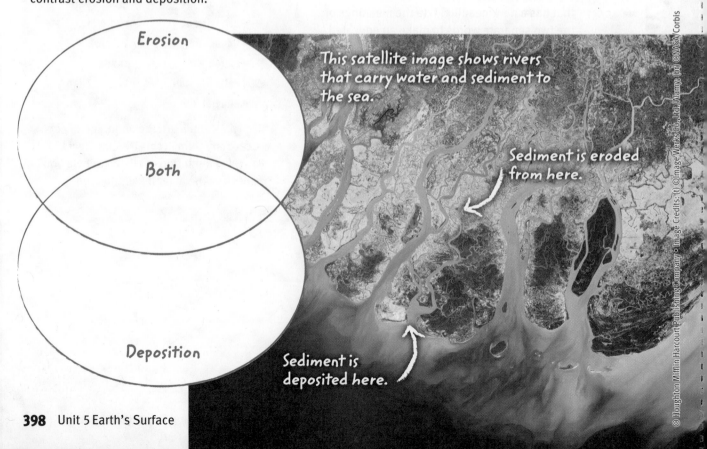

Erosion

Both

Deposition

This satellite image shows rivers that carry water and sediment to the sea.

Sediment is eroded from here.

Sediment is deposited here.

What factors relate to a stream's ability to erode material?

Some streams are able to erode large rocks, while others can erode only very fine sediment. Some streams move many tons of material each day, while others move very little sediment. So what determines how much material a stream can erode? A stream's gradient, discharge, and load are the three main factors that control what sediment a stream can carry.

Gradient

Gradient is the measure of the change in elevation over a certain distance. You can think of gradient as the steepness of a slope. The water in a stream that has a high gradient—or steep slope—moves very rapidly because of the downward pull of gravity. This rapid water flow gives the stream a lot of energy to erode rock and soil. A river or stream that has a low gradient has less energy for erosion, or erosive energy.

Load

Materials carried by a stream are called the stream's *load*. The size of the particles in a stream's load is affected by the stream's speed. Fast-moving streams can carry large particles. The large particles bounce and scrape along the bottom and sides of the streambed. Thus, a stream that has a load of large particles has a high erosion rate. Slow-moving streams carry smaller particles and have less erosive energy.

Discharge

The amount of water that a stream carries in a given amount of time is called *discharge*. The discharge of a stream increases when a major storm occurs or when warm weather rapidly melts snow. As the stream's discharge increases, its erosive energy, speed, and load increase.

Active Reading

6 Explain Why do some streams and rivers cause more erosion and deposition than others?

_____

_____

_____

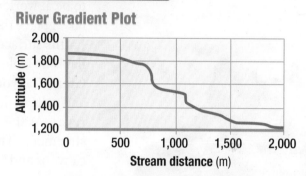

Do the Math

River Gradient Plot

A river gradient plot shows how quickly the elevation of a river falls along its course. The slope of the line is the river's gradient. The line has a steep slope at points along the river where the gradient is steep. The line has a nearly level slope where the river gradient is shallow.

Identify

7 Along this river, at which two approximate altitude ranges are the gradients the steepest?

_____

_____

8 At which altitude ranges would you expect the highest streambed erosion rate?

_____

_____

9 At which altitude ranges would you expect the slowest streambed erosion rate?

_____

_____

Run of a River

What landforms can streams create?

A stream forms as water erodes soil and rock to make a channel. A *channel* is the path that a stream follows. As the stream continues to erode rock and soil, the channel gets wider and deeper. Over time, canyons and valleys can form.

Canyons and Valleys by Erosion

The processes that changed Earth's surface in the past continue to be at work today. For example, erosion and deposition have taken place throughout Earth's history. Six million years ago, Earth's surface in the area now known as the Grand Canyon was flat. The Colorado River cut down into the rock and formed the Grand Canyon over millions of years. Landforms, such as canyons and valleys, are created by the flow of water through streams and rivers. As the water moves, it erodes rock and sediment from the streambed. The flowing water can cut through rock, forming steep canyons and valleys.

Think Outside the Book

10 Apply Discuss with your classmates some landforms near your town that were likely made by flowing water.

Visualize It!

11 Apply On the lines below, label where erosion and deposition are occurring.

Canyon

A _____

B _____

Meander

Floodplains and Marshes by Deposition

When a stream floods, a layer of sediment is deposited over the flooded land. Many layers of deposited sediment can form a flat area called a **floodplain**. Sediment often contains nutrients needed for plant growth. Because of this, floodplains are often very fertile. When sediment builds up in a area of sheltered water, small areas of land form. Plants grow on these small areas. The roots and stems of the plants help to anchor and trap more sediment. Eventually, plants dominate the area. This sheltered, wet, plant-filled area is called a **marsh**.

As a stream flows through an area, its channel may run straight in some parts and curve in other parts. Curves and bends that form a twisting, looping pattern in a stream channel are called *meanders*. The moving water erodes the outside banks and deposits sediment along the inside banks. Over many years, meanders shift position. During a flood, a stream may cut a new channel that bypasses a meander. The cut-off meander forms a crescent-shaped lake, which is called an *oxbow lake*.

Deltas and Alluvial Fans by Deposition

When a stream empties into a body of water, such as a lake or an ocean, its current slows and it deposits its load. Streams often deposit their loads in a fan-shaped pattern called a **delta**. Over time, sediment builds up in a delta, forming new land. Sometimes the new land can extend far into the lake or ocean. A similar process occurs when a stream flows onto a flat land surface from mountains or hills. On land, the sediment forms an alluvial fan. An **alluvial fan** is a fan-shaped deposit that forms on dry land.

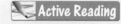

Active Reading

12 Identify As you read, underline the definitions of *marsh*, *delta* and *alluvial fan*.

13 Compare What questions would you ask about an area of deposition to determine whether it was a marsh, a delta, or an alluvial fan?

_____

_____

_____

_____

_____

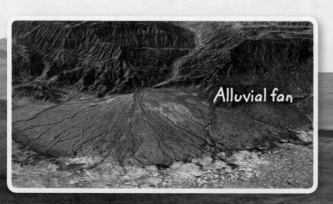

Alluvial fan

Floodplain

C _____

Oxbow lake

Delta

More Waterworks

What landforms are made by groundwater erosion?

As you have learned, rivers cause erosion when water picks up and moves rock and soil. The movement of water underground can also cause erosion. **Groundwater** is the water located within the rocks below Earth's surface. Slightly acidic groundwater can cause erosion by dissolving rock. When underground erosion happens, caves can form. Most of the world's caves formed over thousands of years as groundwater dissolved limestone underground. Although caves are formed by erosion, they also show signs of deposition. Water that drips from cracks in a cave's ceiling leaves behind icicle-shaped deposits known as *stalactites* and *stalagmites*. When the groundwater level is lower than the level of a cave, the cave roof may no longer be supported by the water underneath. If the roof of a cave collapses, it may leave a circular depression called a *sinkhole*.

Active Reading **14 Explain** How does groundwater cause caves to form?

_____

_____

Stalactites are caused by deposition.

Groundwater can erode rock, causing caves to form.

Visualize It!

15 Claims • Evidence • Reasoning Make a claim about what may have happened underground to cause this sinkhole to form. State the evidence for your claim and explain your reasoning.

_____

_____

_____

_____

What forces shape a shoreline?

A **shoreline** is the place where land and a body of water meet. Ocean water along a shoreline moves differently than river water moves. Ocean waves crashing against the shoreline have a great deal of energy. Strong waves may erode material. Gentle waves may deposit materials. In addition to waves, ocean water has *currents,* or streamlike movements of water. Like waves, currents can also erode and deposit materials.

Waves

Waves play a major part in building up and breaking down a shoreline. Waves slow down as they approach a shoreline. The first parts of the shoreline that waves meet are the *headlands,* or pieces of land that project into the water. The slowing waves bend toward the headlands, which concentrates the waves' energy. A huge amount of energy is released when waves crash into headlands, causing the land to erode. The waves striking the areas between headlands have less energy. Therefore, these waves are more likely to deposit materials rather than erode materials.

Currents

When water travels almost parallel to the shoreline very near shore, the current is called a *longshore current*. Longshore currents are caused by waves hitting the shore at an angle. Waves that break at angles move sediment along the coast. The waves push the sand in the same angled direction in which they break. But the return water flow moves sand directly away from the beach. The end result is a zigzag movement of the sand. As sand moves down a beach, the upcurrent end of the beach is eroded away while the downcurrent end of the beach is built up.

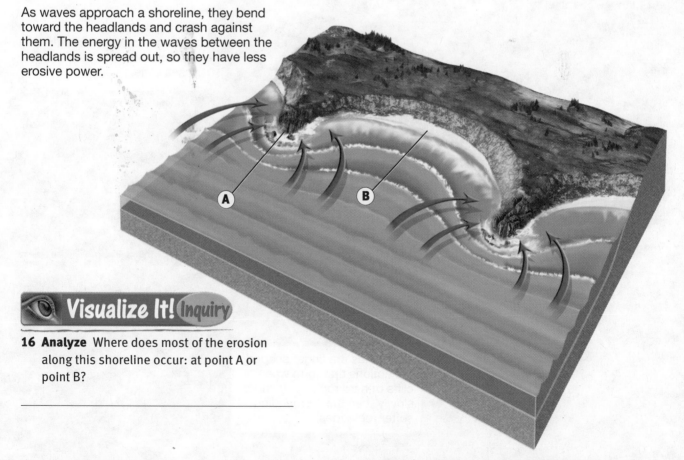

As waves approach a shoreline, they bend toward the headlands and crash against them. The energy in the waves between the headlands is spread out, so they have less erosive power.

Visualize It! Inquiry

16 Analyze Where does most of the erosion along this shoreline occur: at point A or point B?

_____

Surf Versus Turf

What coastal landforms are made by erosion?

Active Reading

17 Identify As you read, underline the sentence that summarizes the factors that determine how fast a shoreline erodes.

Wave erosion produces a variety of features along a shoreline. The rate at which rock erodes depends on the hardness of the rock and the energy of the waves. Gentle waves cause very little erosion. Strong waves from heavy storms can increase the rate of erosion. During storms, huge blocks of rock can be broken off and eroded away. In fact, a severe storm can noticeably change the appearance of a shoreline in a single day.

In addition to wave energy, the hardness of the rock making up the coastline affects how quickly the coastline is eroded. Very hard rock can slow the rate of erosion because it takes a great deal of wave energy to break up hard rock. Soft rock erodes more rapidly. Many shoreline features are caused by differences in rock hardness. Over time, a large area of softer rock can be eroded by strong waves. As a result, part of the shoreline is carved out and forms a bay.

Sea caves form when waves cut large holes into fractured or weak rock along the base of sea cliffs.

Wave-cut platforms form when a sea cliff is worn back from shore, producing a nearly level platform beneath the water at the base of the cliff.

Headlands are finger-shaped projections that form when cliffs of hard rock erode more slowly than the surrounding softer rock does.

Sea Cliffs and Wave-cut Platforms

A *sea cliff* forms when waves erode and undercut rock to make steep slopes. Waves strike the cliff's base, wearing away the rock. This process makes the cliff steeper. As a sea cliff erodes above the waterline, a bench of rock usually remains beneath the water at the cliff's base. This bench is called a *wave-cut platform*. Wave-cut platforms are almost flat because the rocks eroded from the cliff often scrape away at the platform.

Sea Caves, Arches, and Stacks

Sea cliffs seldom erode evenly. Often, headlands form as some parts of a cliff are cut back faster than other parts. As the rock making up sea cliffs and headlands erodes, it breaks and cracks. Waves can cut deeply into the cracks and form large holes. As the holes continue to erode, they become *sea caves*. A sea cave may erode even further and eventually become a *sea arch*. When the top of a sea arch collapses, its sides become *sea stacks*.

18 Summarize Complete the chart by filling in descriptions of each coastal landform.

Coastal Landform	Description
Headland	
Sea cave	
Sea arch	
Sea stack	
Wave-cut platform	

Sea arches form when wave action erodes sea caves until a hole cuts through a headland.

Sea stacks form when the tops of sea arches collapse and leave behind isolated columns of rock.

19 Analyze Which of these features do you think took longer to form: the sea stack, sea arch, or sea cave? Explain.

_____

_____

_____

Shifting Sands

What coastal landforms are made by deposition?

Waves and currents carry a variety of materials, including sand, rock, dead coral, and shells. Often, these materials are deposited on a shoreline, where they form a beach. A **beach** is an area of shoreline that is made up of material deposited by waves and currents. A great deal of beach material is also deposited by rivers and then is moved down the shoreline by currents.

Beaches

You may think of beaches as sandy places. However, not all beaches are made of sand. The size and shape of beach material depend on how far the material has traveled from its source. Size and shape also depend on the type of material and how it is eroded. For example, in areas with stormy seas, beaches may be made of pebbles and boulders deposited by powerful waves. These waves erode smaller particles such as sand.

Visualize It!

20 Infer Would it take more wave energy to deposit sand or the rocks shown on this beach? Explain.

_____

_____

_____

Barrier islands lie nearly parallel to the shore.

Barrier islands are ridges of sand.

Sandbars and Barrier Islands

When waves erode material from the shoreline, longshore currents can transport and deposit this material offshore. This process creates landforms in open water.

A **sandbar** is an underwater or exposed ridge of sand, gravel, or shell material. A **barrier island** is a long, narrow island, usually made of sand, that forms parallel to the shoreline a short distance offshore.

Living on the Edge

Barrier islands are dynamic landforms that are constantly changing shape. What's here today may be gone tomorrow!

Barrier islands

Landform in Limbo

Barrier islands are found all over the world, including the United States. They can be eroded away by tides and large storms. The barrier island at the left was eroded by a hurricane. Because of erosion, the shape of a barrier island is always changing.

Building on Barriers

Barrier islands are popular spots to build vacation homes and hotels. Residents of barrier islands often use anti-erosion strategies to protect their property from erosion by tides and storms. Short-term solutions include using sand bags, like those shown on the right, to slow down erosion.

Extend

Inquiry

21 Explain Give a step-by-step description of how a barrier island could form.

22 Identify Research different technologies and strategies people can use to slow the erosion of a barrier island.

23 Model Choose one of the anti-erosion methods identified in your research and design an experiment to test how well the technology or strategy slows down the process of erosion.

Visual Summary

To complete this summary, fill in the blanks. Then use the key below to check your answers. You can use this page to review the main concepts of the lesson.

Erosion and Deposition by Water

Streams alter the shape of Earth's surface.

24 Caused by erosion: canyons, valleys

Caused by deposition: floodplains, deltas, _____

Groundwater erodes and deposits materials.

25 Caused by erosion: caves, _____

Caused by deposition: stalactites, stalagmites

Waves and currents change the shape of the shoreline.

26 Caused by erosion: bays, inlets, headlands, wave-cut platforms, sea cliffs, sea caves, sea stacks, _____

Caused by deposition: beaches, sandbars, barrier islands

Answers: 24 alluvial fans; 25 sinkholes; 26 sea arches

27 Claims • Evidence • Reasoning How do erosion and deposition work together to form a delta? State your claim. Summarize evidence to support your claim and explain your reasoning.

Lesson Review

Vocabulary

Circle the term that best completes the following sentences.

1 *Erosion/Deposition* occurs when materials drop out of wind or water.

2 When a river flows into an ocean, it slows down and deposits materials in its *alluvial fan/delta*.

3 When a river periodically floods and deposits its sediments, a flat area known as a *floodplain/shoreline* forms over time.

Key Concepts

Complete the table below.

Landform	How It Forms
Canyon	**4 Explain**
Sinkhole	**5 Explain**
Sea cave	**6 Explain**

7 Synthesize How does gravity relate to a stream's ability to erode and deposit materials?

_____

_____

8 Identify What are the two main factors that affect how quickly a coastline erodes?

_____

9 Describe How does a longshore current change a beach?

_____

_____

_____

Critical Thinking

Use this graph, which shows erosion and deposition on a beach, to answer questions 10–11.

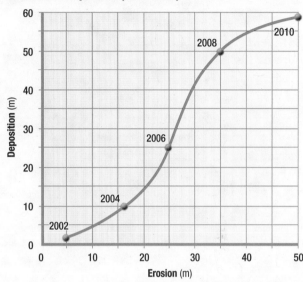

Erosion and Deposition (2002-2010)

10 Analyze In 2004, was there more erosion or deposition taking place?

_____

11 Evaluate Explain how waves and currents are affecting this beach over time.

_____

_____

_____

_____

_____

12 Hypothesize Many communities pump groundwater to irrigate crops and supply homes with water. How do you think overpumping groundwater is related to the formation of sinkholes?

_____

_____

_____

_____

My Notes

Erosion and Deposition by Wind, Ice, and Gravity

ESSENTIAL QUESTION

How do wind, ice, and gravity change Earth's surface?

By the end of this lesson, you should be able to describe erosion and deposition by wind, ice, and gravity as well as identify the landforms that result from these processes.

 S6E5.d Weathering, erosion, and deposition

S6E5.e Effect of natural processes and human activity on Earth's surface

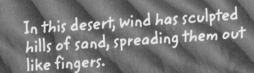

In this desert, wind has sculpted hills of sand, spreading them out like fingers.

Engage Your Brain

1 Predict How do you think wind can erode materials?

_____
_____
_____
_____
_____

2 Infer The dark bands you see in the photo on the right are dirt and rocks frozen in the ice. What do you think will happen to the dirt and rocks when the ice melts?

_____
_____
_____
_____
_____
_____

Active Reading

3 Define In this lesson, you will be learning about how different agents of erosion can abrade rock. Use a dictionary to look up the meaning of the word _abrade_. Record the definition:

_____
_____

Now use the word _abrade_ in your own sentence:

_____
_____
_____

As you read this lesson, circle the word _abrade_ whenever you come across it. Compare the sentences that include this word with the sentence you wrote above.

Vocabulary Terms

• dune	• creep
• loess	• rockfall
• glacier	• landslide
• glacial drift	• mudflow

4 Apply As you learn the definition of each vocabulary term in this lesson, create your own definition or sketch to help you remember the meaning of the term.

Gone with the

How can wind shape Earth?

Have you ever been outside and had a gust of wind blow a stack of papers all over the place? If so, you have seen how wind erosion works. In the same way that wind moved your papers, wind moves soil, sand, and rock particles. When wind moves soil, sand, and rock particles, it acts as an agent of erosion.

Abraded Rock

When wind blows sand and other particles against a surface, it can wear down the surface over time. The grinding and wearing down of rock surfaces by other rock or by sand particles is called *abrasion*. Abrasion happens in areas where there are strong winds, loose sand, and soft rocks. The blowing of millions of grains of sand causes a sandblasting effect. The sandblasting effect slowly erodes the rock by stripping away its surface. Over time, the rock can become smooth and polished.

Desert Pavement

The removal of fine sediment by wind is called *deflation*. This process is shown in the diagram below. During deflation, wind removes the top layer of fine sediment or soil. Deflation leaves behind rock fragments that are too heavy to be lifted by the wind. After a while, these rocks may be the only materials left on the surface. The resulting landscape is known as desert pavement. As you can see in the photo below, desert pavement is a surface made up mostly of pebbles and small, broken rocks.

Wind Direction

Desert Pavement

Visualize It!

5 Describe How did the desert pavement in this photo most likely form? Explain your reasoning.

_____

_____

_____

Wind

Dunes

Wind carries sediment in much the same way that rivers do. Just as rivers deposit their loads, winds eventually drop the materials that they are carrying. For example, when wind hits an obstacle, it slows and drops materials on top of the obstacle. As the material builds up, the obstacle gets larger. This obstacle causes the wind to slow more and deposit more material, which forms a mound. Eventually, the original obstacle is buried. Mounds of wind-deposited sand are called **dunes**. Dunes are common in deserts and along the shores of lakes and oceans.

Generally, dunes move in the same direction the wind is blowing. Usually, a dune's gently sloped side faces the wind. Wind constantly moves material up this side of the dune. As sand moves over the crest of the dune, the sand slides down the slip face and makes a steep slope.

Loess

Wind can carry extremely fine material long distances. Thick deposits of this windblown, fine-grained sediment are known as **loess** (LUHS). Loess can feel like the talcum powder a person may use after a shower. Because wind carries fine-grained material much higher and farther than it carries sand, loess deposits are sometimes found far away from their source. Loess deposits can build up over thousands and even millions of years. Loess is a valuable resource because it forms good soil for growing crops.

6 Infer Why do you think loess can be carried farther than sand?

_____

_____

_____

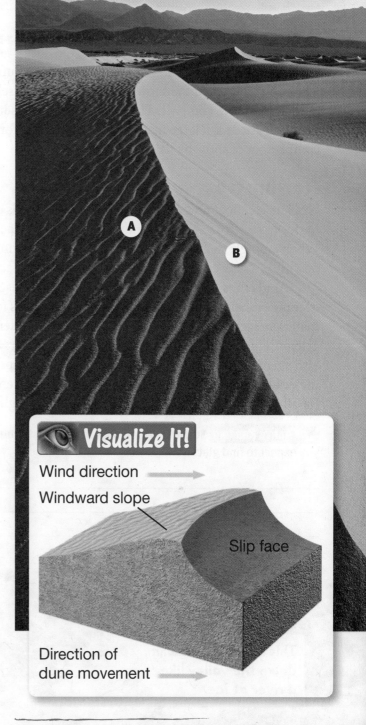

Visualize It!

Wind direction →

Windward slope

Slip face

Direction of dune movement →

7 Determine Look at the photo above the illustration. Which direction does the wind blow across the photographed dune: from left to right or right to left?

_____

_____

8 Identify Which side of the dune in the photograph is the slip face: A or B?

_____

Groovy Glaciers

What kinds of ice shape Earth?

Have you ever made a snowball from a scoop of fluffy snow? If so, you know that when the snow is pressed against itself, it becomes harder and more compact. The same idea explains how a glacier forms. A **glacier** is a large mass of moving ice that forms by the compacting of snow by natural forces.

Flowing Ice

Glaciers can be found anywhere on land where it is cold enough for ice to stay frozen year round. Gravity causes glaciers to move. When enough ice builds up on a slope, the ice begins to move downhill. The steeper the slope is, the faster the glacier moves.

As glaciers move, they pick up materials. These materials become embedded in the ice. As the glacier moves forward, the materials scratch and abrade the rock and soil underneath the glacier. This abrasion causes more erosion. Glaciers are also agents of deposition. As a glacier melts, it drops the materials that it carried. **Glacial drift** is the general term for all of the materials carried and deposited by a glacier.

Active Reading **10 Infer** Where in North America would you expect to find glaciers?

_____

_____

_____

Think Outside the Book

9 Apply Find out whether glaciers have ever covered any parts of the United States. If so, what questions would you ask to determine whether any evidence of past glacial activity exists in these areas today?

As a glacier flowed over this rock, it scratched out these grooves.

This glacier is moving down the valley like a river of ice.

Alpine Glaciers

An alpine glacier is a glacier that forms in a mountainous area. Alpine glaciers flow down the sides of mountains and create rugged landscapes. Glaciers may form in valleys originally created by stream erosion. The flow of water in a stream forms a V-shaped valley. As a glacier slowly flows through a V-shaped valley, it scrapes away the valley floor and walls. The glacier widens and straightens the valley into a broad U-shape. An alpine glacier can also carve out bowl-shaped depressions, called *cirques* (surks), at the head of a valley. A sharp ridge called an *arête* (uh•RAYT) forms between two cirques that are next to each other. When three or more arêtes join, they form a sharp peak called a *horn*.

Visualize It!

11 Summarize Use the illustration below to write a description for each of the following landforms.

Landforms made by alpine glaciers	Description
Arête	
Cirque	
Horn	
U-shaped valley	

Horns are sharp, pyramid-shaped peaks that form when several arêtes join at the top of a mountain.

Arêtes are jagged ridges that form between two or more cirques that cut into the same mountain.

Hanging valleys are small glacial valleys that join the deeper, main valley. Many hanging valleys form waterfalls after the ice is gone.

Cirques are bowl-shaped depressions where glacial ice cuts back into the mountain walls.

U-shaped valleys form when a glacier erodes a river valley. The valley changes from its original V-shape to a U-shape.

Continental Glaciers

Continental glaciers are thick sheets of ice that may spread over large areas, including across entire continents. These glaciers are huge, continuous masses of ice. Continental glaciers create very different landforms than alpine glaciers do. Alpine glaciers form sharp and rugged features, whereas continental glaciers flatten and smooth the landscape. Continental glaciers erode and remove features that existed before the ice appeared. These glaciers smooth and round exposed rock surfaces in a way similar to the way that bulldozers can flatten landscapes.

Erosion and deposition by continental glaciers result in specific, recognizable landforms. Some of the landforms are shown below. Similar landforms can be found in the northern United States, which was once covered by continental glaciers.

Visualize It!

12 Compare What does the formation of erratics and kettle lakes have in common? Explain your reasoning.

_____

_____

_____

_____

_____

_____

Kettle lakes form when chunks of ice are deposited by a glacier and glacial drift builds up around the ice blocks. When the ice melts, a lake forms.

Erratics are large boulders that were transported and deposited by glaciers.

Melting the Ice

A CHANGING WORLD

What would you do if an Ice Age glacial dam broke and let loose millions of gallons of water? Get out of the way and get ready for some erosion!

A Crack in the Ice

During the last Ice Age, a huge ice dam held back Glacial Lake Missoula, a 320-km-long body of water. Then one day, the dam burst. Water roared out, emptying the lake in less than 48 hours!

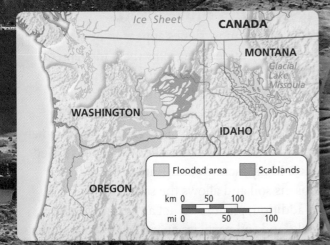

Giant ripple marks from the Missoula floods

Large-Scale Landforms

The erosion caused by the roaring water carved out a landscape of huge waterfalls, deep canyons, and three-story-high ripple marks. Many of these features are in an area called the Scablands.

History Repeats Itself

Lake Missoula eventually reformed behind another ice dam. The breaking of the dam and the floods repeated about 40 more times, ripping away topsoil and exposing and cracking the bedrock.

Extend

Inquiry

13 Relate Where have you seen ripple marks before and how do they compare to the ripple marks shown in the photo on this page?

14 Explain How do you think the three-story-high ripple marks shown here were formed?

15 Model Use sand, pebbles, and other materials to model how a severe flood can alter the landscape. Photograph or illustrate the results of your investigation. Present your results in the form of an animation, slide show, or illustrated report.

Slippery Slopes

How can gravity shape Earth?

Although you can't see it, the force of gravity, like water, wind, and ice, is an agent of erosion and deposition. Gravity not only influences the movement of water and ice, but it also causes rocks and soil to move downslope. This shifting of materials is called *mass movement*. Mass movement plays a major role in shaping Earth's surface.

Slow Mass Movement

Even though most slopes appear to be stable, they are actually undergoing slow mass movement. In fact, all the rocks and soil on a slope travel slowly downhill. The ground beneath the tree shown on the left is moving so slowly that the tree trunk curved as the tree grew. The extremely slow movement of material downslope is called **creep**. Many factors contribute to creep. Water loosens soil and allows the soil to move freely. In addition, plant roots act as wedges that force rocks and soil particles apart. Burrowing animals, such as gophers and groundhogs, also loosen rock and soil particles, making it easier for the particles to be pulled downward.

 **Visualize It!**

16 Analyze As the soil on this hill shifts, how is the tree changing so that it continues to grow upright?

_____

_____

_____

The shape of this tree trunk indicates that creep has occurred along the slope.

© Houghton Mifflin Harcourt Publishing Company • Image Credits: ©ThinkStock/age fotostock

Rapid Mass Movement

The most destructive mass movements happen suddenly and rapidly. Rapid mass movement can be very dangerous and can destroy everything in its path. Rapid mass movement tends to happen on steep slopes because materials are more likely to fall down a steep slope than a shallow slope.

While traveling along a mountain road, you may have noticed signs along the road that warn of falling rocks. A **rockfall** happens when loose rocks fall down a steep slope. Steep slopes are common in mountainous areas. Gravity causes loosened and exposed rocks to fall down steep slopes. The rocks in a rockfall can range in size from small fragments to large boulders.

Another kind of rapid mass movement is a landslide. A **landslide** is the sudden and rapid movement of a large amount of material downslope. As you can see in the photo on the right, landslides can carry away plants. They can also carry away animals, vehicles, and buildings. Heavy rains, deforestation, construction on unstable slopes, and earthquakes increase the chances of a landslide.

A rapid movement of a large mass of mud is a **mudflow**. Mudflows happen when a large amount of water mixes with soil and rock. The water causes the slippery mud to flow rapidly downslope. Mudflows happen in mountainous regions after deforestation has occurred or when a long dry season is followed by heavy rains. Volcanic eruptions or heavy rains on volcanic ash can produce some of the most dangerous mudflows. Mudflows of volcanic origin are called lahars. Lahars can travel at speeds greater than 80 km/h and can be as thick as wet cement.

17 Identify List five events that can trigger a mass movement.

_____

_____

_____

_____

_____

This landslide in California was caused by heavy rains.

 A

 B

Visualize It!

18 Claims • Evidence • Reasoning On which slope, A or B, would a landslide be more likely to occur? Explain your reasoning.

_____

_____

Visual Summary

To complete this summary, fill in the blanks with the correct word or phrase. Then, use the key below to check your answers. You can use this page to review the main concepts of the lesson.

Erosion and Deposition by Wind, Ice, and Gravity

Wind forms dunes and desert pavement.

19 Wind forms dunes through:

_____

20 Wind forms desert pavement through:

_____

Ice erodes and deposits rock.

21 Alpine glaciers make landforms such as:

_____
_____
_____
_____

22 Continental glaciers make landforms such as:

_____
_____

Gravity pulls materials downward.

23 Type of slow mass movement: _____

24 Three major types of rapid mass movement:

_____   _____   _____

25 Summarize Describe the role that gravity plays in almost all examples of erosion and deposition.

Lesson Review

Vocabulary

Use a term from the section to complete each sentence below.

1 When an obstacle causes wind to slow down and deposit materials, the materials pile up and eventually form a _____

2 Large masses of flowing ice called _____ are typically found near Earth's poles and in other cold regions.

3 Very fine sediments called _____ can be carried by wind over long distances.

4 As glaciers retreat, they leave behind deposits of _____

Key Concepts

5 Explain How can glaciers cause deposition?

_____

_____

_____

6 Compare Compare and contrast how wind and glaciers abrade rock.

_____

_____

_____

_____

_____

_____

7 Distinguish What is the difference between creep and a landslide?

_____

_____

_____

_____

Critical Thinking

Use the diagram to answer the question below.

8 Synthesize Which of the four locations would be the best and worst places to build a house? Rank the four locations and explain your reasoning.

_____

_____

_____

_____

_____

9 Integrate Wind erosion occurs at a faster rate in deserts than in places with a thick layer of vegetation covering the ground. Why do you think this is the case?

_____

_____

_____

_____

_____

_____

My Notes

 Lesson 4

Soil Formation

ESSENTIAL QUESTION

How does soil form?

By the end of this lesson, you should be able to describe the physical and chemical characteristics of soil layers and identify the factors that affect soil formation, including the action of living things.

 S6E5.h Composition of soil

Living things, such as this shelf fungus (*Laetiporus sulphureus*), help to break down organic matter. The organic matter mixes with minerals, weathered sediment, water, and air to form soil.

© Houghton Mifflin Harcourt Publishing Company • Image Credits: (bkgd) ©Frank Paul/Alamy

✋ Lesson Labs

Quick Labs
- Observing Life in Soil
- Modeling a Soil Profile
- Observing the Impact of Earthworms on Soil

Field Lab
- Comparing Soil Characteristics

🌎 Engage Your Brain

1 Predict Check T or F to show whether you think each statement is true or false.

T	F	
☐	☐	Soil contains air and water.
☐	☐	Soil does not contain living things.
☐	☐	Soils are the same from place to place.
☐	☐	Climate can affect how fertile soils are.

2 Explain How might the burrows formed by ants affect the soil?

_____

_____

_____

✏️ Active Reading

3 Apply Many scientific words, such as *weather*, have more than one meaning. Use context clues to write your own definition for each meaning of the word *weather*.

Example sentence
The <u>weather</u> outside is nice.

weather:

_____

_____

_____

Example sentence
Wind, water, and plant roots <u>weather</u> rock into sediment.

weather:

_____

_____

_____

Vocabulary Terms

- soil
- humus
- soil profile
- soil horizon

4 Apply As you learn the definition of each vocabulary term in this lesson, write your own definition or sketch to help you remember the meaning of the term.

The Dirt on Soil

What causes soil to form?

Soil is important to your life. You walk on grass that is rooted in soil. You eat foods that need soil in order to grow. But what exactly is soil? Where does it come from? How does it form?

A scientist might define **soil** as a loose mixture of small rock fragments, organic matter, water, and air that can support the growth of vegetation. The very first step in soil formation is the weathering of *parent rock*. Parent rock is the source of inorganic soil particles. Soil forms directly above the parent rock. Soil either develops here, or it is eroded and transported to another location.

Weathering of Parent Rock

Weathering breaks down parent rock into smaller and smaller pieces. These pieces of rock eventually become very small particles that are mixed in with organic matter to form soil. The process of soil formation can take a very long time. The amount of time it takes depends on many factors that you will learn about later in this lesson.

Active Reading

5 Identify As you read, underline the different substances that make up soil.

Soil formation begins when parent rock weathers into small fragments.

Plant roots grow and can break down sediment even further.

Burrowing animals increase the rate of weathering. They mix the soil, allowing more air to enter. They bring sediment to the surface where it is weathered more quickly by water, wind, and organisms.

Decomposition and Mixing by Living Things

Some microorganisms, such as bacteria and fungi, are decomposers that live in soil. These tiny decomposers perform the important task of breaking down the remains of plants and animals. These remains are decayed organic matter called **humus**. Humus is found in the top layer of soils. It is important because it contains nutrients that plants need to grow. Plants take up these nutrients through their roots. When plants or animals die, they are broken down by decomposers, and the nutrients are returned to the soil.

Larger animals, such as earthworms and moles, also live in soil. They loosen and mix the soil as they burrow through it. The mixing increases the amount of air in soil and improves the ability of soil to drain water.

6 Apply How might a fallen leaf eventually become part of soil?

_____

_____

7 Summarize How do decomposers and plants cycle nutrients in soil?

_____

_____

At least a million microorganisms can fit into one spoonful of soil! These tiny organisms have the big job of decomposing plant and animal remains.

Thick Tops, Rocky Bottoms

 Active Reading

8 Identify As you read, underline the factors that affect how long it takes for soils to form and develop.

What factors determine how long it takes for soils to form?

Soil formation and development are processes that take place over a very long period of time. There are four main factors in determining exactly how long these processes take. They include the parent rock type, climate, topography, and plants and animals.

- Rock type: Certain rock types weather at different rates and in different ways. The rate of weathering depends on the structure of the rock and minerals that make up the rock.

- Climate: Soil usually develops more quickly in warm, wet areas than in cold, dry areas.

- Topography: Sediments on steep slopes are often eroded. Soils usually develop faster in flatter areas where sediments are not easily eroded.

- Plants and animals: Plant roots hold sediments in place, allowing soil to develop quickly. Areas teeming with life have higher rates of decomposition and mixing. Soils tend to develop more quickly in these areas. Without a lot of plants and animals, soil tends to develop slowly.

9 Compare List some possible characteristics of an area where soils would develop quickly. Then do the same for an area where soils would develop slowly.

Area where Soils Develop Quickly	Area where Soils Develop Slowly

What are the main soil horizons?

Picture the rich, dark soil in a garden. Now imagine what the soil looks like as you dig deeper beneath the surface. Does the soil look and feel the same as you dig deeper? A vertical section of soil that shows all of the different layers is a **soil profile**. Each layer in the soil profile that has different physical properties is called a **soil horizon**. The main horizons include the A horizon, B horizon, and C horizon. There are many other horizons as well.

A Horizon

The A horizon is at the top of the soil profile. It is often referred to as *topsoil*. Decomposers live in this horizon, so it has the most decayed organic matter. This humus gives it a dark color. Plant roots break up fragments and animals burrow and mix the the soil. These processes increase the rate of weathering, so the A horizon is usually the most developed. As you'll learn later in this lesson, rich soils generally have high amounts of humus. Dead leaves, branches, and other organic matter may cover the surface of the A horizon.

B Horizon

The B horizon lies below the A horizon. It is not as developed as the A horizon and has less humus. Following precipitation events, water seeps down through the A horizon. Water carries material, such as iron minerals and clay, from the A horizon down to the B horizon. This is known as *leaching*. The leached materials commonly give the B horizon a reddish or brownish color.

C Horizon

The C horizon lies below the B horizon. It is the least-developed soil horizon. It contains the largest rock fragments and usually has no organic matter. The C horizon lies directly above the parent rock. Recall that this is the weathered rock from which the soil was formed.

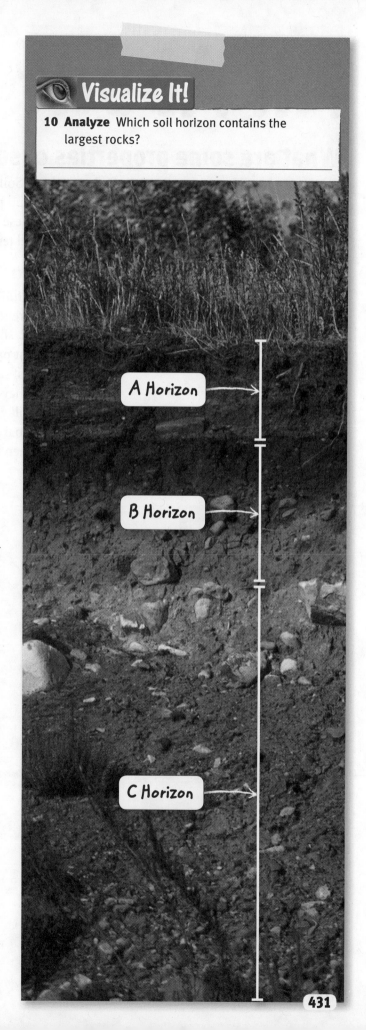

Visualize It!

10 Analyze Which soil horizon contains the largest rocks?

A Horizon

B Horizon

C Horizon

© Houghton Mifflin Harcourt Publishing Company • Image Credits: (r) ©Kenneth W. Fink/Photo Researchers, Inc.

All About Soil

What are some properties of soil?

Plants grow well in some soils and poorly in others. Soils look and feel different. They also contain different minerals and particles. Soil properties are used to classify different soils. These properties include soil texture, color, chemistry, pore space, and fertility.

 **Active Reading**

11 Identify As you read, underline the three kinds of soil particles.

Soil Texture

The term *soil texture* is a property that describes the relative amounts of differently sized soil particles. Soil particles are classified as sand, silt, or clay. Most soils are a mixture of all three. Sand is the largest particle, ranging from 0.05 mm to 2 mm. Soils containing a lot of sand feel coarse. Silt particles are smaller than sand particles. They range from 0.002 mm to 0.05 mm. Silty soils have a smooth, silky feel. At less than 0.002 mm, clay particles are the smallest soil particles. Clayey soils feel very smooth and are usually sticky when they are wet.

Visualize It!

12 Distinguish The last space in each row contains three circles. Fill in the circle that shows the correct relative size of the particle shown in that row.

Particle	Size Range	Relative Size
sand	0.05 mm–2 mm	
silt	0.002 mm–0.05 mm	
clay	less than 0.002 mm	

Soil Color

Soils can be black, brown, red, orange, yellow, gray, and even white. Soil color is a clue to the types and amounts of minerals and organic matter in the soil. Iron minerals make soil orange or reddish. Soils that contain a lot of humus are black or brown. Color can also be a clue about the environmental conditions. Gray soil can indicate that an area is often wet and has poor drainage.

Soils are usually a mixture of colors, such as reddish brown. Scientists use the Munsell System of Color Notation to describe soil colors. The system uses a book of color chips, much like the paint chips found in a paint store. Scientists compare a soil to the color chips in the book to classify soils.

Think Outside the Book

13 Apply Find out about the qualities of your local soil. Describe its texture, color, chemistry, pore space, and fertility. Choose one of these activities to present your description: draw a poster or diagram, create a brochure, or write a poem.

Soil and Climate

Climate can affect how soil forms in different regions on Earth. Warm, rainy regions produce tropical soils and temperate soils. Dry regions produce desert soils and arctic soils.

Tropical Soils form in warm, wet regions. Heavy rains wash away and leach soils, leaving only a thin layer of humus. Soil development is fast in these regions. They are not suitable for growing most crops.

Desert Soils form in dry regions. These soils are shallow and contain little organic matter. Because of the low rainfall, chemical weathering and soil development is slow in desert regions.

Temperate Soils form in regions with moderate rainfall and temperatures. Some temperate soils are dark-colored, rich in organic matter and minerals, and good for growing crops.

Arctic Soils form in cold, dry regions where chemical weathering is slow. They typically do not have well-developed horizons. Arctic soils may contain many rock fragments.

Soil Chemistry

Soil pH is determined by the combination of minerals, sediment, and organic matter found in soil. The pH of soil is a measure of how acidic or basic a soil is. The pH is based on a scale of 0 to 14. If pH is less than 7, the soil is acidic. If pH is above 7, the soil is basic. In the middle of the pH scale is 7, which means the soil is neither acidic nor basic; it is neutral. Scientists measure soil pH to determine whether the soil can support different plants. For example, soybeans grow best in a soil with a pH between 6.0 and 7.0. Peanuts thrive when the pH of soil is between 5.3 and 6.6.

Farmers can adjust the pH of soil to meet the needs of their plants. They can add lime to make acidic soils more basic. They can add acids to make basic soils more acidic.

The pH of a soil can be tested to make sure it will support the plants being grown.

Pore Space

Pore space describes the spaces between soil particles. Water and air are found in the pore spaces of soils. Water and air move easily through soils with many well-connected pore spaces. Soils with this property are well-drained and typically good for plant growth.

Plants need both water and air to grow. About 25 to 60 percent of the volume of most soils is pore space. The best soil for growing most plants has about 50 percent of its volume as pore space, with that volume equally divided between water and air.

Visualize It!

14 Describe Write a caption that describes the pore space for each diagram below.

A _____

_____

_____

B _____

_____

_____

Soil Fertility

Soil fertility describes how well a soil can support plant growth. This quality is affected by factors that include the climate of the area; the amount of humus, minerals, and nutrients in the soil; and the topography of the area.

Fertile soils are often found in areas with moderate rainfall and temperatures. Soils with a lot of humus and the proper proportions of minerals and nutrients have high soil fertility. Soils found in dry areas or on steep hillsides often have low fertility. Farmers can add chemical fertilizers or organic material to soils to improve soil fertility. They also can grow crops, such as legumes, to restore certain nutrients to soil or leave cropland unplanted for a season to replenish its fertility.

Active Reading **15 Apply** What could you do to improve the fertility of the soil in your garden?

_____

_____

This meadow's bluebonnets thrive in well-drained soil. Bluebonnets also grow best in slightly basic soils.

Inquiry

16 Infer Use what you have learned to infer why Soils A and B have the following soils properties.

Soil Properties	Possible Reasons for Soil Properties
Soil A is black, well-drained, and good for growing plants.	
Soil B feels smooth and sticky and is gray in color.	

Visual Summary

To complete this summary, fill in the blanks with the correct word. Then use the key below to check your answers. You can use this page to review the main concepts of the lesson.

Soil Formation

Soil formation involves weathering of rock, addition of organic material, and actions by plants and animals that live in the soil.

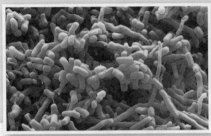

17 In general, soils in cold, dry areas will take _____ to develop than soils in warm, wet areas.

A soil profile commonly has the A horizon, B horizon, and C horizon. They each have distinct physical characteristics.

18 The _____ contains the most organic matter; leaching carries minerals and humus down to the _____.

Characteristics of soil include texture, color, chemistry, pore space, and soil fertility.

19 _____ describes the spaces between soil particles.

Answers: 17 longer; 18 A horizon, B horizon; 19 Pore space

20 Claims • Evidence • Reasoning State how living things can affect the different characteristics and development of soil. Summarize evidence to support your claim and explain your reasoning.

Lesson Review

Vocabulary

Draw a line to connect the following terms to their definitions.

1 soil

2 humus

3 soil profile

4 soil horizon

A decomposed organic matter

B layer of soil with distinct physical properties in a soil profile

C vertical section showing the soil horizons

D mixture of weathered sediment, organic material, water, and air

Key Concepts

5 Identify What is the first step of soil formation?

_____

_____

6 Explain What are the main factors that determine how long it takes for a soil to form and develop?

_____

_____

_____

_____

7 Describe How would a soil that developed in a warm, wet place be different than one that developed in a hot, dry place? Explain your reasoning.

_____

_____

_____

_____

_____

_____

8 Compare How might a dark colored, coarse soil differ from a reddish, smooth soil?

_____

_____

_____

_____

Critical Thinking

Use this table to answer the following question.

Climate Data for Locations A and B		
	Average Yearly Temperature (°C)	Average Yearly Precipitation (cm)
Location A	27	190
Location B	3	26

9 Analyze In which location would soils develop faster? Explain.

_____

_____

_____

_____

10 Infer Which soil would you expect to be better developed: the soil on a hillside or the soil on a valley floor? Explain your reasoning.

_____

_____

_____

_____

11 Synthesize Describe the cycle that involves soil, decomposers, and other living things.

_____

_____

_____

_____

My Notes

Minerals

ESSENTIAL QUESTION

What are minerals, how do they form, and how can they be identified?

By the end of this lesson, you should be able to describe the basic structure of minerals and identify different minerals by using their physical properties.

This cave was once full of water. Over millions of years, dissolved minerals in the water slowly formed these gypsum crystals, which are now considered to be the largest mineral crystals in the world!

S6E5.b Characteristics of minerals

Lesson Labs

Quick Labs
• Cooling Rate and Crystal Size
• Scratch Test

Exploration Lab
• Intrinsic Identification of Minerals

Engage Your Brain

1 Identify Which of the materials listed below is a mineral?

Yes	No	
☐	☐	ice
☐	☐	gold
☐	☐	wood
☐	☐	diamond
☐	☐	table salt

2 Explain Describe how you think the minerals in the picture below may have formed.

_____

_____

_____

Active Reading

3 Synthesize Many of this lesson's vocabulary terms are related to each other. Locate the terms in the Glossary and see if you can find connections between them. When you find two terms that are related to each other, write a sentence using both terms in a way that shows the relationship. An example is done for you.

Example Sentence
Each element is made of only one kind of atom.

_____

_____

_____

_____

Vocabulary Terms

- **mineral**
- **element**
- **atom**
- **compound**
- **matter**
- **crystal**
- **streak**
- **luster**
- **cleavage**

4 Apply As you learn the definition of each vocabulary term in this lesson, create your own definition or sketch to help you remember the meaning of the term.

Animal, Vegetable,

What do minerals have in common?

When you hear the word *mineral,* you may think of sparkling gems. But, in fact, most minerals are found in groups that make up rocks. So what is a mineral? A **mineral** is a naturally occurring, usually inorganic solid that has a definite crystalline structure and chemical composition.

Definite Chemical Composition

To understand what a definite chemical composition is, you need to know a little about elements. **Elements** are pure substances that cannot be broken down into simpler substances by ordinary chemical means. Each element is made of only one kind of atom. All substances are made up of atoms, so **atoms** can be thought of as the building blocks of matter. Stable particles that are made up of strongly bonded atoms are called *molecules.* And, if a substance is made up of molecules of two or more elements, the substance is called a **compound.**

The chemical composition of a mineral is determined by the element or compound that makes up the mineral. For example, minerals such as gold and silver are composed of only one element. Such a mineral is called a *native element.* The mineral quartz is a compound in which silicon atoms can each bond with up to four oxygen atoms in a repeating pattern.

5 Synthesize What is the relationship between elements, atoms, and compounds?

_____

_____

_____

_____

Solid

Matter is anything that has volume and mass. *Volume* refers to the amount of space an object takes up. For example, a golf ball has a smaller volume than a baseball does. Matter is generally found in one of three states: solid, liquid, or gas. A mineral is a solid—that is, it has a definite volume and shape. A substance that is a liquid or a gas is not a mineral. However, in some cases its solid form is a mineral. For instance, liquid water is not a mineral, but ice is because it is solid and has all of the other mineral characteristics also.

Atoms The mineral quartz is made up of atoms of oxygen and silicon.

Oxygen (O)   Silicon (Si)

Compound An atom of silicon can typically bond with up to four oxygen atoms to form a molecule. One or more of these molecules form a compound.

Image Credits: (t) ©Bryan Dadswell/Alamy

© Houghton Mifflin Harcourt Publishing Company

or Mineral?

Usually Inorganic

Most substances made by living things are categorized as organic substances, such as kidney stones and wood. However, a few substances made by animals, such as clam shells, are categorized as inorganic. An inorganic substance is usually one that is not made up of living things or the remains of living things. And, although a few organic substances such as kidney stones are categorized as minerals, most minerals are inorganic. And, unlike clam shells, most of the processes that form minerals usually take place in the non-living environment.

Crystalline Structure

Minerals have a crystalline structure because they are composed of crystals. A **crystal** is a solid, geometric form that results from a repeating pattern of atoms or molecules. A crystal's shape is produced by the arrangement of the atoms or molecules within the crystal. This arrangement is determined by the kinds of atoms or molecules that make up the mineral and the conditions under which it forms. All minerals can be placed into crystal classes according to their specific crystal shape. This diagram shows how silica compounds can be arranged in quartz crystals.

Crystal Structure In crystals, molecules are arranged in a regular pattern.

Naturally Occurring

Minerals are formed by many different natural processes that occur on Earth and throughout the universe. On Earth, the mineral halite, which is used for table salt, forms as water evaporates and leaves behind the salt it contained. Some minerals form as molten rock cools. Talc, a mineral that can be used to make baby powder, forms deep in Earth as high temperature and pressure change the rock. Some of the other ways in which minerals form are on the next page.

6 Classify Circle *Y* for "yes" or *N* for "no" to determine whether the two materials below are minerals.

	Cardboard	Topaz
Definite chemical composition?	Y (N)	(Y) N
Solid?	Y N	(Y) N
Inorganic?	Y N	Y N
Naturally occurring?	Y N	Y N
Crystalline structure?	Y (N)	Y N
Mineral?	Y N	Y N

Mineral Crystal Billions of molecules arranged in a crystalline structure form these quartz crystals.

Crystal Clear!

How are minerals formed?

Minerals form within Earth or on Earth's surface by natural processes. Recall that each type of mineral has its own chemical makeup. Therefore, which types of minerals form in an area depends in part on which elements are present there. Temperature and pressure also affect which minerals form.

As Magma and Lava Cool

Many minerals grow from magma. Magma—molten rock inside Earth—contains most of the types of atoms that are found in minerals. As magma cools, the atoms join together to form different minerals. Minerals also form as lava cools. Lava is molten rock that has reached Earth's surface. Quartz is one of the many minerals that crystallize from magma and lava.

Visualize It!

7 Compare How are the ways in which pluton and pegmatite minerals form similar?

_____

_____

By Metamorphism

Temperature and pressure within Earth cause new minerals to form as bonds between atoms break and reform with different atoms. The mineral garnet can form and replace the minerals chlorite and quartz in this way. At high temperatures and pressures, the element carbon in rocks forms the mineral diamond or the mineral graphite, which is used in pencils.

Cooling Magma Forms Plutons
As magma rises, it can stop moving and cool slowly. This forms rocks like this granite, which contains minerals like quartz, mica, and feldspar.

Cooling Magma Forms Pegmatites
Magma that cools very slowly can form pegmatites. Some crystals in pegmatites, such as this topaz, can grow quite large.

Metamorphism Minerals like these garnets form when temperature and pressure causes the chemical and crystalline makeup of minerals to change.

From Solutions

Water usually has many substances dissolved in it. As water evaporates, these substances form into solids and come out of solution, or *precipitate*. For example, the mineral gypsum often forms as water evaporates. Minerals can also form from hot water solutions. Hot water can dissolve more materials than cold water. As a body of hot water cools, dissolved substances can form into minerals such as dolomite, as they precipitate out of solution.

8 Summarize Describe three ways minerals form.

A _____

_____

B _____

_____

C _____

_____

Precipitating from an Evaporating Solution When a body of salt water evaporates, minerals such as this halite precipitate and are left behind on the shoreline.

Precipitating from a Cooling Solution on Earth's Surface Dissolved materials can come out of a solution and accumulate. Dolomite, can form this way.

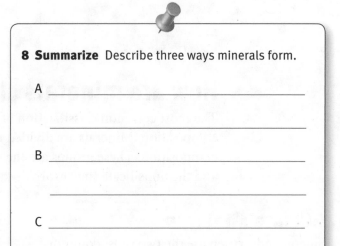

Precipitating from a Cooling Solution Beneath Earth's Surface Water works its way downward and is heated by magma. It then reacts with minerals to form a solution. Dissolved elements, such as gold, precipitate once the fluid cools to form new mineral deposits.

Think Outside the Book

9 Apply Find out what your state mineral is and how it forms.

Sort It Out

How are minerals classified?

The most common classification of minerals is based on chemical composition. Minerals are divided into two groups based on their composition. These groups are the silicate (SIL'ih•kayt) minerals and the nonsilicate (nawn•SIL'ih•kayt) minerals.

Silicate Minerals

Silicon and oxygen are the two most common elements in Earth's crust. Minerals that contain a combination of these two elements are called *silicate minerals*. Silicate minerals make up most of Earth's crust. The most common silicate minerals in Earth's crust are feldspar and quartz. Most silicate minerals are formed from basic building blocks called *silicate tetrahedrons*. Silicate tetrahedrons are made of one silicon atom bonded to four oxygen atoms. Most silicate minerals, including mica and olivine, are composed of silicate tetrahedrons combined with other elements, such as aluminum or iron.

Active Reading **10 Explain** Why is Earth's crust made up mostly of silicate minerals?

_____

_____

The mineral zircon is a silicate mineral. It is composed of the element zirconium and silicate tetrahedrons.

Nonsilicate Minerals

Minerals that do not contain the silicate tetrahedron building block form a group called the *nonsilicate minerals*. Some of these minerals are made up of elements such as carbon, oxygen, fluorine, iron, and sulfur. The table on the next page shows the most important classes of nonsilicate minerals. A nonsilicate mineral's chemical composition determines its class.

Do the Math **You Try It**

11 Calculate Calculate the percent of non-silicates in Earth's crust to complete the graph's key.

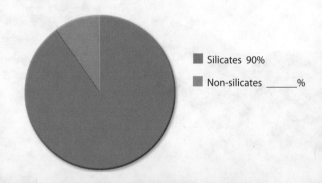

Minerals in Earth's Crust

- Silicates 90%
- Non-silicates _____ %

Classes of Nonsilicate Minerals

Native elements are minerals that are composed of only one element. Copper (Cu) and silver (Ag) are two examples. Native elements are often used to make electronics.

Silver, Ag

Carbonates are minerals that contain carbon (C) and oxygen (O) in the form of the carbonate ion CO_3^{2-}. We use carbonate minerals in cement, building stones, and fireworks.

Calcite, $CaCO_3$

Halides are compounds that form when elements such as fluorine (F) and chlorine (Cl), combine with elements such as calcium (Ca). Halides are used in the chemical industry and in detergents.

Fluorite, CaF_2

Oxides are compounds that form when an element, such as aluminum (Al) or iron (Fe), combines with oxygen. Oxide minerals are used to make abrasives, aircraft parts, and paint.

Corundum, Al_2O_3

Sulfates are minerals that contain sulfur (S) and oxygen (O) in the form of the sulfate ion SO_4^{2-}. Sulfates are used in cosmetics, toothpaste, cement, and paint.

Barite, $BaSO_4$

Sulfides are minerals that contain one or more elements, such as lead (Pb), or iron (Fe), combined with sulfur (S). Sulfide minerals are used to make batteries and medicines.

Pyrite, FeS_2

Visualize It!

12 Classify Examine the chemical formulas for the two minerals at right. Classify the minerals as a silicate or nonsilicate. If it is a nonsilicate, also write its class. Explain your reasoning.

Gypsum, $CaSO_4 \cdot 2H_2O$ Kyanite, Al_2SiO_5

_____   _____

_____   _____

Name That Mineral!

What properties can be used to identify minerals?

If you closed your eyes and tasted different foods, you could probably determine what the foods are by noting properties such as saltiness or sweetness. You can also determine the identity of a mineral by noting different properties. In this section, you will learn about the properties that will help you identify minerals.

Color

The same mineral can come in different colors. For example, pure quartz is colorless. However, impurities can make quartz pink, orange, or many other colors. Other factors can also change a mineral's color. Pyrite is normally golden, but turns black or brown if exposed to air and water. The same mineral can be different colors, and different minerals can be the same color. So, color is helpful but usually not the best way to identify a mineral.

Streak

The color of the powdered form of a mineral is its **streak**. A mineral's streak is found by rubbing the mineral against a white tile called a *streak plate*. The mark left is the streak. A mineral's streak is not always the same as the color of the mineral, but all samples of the same mineral have the same streak color. Unlike the surface of a mineral, the streak is not affected by air or water. For this reason, streak is more reliable than color in identifying a mineral.

Active Reading

13 Identify Underline the name of the property on this page that is most reliable for identifying a mineral.

Visualize It!

14 Claims • Evidence • Reasoning Look at these two mineral samples. What property indicates that they may be the same mineral? Explain your reasoning.

_____

_____

_____

Mineral Lusters

Metallic

Silky

Vitreous

Waxy

Submetallic

Pearly

Resinous

Earthy

Luster

The way a surface reflects light is called **luster**. When you say an object is shiny or dull, you are describing its luster. The two major types of luster are metallic and nonmetallic. Pyrite has a metallic luster. It looks as if it is made of metal. A mineral with a nonmetallic luster can be shiny, but it does not appear to be made of metal. Different types of lusters are shown above.

Cleavage and Fracture

The tendency of a mineral to split along specific planes of weakness to form smooth, flat surfaces is called **cleavage**. When a mineral has cleavage, it breaks along flat surfaces that generally run parallel to planes of weakness in the crystal structure. For example, mica tends to split into parallel sheets. Many minerals, however, do not break along cleavage planes. Instead, they fracture, or break unevenly, into pieces that have curved or irregular surfaces. Scientists describe a fracture according to the appearance of the broken surface. For example, a rough surface has an irregular fracture, and a curved surfaces has a conchoidal (kahn•KOY•duhl) fracture.

Visualize It!

15 Identify Write the correct description, either *cleavage* or *fracture*, under the two broken mineral crystals shown here.

Cleavage

Fracture

© Houghton Mifflin Harcourt Publishing Company • Image Credits: (metallic) ©Steve Sant/Alamy; (silky) ©Lester V. Bergman/Corbis; (vitreous) ©Joel Arem/Photo Researchers, Inc.; (waxy) ©Scenics & Science/Alamy; (submetallic) ©Harry Tayor/Dorling Kindersley/Getty Images; (pearly) ©GC Minerals/Alamy; (resinous) ©MarcelClemens/Shutterstock; (earthy) ©Leslie Garland Picture Library/Alamy; (br) ©USGS

Mohs Scale

1	Talc
2	Gypsum
3	Calcite
4	Fluorite
5	Apatite
6	Feldspar
7	Quartz
8	Topaz
9	Corundum
10	Diamond

Your fingernail has a hardness of about 2.5, so it can scratch talc and gypsum.

A steel file has a hardness of about 6.5. You can scratch feldspar with it.

Diamond is the hardest mineral. Only a diamond can scratch another diamond.

Visualize It!

16 Determine A mineral can be scratched by calcite but not by a fingernail. What is its approximate hardness?

_____

Density

If you pick up a golf ball and a table-tennis ball, which will feel heavier? Although the balls are of similar size, the golf ball will feel heavier because it is denser. *Density* is the measure of how much matter is in a given amount of space. Density is usually measured in grams per cubic centimeter. Gold has a density of 19 g/cm³. The mineral pyrite looks very similar to gold, but its density is only 5 g/cm³. Because of this, density can be used to tell gold from pyrite. Density can also be used to tell many other similar-looking minerals apart.

Hardness

A mineral's resistance to being scratched is called its *hardness*. To determine the hardness of minerals, scientists use the Mohs hardness scale, shown at left. Notice that talc has a rating of 1 and diamond has a rating of 10. The greater a mineral's resistance to being scratched, the higher its hardness rating. To identify a mineral by using the Mohs scale, try to scratch the surface of a mineral with the edge of one of the 10 reference minerals. If the reference mineral scratches your mineral, the reference mineral is as hard as or harder than your mineral.

Special Properties

All minerals exhibit the properties that were described earlier in this section. However, a few minerals have some additional, special properties that can help identify those minerals. For example, the mineral magnetite is a natural magnet. The mineral calcite is usually white in ordinary light, but in ultraviolet light, it often appears red. Another special property of calcite is shown below.

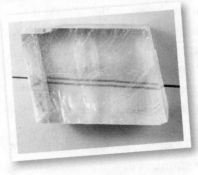

A clear piece of calcite placed over an image will cause a double image.

Why It Matters

Made from Minerals

Many minerals contain useful substances. Rutile and several other minerals contain the metal titanium. Titanium can resist corrosion and is about as strong as steel, but it is 47% lighter than steel. These properties make titanium very valuable.

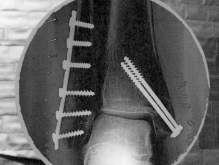

Devices for Doctors

Surgical procedures like joint replacements require metal implantations. Titanium is used because it can resist body fluid corrosion and its low density and elasticity is similar to human bone.

Marvels for Mechanics

Motorcycle exhaust pipes are often made out of titanium, which dissipates heat better than stainless steel.

An Aid to Architects

Titanium doesn't just serve practical purposes. Architect Frank Gehry used titanium panels to cover the outside of the Guggenheim Museum in Bilbao, Spain. He chose titanium because of its luster.

Extend

Inquiry

17 Infer How do you think the density of titanium-containing minerals would compare to the density of minerals used to make steel? Explain.

18 List Research some other products made from minerals. Make a list summarizing your research.

19 Determine Choose one of the products you researched. How do the properties of the minerals used to make the product contribute to the product's characteristics or usefulness?

Visual Summary

To complete this summary, fill in the blanks with the correct words or phrase. Then use the key below to check your answers. You can use this page to review the main concepts of the lesson.

Minerals make up Earth's crust.

20 A mineral:

- has a definite chemical composition
- is a solid
- is usually inorganic
- is formed in nature
- _____

Minerals are classified by composition.

21 Minerals are classified in two groups as:

Quartz, SiO_2 Calcite, $CaCO_3$

Minerals

Minerals form by natural processes.

22 Minerals form by:

- metamorphism
- the cooling of magma and lava
- _____

Minerals are identified by their properties.

23 Properties used to identify minerals include:

- color and luster
- _____
- cleavage or fracture
- density and hardness
- special properties

Answers: 20 has a crystalline structure; 21 silicates (left), nonsilicates (right); 22 precipitating from solutions; 23 streak

24 **Claims • Evidence • Reasoning** Ice (H_2O) is a mineral. State whether it is a silicate or a nonsilicate and list two of its properties. Summarize evidence to support your claim and explain your reasoning.

Lesson Review

Vocabulary

Fill in the blank with the term that best completes the following sentence.

1 The way light bounces off a mineral's surface is described by the mineral's _____

2 The color of a mineral in powdered form is the mineral's _____

3 Each element is made up of only one kind of _____

Key Concepts

4 Explain How could you determine whether an unknown substance is a mineral?

_____
_____
_____
_____
_____

5 Determine If a substance is a mineral, how could you identify what type of mineral it is?

_____
_____
_____

6 Organize In the space below, draw a graphic organizer showing how minerals can be classified. Be sure to include the six main classes of nonsilicate minerals.

Critical Thinking

Use the diagram below to answer question 7.

Carbon Bonds in Graphite

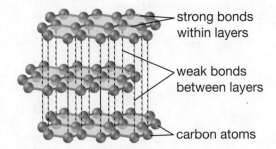

strong bonds within layers

weak bonds between layers

carbon atoms

7 Evaluate The diagram above shows the crystal structure of graphite, a mineral made up of carbon atoms that are bonded together in a regular pattern. Do you think graphite would most likely display cleavage or fracture? Explain your answer.

_____
_____
_____
_____
_____

8 Infer How do you think the hardness and density of a mineral that formed through metamorphism would compare to a mineral that formed through evaporation? Explain.

_____
_____
_____
_____
_____
_____
_____
_____

My Notes

The Rock Cycle

ESSENTIAL QUESTION

What is the rock cycle?

By the end of this lesson, you should be able to describe the series of processes and classes of rocks that make up the rock cycle.

S6E5.b Characteristics of minerals

S6E5.c Rock formation and the rock cycle

It may be hard to believe, but these mountains actually move. Wyoming's Teton Mountains rise by millimeters each year. An active fault is uplifting the mountains. In this lesson, you will learn about uplift and other processes that change rock.

Lesson Labs

Quick Labs
- Crayon Rock Cycle
- Modeling Weathering

 Engage Your Brain

1 Describe Fill in the blank with the word or phrase that you think correctly completes the following sentences.

Most of Earth is made of _____

Rock is _____ changing.

The three main classes of rock are igneous, metamorphic, and _____

2 Describe Write your own caption for this photo.

_____

_____

_____

 Active Reading

3 Synthesize Many English words have their roots in other languages. Use the Latin words below to make an educated guess about the meaning of the words *erosion* and *deposition*.

Latin Word	Meaning
erosus	eaten away
depositus	laid down

Vocabulary Terms
- weathering
- erosion
- deposition
- igneous rock
- sedimentary rock
- metamorphic rock
- rock cycle
- uplift
- subsidence
- rift zone

4 Apply As you learn the definition of each vocabulary term in this lesson, create your own definition or sketch to help you remember the meaning of the term.

Erosion:

_____

_____

Deposition:

_____

_____

Let's Rock!

What is rock?

The solid parts of Earth are made almost entirely of rock. Scientists define rock as a naturally occurring solid mixture of one or more minerals that may also include organic matter. Most rock is made of minerals, but some rock is made of nonmineral material that is not organic, such as glass. Rock has been an important natural resource as long as humans have existed. Early humans used rocks as hammers to make other tools. For centuries, people have used different types of rock, including granite, marble, sandstone, and slate, to make buildings, such as the pyramids shown below.

It may be hard to believe, but rocks are always changing. People study rocks to learn how areas have changed through time.

5 List How is rock used today?

_____

_____

_____

_____

The ancient Egyptians used a rock called limestone to construct the Great Sphinx and the pyramids at Giza.

These rock formations in Goreme, Turkey, are known as fairy chimneys. They were shaped by erosion.

Think Outside the Book

6 Design Create a travel brochure for Goreme, Turkey.

What processes change rock?

Natural processes make and destroy rock. They change each type of rock into other types of rock and shape the features of our planet. These processes also influence the type of rock that is found in each area of Earth's surface.

Active Reading **7 Identify** As you read, underline the processes and factors that can change rock.

Weathering, Erosion, and Deposition

The process by which water, wind, ice, and changes in temperature break down rock is called **weathering**. Weathering breaks down rock into fragments called *sediment*. The process by which sediment is moved from one place to another is called **erosion.** Water, wind, ice, and gravity can erode sediments. These sediments are eventually deposited, or laid down, in bodies of water and other low-lying areas. The process by which sediment comes to rest is called **deposition.**

Temperature and Pressure

Rock that is buried can be squeezed by the weight of the rock or the layers of sediment on top of it. As pressure increases with depth beneath Earth's surface, so does temperature. If the temperature and pressure are high enough, the buried rock can change into metamorphic rock. In some cases, the rock gets hot enough to melt and forms *magma*, or molten rock. If magma reaches Earth's surface, it is called *lava*. The magma or lava eventually cools and solidifies to form new rock.

Classified Information!

What are the classes of rocks?

Rocks fall into three major classes based on how they form. **Igneous rock** forms when magma or lava cools and hardens to become solid. It forms beneath or on Earth's surface. **Sedimentary rock** forms when minerals that form from solutions or sediment from older rocks get pressed and cemented together. **Metamorphic rock** forms when pressure, temperature, or chemical processes change existing rock. Each class can be divided further, based on differences in the way rocks form. For example, some igneous rocks form when lava cools on Earth's surface, and others form when magma cools deep beneath the surface. Therefore, igneous rock can be classified based on how and where it forms.

Active Reading

8 Identify As you read the paragraph, underline the three main classes of rocks.

Think Outside the Book Inquiry

9 Claims • Evidence • Reasoning With a classmate, discuss the processes that might have shaped the rock formations in the Valley of Fire State Park. Summarize the evidence to support your claim about the processes and explain your reasoning.

These formations in Valley of Fire State Park in Nevada are made of sandstone, a sedimentary rock.

Sedimentary

Sedimentary rock is composed of minerals formed from solutions or sediments from older rock. Sedimentary rock forms when the weight from above presses down on the layers of minerals or sediment, or when minerals dissolved in water solidify between sediment pieces and cement them together.

Sedimentary rocks are named according to the size and type of the fragments they contain. For example, the rock shown here is made of sand and is called sandstone. Rock made primarily of the mineral calcite (calcium carbonate) is called limestone.

sandstone

Enchanted Rock in Texas is a large dome made of granite, an intrusive igneous rock.

Igneous Rock

Igneous rock forms from cooling lava and magma. As molten rock cools and becomes solid, the minerals crystallize and grow. The longer the cooling takes, the more time the crystals have to grow. The granite shown here cooled slowly and is made of large crystals. Rock that forms when magna cools beneath Earth's surface is called intrusive igneous rock. Rock that forms when lava cools on Earth's surface is called extrusive igneous rock.

granite

Metamorphic Rock

Metamorphic rock forms when high temperature and pressure change the texture and mineral content of rock. For example, a rock can be buried in Earth's crust, where the temperature and pressure are high. Over millions of years, the solid rock changes, and new crystals are formed. Metamorphic rocks may be changed in four ways: by temperature, by pressure, by temperature and pressure combined, or by fluids or other chemicals. Gneiss, shown here, is a metamorphic rock. It forms at high temperatures deep within Earth's crust.

gneiss

Gneiss is a metamorphic rock that is made up of bands of light and dark minerals.

10 Compare Fill in the chart to compare and contrast sedimentary, igneous, and metamorphic rock.

Classes of Rocks

Sedimentary rock	Igneous rock	Metamorphic rock

What is the rock cycle?

Active Reading **11 Apply** As you read, underline the rock types that metamorphic rock can change into.

Rocks may seem very permanent, solid, and unchanging. But over millions of years, any of the three rock types can be changed into another of the three types. For example, igneous rock can change into sedimentary or metamorphic rock, or back into another kind of igneous rock. This series of processes in which rock changes from one type to another is called the **rock cycle**. Rocks may follow different pathways in the cycle. Examples of these pathways are shown here. Factors, including temperature, pressure, weathering, and erosion, may change a rock's identity. Where rock is located on a tectonic plate and whether the rock is at Earth's surface also influence how it forms and changes.

When igneous rock is exposed at Earth's surface, it may break down into sediment. Igneous rock may also change directly into metamorphic rock while still beneath Earth's surface. It may also melt to form magma that becomes another type of igneous rock.

When sediment is pressed together and cemented, the sediment becomes sedimentary rock. With temperature and pressure changes, sedimentary rocks may become metamorphic rocks, or they may melt and become igneous rock. Sedimentary rock may also be broken down at Earth's surface and become sediment that forms another sedimentary rock.

Under certain temperature and pressure conditions, metamorphic rock will melt and form magma. Metamorphic rock can also be altered by heat and pressure to form a different type of metamorphic rock. Metamorphic rock can also be broken down by weathering and erosion to form sediment that forms sedimentary rock.

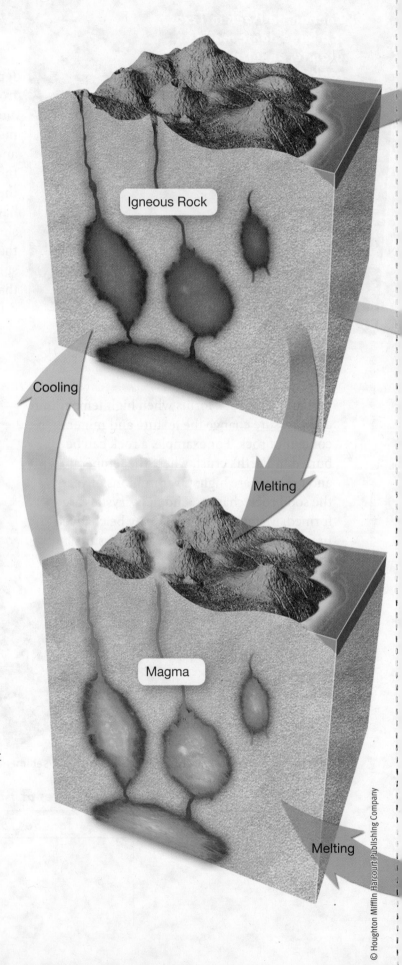

Igneous Rock

Cooling

Melting

Magma

Melting

(A) _____

_____

Visualize It!

12 Apply Label the missing rock type (B) and processes (A and C) on the diagram of the rock cycle.

(B) _____

Temperature and pressure

(C) _____

_____

_____

Weathering, erosion, and deposition

Melting

Think Outside the Book

13 Apply Write a series of blog entries from the viewpoint of igneous rock that is changing into sedimentary rock.

Metamorphic Rock

14 Identify List one process that happens above Earth's surface.

_____

List one process that happens below Earth's surface.

_____

How do tectonic plate motions affect the rock cycle?

Tectonic plate motions can move rock around. Rock that was beneath Earth's surface may become exposed to wind and rain. Sediment or rock on Earth's surface may be buried. Rock can also be changed into metamorphic rock by tectonic plate collisions because of increased temperature and pressure.

By Moving Rock Up or Down

There are two types of vertical movements in Earth's crust: uplift and subsidence. **Uplift** is the rising of regions of the crust to higher elevations. Uplift increases the rate of erosion on rock. **Subsidence** is the sinking of regions of the crust to lower elevations. Subsidence leads to the formation of basins where sediment can be deposited.

By Pulling Apart Earth's Surface

A **rift zone** is an area where a set of deep cracks form. Rift zones are common between tectonic plates that are pulling apart. As they pull apart, blocks of crust in the center of the rift zone subside and the pressure on buried rocks is reduced. The reduction in pressure allows rock below Earth's surface to rise up. As the rock rises, it undergoes partial melting and forms magma. Magma can cool below Earth's surface to form igneous rock. If it reaches the surface, magma becomes lava, which can also cool to form igneous rock.

15 Compare How does uplift differ from subsidence?

_____

_____

_____

16 Predict Label uplift and subsidence on this diagram. What pathway in the rock cycle might rock take next if it is subjected to uplift? Explain your reasoning.

_____

_____

_____

_____

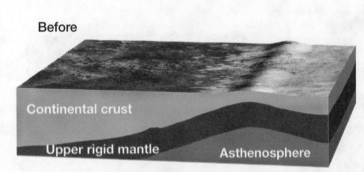

Before

Continental crust

Upper rigid mantle   Asthenosphere

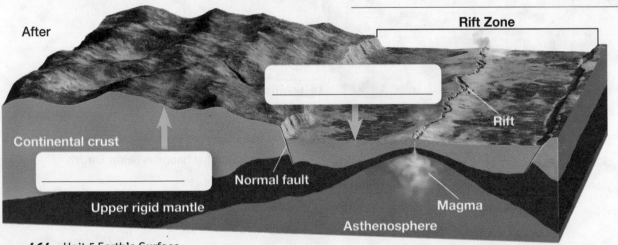

After

Rift Zone

Continental crust

Upper rigid mantle

Normal fault

Rift

Magma

Asthenosphere

Cliff Dwellings

Can you imagine living on the side of a cliff? Some ancient peoples could! They created dwellings from cliff rock. They also decorated rock with art, as you can see in the pictographs shown below.

Cliff Palace
This dwelling in Colorado is called the Cliff Palace. It was home to the Ancient Puebloans from about 550 to 1300 CE.

Cliff Art
These pictographs are located at the Gila Cliff Dwellings in New Mexico.

A Palace in Rock
Ancient cliff dwellings are also found outside the United States. These dwellings from about 70 CE are located in Petra, Jordan.

Extend

Inquiry

17 Identify Describe how ancient people used rock to create shelter.

18 Research Find out how people lived in one of the cliff dwelling locations. How did living in a rock environment affect their daily lives?

19 Produce Illustrate how the people lived by doing one of the following: write a play, write a song, or create a graphic novel.

Visual Summary

To complete this summary, use what you know about the rock cycle to fill in the blanks below. Then use the key below to check your answers. You can use this page to review the main concepts of the lesson.

Each rock type can change into another of the three types.

20 When sediment is pressed together and cemented, the sediment becomes

_____

21 When lava cools and solidifies,

_____ forms.

22 Metamorphic rock can be altered by temperature and pressure to form a different type of

_____

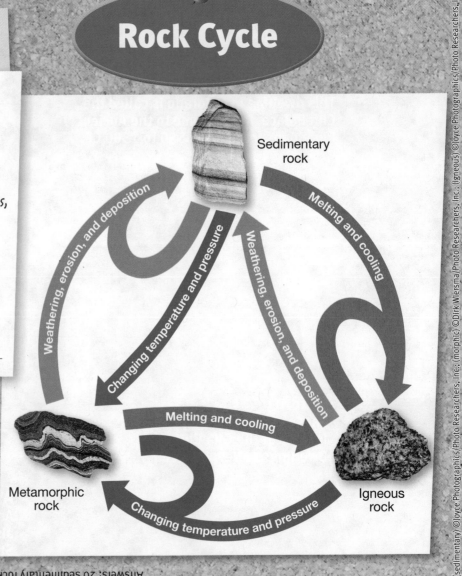

Rock Cycle

Sedimentary rock

Weathering, erosion, and deposition

Melting and cooling

Changing temperature and pressure

Weathering, erosion, and deposition

Melting and cooling

Metamorphic rock

Changing temperature and pressure

Igneous rock

Answers: 20 sedimentary rock; 21 Igneous rock; 22 metamorphic rock

23 Explain What factors and processes can affect the pathway that igneous rock takes in the rock cycle?

Lesson Review

Vocabulary

In your own words, define the following terms.

1 Rock cycle

_____

_____

2 Weathering

_____

_____

3 Rift zone

_____

_____

Key Concepts

Use these photos to classify the rock as sedimentary, igneous, or metamorphic.

Example	Type of rock
4 Classify This rock is made up of the mineral calcite, and it formed from the remains of organisms that lived in water.	
5 Classify Through high temperature and pressure, this rock formed from a sedimentary rock.	
6 Classify This rock is made of tiny crystals that formed quickly when molten rock cooled at Earth's surface.	

7 Describe How can sedimentary rock become metamorphic rock? Explain your reasoning.

_____

_____

_____

8 Explain How can subsidence lead to the formation of sedimentary rock?

_____

_____

_____

9 Explain Why are rift zones common places for igneous rock to form?

_____

_____

_____

Critical Thinking

10 Hypothesize What would happen to the rock cycle if erosion did not occur?

_____

_____

_____

11 Criticize A classmate states that igneous rock must always become sedimentary rock next, according to the rock cycle. Explain why this statement is not correct.

_____

_____

_____

12 Predict Granite is an igneous rock that forms from magma cooled below Earth's surface. Why would granite have larger crystals than igneous rocks formed from lava cooled above Earth's surface?

_____

_____

_____

My Notes

Analyzing Technology

Skills
Identify risks
Identify benefits
✓ Evaluate cost of technology
✓ Evaluate environmental impact
✓ Propose improvements
Propose risk reduction
✓ Compare technology
✓ Communicate results

Objectives
• Analyze the life cycle of an aluminum can.
• Analyze the life cycle of a glass bottle.
• Evaluate the cost of recycling versus disposal of technology.
• Analyze the environmental impact of technology.

Analyzing the Life Cycles of Aluminum and Glass

A life cycle analysis is a way to evaluate the real cost of a product. The analysis considers how much money an item costs to make. It also examines how making the product affects the economy and the environment through the life of the product. Engineers, scientists, and technologists use this information to improve processes and to compare products.

Costs of Production

Have you ever wondered where an aluminum soda can comes from? Have you wondered where the can goes when you are done with it? If so, you have started a life cycle analysis by asking the right questions. Aluminum is a metal found in a type of rock called *bauxite*. To get aluminum, first bauxite must be mined. The mined ore is then shipped to a processing plant. There, the bauxite is melted to get aluminum in a process called *smelting*. After smelting, the aluminum is processed. It may be shaped into bicycle parts or rolled into sheets to make cans. Every step in the production involves both financial costs and environmental costs that must be considered in a life cycle analysis.

Many bicycles are made of aluminum because it is lightweight and strong.

Costs of Disposal

After an aluminum can is used it can travel either to a landfill or to a recycling plant. The process of recycling an aluminum can does require the use of some energy. However, the financial and environmental costs of disposing of a can and mining ore are much greater than the cost of recycling a can. Additionally, smelting bauxite produces harmful wastes. A life cycle analysis of an aluminum can must include the cost and environmental effects of mining, smelting, and disposing of the aluminum can.

1 Analyze After a can is recycled, which steps are no longer part of the life cycle?

_____

_____

_____

_____

_____

Bauxite mining

Most bauxite mining occurs far away from where aluminum is used. Large ships or trains transport the ore before it is made into aluminum products.

Aluminum is one of the easiest materials to recycle. Producing a ton of aluminum by shredding and remelting uses about 5% of the energy needed to process enough bauxite to make a ton of aluminum.

Smelting

Fabrication

Remelting

Shredding

Recycling

Life Cycle of an Aluminum Can

Manufacturing

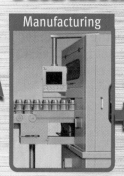

Consumer use

2 Evaluate In the life cycle shown here, which two steps could include an arrow to indicate disposal?

_____

_____

✋ **You Try It!** ➡

Now it's your turn to analyze the life cycle of a product.

✋ You Try It!

Now, apply what you have learned about the life cycle of aluminum to analyze the life cycle of a glass bottle. Glass is made by melting silica from sand or from mineral deposits mined from the Earth. A kiln heats the silica until it melts to form a red-hot glob. Then, the glass is shaped and cooled to form useful items.

① Evaluate Cost of Technology

As a group, discuss the steps that would be involved in making a glass bottle. List the steps in the space below. Start with mining and end at a landfill. Include as many steps in the process as you can think of. Beside each step, tell whether there would be financial costs, environmental costs, or both.

Life Cycle of a Glass Bottle

② Evaluate Environmental Impact

Use the table below to indicate which of the steps listed above would have environmental costs, and what type of cost would be involved. A step can appear in more than one column.

Cause pollution	Consume energy	Damage habitat

③ Propose Improvements

In your group, discuss how you might improve the life cycle of a glass bottle and reduce the impact on the environment. Draw a life cycle that includes your suggestions for improvement.

④ Compare Technology

How does your improved process decrease the environmental effects of making and using glass bottles?

_____

_____

_____

_____

⑤ Communicate Results

Imagine that you are an accountant for a company that produces glass bottles. In the space below, write an argument for using recycled glass that is based on financial savings for your company.

_____

_____

_____

_____

Three Classes of Rock

ESSENTIAL QUESTION

How do rocks form?

By the end of this lesson, you should be able to describe the formation and classification of sedimentary, igneous, and metamorphic rocks.

Wind and water have eroded the softer rock surrounding Ship Rock, an igneous landform in New Mexico.

 S6E5.c Rock formation and the rock cycle

Lesson Labs

Quick Labs
- Stretching Out
- Observing Rocks

S.T.E.M. Lab
- Modeling Rock Formation

Engage Your Brain

1 Predict Check T or F to show whether you think each statement is true or false.

T **F**

☐ ☐ All rocks form deep beneath Earth's surface.

☐ ☐ Some rocks are made up of materials from living things.

☐ ☐ Some rocks take millions of years to form.

☐ ☐ All rocks are made up of the same kinds of minerals.

☐ ☐ Some rocks form from particles of other rocks.

2 Identify How do you think rocks might form as a result of the volcanic activity shown here?

_____

_____

_____

_____

Active Reading

3 Apply Use context clues to write your own definition for the words *composition* and *texture*.

Example sentence:
The <u>composition</u> of the trail mix was 50% nuts, 30% dried fruit, and 20% granola.

composition:

_____

_____

Example sentence:
Because glass is smooth, flat, and shiny, it has a much different <u>texture</u> than wood does.

texture:

_____

_____

Vocabulary Terms
- rock
- texture
- composition

4 Apply As you learn the definition of each vocabulary term in this lesson, create your own definition or sketch to help you remember the meaning of the term.

A Rocky World

How are rocks classified?

A combination of one or more minerals or organic matter is called **rock**. Scientists divide rock into three classes based on how each class of rock forms. The three classes of rock are igneous, sedimentary, and metamorphic. Each class of rock can be further divided into more specific types of rock. For example, igneous rocks can be divided based on where they form. All igneous rock forms when molten rock cools and solidifies. However, some igneous rocks form on Earth's surface and others form within Earth's crust. Sedimentary and metamorphic rocks are also divided into more specific types of rock. How do scientists understand how to classify rocks? They observe their composition and texture.

By Mineral Composition

The minerals and organic matter a rock contains determine the **composition**, or makeup, of that rock, as shown below. Many rocks are made up mostly of the minerals quartz and feldspar, which contain a large amount of the compound silica. Other rocks have different compositions. The limestone rock shown below is made up mostly of the mineral calcite.

Active Reading

5 Identify As you read, underline two properties that are used to classify rock.

Do the Math

6 Graph Fill in the percentage grid on the right to show the amounts of calcite and aragonite in limestone.

Composition of a Sample of Granite

- Feldspar 65%
- Quartz 25%
- Mica 10%

Composition of a Sample of Limestone

- Calcite 95%
- Aragonite 5%

Granite is made of silica minerals.

Limestone is made of carbonate minerals.

By Texture

The size, shape, and positions of the grains that make up a rock determine a rock's **texture**. Coarse-grained rock has large grains that are easy to see with your eyes. Fine-grained rock has small grains that can only be seen by using a hand lens or microscope. The texture of a rock may give clues as to how and where it formed. Igneous rock can be fine-grained or coarse-grained depending on the time magma takes to cool. The texture of metamorphic rock depends on the rock's original composition and the temperature and pressure at which the rock formed. The rocks shown below look different because they formed in different ways.

Visualize It!

7 Describe Observe the sedimentary rocks on this page and describe their texture as coarse-grained, medium-grained, or fine-grained.

This mudstone is made up of microscopic particles of clay.

B _____

_____

This sandstone formed from sand grains that once made up a sand dune.

A _____

_____

This breccia is composed of broken fragments of rock cemented together.

C _____

_____

The Furnace Below

What are two kinds of igneous rock?

Igneous rock forms when hot, liquid magma cools into solid rock. Magma forms when solid rock melts below Earth's surface. Magma flows through passageways up toward Earth's surface. Magma can cool and harden below Earth's surface, or it can make its way above Earth's surface and become lava.

Intrusive Igneous Rock

When magma does not reach Earth's surface, it cools in large chambers, in cracks, or between layers in the surrounding rock. When magma pushes into, or intrudes, surrounding rock below Earth's surface and cools, the rock that forms is called *intrusive igneous rock*. Magma that is well insulated by surrounding rock cools very slowly. The minerals form large, visible crystals. Therefore, intrusive igneous rock generally has a coarse-grained texture. Examples of intrusive igneous rock are granite and diorite. A sample of diorite is shown at the left.

Diorite is an example of intrusive igneous rock.

8 Infer What evidence supports the claim that diorite is an intrusive igneous rock?

_____

Deep Inside Earth The amount of time magma takes to cool determines the texture of an igneous rock.

Crystals Slow-cooling magma has time to form large mineral crystals. The resulting rock is coarse-grained.

Magma chamber Magma chambers deep inside Earth contain pools of molten rock. Magma cools slowly in large chambers such as this.

© Houghton Mifflin Harcourt Publishing Company • Image Credits: ©Dirk Wiersma/Photo Researchers, Inc.

© Houghton Mifflin Harcourt Publishing Company • Image Credits: (t) ©Images & Volcans/Photo Researchers, Inc.; (b) ©Harry Taylor/Dorling Kindersley/Getty Images

Near or at Earth's Surface
Fine-grained igneous rock forms as lava cools quickly at Earth's surface.

Extrusive Igneous Rock

Igneous rock that forms when lava erupts, or extrudes, onto Earth's surface is called *extrusive igneous rock*. Extrusive igneous rock is common around the sides and bases of volcanoes. Lava cools very quickly at Earth's surface. So, there is very little time for crystal formation. Because there is little time for crystals to form, extrusive rocks are made up of very small crystals and have a fine-grained texture. Obsidian (ahb•SID•ee•uhn) is an extrusive rock that cools so rapidly that no crystals form. Obsidian looks glassy, so it is often called *volcanic glass*. Other common extrusive igneous rocks are basalt and andesite.

Lava flows form when lava erupts from a volcano. The photo above shows an active lava flow. Sometimes lava erupts and flows from long cracks in Earth's crust called *fissures*. It also flows on the ocean floor at places where tension is causing Earth's crust to pull apart.

Active Reading **9 Explain** How does the rate at which magma cools affect the texture of igneous rock?

_____

_____

Basalt is an example of extrusive igneous rock.

10 Compare Use the Venn diagram to compare and contrast intrusive igneous rock and extrusive igneous rock.

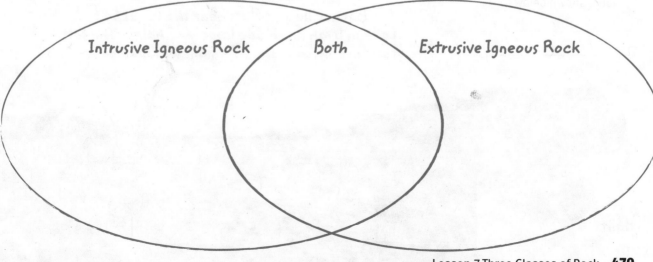

Intrusive Igneous Rock   Both   Extrusive Igneous Rock

Lay It On!

Horizontal layers of clastic sedimentary rocks and volcanic ash are exposed at Badlands National Park in South Dakota.

Sandstone

What are three types of sedimentary rock?

All the processes that form sedimentary rock occur mainly at or near the surface of Earth. Some of these processes include weathering, erosion, deposition, burial, and cementation. Based on the way that they form, scientists classify sedimentary rocks as clastic, chemical, and organic sedimentary rock.

Clastic Sedimentary Rock

Clastic sedimentary rock forms when sediments are buried, compacted, and cemented together by calcite or quartz. The size of the sediment, or clasts, that makes up the rock is used to classify clastic sedimentary rocks. Fine-grained sedimentary rocks, in which grains are too small to be seen, include mudstone, siltstone, and shale. Sandstone, which is shown at the left, is a medium-grained clastic sedimentary rock with visible grains. Breccia and conglomerate are coarse-grained clastic sedimentary rocks made of large particles, such as pebbles, cobbles, and boulders.

Chemical Sedimentary Rock

Chemical sedimentary rocks form when water, usually seawater, evaporates. Most water contains dissolved minerals. As water evaporates, the minerals in water become concentrated to the point that they precipitate out of solution and crystallize. Halite, or rock salt, is an example of chemical sedimentary rock. It is made of sodium chloride, NaCl. Halite forms when sodium ions and chlorine ions in shallow bodies of water become so concentrated that halite crystallizes from solution.

 Visualize It!

11 Identify How would you describe the texture of the halite shown below?

_____

_____

The Bonneville Salt Flats near the Great Salt Lake in Utah are made largely of halite. The salt flats are the remains of an ancient lake bed.

Halite

The White Cliffs of Dover on the English sea coast are made up of the skeletons of the marine alga that is shown below.

Skeleton of a marine alga

Organic Sedimentary Rock

Organic sedimentary rock forms from the remains or fossils, of once-living plants and animals. Most limestone forms from the fosssils of organisms that once lived in the ocean. Over time, the skeletons of these marine organisms, which are made of calcium carbonate, collect on the ocean floor. These animal remains, together with sediment, are eventually buried, compacted, and cemented together to form *fossiliferous* [fahs•uh•LIF•er•uhs] limestone.

Coquina is a fossiliferous limestone that consists of the shells of marine mollusks that have been cemented together by calcite. Chalk is a soft, white limestone that is made up of the skeletons of microorganisms that collect in huge numbers on the floor of the deep ocean.

Coal is another type of organic sedimentary rock. It forms when plant material is buried and changes into coal as a result of increasing heat and pressure. This process occurs over millions of years.

Active Reading **12 Identify** What are two types of organic sedimentary rock?

_____

_____

13 Compare Use the table to compare and contrast clastic, chemical, and organic sedimentary rock.

Three Types of Sedimentary Rock

Clastic	Chemical	Organic

The Heat Is On!

Sedimentary shale

Slate

Phyllite

When shale is exposed to increasing temperature and pressure, different foliated metamorphic rocks form.

What are two types of metamorphic rock?

As a rock is exposed to high temperature and pressure, the crystal structures of the minerals in the rock change to form new minerals. This process results in the formation of metamorphic rock, which has either a foliated texture or a nonfoliated texture.

Foliated Metamorphic Rock

The metamorphic process in which mineral grains are arranged in planes or bands is called *foliation* (foh•lee•AY•shuhn). Foliation occurs when pressure causes the mineral grains in a rock to realign to form parallel bands.

Metamorphic rocks with a foliated texture include slate, phyllite, schist (SHIST), and gneiss (NYS). Slate and phyllite are commonly produced when shale, a fine-grained sedimentary rock, is exposed to an increase in temperature and pressure. The minerals in slate and phyllite are squeezed into flat, sheet-like layers. With increasing temperature and pressure, phyllite may become schist, a coarse-grained foliated rock. With further increases in temperature and pressure, the minerals in schist separate into alternating bands of light and dark minerals. Gneiss is a coarse-grained, foliated rock that forms from schist. Slate, phyllite, schist, and gneiss can all begin as shale, but they are very different rocks. Each rock forms under a certain range of temperatures and pressures, and contains different minerals.

Schist

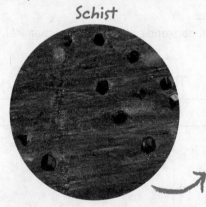

Gneiss

14 Describe What happens to the minerals as gneiss forms from schist?

_____

_____

Image Credits: (t) ©HMH; (tc) ©HMH; (bl) ©HMH; (bc) ©HMH; (br) ©Krystyna Szulecka Photography/Alamy

Nonfoliated Metamorphic Rock

Metamorphic rocks that do not have mineral grains that are aligned in planes or bands are called *nonfoliated*. Nonfoliated metamorphic rocks are commonly made of one or only a few minerals. During metamorphism, mineral grains or crystals may change size or shape, and some may change into another mineral.

Two common nonfoliated metamorphic rocks are quartzite and marble. Quartzite forms when quartz sandstone is exposed to high temperature and pressure. This causes the sand grains to grow larger and the spaces between the sand grains disappear. For that reason, quartzite is very hard and not easily broken down.

When limestone undergoes metamorphism, the limestone becomes marble. During the process of metamorphism, the calcite crystals in the marble grow larger than the calcite grains in the original limestone.

The mineral grains in quartzite (top) and crystals in marble (bottom) do not form bands.

![Active Reading] **15 Apply** What are two characteristics of nonfoliated metamorphic rocks?

_____

_____

Marble is a nonfoliated metamorphic rock that forms when limestone is metamorphosed. Marble is used to build monuments and statues.

Think Outside the Book Inquiry

16 Apply With a classmate, discuss how different types of rocks can be used as building or construction materials.

© Houghton Mifflin Harcourt Publishing Company • Image Credits: (t) ©Colin Keates/Natural History Museum London/Dorling Kindersley/Getty Images; (c) ©HMH; (b) ©Grant Faint/The Image Bank/Getty Images

Visual Summary

To complete this summary, fill in the blanks. Then, use the key below to check your answers. You can use this page to review the main concepts of the lesson.

Sedimentary rock may form from layers of sediment that are cemented together.

17 Sedimentary rocks can be classified into three groups:

_____,

_____, and

_____

Three Classes of Rock

Igneous rock forms from magma or lava that has cooled and hardened.

18 Igneous rocks can be classified into two groups:

_____

and _____

Metamorphic rock forms under high temperature or pressure deep within Earth's crust.

19 Metamorphic rocks can be classified into two groups:

_____

and _____

Answers: 17 clastic, chemical, organic; 18 intrusive, extrusive; 19 foliated, nonfoliated

20 Claims • Evidence • Reasoning While hiking in the mountains, you see a large outcrop of marble. State a process by which the metamorphic rock marble forms from the sedimentary rock limestone. Summarize evidence to support your claim and explain your reasoning.

Lesson Review

Vocabulary

Fill in the blank with the term that best completes the following sentence.

1 Sedimentary rocks that are made up of large pebbles and stones have a coarse-grained

_____

2 Most granite has a _____ of quartz, mica, and feldspar.

3 _____ can be considered to be mixtures of minerals.

Key Concepts

4 Summarize How does the cooling rate of magma or lava affect the texture of the igneous rock that forms?

_____

_____

_____

_____

_____

_____

5 Describe How does clastic sedimentary rock form?

_____

_____

_____

6 Explain What is the difference between foliated and nonfoliated metamorphic rock?

_____

_____

_____

_____

_____

Critical Thinking

Use this photo to answer the following questions.

7 Identify What type of rock is shown here? What evidence supports your claim?

_____

_____

_____

_____

8 Describe How did this rock form? Explain your reasoning.

_____

_____

_____

9 Infer Suppose this rock was exposed to high temperatures and pressure. What would most likely happen to it?

_____

_____

_____

10 Infer What information can a foliated metamorphic rock provide you about the conditions under which it formed?

_____

_____

_____

_____

_____

My Notes

Lesson 1
ESSENTIAL QUESTION
How does weathering change Earth's surface?

Analyze the effects of physical and chemical weathering on Earth's surface, including examples of each kind of weathering.

Lesson 2
ESSENTIAL QUESTION
How does water change Earth's surface?

Relate the processes of erosion and deposition by water to the landforms that result from these processes.

Lesson 3
ESSENTIAL QUESTION
How do wind, ice, and gravity change Earth's surface?

Describe erosion and deposition by wind, ice, and gravity as well as identify the landforms that result from these processes.

Lesson 4
ESSENTIAL QUESTION
How does soil form?

Describe the physical and chemical characteristics of soil layers and identify the factors that affect soil formation, including the action of living things.

Lesson 5
ESSENTIAL QUESTION
What are minerals, how do they form, and how can they be identified?

Describe the basic structures of minerals and identify different minerals by using their physical properties.

Lesson 6
ESSENTIAL QUESTION
What is the rock cycle?

Describe the series of processes and classes of rocks that make up the rock cycle.

Lesson 7
ESSENTIAL QUESTION
How do rocks form?

Describe the formation and classification of sedimentary, igneous, and metamorphic rocks.

Think Outside the Book

2 Synthesize Choose one of these activities to help synthesize what you have learned in this unit.

☐ Using what you learned in lessons 1, 3, and 4, explain the role that physical weathering plays in soil formation by making a flipbook.

☐ Using what you learned in lessons 5, 6, and 7, plan an investigation to identify minerals present in rocks from your local area. Conduct your investigation and write a short essay to summarize the results.

Connect ESSENTIAL QUESTIONS
Lessons 1 and 3

1 Synthesize Explain how gravity causes erosion.

_____

_____

Unit 5 Review

Name _____

Vocabulary

Fill in each blank with the term that best completes the following sentences.

1 _____ is the dark, organic-rich material formed as a top layer in soil from the decayed remains of plants and animals.

2 The process by which rocks break down as a result of chemical reactions is called _____.

3 A _____ is a naturally occurring, solid combination of one or more minerals or organic matter.

4 The rock material deposited by glaciers as they melt and retreat is called _____.

5 _____ is a physical property used to describe how the surface of a mineral reflects light.

Key Concepts

Read each question below, and circle the best answer.

6 Which term describes the ability a soil has to support plant growth?

   A chemistry

   B fertility

   C texture

   D pore space

7 What are two processes that result in rocks being broken down into smaller pieces?

   A sunlight and glacial melting

   B chemical weathering and physical weathering

   C chemical weathering and deposition

   D physical weathering and humus

8 The table below lists five classes of nonsilicate minerals.

Class	Description	Example
Carbonates	contain carbon and oxygen compounds	calcite
Halides	contain ions of chlorine, fluorine, iodine, and bromine	halite
Native elements	contain only one type of atom	gold
Oxides	contain oxygen compounds	hematite
Sulfides	contain sulfur compounds	pyrite

There are actually six classes of nonsilicate minerals. Which class is missing from this chart?

A feldspars

B micas

C silicates

D sulfates

9 This diagram shows a landform called an alluvial fan.

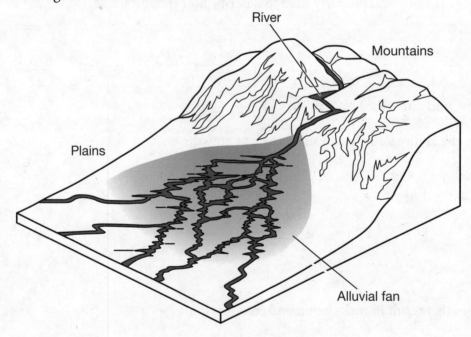

How does an alluvial fan form?

A It forms where a stream enters an ocean or lake, slows down, and deposits sediments there over time.

B It forms from a stream overflowing and depositing sediments.

C It forms where part of a meandering stream is cut off.

D It forms where a stream reaches a flat area of land, slows down, and deposits sediments there over time.

10 While walking along a seashore, Antonio determined that the shore has been affected by stormy seas and rough waves. What did Antonio observe?

A The beach was sandy.   **C** The beach was rocky.

B There were sandbars.   **D** There was a sea stack.

11 Landslides, rockfalls, and creep are examples of erosion and deposition by which erosion agent?

A gravity   **C** oxidation

B solar energy   **D** wind

12 Granite can form when magma cools within Earth. Basalt can form when lava cools on Earth's surface. What do granite and basalt have in common?

A They are igneous.

B They are old.

C They are fossils.

D They are intrusive.

13 A student is trying to identify a mineral in science class.

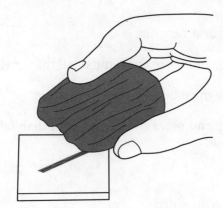

What property of the mineral is the student testing?

A cleavage   **C** luster

B color   **D** streak

14 The diagram below shows a landform called a sinkhole.

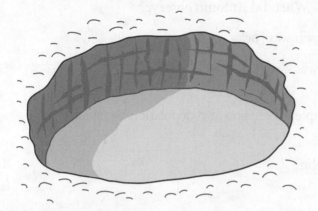

How does a sinkhole form?

A Stalactites erode the ceiling of a cavern.

B A flowing stream in the mountains erodes sediment and the ground caves in.

C Underground water erodes rock forming a cavern, and over time the cavern's roof collapses.

D A flowing stream erodes soil and rock making the stream deeper and wider.

15 A glacier is a large mass of moving ice. What conditions are necessary for a glacier to form?

A The weather must be below freezing and very dry.

B The weather must be below freezing, and more snow must fall than melt.

C The weather must be mild, and there must be a lot of precipitation.

D The weather must be below freezing, and more snow must melt than fall.

Critical Thinking

Answer the following questions in the space provided.

16 Explain whether water is a cause of either chemical weathering, physical weathering, or both.

_____

_____

_____

_____

17 Below is a diagram of the soil profile of three layers of soil.

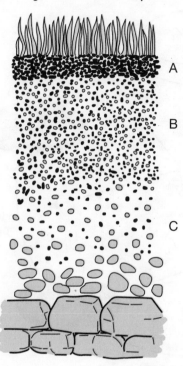

Describe the characteristics and properties of the three layers of soil.

_____

_____

_____

_____

_____

18 You are standing by a cliff far away from the ocean. You see a sedimentary layer with shells in it. You are told the shells are from oceanic organisms. How do you think this layer formed?

_____

_____

_____

_____

19 The diagram below shows the rock cycle.

The rock cycle describes how rocks change. What conditions must be present for igneous or sedimentary rock to change into metamorphic rock? Name two ways that this could happen.

_____

_____

_____

Connect **ESSENTIAL QUESTIONS**
Lessons 2 and 3

Answer the following question in the space provided.

20 How can water and gravity work together to erode soil, sediment, and rock? Give two examples. _____

_____

_____

Explain how water deposits soil, sediment, and rock. Give two examples. _____

_____

_____

_____

The Restless Earth

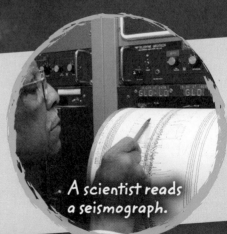

Big Idea

Earth's surface has changed over time as a result of the movement of tectonic plates and other natural processes.

S6E5., S6E5.a, S6E5.e, S6E5.f, S6E5.g

The Cleveland volcano in Alaska erupts.

A scientist reads a seismograph.

What do you think?

Earth is continuously changing. How can volcanoes and earthquakes change Earth's landscape? How do we know how the Earth has changed? As you explore the unit, gather evidence to help you state and support claims to answer these questions.

Unit 6
The Restless Earth

CITIZEN SCIENCE
Stable Structures

The building on the right, located in San Francisco, was engineered to protect it from earthquakes.

① Think About It

A People in different parts of the United States—and all over the world—need to make buildings earthquake-proof. Where would it be of most importance to have earthquake-proof buildings?

_____

_____

B The taller the building, the more difficult it is to make it safe during an earthquake. Why do you think this is?

_____

_____

_____

C Some materials survive the shaking from an earthquake, while others crumble or crack. What materials might withstand an earthquake? Why?

_____

_____

_____

_____

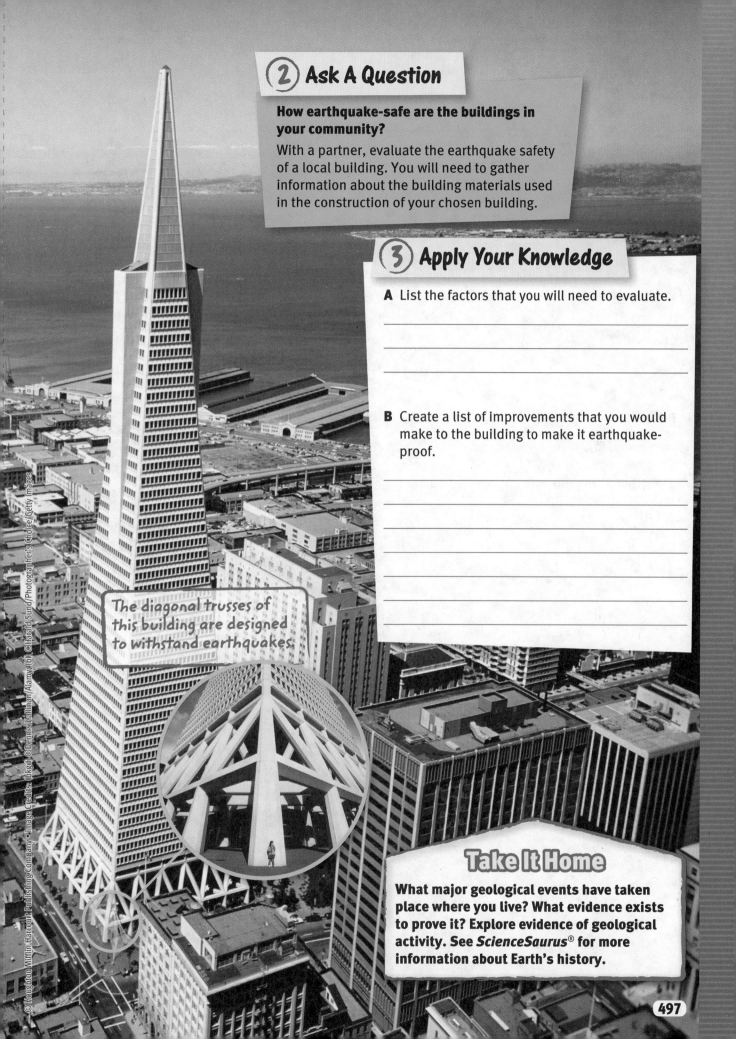

② Ask A Question

How earthquake-safe are the buildings in your community?

With a partner, evaluate the earthquake safety of a local building. You will need to gather information about the building materials used in the construction of your chosen building.

③ Apply Your Knowledge

A List the factors that you will need to evaluate.

_____

_____

_____

B Create a list of improvements that you would make to the building to make it earthquake-proof.

_____

_____

_____

_____

_____

_____

_____

_____

The diagonal trusses of this building are designed to withstand earthquakes.

Take It Home

What major geological events have taken place where you live? What evidence exists to prove it? Explore evidence of geological activity. See *ScienceSaurus®* for more information about Earth's history.

Earth's Layers

ESSENTIAL QUESTION

What are Earth's layers?

By the end of this lesson, you should be able to identify Earth's compositional and physical layers and describe their properties.

S6E5.a Earth's layers

If you could dig below this canyon, you would discover that Earth is made up of different layers below its surface.

Lesson Labs

Quick Labs
• Layers of Earth
• Ordering Earth's Layers

S.T.E.M. Lab
• Models of Earth

Engage Your Brain

1 Predict Check T or F to show whether you think each statement is true or false.

T	F	
☐	☐	The outermost layer of solid Earth is sometimes called the crust.
☐	☐	The crust is the densest layer.
☐	☐	The mantle is the layer between the crust and the core.
☐	☐	Earth's core is divided into five parts.

2 Describe If you were asked to describe this apple, how many layers would you say it has? How would you describe the layers?

_____
_____
_____
_____
_____
_____

Active Reading

3 Synthesize You can often define an unknown word if you know the meaning of its word parts. Use the word parts and sentence below to make an educated guess about the meaning of the word *mesosphere*.

Word part	Meaning
meso-	middle
-sphere	ball

Example sentence
The <u>mesosphere</u> is more than 2,000 km thick.

mesosphere:

_____
_____
_____

Vocabulary Terms

• crust   • lithosphere
• mantle   • asthenosphere
• convection   • mesosphere
• core

4 Distinguish Many of this lesson's vocabulary terms refer to Earth's layers. Make a list of questions to help you compare and contrast each layer as you learn the meaning of each term.

Peeling the Layers

What is inside Earth?

If you tried to dig to the center of Earth, what do you think you would find? Would Earth be solid or hollow? Would it be made of the same material throughout? Actually, Earth is made of several layers. The materials that make up each layer have characteristic properties that vary from layer to layer. Scientists think about Earth's layers in two ways—in terms of their chemical composition and in terms of their physical properties.

Think Outside the Book Inquiry

5 Analyze With a classmate, discuss why scientists might have two ways for thinking about Earth's layers. Support your claims with evidence.

What are Earth's compositional layers?

Earth can be divided into three layers based on chemical composition. These layers are called the *crust*, the *mantle*, and the *core*. Each compositional layer is made up of a different mixture of chemicals.

Earth is divided into three layers based on the chemical composition of each layer.

core

mantle

crust

continental crust

oceanic crust

mantle

Continental crust is thicker than oceanic crust.

Crust

The outermost solid layer of Earth is the **crust.** There are two types of crust—continental and oceanic. Both types are made mainly of the elements oxygen, silicon, and aluminum. However, the denser oceanic crust has almost twice as much iron, calcium, and magnesium. These elements form minerals that are denser than those in the continental crust.

Mantle

The **mantle** is located between the core and the crust. It is a region of hot, slow-flowing, solid rock. When convection takes place in the mantle, cooler rock sinks and warmer rock rises. **Convection** is the movement of matter that results from differences in density caused by variations in temperature. Scientists can learn about the mantle by observing mantle rock that has risen to Earth's surface. The mantle is denser than the crust. It contains more magnesium and less aluminum and silicon than the crust does.

Core

The **core** extends from below the mantle to the center of Earth. Scientists think that the core is made mostly of iron and some nickel. Scientists also think that it contains much less oxygen, silicon, aluminum, and magnesium than the mantle does. The core is the densest layer. It makes up about one-third of Earth's mass.

Active Reading **7 Identify** What element makes up most of Earth's core? _____

What are Earth's physical layers?

Earth can also be divided into layers based on physical properties. The properties considered include whether the layer is solid or liquid, and how the layer moves or transmits waves. The five physical layers are the *lithosphere, asthenosphere, mesosphere, outer core*, and *inner core*.

Active Reading **8 Label** Write the names of the compositional layers shown below in the spaces provided.

Visualize It!

9 Claims • Evidence • Reasoning Which of Earth's compositional layers make up the lithosphere? Explain your reasoning.

_____

_____

Lithosphere

The outermost, rigid layer of Earth is the **lithosphere.** The lithosphere is made of two parts—the crust and the rigid, upper part of the mantle. The lithosphere is divided into pieces called *tectonic plates*.

A _____

Asthenosphere

The **asthenosphere** is a layer of weak or soft mantle that is made of rock that flows slowly. Tectonic plates move on top of this layer.

Mesosphere

The strong, lower part of the mantle is called the **mesosphere.** Rock in the mesosphere flows more slowly than rock in the asthenosphere does.

B _____

Outer Core

The outer core is the liquid layer of Earth's core. It lies beneath the mantle and surrounds the inner core.

Inner Core

The inner core is the solid, dense center of our planet that extends from the bottom of the outer core to the center of Earth, which is about 6,380 km beneath the surface.

C _____

 **Do the Math** Sample Problem

Here's an example of how to find the percentage thickness of the core that is the outer core.

Physical	Compositional
Continental lithosphere (150 km)	Continental crust (30 km)
Asthenosphere (250 km)	Mantle (2,900 km)
Mesosphere (2,550 km)	
Outer core (2,200 km)	Core (3,430 km)
Inner core (1,230 km)	

Identify

A. What do you know?
core = 3,430 km   outer core = 2,200 km

B. What do you want to find out?
Percentage of core that is outer core

Plan

C. Write the formula:

Percentage (%) of core that is outer core =

$\left(\dfrac{\text{thickness of outer core}}{\text{thickness of core}}\right) \times 100\%$

D. Substitute into the formula:

$\% = \dfrac{(2{,}200)}{(3{,}430)} \times 100\%$

Solve

E. Calculate and simplify:

$\% = 0.6414 \times 100\% = 64.14\%$

Answer: 64.14%

 **Do the Math** You Try It

10 Calculate What percentage thickness of the continental lithosphere is continental crust?

Identify

A. What do you know?

B. What do you want to find out?

Plan

C. Write the formula:

D. Substitute into the formula:

Solve

E. Calculate and simplify:

Answer:

Visual Summary

To complete this summary, fill in the blanks with the correct word or phrase. Then, use the key below to check your answers. You can use this page to review the main concepts of the lesson.

Earth is divided into three compositional layers.

11 The outermost compositional layer of the Earth is the _____ .

12 The _____ is denser than the crust and contains more magnesium.

Earth is divided into five physical layers.

13 The _____ is divided into pieces called tectonic plates.

14 The _____ core is the liquid layer of Earth's core.

Earth's Layers

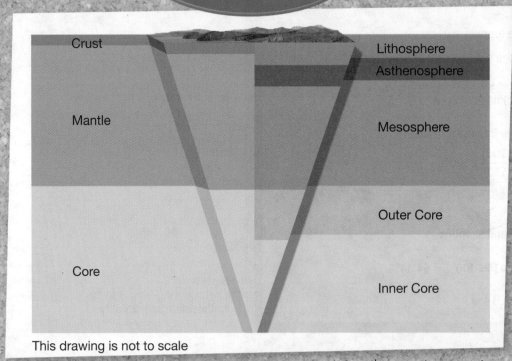

Crust

Mantle

Core

Lithosphere

Asthenosphere

Mesosphere

Outer Core

Inner Core

This drawing is not to scale

15 **Synthesize** Which physical layers correspond to which compositional layers?

Lesson Review

Vocabulary

Fill in the blank with the term that best completes the following sentence.

1 The ___Outer crust___ is a region of hot, slow-flowing, solid rock between the core and the crust.

2 The ___inner crust___ is the densest compositional layer and makes up one-third of Earth's mass.

3 The ___crust___ is the outermost, rigid physical layer of Earth.

Key Concepts

Use this diagram to answer the following questions.

4 Identify Which model of Earth's interior does this image show?

___3 main layers - crust, mantle, core___

5 Identify Which of these layers is made mostly of iron and nickel?

_____

6 Compare Explain the differences between the inner core and the outer core.

___Outer core is mostly made of___
___liquid and inner core is made___
___of motion___

Critical Thinking

7 Compare Explain the difference between the lithosphere and the crust.

___crust is above the___
___lithosphere___

_____

8 Predict Scientists find dense rock on Earth's surface that is made of magnesium and smaller amounts of aluminum and silicon. What layer of Earth might this rock help scientists study? Explain your reasoning.

_____
_____
_____
_____
_____

9 Distinguish Suppose you were asked to identify one of Earth's layers based on its properties. List two questions you might ask to identify the layer. How would the answer to each question help you identify the layer?

_____
_____
_____
_____
_____
_____
_____
_____
_____

My Notes

Lesson 2

Geologic Change over Time

ESSENTIAL QUESTION

How do we learn about Earth's history?

By the end of this lesson, you should be able to explain how Earth materials, such as rock, fossils, and ice, show that Earth has changed over time.

Scientists learn about Earth's history by studying materials such as these rhinoceros fossils in Nebraska.

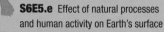

S6E5.e Effect of natural processes and human activity on Earth's surface

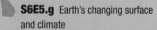

S6E5.g Earth's changing surface and climate

Lesson Labs

Quick Labs
• Modeling the Fossil Record
• Fossil Flipbooks

S.T.E.M. Lab
• Exploring Landforms

Engage Your Brain

1 Predict Check T or F to show whether you think each statement is true or false.

T	F	
☐	☐	Once rock forms, it never changes.
☐	☐	Fossils can tell us which animals lived at a certain time.
☐	☐	The climate is exactly the same all over the world.
☐	☐	A volcano erupting is an example of a geologic process.

2 Explain What can you infer about the environment in which this fossil probably formed?

_____

_____

_____

Active Reading

3 Synthesize You can often define an unknown word if you know the meaning of its word parts. Use the word parts and sentence below to make an educated guess about the meaning of the word *uniformitarianism*.

Word part	Meaning
uniform-	the same in all cases and at all times
-ism	a system of beliefs or actions

Vocabulary Terms

- uniformitarianism
- fossil
- trace fossil
- Pangaea
- climate
- ice core

4 Identify This list contains vocabulary terms you'll learn in this lesson. As you read, circle the definition of each term.

Example sentence
The idea that erosion has occurred the same way throughout Earth's history is an example of <u>uniformitarianism</u>.

uniformitarianism:

_____

_____

Been There,

This inactive volcano last erupted over 4,000 years ago.

This is an active volcano.

What is the principle of uniformitarianism?

The principle of **uniformitarianism** (yoo•nuh•fohr•mih•TAIR•ee•uh•niz•uhm) states that geologic processes that happened in the past can be explained by current geologic processes. Processes such as volcanism and erosion that go on today happened in a similar way in the past. Because geologic processes tend to happen at a slow rate, this means that Earth must be very old. In fact, scientists have shown that Earth is about 4.6 billion years old.

Most geologic change is slow and gradual, but sudden changes have also affected Earth's history. An asteroid hitting Earth may have led to the extinction of the dinosaurs. However, scientists see these as a normal part of geologic change.

Active Reading **5 Describe** In your own words, describe the principle of uniformitarianism.

_____
_____
_____
_____

Visualize It!

6 Identify How do these photos show the principle of uniformitarianism?

_____
_____
_____

Done That

How do organisms become preserved as fossils?

Fossils are the traces or remains of organisms that lived long ago, most commonly preserved in sedimentary rock. Fossils may be skeletons or body parts, shells, burrows, or ancient coral reefs. Fossils form in many different ways.

Visualize It!

Trapped in Amber

Imagine that an insect is caught in soft, sticky tree sap. Suppose that the insect is covered by more sap, which hardens with the body of the insect inside. Amber is formed when hardened tree sap is buried and preserved in sediment. Some of the best insect fossils, such as the one shown below, are found in amber. Fossil spiders, frogs, and lizards have also been found in amber.

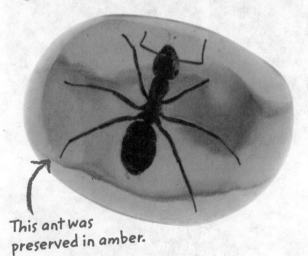

This ant was preserved in amber.

7 Analyze What features of the ant can you still see in this fossil?

_____

_____

_____

Trapped in Asphalt

There are places where asphalt wells up at Earth's surface in thick, sticky pools. One such place is La Brea Tar Pits in California. These asphalt pools have trapped and preserved many fossils over the past 40,000 years, such as the one shown below. Fossils such as these show a lot about what life was like in Southern California in the past.

This water beetle was preserved in asphalt.

8 Describe How did this organism become a fossil?

_____

_____

_____

_____

Buried in Rock

When an organism dies, it often starts to decay or is eaten by other organisms. Sometimes, however, organisms are quickly buried by sediment when they die. The sediment slows down decay and can protect parts of the body from damage. Hard parts of organisms, such as shells and bones, do not break down as easily as soft parts do. So, when sediments become rock, the hard parts of animals are preserved and become part of the rock as the sediments harden.

Visualize It! **9 Analyze** What part of the organism was preserved as a fossil in this rock?

_____

_____

Ammonites once lived in shells in ancient seas.

Become Frozen

In very cold places on Earth, the soil can be frozen all the time. An animal that dies there may also be frozen. It is frozen with skin and flesh, as well as bones. Because cold temperatures slow down decay, many types of frozen fossils are preserved from the last ice age.

Visualize It! **10 Compare** What information can this fossil give that fossils preserved in rock cannot? Support your claim with evidence.

_____

_____

_____

This frozen mammoth was discovered in Siberia.

Become Petrified

Petrification (pet•ruh•fi•KAY•shuhn) happens when an organism's tissues are replaced by minerals. In some petrified wood, minerals have replaced all of the wood. A sample of petrified wood is shown at the right. This wood is in the Petrified Forest National Park in Arizona.

A similar thing happens when the pore space in an organism's hard tissue, such as bone, is filled up with minerals.

This petrified wood is in Arizona.

What are trace fossils?

Active Reading 11 **Identify** As you read, underline examples of trace fossils.

Fossils of organisms can tell us a lot about the bodies of life forms. Another type of fossil may also give evidence about how some animals behaved. A **trace fossil** is a fossilized structure that formed in sedimentary rock by animal activity on or in soft sediment.

Tracks, like the ones across this page, are one type of trace fossil. They are footprints made by animals in soft sediment that later became hard rock. Tracks show a lot about the animal that made them, such as how it lived, how big it was, and how fast it moved. For example, scientists have found paths of tracks showing that a group of dinosaurs moved in the same direction. This has led scientists to hypothesize that some dinosaurs moved in herds.

Burrows are another kind of trace fossil. Burrows are pathways or shelters made by animals, such as clams on the sea floor or rodents on land, that dig in sediment. Some scientists also classify animal dung, called coprolite (KAHP•ruh•lyt), as a trace fossil. Some coprolites are shown at the right.

These tracks were made by dinosaurs that once lived in Utah.

Visualize It! (Inquiry)

12 **Illustrate** Draw two sets of tracks that represent what you might leave for future scientists to study. Draw one set of you walking and another set of you running.

Walking

_____

Running

Time Is on Our Side

Visualize It!

13 Infer What do these fossils of tropical plants from Antarctica tell you about what the climate was once like?

_____

_____

_____

A piece of Antarctica's past

Antarctica today

Active Reading

14 Identify As you read, underline two types of changes on Earth that fossils can give information about.

What can fossils tell us?

All of the fossils that have been discovered on Earth are called the *fossil record*. The fossil record shows part of the history of life on Earth. It is only part of the history because some things are still unknown. Not all the organisms that ever lived have left behind fossils. Also, there are many fossils that have not been discovered yet. Even so, fossils that are available do provide important information about Earth's history.

Fossils can tell scientists about environmental changes over time. The types of fossils preserved in sedimentary rock show what the environment was like when the organisms were alive. For example, fish fossils indicate that an aquatic environment was present. Palm fronds mean a tropical environment was present. Scientists have found fossils of trees and dinosaurs in Antarctica, so the climate there must have been warm in the past.

Fossils can also tell scientists how life forms have changed over time. Major changes in Earth's environmental conditions and surface can influence an organism's survival and the types of adaptations that a species must have to survive. To learn about how life on Earth has changed, scientists study relationships between different fossils and between fossils and living organisms.

How does sedimentary rock show Earth's history?

Rock and mineral fragments move from one place to another during erosion. Eventually, this sediment is deposited in layers. As new layers of sediment are deposited, they cover older layers. Older layers become compacted. Dissolved minerals, such as calcite and quartz, separate from water that passes through the sediment. This forms a natural cement that holds the rock and mineral fragments together in sedimentary rock.

Scientists use different characteristics to classify sedimentary rock. These provide evidence of the environment that the sedimentary rock formed in.

Composition

The composition of sedimentary rock shows the source of the sediment that makes up the rock. Some sedimentary rock forms when rock or mineral fragments are cemented together. Sandstone, shown below, forms when sand grains are deposited and buried, then cemented together. Other sedimentary rock forms from the remains of once-living plants and animals. Most limestone forms from the remains of animals that lived in the ocean. Another sedimentary rock, called coal, forms underground from partially decomposed plant material that is buried beneath sediment.

Active Reading 15 **Describe** What processes can cause rock to break apart into sediment?

_____

_____

_____

Texture and Features

The texture of sedimentary rock shows the environment in which the sediment was carried and deposited. Sedimentary rock is arranged in layers. Layers can differ from one another, depending on the kind, size, and color of their sediment. Features on sedimentary rock called *ripple marks* record the motion of wind or water waves over sediment. An example of sedimentary rock with ripple marks is shown below. Other features, called *mud cracks,* form when fine-grained sediments at the bottom of a shallow body of water are exposed to the air and dry out. Mud cracks show that an ancient lake, stream, or ocean shoreline was once a part of an area.

Visualize It!

16 **Identify** Which arrow shows the direction that water was moving to make these ripple marks?

These are ripple marks in sandstone.

Sandstone

What do Earth's surface features tell us?

Earth's surface is always changing. Continents change position continuously as tectonic plates move across Earth's surface.

Continents Move

The continents have been moving throughout Earth's history. For example, at one time the continents formed a single landmass called **Pangaea** (pan•JEE•uh). Pangaea broke apart about 200 million years ago. Since then, the continents have been slowly moving to their present locations, and continue to move today.

Evidence of Pangaea can be seen by the way rock types, mountains, and fossils are now distributed on Earth's surface. For example, mountain-building events from tectonic plate movements produced different mountain belts on Earth. As the map below shows, rock from one of these mountain belts is now on opposite sides of the Atlantic Ocean. Scientists think this mountain belt separated as continents have moved to their current locations.

Today's continents were once part of a landmass called Pangaea.

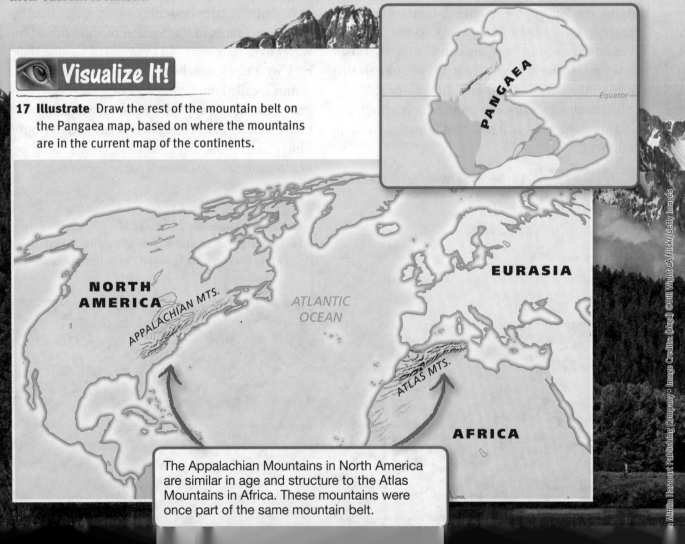

Visualize It!

17 Illustrate Draw the rest of the mountain belt on the Pangaea map, based on where the mountains are in the current map of the continents.

The Appalachian Mountains in North America are similar in age and structure to the Atlas Mountains in Africa. These mountains were once part of the same mountain belt.

Landforms Change over Time

The movement of tectonic plates across Earth has resulted in extraordinary events. When continental plates collide, mountain ranges such as the ones shown below can form. As they pull apart, magma can be released in volcanic eruptions. When they grind past one another, breaks in Earth's surface form, where earthquakes can occur. Collisions between oceanic and continental plates can also cause volcanoes and the formation of mountains.

In addition to forces that build up Earth's surface features, there are forces that break them down as well. Weathering and erosion always act on Earth's surface, changing it with time. For example, high, jagged mountains can become lower and more rounded over time. So, the height and shape of mountains can tell scientists about the geologic history of mountains.

Think Outside the Book

19 **Support** Find out about how the continents continue to move today. Draw a map that shows the relative motion along some of the tectonic plate boundaries.

Visualize It!

18 **Analyze** Label the older and younger mountains below. Explain how you decided which was older and which was younger. Use evidence to support your claim.

_____

_____

_____

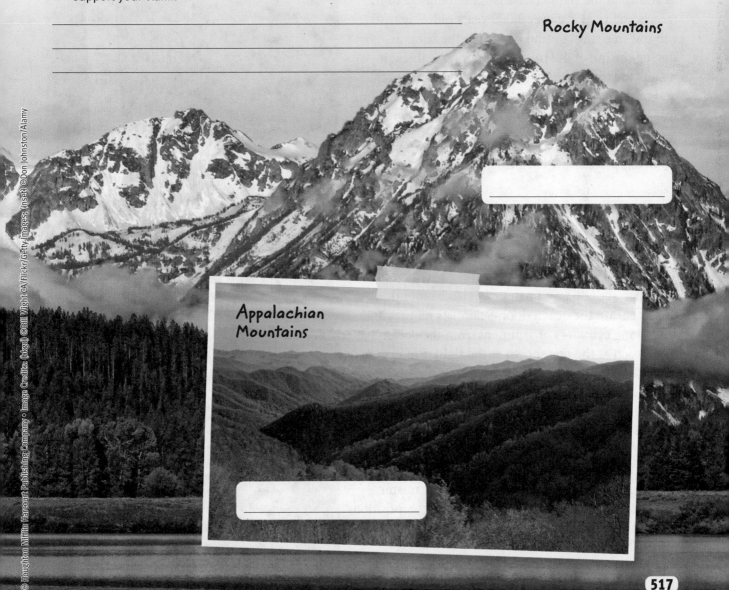

Rocky Mountains

Appalachian Mountains

Back to the Future

What do other materials tell us about Earth's climate history?

The **climate** of an area describes the weather conditions in the area over a long period of time. Climate is mostly determined by temperature and precipitation. In addition to using fossils, scientists also analyze other materials to study how Earth's climate and environmental conditions have changed over time.

Active Reading

20 Identify As you read the next two pages, underline the evidence that scientists use to learn about Earth's climate history.

Trees

When most trees grow, a new layer of wood is added to the trunk every year. This forms rings around the circumference (suhr•KUHM•fuhr•uhns) of the tree, as shown at the right. These rings tell the age of the tree. Some trees are over 2,000 years old. Scientists can use tree rings to find out about the climate during the life of the tree. If a tree ring is thick, it means the tree grew well—there was plenty of rain and favorable temperatures existed at that time. Thin tree rings mean the growing conditions were poor.

Visualize It! 21 Analyze What is the time frame for which this tree can give information about Earth's climate?

1996
1976
1969
1950
1941
1935
1923
1914
1907
1890
1687
1874
1862
1849
1844
1832
1827
1806
1705

Tree rings tell the age of a tree and what the climate was like.

Sea-Floor Sediments

Evidence about past climates can also be found deep beneath the ocean floor. Scientists remove and study long cylinders of sediment from the ocean floor, such as the one shown at the right. Preserved in these sediments are fossil remains of microscopic organisms that have died and settled on the ocean floor. These remains build up in layers, over time. If certain organisms are present, it can mean that the climate was particularly cold or warm at a certain time. The chemical composition of sediments, especially of the shells of certain microorganisms, can also be important. It shows what the composition was of the ocean water and atmosphere when the organisms were alive.

These scientists are studying sediment from the Ross Sea in Antarctica.

Ice

Icecaps are found in places such as Iceland and islands in the Arctic. The icecaps formed as older snow was squeezed into ice by new snow falling on top of it. Scientists can drill down into icecaps to collect a long cylinder of ice, called an **ice core**.

Ice cores, such as the ones shown in these photographs, give a history of Earth's climate over time. Some ice cores have regular layers, called bands, which form each year. Band size shows how much precipitation fell during a given time. The composition of water and concentration of gases in the ice core show the conditions of the atmosphere at the time that the ice formed.

Scientists study ice cores to find out about amounts of precipitation in the past.

---

22 Evaluate Fill in the table by reading the evidence and suggesting what it could mean.

Evidence	What it could mean
A. A scientist finds a fossil of a shark tooth in a layer of rock that is high in the mountains.	
B. Rocks from mountains on two different continents were found to have formed at the same time and to have the same composition.	
C. Upon studying an ice core, scientists find that a particular band is very wide.	

Visual Summary

To complete this summary, check the box that indicates true or false. Then use the key below to check your answers. You can use this page to review the main concepts of the lesson.

Fossils give information about changes in Earth's environments and life forms.

23 Trace fossils give information about animal activity and movement.

☐ True
☐ False

Studying Earth's History

Sedimentary rocks provide information about Earth's geologic history.

24 These are ripple marks in sedimentary rock.

☐ True
☐ False

Earth's surface features reflect its geologic history.

25 Tall, jagged mountains are older than rounded, smaller mountains.

☐ True
☐ False

Besides fossils, other materials give information about Earth's climate history.

26 Scientists study the width of tree rings to learn about past climate conditions.

☐ True
☐ False

Answers: 23 T; 24 T; 25 F; 26 T

27 **Claims • Evidence • Reasoning** Describe three different materials that can be used to study Earth's history. Make a claim about how they provide information about the Earth. Support your claim with evidence and explain your reasoning.

Lesson Review

Vocabulary

In your own words, define the following terms.

1 uniformitarianism _____

_____

2 trace fossil _____

_____

Key Concepts

3 Identify How old is Earth?

_____

4 Explain How can sedimentary rock show Earth's history?

_____

_____

_____

_____

5 List Name three examples of trace fossils.

_____

_____

6 Explain Name five ways that organisms can be preserved as fossils, and explain what fossils can show about Earth's history.

_____

_____

_____

_____

_____

7 Describe How do Earth's surface features indicate changes over time?

_____

_____

_____

8 Describe What are two ways that scientists can study Earth's climate history?

_____

_____

_____

_____

Critical Thinking

9 Justify Is a piece of pottery an example of a fossil? Explain your reasoning.

_____

_____

_____

_____

Use this photo to answer the following questions.

10 Synthesize How does the erosion of these mountains support the principle of uniformitarianism?

_____

_____

_____

11 Infer The type and age of rocks found in this mountain range are also found on another continent. What might this mean?

_____

_____

_____

_____

My Notes

Plate Tectonics

ESSENTIAL QUESTION

What is plate tectonics?

By the end of this lesson, you should be able to explain the theory of plate tectonics, to describe how tectonic plates move, and to identify geologic events that occur because of tectonic plate movement.

The San Andreas Fault is located where two tectonic plates slide past each other.

The course of this river has been shifted as a result of tectonic plate motion.

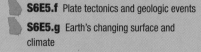

S6E5.f Plate tectonics and geologic events

S6E5.g Earth's changing surface and climate

✋ **Lesson Labs**

Quick Labs
• Tectonic Ice Cubes
• Mantle Convection
• Reconstructing Land Masses

Exploration Lab
• Sea-floor Spreading

🧠 Engage Your Brain

1 Identify Check T or F to show whether you think each statement is true or false.

T   F

☐   ☐   Earth's surface is all one piece.

☐   ☐   Scientists think the continents once formed a single landmass.

☐   ☐   The seafloor is smooth and level.

☐   ☐   All tectonic plates are the same.

2 Predict Imagine that ice cubes are floating in a large bowl of punch. If there are enough cubes, they will cover the surface of the punch and bump into one another. Parts of the cubes will be below the surface of the punch and will displace the punch. Will some cubes displace more punch than others? Explain your answer.

_____

_____

_____

_____

_____

_____

✏️ Active Reading

3 Apply Many scientific words, such as *divergent* and *convergent,* also have everyday meanings or are related to words with everyday meanings. Use context clues to write your own definition for each underlined word.

Example sentence
They argued about the issue because their opinions about it were <u>divergent</u>.

divergent:

_____

_____

Example sentence

The two rivers <u>converged</u> near the town.

convergent:

_____

_____

Vocabulary Terms

• Pangaea
• sea-floor spreading
• plate tectonics
• tectonic plates
• convergent boundary
• divergent boundary
• transform boundary
• convection

4 Identify This list contains key terms you'll learn in this lesson. As you read, underline the definition of each term.

Puzzling Evidence

What evidence suggests that continents move?

Have you ever looked at a map and noticed that the continents look like they could fit together like puzzle pieces? In the late 1800s, Alfred Wegener proposed his hypothesis of continental drift. He proposed that the continents once formed a single landmass, broke up, and drifted. This idea is supported by several lines of evidence. For example, fossils of the same species are found on continents on different sides of the Atlantic Ocean. These species could not have crossed the ocean. The hypothesis is also supported by the locations of mountain ranges and rock formations and by evidence of the same ancient climatic conditions on several continents.

Geologic evidence supports the hypothesis of continental drift.

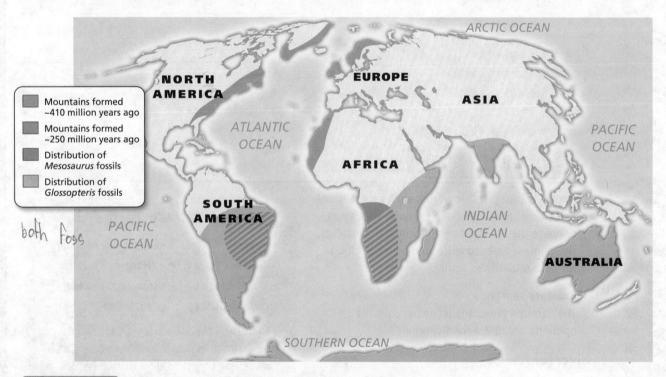

Key:
- Mountains formed ~410 million years ago
- Mountains formed ~250 million years ago
- Distribution of *Mesosaurus* fossils
- Distribution of *Glossopteris* fossils

both foss

👁 **Visualize It!** 5 **Summarize** Using the map and its key, complete the table to describe evidence that indicates each continent pair was once joined.

	Fossil evidence	Mountain evidence
South America and Africa	both fossils are found in both continent	no evidence
North America and Europe	both mountains formed 410 million years ago	no evidence

What is Pangaea?

Active Reading 6 **Identify** As you read, underline the description of how North America formed from Pangaea.

Using evidence from many scientific fields, scientists can construct a picture of continental change throughout time. Scientists think that about 245 million years ago, the continents were joined in a single large landmass they call **Pangaea** (pan•JEE•uh). As the continents collided to form Pangaea, mountains formed. A single, large ocean called Panthalassa surrounded Pangaea.

About 200 million years ago, a large rift formed and Pangaea began to break into two continents—*Laurasia* and *Gondwana*. Then, Laurasia began to drift northward and rotate slowly, and a new rift formed. This rift separated Laurasia into the continents of North America and Eurasia. The rift eventually formed the North Atlantic Ocean. At the same time, Gondwana also broke into two continents. One continent contained land that is now the continents of South America and Africa. The other continent contained land that is now Antarctica, Australia, and India.

About 150 million years ago, a rift between Africa and South America opened to form the South Atlantic Ocean. India, Australia, and Antarctica also began to separate from each other. As India broke away from Australia and Antarctica, it started moving northward, toward Eurasia.

As India and the other continents moved into their present positions, new oceans formed while others disappeared. In some cases, continents collided with other continents. About 50 million years ago, India collided with Eurasia, and the Himalaya Mountains began to form. Mountain ranges form as a result of these collisions, because a collision welds new crust onto the continents and uplifts some of the land.

The Breakup of Pangaea

245 million years ago

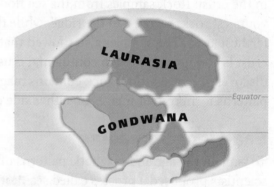

200 million years ago

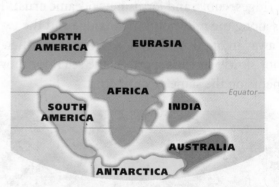

65 million years ago

3 million years ago

What discoveries support the idea of continental drift?

Wegener's ideas of continental drift were pushed aside for many years because scientists could not determine how continents moved. Then, in the mid-1900s, scientists began mapping the sea floor. They expected the floor to be smooth and level. Instead, they found huge under-water mountain ranges called *mid-ocean ridges*. The discovery of mid-ocean ridges eventually led to the theory of plate tectonics, which built on some of Wegener's ideas.

7 Summarize Why would many scientists not accept the hypothesis of continental drift?

Age and Magnetic Properties of the Sea Floor

Scientists learned that the mid-ocean ridges form along cracks in the crust. Rock samples from the sea floor revealed that the youngest rock is closest to the ridge, while the oldest rock is farthest away. The samples also showed that even the oldest ocean crust is young compared to continental crust. Scientists also discovered that sea-floor rock contains magnetic patterns. These patterns form mirror images on either side of a mid-ocean ridge.

Sea-Floor Spreading

To explain the age and magnetic patterns of sea-floor rocks, scientists proposed a process called **sea-floor spreading**. In this process, molten rock from inside Earth rises through the cracks in the ridges, cools, and forms new oceanic crust. The old crust breaks along the mid-point of the ridge and the two pieces of crust move away in opposite directions from each other. In this way, the sea floor slowly spreads apart. As the sea floor moves, so do the continents on the same piece of crust.

This map shows where mid-ocean ridges are located.

Ocean Trenches

If the sea floor has been spreading for millions of years, why is Earth not getting larger? Scientists discovered the answer when they found huge trenches, like deep canyons, in the sea floor. At these sites, dense oceanic crust is sinking into the asthenosphere as shown in the diagram below. Older crust is being destroyed at the same rate new crust is forming. Thus, Earth remains the same size.

With this new information about the sea floor, sea-floor spreading, and ocean trenches, scientists could begin to understand how continents were able to move.

Active Reading

8 Identify Why is Earth not getting larger if the sea floor is spreading?

_____

_____

_____

Visualize It!

9 Provide Label the youngest rock and the oldest rock on this diagram of sea-floor spreading.

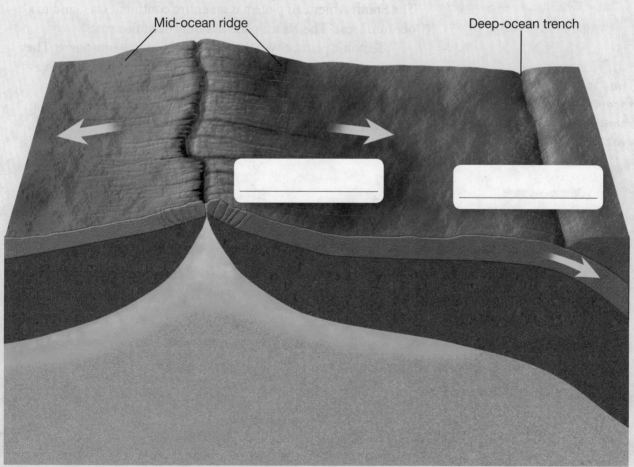

Sea-floor spreading takes place at mid-ocean ridges.

Mid-ocean ridge

Deep-ocean trench

© Houghton Mifflin Harcourt Publishing Company

A Giant Jigsaw

What is the theory of plate tectonics?

As scientists' understanding of continental drift, mid-ocean ridges, and sea-floor spreading grew, scientists formed a theory to explain these processes and features. **Plate tectonics** describes large-scale movements of Earth's lithosphere, which is made up of the crust and the rigid, upper part of the mantle. Plate tectonics explains how and why features in Earth's crust form and continents move.

What is a tectonic plate?

The lithosphere is divided into pieces called **tectonic plates.** These plates move around on top of the asthenosphere. The plates are moving in different directions and at different speeds. Each tectonic plate fits together with the plates that surround it. The continents are located on tectonic plates and move around with them. The major tectonic plates include the Pacific, North American, Nazca, South American, African, Australian, Eurasian, Indian, and Antarctic plates. Not all tectonic plates are the same. The South American plate has an entire continent on it and has oceanic crust. The Nazca plate has only oceanic crust.

Tectonic plates cover the surface of the asthenosphere. They vary in size, shape, and thickness. Thick tectonic plates, such as those with continents, displace more asthenosphere than thin oceanic plates do. But, oceanic plates are much more dense than continental plates are.

The Andes Mountains formed where the South American plate and Nazca plate meet.

© Houghton Mifflin Harcourt Publishing Company • Image Credits: ©Emil von Maltitz/Gallo Images/Getty Images

12 Locate Which letter marks where the Andes Mountains are located on the map of tectonic plates, A, B, or C? _____

The tectonic plates fit together like the pieces of a jigsaw puzzle.

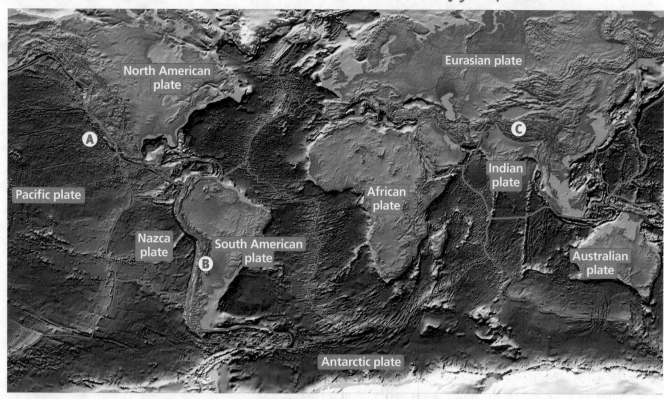

North American plate

Eurasian plate

C

Indian plate

Pacific plate

African plate

Nazca plate

South American plate

B

Australian plate

Antarctic plate

A

The thickest part of the South American plate is the continental crust. The thinnest part of this plate is in the Atlantic Ocean.

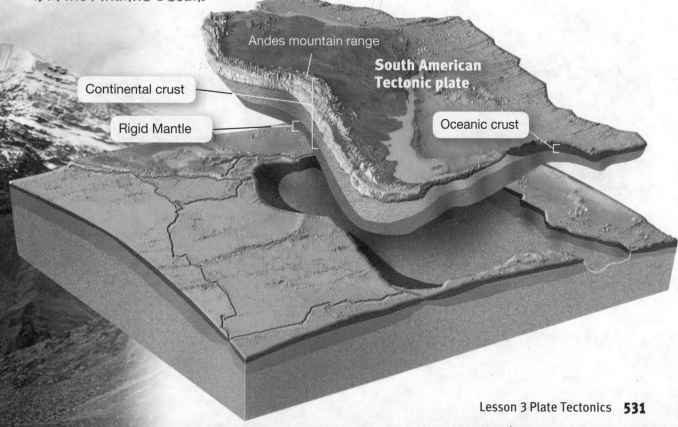

Andes mountain range

South American Tectonic plate

Continental crust

Rigid Mantle

Oceanic crust

Boundaries

What are the three types of plate boundaries?

The most dramatic changes in Earth's crust occur along plate boundaries. Plate boundaries may be on the ocean floor, around the edges of continents, or even within continents. There are three types of plate boundaries: divergent boundaries, convergent boundaries, and transform boundaries. Each type of plate boundary is associated with characteristic landforms.

Active Reading

13 Identify As you read, underline the locations where plate boundaries may be found.

Convergent Boundaries

Convergent boundaries form where two plates collide. Three types of collisions can happen at convergent boundaries. When two tectonic plates of continental lithosphere collide, they buckle and thicken, which pushes some of the continental crust upward. When a plate of oceanic lithosphere collides with a plate of continental lithosphere, the denser oceanic lithosphere sinks into the asthenosphere. Boundaries where one plate sinks beneath another plate are called subduction zones. When two tectonic plates of oceanic lithosphere collide, one of the plates subducts, or sinks, under the other plate.

Inquiry

14 Infer Why do you think the denser plate subducts in a collision?

_____

_____

_____

Continent-Continent Collisions
When two plates of continental lithosphere collide, they buckle and thicken. This causes mountains to form.

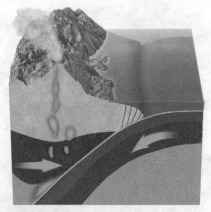

Continent-Ocean Collisions
When a plate of oceanic lithosphere collides with a plate of continental lithosphere, the oceanic lithosphere subducts because it is denser.

Ocean-Ocean Collisions
When two plates of oceanic lithosphere collide, the older, denser plate subducts under the other plate.

Divergent Boundaries

At a **divergent boundary**, two plates move away from each other. This separation allows the asthenosphere to rise toward the surface and partially melt. This melting creates magma, which erupts as lava. The lava cools and hardens to form new rock on the ocean floor.

As the crust and the upper part of the asthenosphere cool and become rigid, they form new lithosphere. This lithosphere is thin, warm, and light. This warm, light rock sits higher than the surrounding sea floor because it is less dense. It forms mid-ocean ridges. Most divergent boundaries are located on the ocean floor. However, rift valleys may also form where continents are separated by plate movement.

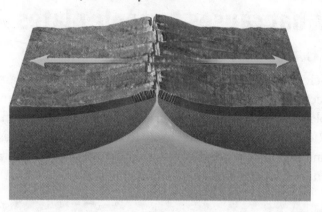

At divergent boundaries, plates separate.

Transform Boundaries

A boundary at which two plates move past each other horizontally is called a **transform boundary**. However, the plate edges do not slide along smoothly. Instead, they scrape against each other in a series of sudden slippages of crustal rock that are felt as earthquakes. Unlike other types of boundaries, transform boundaries generally do not produce magma. The San Andreas Fault in California is a major transform boundary between the North American plate and the Pacific plate. Transform motion also occurs at divergent boundaries. Short segments of mid-ocean ridges are connected by transform faults called fracture zones.

At transform boundaries, plates slide past each other horizontally.

![Active Reading]

15 Compare How are transform boundaries different from convergent and divergent boundaries? Support your claim with evidence.

_____

_____

_____

Hot Plates

What causes tectonic plates to move?

Scientists have proposed three mechanisms to explain how tectonic plates move over Earth's surface. Mantle convection drags plates along as mantle material moves beneath tectonic plates. Ridge push moves plates away from mid-ocean ridges as rock cools and becomes more dense. Slab pull tugs plates along as the dense edge of a plate sinks beneath Earth's surface.

Active Reading

16 Identify As you read, underline three mechanisms scientists have proposed to explain plate motion.

Ridge push

Ridge push

Mantle Convection

As atoms in Earth's core and mantle undergo radioactive decay, energy is released as heat. Some parts of the mantle become hotter than others parts. The hot parts rise as the sinking of cooler, denser material pushes the heated material up. This kind of movement of material due to differences in density is called **convection**. It was thought that as the mantle convects, or moves, it would drag the overlying tectonic plates along with it. However, this hypothesis has been criticized by many scientists because it does not explain the huge amount of force that would be needed to move plates.

Ridge Push

Newly formed rock at a mid-ocean ridge is warm and less dense than older, adjacent rock. Because of its lower density, the new rock rests at a higher elevation than the older rock. The older rock slopes downward away from the ridge. As the newer, warmer rock cools, it also becomes more dense. These cooling and increasingly dense rocks respond to gravity by moving down the slope of the asthenosphere, away from the ridge. This force, called ridge push, pushes the rest of the plate away from the mid-ocean ridge.

Slab Pull

At subduction zones, a denser tectonic plate sinks, or subducts, beneath another, less dense plate. The leading edge of the subducting plate is colder and denser than the mantle. As it sinks, the leading edge of the plate pulls the rest of the plate with it. This process is called slab pull. In general, subducting plates move faster than other plates do. This evidence leads many scientists to think that slab pull may be the most important mechanism driving tectonic plate motion.

Slab pull

17 Compare Complete the chart with brief descriptions to compare and contrast mantle convection, ridge push, and slab pull.

Mechanisms

Mantle convection	Ridge push	Slab pull

Visual Summary

To complete this summary, fill in the blanks to complete the label or caption. Then use the key below to check your answers. You can use this page to review the main concepts of the lesson.

Plate Tectonics

The continents were joined in a single landmass.

18 Scientists call the landmass _____

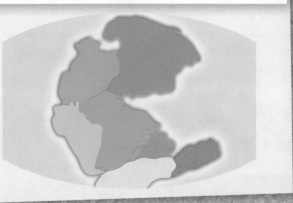

Tectonic plates differ in size and composition.

19 The United States lies on the _____ plate.

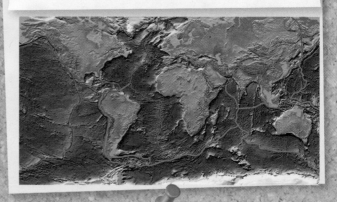

There are three types of plate boundaries: convergent, divergent, and transform.

20 This image shows a _____ boundary.

Three mechanisms may drive plate motion. These are mantle convection, slab pull, and ridge push.

21 The mechanism that scientists think is most important is _____

Answers: 18 Pangaea; 19 North American; 20 transform; 21 slab pull

22 **Claims • Evidence • Reasoning** How does the flow of energy as heat in Earth's interior contribute to the movement of tectonic plates? Make a claim about what would happen if convection within the Earth did not occur. Summarize evidence to support the claim and explain your reasoning.

Lesson Review

Vocabulary

Fill in the blanks with the term that best completes the following sentences.

1 The lithosphere is divided into pieces called

_____

2 The theory that describes large-scale movements of Earth's lithosphere is called

_____

3 The movement of material due to differences in density that are caused by differences in temperature is called _____

_____

Key Concepts

Use this diagram to answer the following questions.

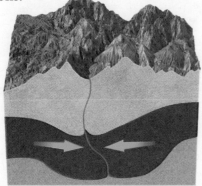

4 Identify What type of plate boundary is shown?

_____

5 Identify Which types of lithosphere are colliding at this boundary?

_____

_____

_____

6 Identify What landforms are likely to form at this boundary?

_____

_____

_____

7 Describe How is continental lithosphere different from oceanic lithosphere?

_____

_____

_____

8 Compare How are convergent boundaries different from divergent boundaries?

_____

_____

_____

_____

Critical Thinking

9 Analyze Why does cool rock material sink when convection takes place in the mantle? Explain your reasoning.

_____

_____

_____

_____

_____

_____

_____

_____

10 Defend A classmate states that continental drift could not be possible because it would take far too much force to move tectonic plates. Describe the hypotheses scientists use to explain the movement of tectonic plates. Which hypothesis do many scientists think may explain the great force needed to move plates?

_____

_____

_____

_____

_____

_____

_____

My Notes

Mountain Building

ESSENTIAL QUESTION

How do mountains form?

By the end of this lesson, you should be able to describe how the movement of Earth's tectonic plates causes mountain building.

S6E5.f Plate tectonics and geologic events

The highest peak in the Alps mountain range is Mont Blanc at just over 4,800 m tall.

Engage Your Brain

1 Predict Check T or F to show whether you think each statement is true or false.

T	F	
☐	☐	Mountains can originate from a level surface that is folded upward.
☐	☐	Rocks can be pulled apart by the movement of tectonic plates.
☐	☐	All mountains are created by volcanoes.
☐	☐	A mountain range can form only at the edge of a tectonic plate.

2 Hypothesize The Appalachian Mountains were once taller than the Rocky Mountains. What do you think happened to the mountains? Explain.

_____

_____

_____

Rocky Mountains

Appalachian Mountains

Active Reading

3 Compare The terms *compression* and *tension* have opposite meanings. Compare the two sentences below, then write your own definition for *compression* and *tension*.

Vocabulary	Sentence
compression	The stack of books on Jon's desk caused the bottom book to be flattened by <u>compression</u>.
tension	Keisha pulled the piece of string so hard, the <u>tension</u> caused the string to break.

Vocabulary Terms
- deformation
- folding
- fault
- shear stress
- tension
- compression

4 Apply As you learn the definition of each vocabulary term in this lesson, create your own definition or sketch to help you remember the meaning of the term.

compression:

_____

_____

tension:

_____

_____

Stressed Out

How can tectonic plate motion cause deformation?

The movement of tectonic plates places stress on rocks. A tectonic plate is a block of lithosphere that consists of crust and the rigid outermost part of the mantle. *Stress* is the amount of force per unit area that is placed on an object. Rocks can bend or break under stress. In addition, low temperatures make materials more brittle, or easily broken. High temperatures can allow rock to bend.

When a rock is placed under stress, it deforms, or changes shape. **Deformation** (dee•fohr•MAY•shuhn) is the process by which rocks change shape when under stress. Rock can bend if it is placed under high temperature and pressure for long periods of time. If the stress becomes too great, or is applied quickly, rock can break. When rocks bend, folds form. When rocks break, faults form.

5 Identify As you read, list some objects near you that can bend or break from deformation.

_____

_____

_____

_____

_____

By applying stress, the boy is causing the spaghetti to deform. Similarly, stress over a long period of time can cause rock to bend.

Like the spaghetti, stress over a short period of time or great amounts of stress can cause rock to break.

Visualize It!

6 Describe How can the same material bend in one situation but break in another? Explain your reasoning.

_____

_____

_____

_____

What are two kinds of folds?

Folded rock layers appear bent or buckled. **Folding** occurs when rock layers bend under stress. The bends are called *folds*. Scientists assume that all rock layers start out as horizontal layers deposited on top of each other over time. Sometimes, different layers of rocks can still be seen even after the rocks have been folded. When scientists see a fold, they know that deformation has happened. Two common types of folds are synclines and anticlines.

Synclines and Anticlines

Folds are classified based on the age of the rock layers. In a *syncline* (SIN•klyn), the youngest layers of rock are found at the core of a fold. The oldest layers are found on the outside of the fold. Synclines usually look like rock layers that are arched upward, like a bowl. In an *anticline* (AN•tih•klyn), the oldest layers of rock are found at the core of the fold. The youngest layers are found on the outside of the fold. Anticlines often look like rock layers that are arched downwards and high in the middle. Often, both types of folds will be visible in the same rock layers, as shown below.

Think Outside the Book

7 Model Stack several sheets of paper together. Apply stress to the sides of the paper to create a model of a syncline and an anticline. Share your model with your teacher.

The hinge is the middle point of the bend in a syncline or anticline.

8 Identify Rock layers are labeled on the image below. Which rock layers are the youngest and oldest?

_____

_____

How do you know? _____

_____

_____

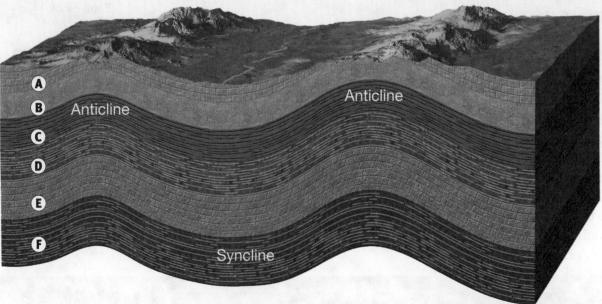

Anticline

Anticline

Ⓐ
Ⓑ
Ⓒ
Ⓓ
Ⓔ
Ⓕ

Syncline

Faulted

What are the three kinds of faults?

Rock can be under so much stress that it cannot bend and may break. The crack that forms when large blocks of rock break and move past each other is called a **fault**. The blocks of rock on either side of the fault are called *fault blocks*. The sudden movement of fault blocks can cause earthquakes.

Any time there is a fault in Earth's crust, rocks tend to move in predictable ways. Earth has three main kinds of faults: strike-slip faults, normal faults, and reverse faults. Scientists classify faults based on the way fault blocks move relative to each other. The location where two fault blocks meet is called the *fault plane*. A fault plane can be oriented horizontally, vertically, or at any angle in between. For any fault except a perfectly vertical fault, the block above the fault plane is called the *hanging wall*. The block below the fault plane is the *footwall*.

The movement of faults can create mountains and other types of landforms. At any tectonic plate boundary, the amount of stress on rock is complex. Therefore, any of the three types of faults can occur at almost all plate boundaries.

Active Reading

9 Identify As you read, underline the direction of movement of the fault blocks in each type of fault.

Strike-Slip Faults

In a strike-slip fault, the fault blocks move past each other horizontally. Strike-slip faults form when rock is under shear stress. **Shear stress** is stress that pushes rocks in parallel but opposite directions as seen in the image. As rocks are deformed deep in Earth's crust, energy builds. The release of this energy can cause earthquakes as the rocks slide past each other. Strike-slip faults are common along transform boundaries, where tectonic plates move past each other. The San Andreas Fault system in California is an example of a strike-slip fault.

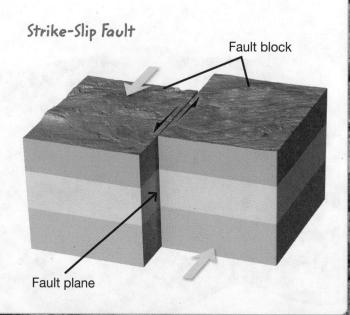
Strike-Slip Fault
Fault block
Fault plane

Normal Faults

In the normal fault shown on the right, the hanging wall moves down relative to the footwall. The faults are called normal because the blocks move in a way that you would *normally* expect as a result of gravity. Normal faults form when the rock is under tension. **Tension** (TEN•shuhn) is stress that stretches or pulls rock apart. Therefore, normal faults are common along divergent boundaries. Earth's crust can also stretch in the middle of a tectonic plate. The Basin and Range area of the southwestern United States is an example of a location with many normal fault structures.

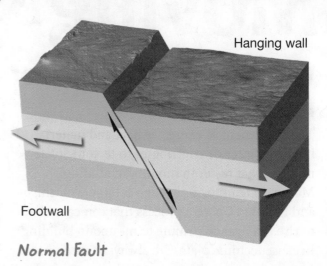

Hanging wall

Footwall

Normal Fault

Reverse Faults

In the reverse fault shown on the right, the hanging wall moves up relative to the footwall. The faults are called reverse because the hanging blocks move up, which is the reverse of what you would expect as a result of gravity. Reverse faults form when rocks undergo compression. **Compression** (kuhm•PRESH•uhn) is stress that squeezes or pushes rock together. Reverse faults are common along convergent boundaries, where two plates collide. The San Gabriel Mountains in the United States are caused by reverse faults.

Reverse Fault

👁 **Visualize It!**

10 **Identify** Label the fault plane, hanging wall, and footwall on the reverse fault to the right.

Think Outside the Book Inquiry

11 **Compile** Create a memory matching game of the types of faults. Create as many cards as you can with different photos, drawings, or written details about the types of faults. Use the cards to quiz yourself and your classmates.

Moving On Up

What are the three kinds of mountains?

The movement of energy as heat and material in Earth's interior contributes to tectonic plate motions that result in mountain building. Mountains can form through folding, volcanism, and faulting. *Uplift*, a process that can cause land to rise can also contribute to mountain building. Because tectonic plates are always in motion, some mountains are constantly being uplifted.

Active Reading **12 Identify** As you read, underline examples of folded, volcanic, and fault-block mountains.

Folded Mountains

Folded mountains form when rock layers are squeezed together and pushed upward. They usually form at convergent boundaries, where plates collide. For example, the Appalachian Mountains (ap•uh•LAY•chun) formed from folding and faulting when the North American plate collided with the Eurasian and African plates millions of years ago.

In Europe, the Pyrenees (PIR•uh•neez) are another range of folded mountains, as shown below. They are folded over an older, pre-existing mountain range. Today, the highest peaks are over 3,000 m tall.

The Pyrenees Mountains are folded mountains that separate France from Spain.

Visualize It!

13 Describe What evidence do you see that the Pyrenees Mountains are folded mountains? Explain your reasoning.

_____

_____

_____

Volcanic Mountains

Volcanic mountains form when melted rock erupts onto Earth's surface. Many major volcanic mountains are located at convergent boundaries. Volcanic mountains can form on land or on the ocean floor. Volcanoes on the ocean floor can grow so tall that they rise above the surface of the ocean, forming islands. Most of Earth's active volcanoes are concentrated around the edge of the Pacific Ocean. This area is known as the Ring of Fire. Many volcanoes, including Mt. Griggs in the image to the right, are located on the Northern rim of the Pacific plate in Alaska.

Mt. Griggs volcano on the Alaskan Peninsula is 2,317 m high.

The Teton Mountains in Wyoming are fault-block mountains.

Fault-Block Mountains

Fault-block mountains form when tension makes the lithosphere break into many normal faults. Along the faults, pieces of the lithosphere drop down compared with other pieces. The pieces left standing form fault-block mountains. The Teton Mountains (TEE•tuhn) and the Sierra Nevadas are fault-block mountains.

14 Identify Draw a simple version of each type of mountain below.

Folded	Volcanic	Faulted

Visual Summary

To complete this summary, fill in the blanks with the correct word or phrase. Then use the key below to check your answers. You can use this page to review the main concepts of the lesson.

Mountain Building

Rocks can bend or break under stress.

15 The process by which rocks change shape under stress is called _____

Folds occur when rock layers bend.

16 A rock structure with the oldest rocks at the core of the fold is called a/an _____

Faults occur when rock layers break.

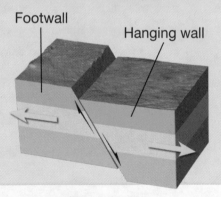

Footwall

Hanging wall

17 The type of fault pictured is a _____ fault.

Mountains form through folding, volcanism, and faulting.

18 The type of mountains pictured are _____ mountains.

Answers: 15 deformation; 16 anticline; 17 normal; 18 fault-block

19 Synthesize The middle of tectonic plates tend to have fewer mountains than locations near tectonic plate boundaries. What might be one possible explanation for this?

Lesson Review

Vocabulary

Fill in the blank with the term that best completes the following sentences.

1 A normal fault is a result of a type of stress known as _____

2 A strike-slip fault is a result of _____ stress.

3 A reverse fault is caused by a type of stress known as _____

Key Concepts

Fill in the table below by identifying the type of mountain described in the example question.

Example	Type of Mountain
4 Identify The Basin and Range province is characterized by many normal faults.	
5 Identify The Cascade Range in the United States has many eruptive mountains.	
6 Identify The Pyrenees Mountains have many syncline and anticline structures.	

7 Describe How does the movement of tectonic plates cause deformation in rock?

_____

_____

_____

8 Compare How do folded, volcanic, and fault-block mountains differ?

_____

_____

_____

Critical Thinking

Use the diagram below to answer the following questions.

9 Correlate What type of stress caused the fault shown in the image?

_____

10 Apply Along which type of tectonic plate boundary would this fault be common? How do you know?

_____

_____

_____

11 Analyze Can rock undergo compression, tension, and shear stress all at once? Explain.

_____

_____

_____

_____

12 Claims • Evidence • Reasoning Imagine you are walking along a roadway and see a syncline. What can you conclude about the formation of that fold? Explain your reasoning.

_____

_____

_____

_____

My Notes

Lesson **5**

Volcanoes

ESSENTIAL QUESTION

How do volcanoes change Earth's surface?

By the end of this lesson, you should be able to describe what the various kinds of volcanoes and eruptions are, where they occur, how they form, and how they change Earth's surface.

S6E5.f Plate tectonics and geologic events

The Arenal volcano in Costa Rica has been active since 1968. The volcano has erupted on and off for over 7,000 years.

© Houghton Mifflin Harcourt • Image Credits: (bkgd) ©Schafer & Hill/Stone/Getty Images

Lesson Labs

Quick Labs
• Modeling an Explosive Eruption
• Volcano Mapping
Exploration Lab
• Modeling Lava Viscosity

Engage Your Brain

1 Predict Check T or F to show whether you think each statement is true or false.

T	F	
☐	☐	Volcanoes create new landforms such as mountains.
☐	☐	Tectonic plate boundaries are the only locations where volcanoes form.
☐	☐	Volcanic eruptions are often accompanied by earthquakes.
☐	☐	Volcanoes form new rocks and minerals.

2 Hypothesize You are a news reporter assigned to cover a story about the roadway in the image below. Describe what you think happened in this photo.

_____

_____

_____

Active Reading

3 Synthesize You can often define an unknown word if you know the meaning of its word parts. Use the word parts and sentence below to make an educated guess about the meaning of the word *pyroclastic*.

Word part	Meaning
pyro-	heat or fire
-clastic	pieces

Example sentence
Pyroclastic material was ejected into the atmosphere with explosive force during the eruption of the volcano.

pyroclastic:

_____

_____

Vocabulary Terms

• volcano   • vent
• magma   • tectonic plate
• lava   • hot spot

4 Apply As you learn the definition of each vocabulary term in this lesson, create your own definition or sketch to help you remember the meaning of the term.

Magma MAGIC

What is a volcano?

What do volcanoes look like? Most people think of a steep mountain with smoke coming out of the top. In fact, a **volcano** is any place where gas, ash, or melted rock come out of the ground. A volcano can be a tall mountain, as shown below, or a small crack in the ground. Volcanoes occur on land and underwater. There are even volcanoes on other planets. Not all volcanoes actively erupt. Many are *dormant*, meaning an eruption has not occurred in a long period of time.

Volcanoes form as rock below the surface of Earth melts. The melted rock, or **magma**, is less dense than solid rock, so it rises toward the surface. **Lava** is magma that has reached Earth's surface. Lava and clouds of ash can erupt from a **vent**, or opening of a volcano.

👁 Visualize It!

5 Identify Label the parts of the volcano. Include the following terms: *magma, lava, vent, ash cloud*.

Lava can reach temperatures of more than 1,200 °C.

What are the kinds of volcanic landforms?

The location of a volcano and the composition of magma determine the type of volcanic landforms created. Shield volcanoes, cinder cones, composite volcanoes, lava plateaus, craters, and calderas are all types of volcanic landforms.

Volcanic Mountains

Materials ejected from a volcano may build up around a vent to create volcanic mountains. *Viscosity* (vyz•SKAHZ•ih•tee) is the resistance of a liquid material, such as lava, to flow. The viscosity of lava determines the explosiveness of an eruption and the shape of the resulting volcanic mountain. Low-viscosity lava flows easily, forms low slopes, and erupts without large explosions. High-viscosity lava does not flow easily, forms steep slopes, and can erupt explosively. *Pyroclastic materials* (py•roh•KLAHZ•tyk*)*, or hot ash and bits of rock, may also be ejected into the atmosphere.

Active Reading

7 Identify As you read, underline the main features of each type of volcanic mountain.

© Houghton Mifflin Harcourt Publishing Company • Image Credits: (tl) ©Bernd Mellmann/Alamy; (lc) ©Gary Flegehen/All Canada Photos/age fotostock; (lb) ©Tom Mareschal/Alamy

Think Outside the Book · Inquiry

6 Apply Small fragments of rock material that are ejected from a volcano are known as *volcanic ash*. Volcanic ash is a form of pyroclastic material. The material does not dissolve in water and is very abrasive, meaning it can scratch surfaces. Ash can build up to great depths in locations around a volcano. Write a cleanup plan for a town that explains how you might safely remove and dispose of volcanic ash.

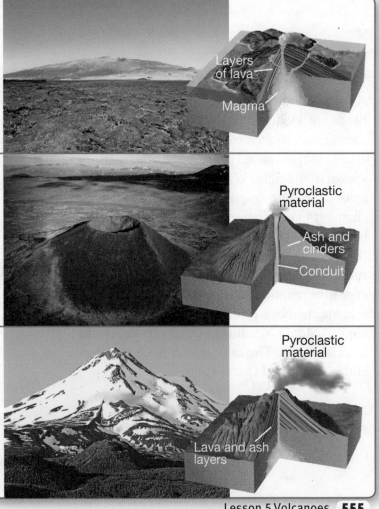

- **Shield Volcanoes** Volcanoes with a broad base and gently sloping sides are *shield volcanoes*. Shield volcanoes cover a wide area and generally form from mild eruptions. Layers of lava flow out from the vent, harden, and slowly build up to form the cone. The Hawaiian Islands are shield volcanoes.

Layers of lava

Magma

- **Cinder Cones** Sometimes, ash and pieces of lava harden in the air and can fall to the ground around a small vent. The hardened pieces of lava are called cinders. The cinders and ash build up around the vent and form a steep volcano called a *cinder cone*. A cinder cone can also form at a side vent on other volcanic mountains, such as on shield or composite volcanoes.

Pyroclastic material

Ash and cinders

Conduit

- **Composite Volcanoes** Alternating layers of hardened lava flows and pyroclastic material create *composite volcanoes* (kuhm•PAHZ•iht). During a mild eruption, lava flows cover the sides of the cone. During an explosive eruption, pyroclastic material is deposited around the vent. Composite volcanoes commonly develop into large and steep volcanic mountains.

Pyroclastic material

Lava and ash layers

Fissures and Lava Plateaus

Fissure eruptions (FIH•shohr ee•RUHP•shuhnz) happen when lava flows from giant cracks, or *fissures*, in Earth's surface. The fissures are found on land and on the ocean floor. A fissure eruption has no central opening. Lava flows out of the entire length of the fissure, which can be many kilometers long. As a result, a thick and mostly flattened layer of cooled lava, called a *lava plateau* (plah•TOH), can form. One example of a lava plateau is the Columbia Plateau Province in Washington, Oregon, and Idaho, as shown to the right.

The Palouse Falls in Washington plunge deep into exposed layers of the Columbia lava plateau.

Craters and Calderas

A *volcanic crater* is an opening or depression at the top of a volcano caused by eruptions. Inside the volcano, molten rock can form an expanded area of magma called a *magma chamber*, as shown to the right. When the magma chamber below a volcano empties, the roof of the magma chamber may collapse and leave an even larger, basin-shaped depression called a *caldera* (kahl•DAHR•uh). Calderas can form from the sudden drain of a magma chamber during an explosive eruption or from a slowly emptied magma chamber. More than 7,000 years ago, the cone of Mount Mazama in Oregon collapsed to form a caldera. The caldera later filled with water and is now called Crater Lake.

A caldera can be more than 100 km in diameter.

 **Visualize It!**

8 Describe How does the appearance of land surfaces change before and after a caldera forms?

_____

_____

_____

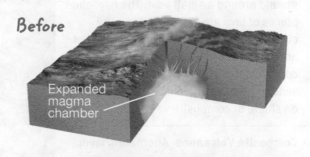

Before

Expanded magma chamber

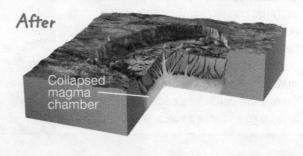

After

Collapsed magma chamber

ERUPTION!

Where do volcanoes form?

Volcanoes can form at plate boundaries or within the middle of a plate. Recall that **tectonic plates** are giant sections of lithosphere on Earth's surface. Volcanoes can form at *divergent plate boundaries* where two plates are moving away from each other. Most fissure eruptions occur at divergent boundaries. Shield volcanoes, fissure eruptions, and cinder cones can also occur away from plate boundaries within a plate at *hot spots*. The type of lava normally associated with these volcanoes has a relatively low viscosity, few trapped gases, and is usually not explosive.

Composite volcanoes are most common along *convergent plate boundaries* where oceanic plates subduct. In order for the rock to melt, it must be hot and the pressure on it must drop, or water and other fluids must be added to it. Extra fluids from ocean water form magma of higher viscosity with more trapped gases. Thus, composite volcanoes produce the most violent eruptions. The *Ring of Fire* is a name used to describe the numerous explosive volcanoes that form on convergent plate boundaries surrounding the Pacific Ocean.

📎 **Active Reading**

9 Identify As you read, underline three locations where volcanoes can form.

Plate Tectonic Boundaries and Volcano Locations Worldwide

Visualize It!

10 Describe How do the locations of volcanoes relate to tectonic plate boundaries?

_____

_____

_____

At Divergent Boundaries

At divergent boundaries, plates move away from each other. The lithosphere stretches and gets thinner, so the pressure on the mantle rock below decreases. As a result, the asthenosphere bulges upward and magma forms. This magma rises through fissures in the lithosphere, out onto the land or the ocean floor.

Most divergent boundaries are on the ocean floor. When eruptions occur in these areas, undersea volcanoes develop. These volcanoes and other processes lead to the formation of a long, underwater mountain range known as a *mid-ocean ridge*. Two examples of mid-ocean ridges are the East Pacific Rise in the Pacific Ocean and the Mid-Atlantic Ridge in the Atlantic Ocean. The youngest rocks in the ocean are located at mid-ocean ridges.

Shield volcanoes and cinder cones are common in Iceland, where the Mid-Atlantic Ridge runs through the country. As the plates move away from each other, new crust forms. When a divergent boundary is located in the middle of a continent, the crust stretches until a rift valley is formed, as shown below.

Active Reading **11 Identify** What types of volcanic landforms occur at divergent plate boundaries?

_____

_____

_____

Divergent plate boundaries create fissure eruptions and shield volcanoes.

Fissure

The Great Rift Valley in Africa is a location where the crust is stretching and separating.

Tectonic plates move away from each other at divergent boundaries.

At Convergent Boundaries

At convergent boundaries, two plates move toward each other. In most cases, one plate sinks beneath the other plate. As the sinking plate dives into the mantle, fluids in the sinking plate become super heated and escape. These escaping fluids cause the rock above the sinking plate to melt and form magma. This magma rises to the surface and erupts to form volcanoes.

The magma that forms at convergent boundaries has a high concentration of fluids. As the magma rises, decreasing pressure causes the fluid trapped in the magma to form gas bubbles. But, because the magma has a high viscosity, these bubbles cannot escape easily. As the bubbles expand, the magma rises faster. Eventually, the magma can erupt explosively, forming calderas or composite volcanoes. Gas, ash, and large chunks of rock can be blown out of the volcanoes. The Cascade Range is a chain of active composite volcanoes in the northwestern United States, as shown to the right. In 1980, Mt. St. Helens erupted so violently that the entire top of the mountain was blown away.

12 Identify Draw two arrows in the white boxes to indicate the direction of motion of the plates that formed the Cascade volcanoes.

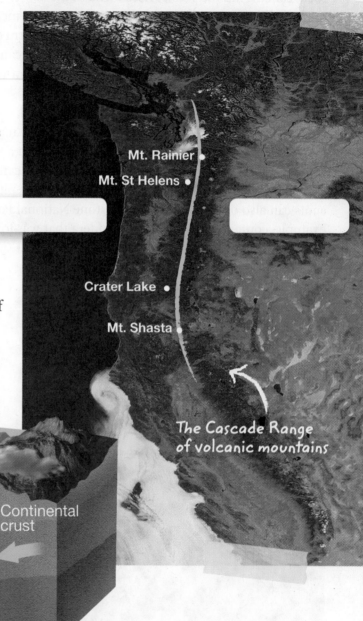

Mt. Rainier

Mt. St Helens

Crater Lake

Mt. Shasta

The Cascade Range of volcanic mountains

Tectonic plates move toward each other at convergent boundaries.

Oceanic crust

Continental crust

13 Summarize List the characteristics of divergent-boundary volcanoes and convergent-boundary volcanoes below.

Volcanoes at divergent boundaries	Volcanoes at convergent boundaries

At Hot Spots

Volcanoes can form within a plate, away from the plate boundaries. A **hot spot** is a location where a column of extremely hot mantle rock, called a *mantle plume*, rises through the asthenosphere. As the hot rock reaches the base of the lithosphere, it melts partially to form magma that can rise to the surface and form a volcano. Eruptions at a hot spot commonly form shield volcanoes. As tectonic plates move over a mantle plume, chains of volcanic mountains can form, as shown below.

The youngest Hawaiian island, the Big Island, is home to Kilauea (kih•loh•AY•uh). The Kilauea volcano is an active shield volcano located over a mantle plume. To the north and west of Kilauea is a chain of progressively-older shield volcanoes. These volcanoes were once located over the same mantle plume. Hot spots can also occur on land. Yellowstone National Park, for example, contains a huge volcanic caldera that was formed by the same mantle plume that created the Columbia Plateau.

Visualize It!

14 Analyze Which location, *A*, *B*, or *C*, do you think is the oldest volcano? Explain your reasoning.

_____

_____

_____

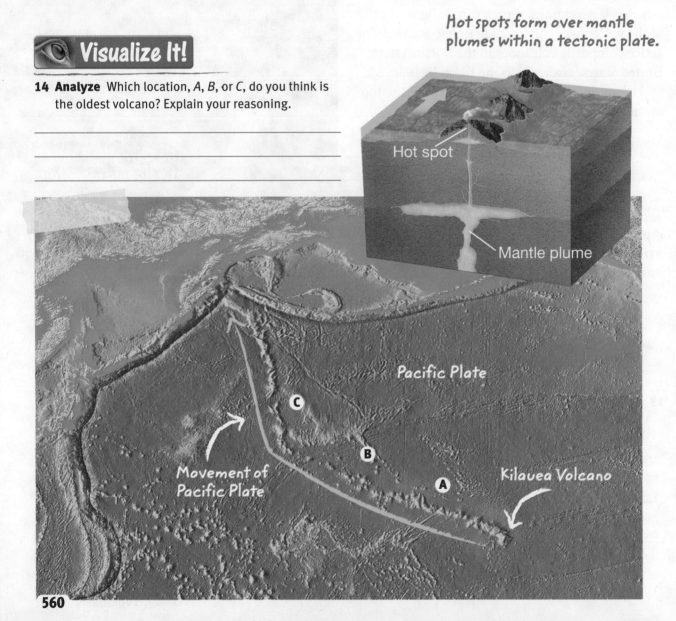

Hot spots form over mantle plumes within a tectonic plate.

Hot spot

Mantle plume

Pacific Plate

Movement of Pacific Plate

Kilauea Volcano

Living Near a Volcano

Volcanoes occur around the world. Many people live near volcanoes because the soils around a volcano can be very rich with essential minerals. These minerals make the soils fertile for growing a variety of crops. Living near a volcano also has its hazards. Sudden and unexpected eruptions can cause people to lose their homes and their lives.

Not All Bad
Volcanic rocks are used in jewelry, in making concrete, and in water filtration systems. Even cat litter and facial scrubs can contain volcanic rock.

Destruction
Earthquakes, fires, ash, and lava flows during an eruption can destroy entire cities.

Ash in the Air
Volcanic ash can cause breathing problems, bury crops, and damage engines. The weight of falling ash can cause buildings to collapse.

Extend

Inquiry

15 Identify Are all characteristics of volcanoes dangerous?

16 Apply Research the eruption of a specific volcano of your choice. Describe how the volcano affected the environment and the people near the volcano.

17 Design Create a poster that outlines a school safety plan for events that can occur before, during, and after a volcanic eruption.

Visual Summary

To complete this summary, check the box that indicates true or false. Then, use the key below to check your answers. You can use this page to review the main concepts of the lesson.

Lava and magma are different.

T F

18 ☐ ☐ Lava is inside Earth's crust and may contain trapped gases.

The three types of volcanic mountains are shield volcanoes, cinder cones, and composite volcanoes.

T F

19 ☐ ☐ The type of volcano shown is a shield volcano.

Volcanoes

Volcanoes can form at tectonic plate boundaries.

ASIA

NORTH AMERICA

PACIFIC OCEAN

AUSTRALIA

T F

20 ☐ ☐ At divergent plate boundaries, plates move toward each other.

Volcanoes can form at hot spots.

Hot spot

Mantle plume

T F

21 ☐ ☐ Hot spots are restricted to tectonic plate boundaries.

Answers: 18 False; 19 True; 20 False; 21 False

22 **Explain** How do volcanoes contribute to the formation of new landforms?

Lesson Review

Vocabulary

Write 1 or 2 sentences that describe the differences between the two terms.

1 magma   lava

_____

_____

2 volcano   vent

_____

_____

3 tectonic plate   hot spot

_____

_____

Key Concepts

Use the image to answer the following question.

4 Identify How did the composite volcano in the image get its layered interior?

_____

_____

_____

5 Claims • Evidence • Reasoning Is pyroclastic material likely to form from low-viscosity lava or high-viscosity lava? Use evidence to support your claim, and explain your reasoning.

_____

_____

_____

Describe the location and characteristics of the types of volcanic landforms in the table below.

Volcanic landform	Description
6 Hot-spot volcanoes	
7 Cinder cones	
8 Calderas	

Critical Thinking

9 Hypothesize In Iceland, the Mid-Atlantic Ridge runs through the center of the country. What can you conclude about the appearance of Iceland many thousands of years from now?

_____

_____

_____

_____

10 Analyze Why do you think the location surrounding the Pacific Ocean is known as the Ring of Fire?

_____

_____

_____

_____

My Notes

Lesson 6

Earthquakes

ESSENTIAL QUESTION

Why do earthquakes happen?

By the end of this lesson, you should be able to describe the causes of earthquakes and to identify where earthquakes happen.

S6E5.f Plate tectonics and geologic events

The 1995 Kobe earthquake in Japan destroyed more than 200,000 buildings and structures including this railroad track.

Engage Your Brain

1 Predict Fill in any words or numbers that you think best complete each of the statements below.

Each year there are approximately _____ earthquakes detected around the world.

In the United States, the state with the most earthquakes on average is _____

Every year, earthquakes cause _____ of dollars in damages in the United States.

Most earthquakes only last for several _____ of time.

2 Analyze Using the image, list in column 1 some of the hazards that can occur after an earthquake. In column 2, explain why you think these items or situations would be hazardous.

Hazards	Why?

Active Reading

3 Synthesize You can often define an unknown word if you know the meaning of its word parts. Use the word parts and sentence below to make an educated guess about the meaning of the word *epicenter*.

Word part	Meaning
epi-	on, upon, or over
-center	the middle

Example sentence
The <u>epicenter</u> of the earthquake was only 3 km from our school.

epicenter:

_____

_____

Vocabulary Terms

- earthquake
- focus
- epicenter
- tectonic plate boundary
- fault
- deformation
- elastic rebound

4 Apply As you learn the definition of each vocabulary term in this lesson, create your own definition or sketch to help you remember the meaning of the term.

Let's Focus

What is an earthquake?

Earthquakes can cause extreme damage and loss of life. **Earthquakes** are ground movements that occur when blocks of rock in Earth move suddenly and release energy. The energy is released as seismic waves which cause the ground to shake and tremble.

Earthquake waves can be tracked to a point below Earth's surface known as the *focus*. The **focus** is a place within Earth along a fault at which the first motion of an earthquake occurs. Motion along a fault causes stress. When the stress on the rock is too great, the rock will rupture and cause an earthquake. The earthquake releases the stress. Directly above the focus on Earth's surface is the **epicenter** (EP•ih•sen•ter). Seismic waves flow outward from the focus in all directions.

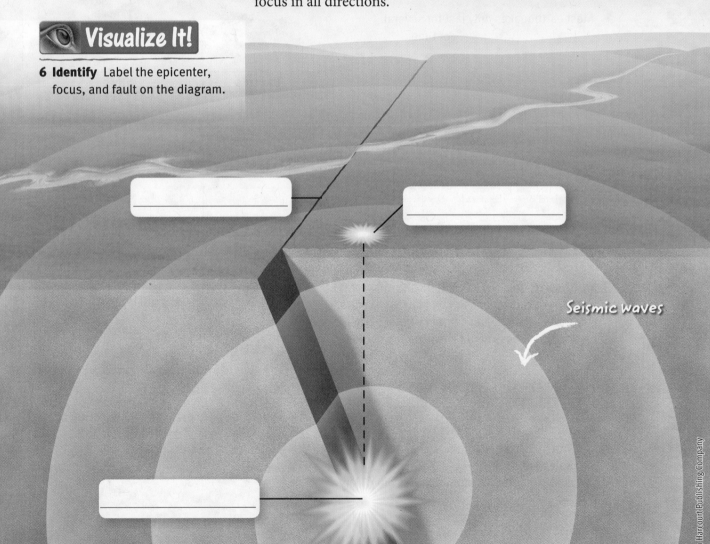

Seismic waves

What causes earthquakes?

Most earthquakes occur near the boundaries of tectonic plates. A **tectonic plate boundary** is where two or more tectonic plates meet. As tectonic plates move, pressure builds up near the edges of the plates. These movements break Earth's crust into a series of faults. A **fault** is a break in Earth's crust along which blocks of rock move. The release of energy that accompanies the movement of the rock along a fault causes an earthquake.

Elastic Rebound

When rock is put under tremendous pressure, stress may deform, or change the shape of, the rock. **Deformation** (dee•fohr•MAY•shuhn) is the process by which rock becomes deformed and changes shape due to stress. As stress increases, the amount of energy that is stored in the rock increases, as seen in image B to the right.

Stress can change the shape of rock along a fault. Once the stress is released, rock may return to its original shape. When rock returns to nearly the same shape after the stress is removed, the process is known as *elastic deformation*. Imagine an elastic band that is pulled tight under stress. Once stress on the elastic band is removed, there is a *snap!* The elastic band returns to its original shape. A similar process occurs during earthquakes.

Similar to an elastic band, rock along tectonic plate boundaries can suddenly return to nearly its original shape when the stress is removed. The sudden *snap* is an earthquake. The return of rock to its original shape after elastic deformation is called **elastic rebound**. Earthquakes accompany the release of energy during elastic rebound. When the rock breaks and rebounds, it releases energy as seismic waves. The seismic wave energy radiates from the focus of the earthquake in all directions. This energy causes the ground to shake for a short time. Most earthquakes last for just a few seconds.

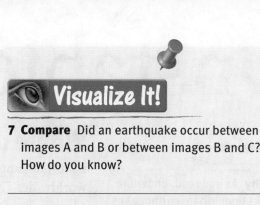

Visualize It!

7 Compare Did an earthquake occur between images A and B or between images B and C? How do you know?

_____

_____

_____

A

Along a fault, rocks are pushed or pulled in different directions and at different speeds.

B

As stress increases and energy builds within the rock, the rock deforms but remains locked in place.

C

Too much stress causes the rock to break and rebound to its original shape, releasing energy.

Unstable Ground

Active Reading

8 Identify As you read, underline the locations where earthquakes occur.

Where do earthquakes happen?

Each year, approximately 500,000 earthquakes are detected worldwide. The map below shows some of these earthquakes. Movement of material and energy in the form of heat in Earth's interior contribute to plate motions that result in earthquakes.

Most earthquakes happen at or near tectonic plate boundaries. Tectonic plate boundaries are areas where Earth's crust experiences a lot of stress. This stress occurs because the tectonic plates are colliding, separating, or grinding past each other horizontally. There are three main types of tectonic plate boundaries: divergent, convergent, and transform. The movement and interactions of the plates causes the crust to break into different types of faults. Earthquakes happen along these faults.

Plate Tectonic Boundaries and Earthquake Locations Worldwide

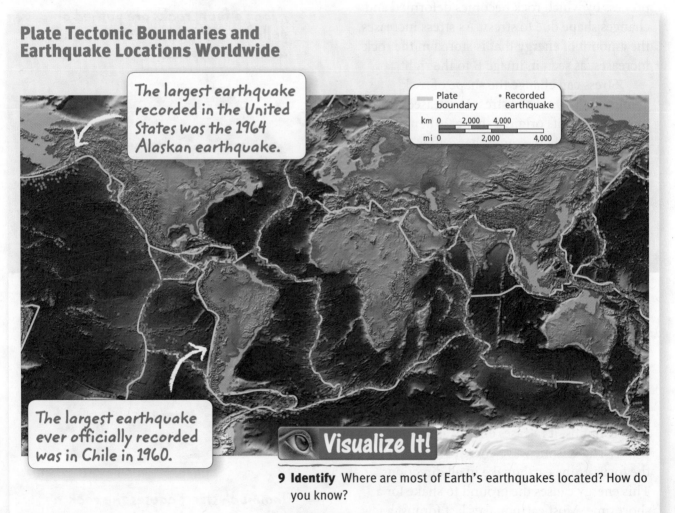

The largest earthquake recorded in the United States was the 1964 Alaskan earthquake.

The largest earthquake ever officially recorded was in Chile in 1960.

Plate boundary	• Recorded earthquake
km 0 2,000 4,000	
mi 0 2,000 4,000	

Visualize It!

9 Identify Where are most of Earth's earthquakes located? How do you know?

_____

_____

_____

At Divergent Boundaries

At a divergent boundary, plates pull apart, causing the crust to stretch. Stress that stretches rock and makes rock thinner is called *tension*. Normal faults commonly result when tension pulls rock apart.

Most of the crust at divergent boundaries is thin, so the earthquakes tend to be shallow. Most earthquakes at divergent boundaries are no more than 20 km deep. A mid-ocean ridge is an example of a divergent boundary where earthquakes occur.

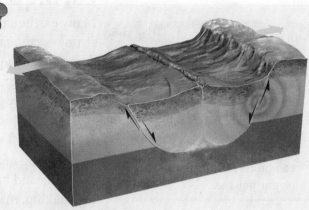

At divergent boundaries, earthquakes are common along _____ faults.

At Convergent Boundaries

Convergent plate boundaries occur when plates collide, causing rock to be squeezed. Stress that shortens or squeezes an object is known as *compression*. Compression causes the formation of reverse faults. Rocks are thrust over one another at reverse faults.

When two plates come together, both plates may crumple up to form mountains. Or one plate can subduct, or sink, underneath the other plate and into the mantle. The earthquakes that happen at convergent boundaries can be very strong. Subduction zone earthquakes occur at depths of up to 700 km.

At convergent boundaries, earthquakes are common along _____ faults.

At Transform Boundaries

A transform boundary is a place where two tectonic plates slide past each other horizontally. Stress that distorts a body by pushing different parts of the body in opposite directions is called *shear stress*. As the plates move, rocks on both sides of the fault are sheared, or broken, as they grind past one another in opposite directions.

Strike–slip faults are common at transform boundaries. Most earthquakes along the faults at transform boundaries are relatively shallow. The earthquakes are generally within the upper 50 km of the crust.

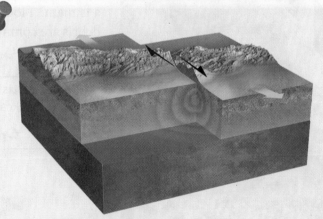

At transform boundaries, earthquakes are common along _____ faults.

What are some effects of earthquakes?

Many earthquakes do not cause major damage. However, some strong earthquakes can cause billions of dollars in property damage. Earthquakes may even cause human injuries and loss of life. In general, areas closest to the epicenter of an earthquake experience the greatest damage.

Danger to People and Structures

The shaking of an earthquake can cause structures to move vertically and horizontally. When structures cannot withstand the shaking, major destruction can occur. Following the release of seismic waves, buildings can shake so violently that a total or partial collapse can happen, as shown at left.

Much of the injury and loss of life that happen during and after earthquakes is caused by structures that collapse. In addition, fires, gas leaks, floods, and polluted water supplies can cause secondary damages following an earthquake. The debris left after an earthquake can take weeks or months to clean up. Bridges, roadways, homes, and entire cities can become disaster zones.

Tsunamis

An earthquake under the ocean can cause a vertical movement of the sea floor that displaces an enormous amount of water. This displacement may cause a tsunami to form. A *tsunami* (tsoo•NAH•mee) is a series of extremely long waves that can travel across the ocean at speeds of up to 800 km/h. Tsunami waves travel outward in all directions from the point where the earthquake occurred. As the waves approach a shoreline, the size of the waves increases. The waves can be taller than 30 m. Tsunami waves can cause major destruction and take many lives as they smash and wash away anything in their path. Many people may drown during a tsunami. Floods, polluted water supplies, and large amounts of debris are common in the aftermath.

11 **Design** You are an emergency management professional. You have been assigned to create an earthquake safety brochure for your town. Create a brochure that demonstrates ways people can protect themselves during an earthquake.

Think Outside the Book Inquiry

Although most of this building is left standing, the entire area is a hazard to citizens in the town.

12 **Identify** List some of the hazards associated with earthquakes on land and underwater.

On Land	Underwater

A CHANGING WORLD

Killer Quake

Imagine losing half the people in your city. On December 26, 2004, a massive tsunami destroyed approximately one-third of the buildings in Banda Aceh, Indonesia, and wiped out half the population.

Before

INDIA
MYANMAR
BANGLADESH
THAILAND
Andaman Is.
SRI LANKA
Nicobar Is.
MALDIVES
Banda Aceh
MALAYSIA
INDONESIA
INDIAN OCEAN

● Epicenter
━ Affected coastal areas

How Tsunamis Form
In the ocean, tsunami waves are fast but not very tall. As the waves approach a coast, they slow down and get much taller.

Before the Earthquake
The Banda Aceh tsunami resulted from a very strong earthquake in the ocean. Banda Aceh was very close to the epicenter.

Major Damages
The destruction to parts of Asia were so massive that geographers had to redraw the maps of some of the countries.

After

Extend

Inquiry

13 Identify In what ocean did the earthquake occur?

14 Research Investigate one other destructive tsunami and find out where the earthquake that caused it originated.

15 Debate Many of the people affected by the tsunami were poor. Why might earthquakes be more damaging in poor areas of the world? Explain your reasoning.

Visual Summary

To complete this summary, fill in the correct word. Then use the key below to check your answers. You can use this page to review the main concepts of the lesson.

Earthquakes

Earthquakes occur along faults.

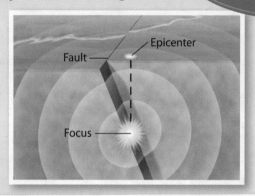

Epicenter

Fault

Focus

16 The epicenter of an earthquake is directly above the _____

Rocks break and snap back to their original shape in an earthquake.

17 Earthquakes happen when rocks bend and snap back in a process called _____

Earthquakes usually happen along plate boundaries.

18 The three types of plate boundaries are

_____

_____

_____

Earthquakes can cause a lot of damage.

19 An example of the dangers of earthquakes is _____

Answers: 16 focus; 17 elastic rebound; 18 divergent, convergent, and transform; 19 building collapse

20 Claims • Evidence • Reasoning Can earthquakes be prevented? Use evidence to support your claim, and explain your reasoning.

Lesson Review

Vocabulary

In your own words, define the following terms.

1 Elastic rebound

_____

_____

_____

2 Focus

_____

_____

_____

3 Fault

_____

_____

_____

Key Concepts

Example	Type of Boundary
4 Identify Most of the earthquakes in Japan are a result of one plate sinking under another.	
5 Identify The African Rift Valley is a location where plates are moving apart.	
6 Identify The San Andreas fault is a location where tectonic plates move horizontally past each other.	

7 Explain What causes an earthquake?

_____

_____

_____

_____

Critical Thinking

Use the image to answer the following questions.

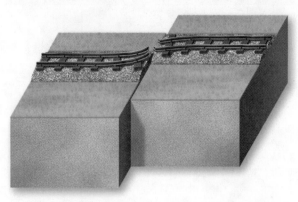

8 Analyze How does the image demonstrate that deformation has taken place? Explain your reasoning.

_____

_____

_____

_____

9 Apply How does Earth's surface and the structures on the surface change as a result of an earthquake?

_____

_____

_____

_____

_____

_____

10 Hypothesize Why do you think there is often only a short amount of time to evacuate an area before an earthquake?

_____

_____

_____

_____

My Notes

Engineering Design Process

Skills
Identify a need
Conduct research
✓ Brainstorm solutions
✓ Select a solution
Design a prototype
✓ Build a prototype
✓ Test and evaluate
✓ Redesign to improve
✓ Communicate results

Objectives
• Explain how scientists measure the energy of earthquakes.
• Design a model seismometer to measure motion.
• Test and modify a prototype to achieve a desired result.

Building a Seismometer

An earthquake occurs when rocks beneath the ground move suddenly. The energy of this movement travels through Earth in waves. Sometimes the shaking is detected hundreds or thousands of miles away from the origin of the earthquake. Scientists can learn about earthquakes by measuring the earthquake waves.

Measuring Motion

A seismometer is a device for measuring the motion of the ground beneath it. To develop seismometers, scientists had to solve a problem: How do you keep one part of the device from moving when the ground moves? The solution can be seen in the design shown here. A spring separates a heavy weight from the frame of the seismometer. Attached to the weight is a pen. The tip of the pen touches the surface of a circular drum that is covered in paper and slowly turning. When the ground moves, the frame and the rotating drum move along with it. The spring absorbs the ground's movement, so the weight and pen do not move. The pen is always touching the paper on the rotating drum. When the ground is not moving, the pen draws a straight line. When the ground moves, the pen draws this movement.

Waves move the instrument, but the spring and weight keep the pen still.

1 Infer This instrument measures the up-and-down motion of earthquake waves. How would you have to change the instrument to measure side-to-side motion of an earthquake?

_____

_____

_____

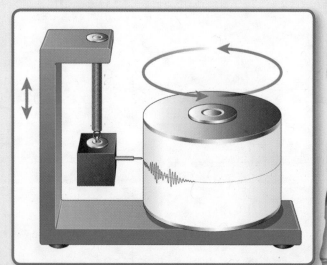

2 Infer In the oval below, write *moves* or *still* to indicate whether the labeled part moves during an earthquake or remains still.

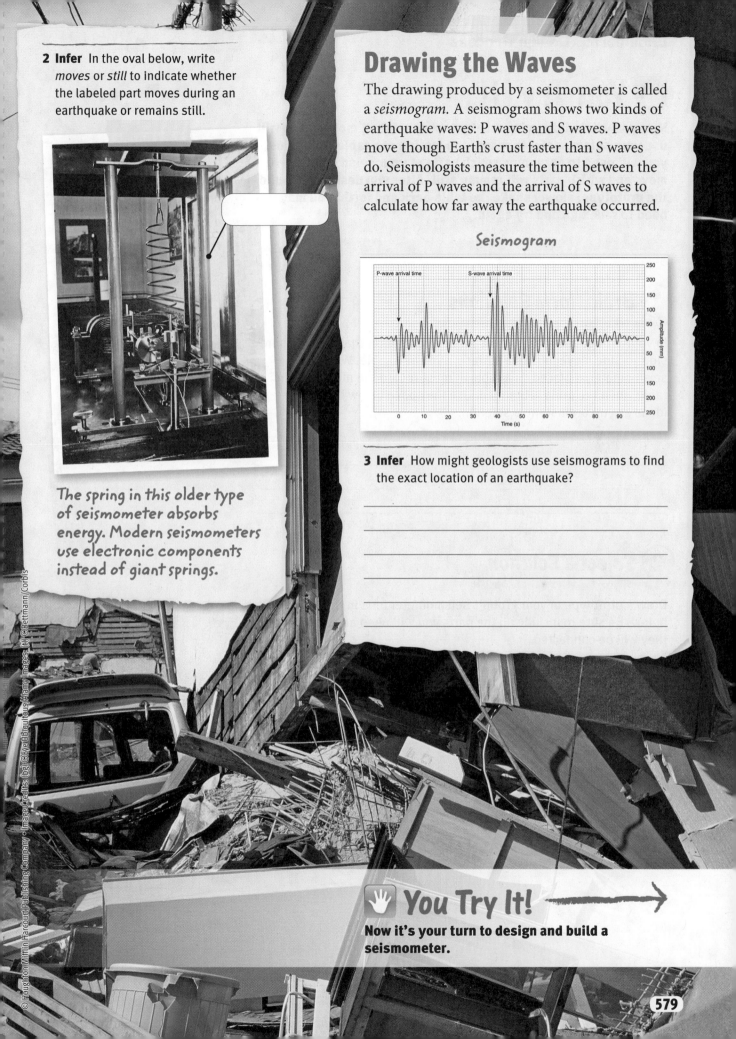

The spring in this older type of seismometer absorbs energy. Modern seismometers use electronic components instead of giant springs.

Drawing the Waves

The drawing produced by a seismometer is called a *seismogram*. A seismogram shows two kinds of earthquake waves: P waves and S waves. P waves move though Earth's crust faster than S waves do. Seismologists measure the time between the arrival of P waves and the arrival of S waves to calculate how far away the earthquake occurred.

Seismogram

3 Infer How might geologists use seismograms to find the exact location of an earthquake?

_____

_____

_____

_____

_____

_____

👋 **You Try It!** ⟶

Now it's your turn to design and build a seismometer.

You Try It!

Now you will build a seismometer that can detect motion. You will use your seismometer to record the motion of a table. To do this, you will need to determine which parts of your seismometer will move and which parts will remain still. After you design and build the prototype, slowly shake the table back and forth. You may need to redesign and try again.

You Will Need

✓ large square wooden frame

✓ metal weights

✓ string

✓ fine point felt tip pen

✓ long strips or roll of paper

✓ tape

✓ various hooks and hardware

1 Brainstorm Solutions

In your group, brainstorm ideas for a seismometer that will measure side-to-side movement of a surface, such as a table. When the seismometer is placed on a table, it must record the motion of the table when the table is bumped. Use the space below to record ideas as you brainstorm a solution.

_____

_____

_____

2 Select a Solution

Draw a prototype of your group's seismometer idea in the space below. Be sure to include all the parts you will need and show how they will be connected.

(3) Build a Prototype

In your group, build the seismometer. As the group builds it, are there some aspects of the design that cannot be assembled as predicted? What did the group have to revise in the prototype?

_____

_____

_____

_____

(4) Test and Evaluate

Bump or shake the table under the seismometer. Did the prototype record any motion on the paper strip? If not, what can you revise?

_____

_____

_____

_____

(5) Redesign to Improve

Choose one aspect to revise, and then test again. Keep making revisions, one at a time, until your seismometer records the motion of the table. How many revisions did the group make?

_____

_____

(6) Communicate Results

Report your observations about the prototype seismometer. Include changes that improved its performance or decreased its performance. Propose ways that you could have built a more accurate seismometer. Describe what additional materials you would need and what they would be used for.

_____

_____

_____

_____

_____

Unit 6 〉Big Idea〉 Earth's surface has changed over time as a result of the movement of tectonic plates and other natural processes.

Lesson 1
ESSENTIAL QUESTION
What are Earth's layers?

Identify Earth's compositional and physical layers and describe their properties.

Lesson 2
ESSENTIAL QUESTION
How do we learn about Earth's history?

Explain how Earth materials, such as rock, fossils, and ice, show that Earth has changed over time.

Lesson 3
ESSENTIAL QUESTION
What is plate tectonics?

Explain the theory of plate tectonics and plate movement, and identify the geologic events caused by this.

Lesson 4
ESSENTIAL QUESTION
How do mountains form?

Describe how the movement of Earth's tectonic plates causes mountain building.

Lesson 5
ESSENTIAL QUESTION
How do volcanoes change Earth's surface?

Describe what the various kinds of volcanoes and eruptions are, where they occur, how they form, and how they change Earth's surface.

Lesson 6
ESSENTIAL QUESTION
Why do earthquakes happen?

Describe the causes of earthquakes and identify where earthquakes happen.

Connect ESSENTIAL QUESTIONS
Lessons 3 and 6

1 Synthesize Explain why tectonic plate boundaries are areas of intense geological activity.

_____

_____

_____

_____

Think Outside the Book

2 Synthesize Choose one of these activities to help synthesize what you have learned in this unit.

☐ Using what you learned in lessons 3, 4, 5, and 6, prepare a poster presentation that summarizes plate tectonic activity at convergent boundaries.

☐ Using what you learned in lessons 3, 4, and 6, prepare a poster presentation that summarizes plate tectonics at divergent boundaries.

Unit 6 Review

Name _____

Vocabulary

Fill in each blank with the term that best completes the following sentences.

1 The hot, convecting _____ is the layer of rock between the
Earth's crust and core.

2 _____ is the theory that explains how large
pieces of Earth's outermost layer move and change shape.

3 _____ is the bending of rock layers due to stress.

4 A(n) _____ is a vent or fissure in the Earth's surface
through which magma and gases are expelled.

5 A(n) _____ is a movement or trembling of the ground
that is caused by a sudden release of energy when rocks move along a fault.

Key Concepts

Read each question below, and circle the best answer.

6 What is the difference between lava and magma?

A Magma is found above Earth's surface and lava is found below Earth's surface.

B Lava is a solid material and magma is a liquid material.

C Magma is found below Earth's surface and lava is found above Earth's surface.

D Magma only erupts in the ocean and lava only erupts on land.

7 Tectonic plates are made of continental crust, oceanic crust, or a combination of
the two. Besides their locations, how else are these two kinds of crust different?

A Tectonic plates made of continental crust are larger than plates made of oceanic
crust.

B Tectonic plates made of continental crust are smaller than plates made of
oceanic crust.

C Continental crust is thicker than oceanic crust.

D Continental crust is thinner than oceanic crust.

8 Which of these choices names two kinds of trace fossils?

   A tracks and burrows   **C** bee and beetle in amber

   B shells and bones   **D** petrified and mummified fossils

9 Earth's surface features slowly change over time. For example, sharp, jagged mountain ranges become lower and more rounded over time. What is responsible for this change in their shape?

   A weathering and erosion   **C** movement of continents

   B deposition   **D** collisions between continental plates

10 Volcanic eruptions can have many characteristics. They can be slow, fast, calm, explosive, or a combination of these. Which type of eruption is associated with the release of pyroclastic materials?

   A a calm eruption

   B an explosive eruption

   C a fast eruption

   D a slow eruption

11 What happens at a divergent tectonic plate boundary?

   A Two tectonic plates move horizontally past one another.

   B Two tectonic plates pull away from each other, forming a rift valley or mid-ocean ridge.

   C Two tectonic plates come together to form one plate.

   D Two tectonic plates collide, causing subduction.

12 The figure below shows an arch, a geologic formation made over a long period of time by a process that supports the principle of uniformitarianism.

Which process below formed the arch shown in the figure?

A precipitation   **C** erosion

B deposition   **D** volcanism

13 Which of the following is a major difference between Earth's inner core and Earth's outer core?

A The inner core is liquid and the outer core is solid.

B The inner core is solid and the outer core is liquid.

C The inner core is gas and the outer core is solid.

D The inner core is solid and the outer core is gas.

14 Volcanic islands can form over hot spots. The Hawaiian Islands started forming over a hot spot in the Pacific Ocean millions of years ago. What process causes the hot, solid rock to rise through the mantle at these locations?

A condensation   **C** convection

B conduction   **D** radiation

15 Earth's three compositional layers are the mantle, core, and crust.

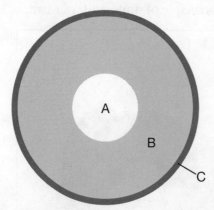

Which statement below is correct?

A A is the crust, B is the core, and C is the mantle.

B A is the core, B is the mantle, and C is the crust.

C A is the inner core, B is the outer core, and C is the mantle.

D A is the core, B is the crust, and C is the mantle.

16 Earth can be divided into five layers: lithosphere, asthenosphere, mesosphere, outer core, and inner core. Which properties are used to make these divisions?

A compositional properties   **C** chemical properties

B physical properties   **D** elemental properties

17 This diagram shows the formation of a fault-block mountain. Arrows outside of the blocks show the directions of force. Arrows inside the blocks show the directions of movement. The blocks *K* and *L* move along a line marked *J*.

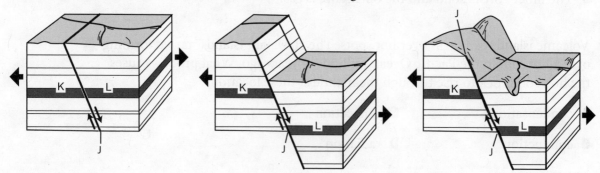

What does the line marked by the letter *J* represent?

A a river   **C** the fault line

B a rock layer   **D** the focus

18 The map below shows the epicenters of some major earthquakes of 2003.

Locations of Major Earthquakes in 2003

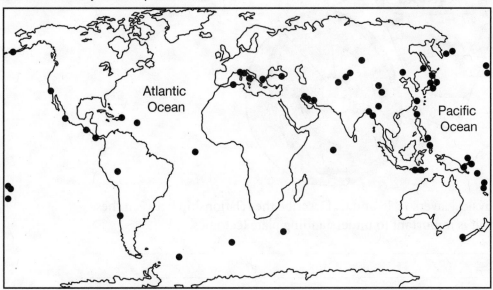

What is the most likely reason that there were no major earthquakes recorded in the interior of the continent of Africa?

A There are no faults in Africa.

B The landmass of Africa is too large to be affected by earthquakes.

C The plate boundary inside Africa is too small to form earthquakes.

D No major plate boundaries cut through the continent of Africa.

Critical Thinking

Answer the following questions in the space provided.

19 Explain how a convergent boundary is different from a transform boundary. Then, name one thing that commonly occurs along both convergent boundaries and transform boundaries.

_____

_____

_____

_____

_____

_____

20 The diagram below shows the five physical layers of Earth.

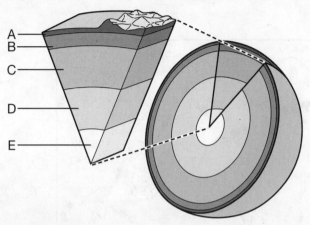

Identify the physical layers A, B, and C. Describe the relationship between these layers and how it is important to understanding plate tectonics.

_____

_____

_____

_____

21 What evidence do we have that the surface of the Earth has changed over time? Explain how the principle of uniformitarianism applies to this evidence.

_____

_____

_____

_____

Connect ESSENTIAL QUESTIONS
Lessons 4 and 5

Answer the following question in the space provided.

22 Explain how forces from tectonic plate movement can build these three types of mountains: folded mountains, fault-block mountains, and volcanic mountains.

_____

_____

_____

_____

_____

Earth's Resources

Common building materials such as lumber, bricks, and glass are all made from natural resources.

Big Idea

Humans use natural resources for materials and energy, and also affect the environment with their population growth.

S6E5., S6E5.e, S6E6., S6E6.a, S6E6.b

Wood for buildings comes from forests that have to be managed wisely.

What do you think?

Humans affect Earth's surface when they harvest its resources and through other activities. What happens when these resources are used up? How do humans affect the environment? As you explore the unit, gather evidence to help you state and support claims to answer these questions.

Energy Sources

The world is filled with valuable resources. How we use, reuse, or use up those resources is important to this and future generations.

① Think About It

Every time you walk into school on a normal school day, the lights are on, the rooms are comfortable, and there are material resources available for teacher and student use. Where does your school get its energy? Is it from a renewable or nonrenewable resource? Could the energy be used more efficiently?

_____

_____

_____

_____

The type of lighting as well as the quality of doors and windows can make a difference in a building's energy costs and efficiency.

② Ask a Question

What is the energy source for your school's heating and cooling system?

With a partner or as a class, learn more about the source of energy for your school's heating and cooling system and the energy efficiency of your school building. As you talk about it, consider the items below.

Things to Consider

☐ Does your school have more than one energy source?

☐ Is your school building energy efficient?

Many older schools have been modified with new windows, doors, and insulation. These changes were made to save on heating and cooling costs and to provide a more comfortable learning environment.

③ Make a Plan

Once you have learned about your school building's energy efficiency, develop a proposal for your principal. Propose an alternative energy source for the heating and cooling system and ways to improve the building's energy efficiency.

A Describe the current energy source for your school's heating and cooling system.

_____

_____

B Describe one alternative energy source your school could use.

_____

_____

C List any noted energy inefficiencies and suggestions for improvements.

_____

_____

Ideas for saving resources can help schools save money.

Take It Home

What energy sources supply your home? With an adult, talk about possible ways to improve energy efficiency where you live. See *ScienceSaurus®* for more information about energy conservation.

Nonrenewable Energy Resources

ESSENTIAL QUESTION

How do we use nonrenewable energy resources?

By the end of this lesson, you should be able to describe how humans use energy resources and the role of nonrenewable energy resources in society.

The energy that lights up this city and powers the vehicles comes from energy resources. Most of our energy resources are being used up faster than natural processes can replace them.

 S6E6.a Renewable and nonrenewable energy resources

Engage Your Brain

1 Identify Unscramble the letters below to find substances that are nonrenewable resources.

ALCO _____

AUNTRLA SGA _____

NUUIMAR _____

MLPEOUTRE _____

2 Describe Write your own caption for this photo.

_____

_____

_____

Active Reading

3 Synthesize Many English words have their roots in other languages. Use the Latin word below to make an educated guess about the meaning of the word *fission*.

Latin word	Meaning
fissus	to split

Example sentence
An atomic nucleus can undergo <u>fission</u>.

fission:

_____

_____

Vocabulary Terms

- natural resource
- energy resource
- renewable resource
- nonrenewable resource
- fossil fuel
- nuclear energy
- fission

4 Identify This list contains the vocabulary terms you'll learn in this lesson. As you read, circle the definition of each term.

Be Resourceful!

What are the two main types of nonrenewable energy resources?

A **natural resource** is any natural material that is used by humans. Natural resources include air, soil, minerals, water, oil, plants, and animals. An **energy resource** is a natural resource that humans use to generate energy and can be renewable or nonrenewable. **Renewable resources** are replaced by natural processes at least as quickly as they are used. **Nonrenewable resources** are used up faster than they can be replaced. Most of the energy used in the United States comes from nonrenewable resources.

Fossil Fuels

A **fossil fuel** is a nonrenewable energy resource that forms from the remains of organisms that lived long ago. Fossil fuels release energy when they are burned. This energy can be converted to electricity or used to power engines. Fossil fuels are the most commonly used energy resource because they are relatively inexpensive to locate and process.

Nuclear Fuel

The energy released when the nuclei of atoms are split or combined is called **nuclear energy**. This energy can be obtained by two kinds of nuclear reactions—fusion and fission. Today's nuclear power plants use fission, because the technology for fusion power plants does not currently exist. The most common nuclear fuel is uranium. Uranium is obtained by mining and processing uranium ore, which is a nonrenewable resource.

Do the Math

You Try It

Nonrenewable Energy Resources Consumed in the U.S. in 2009

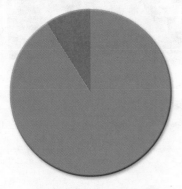

■ Fossil Fuels 90.37%
■ Nuclear Fuel 9.63%

5 Calculate In 2009, 86.8 quadrillion BTUs of the energy used in the United States was produced from nonrenewable energy resources. Using the graph above, calculate how much of this energy was produced from nuclear fuel.

6 Compare Fill in the Venn diagram to compare and contrast fossil fuels and nuclear fuel.

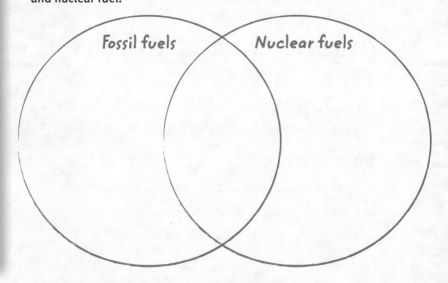

Fossil fuels   Nuclear fuels

What are the three main types of fossil fuels?

All living things contain the element carbon. Fossil fuels form from the remains of living things, so they also contain carbon. Most of this carbon is in the form of hydrocarbons, which are compounds made of hydrogen and carbon. Fossil fuels can be liquids, gases, or solids. Fossil fuels include petroleum, natural gas, and coal.

Active Reading **7 Identify** As you read, underline the state of matter for each fossil fuel.

Petroleum

Petroleum, or *crude oil*, is a liquid mixture of complex hydrocarbon compounds. Crude oil is extracted from the ground by drilling then processed for use. This process, called *refining*, separates the crude oil into different products such as gasoline, kerosene, and diesel fuel. More than 35 percent of the world's energy comes from crude oil products. Crude oil is also used to make products such as ink, bubble gum, and plastics.

This crude oil will be refined into gasoline, diesel fuel, heating oil, kerosene, and other products.

Natural Gas

Natural gas is a mixture of gaseous hydrocarbons. Most natural gas is used for heating and cooking, but some is used to generate electricity. Also, some vehicles use natural gas as fuel.

Methane is the main component of natural gas. Butane and propane can also be separated from natural gas. Butane and propane are used as fuel for camp stoves and outdoor grills. Some rural homes also use propane as a heating fuel.

Natural gas is a popular fuel for cooking because it is inexpensive.

Coal

The fossil fuel most widely used for generating electrical power is a solid called coal. Coal was once used to heat homes and for transportation. In fact, many trains in the 1800s and early 1900s were pulled by coal-burning steam locomotives. Now, most people use gasoline for transportation fuel. But more than half of our nation's electricity comes from coal-burning power plants.

Coal is a fossil fuel often used to generate electricity.

How do fossil fuels form?

How might a sunny day 200 million years ago relate to your life today? If you traveled to school by bus or car, you likely used energy from sunlight that warmed Earth that long ago.

Fossil fuels form over millions of years from the buried remains of ancient organisms. Fossil fuels differ in the kinds of organisms from which they form and in how they form. This process is continuing, too. The fossil fuels forming today will be available for use in a few million years!

Petroleum and Natural Gas Form from Marine Organisms

Petroleum and natural gas form mainly from the remains of microscopic sea organisms. When these organisms die, their remains sink and settle on the ocean floor. There, the dead organisms are gradually buried by sediment. The sediment is compacted by more layers of dead organisms and sediment. Over time the sediment layers become layers of rock.

Over millions of years, heat and pressure turn the remains of the organisms into petroleum and natural gas. The petroleum and natural gas, along with groundwater, flow into pores in the rock. A rock with pores is a *permeable rock*. Permeable rocks become reservoirs where the petroleum and natural gas are trapped and concentrated over time. Humans can extract the fuels from these reservoirs.

Think Outside the Book Inquiry

8 Claims • Evidence • Reasoning
With a classmate, state how the process of petroleum formation might affect oil availability in the future. Provide evidence to support your claim and explain your reasoning.

Petroleum and Natural Gas Formation

❶ Microscopic marine organisms die and settle to the bottom of the sea.

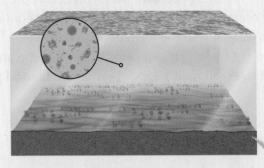

❷ Layers of sediment slowly bury the dead marine organisms.

❸ Heat and pressure on these layers slowly turn the remains of these organisms into petroleum and natural gas.

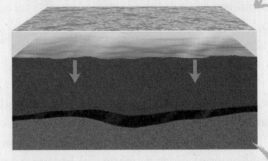

❹ Petroleum and natural gas flow through permeable rocks, where they are trapped and become concentrated into reservoirs.

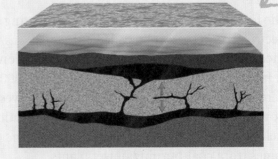

Coal Formation

1 **Peat** Partially decayed swamp plants sink and change into peat.

2 **Lignite** As sediment buries the peat, increases in temperature and pressure change peat to lignite.

3 **Bituminous Coal** As sediment builds, increased temperature and pressure change lignite to bituminous coal.

4 **Anthracite** As sediments accumulate and temperature and pressure rise, bituminous coal changes to anthracite.

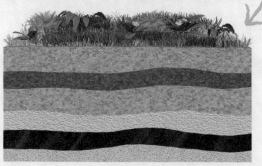

Coal Forms from Plant Remains

Active Reading **9 Identify** As you read, underline the factors that convert the buried plants into coal.

Coal is formed over millions of years from the remains of swamp plants. When the plants die, they sink to the swamp floor. Low oxygen levels in the water keep many plants from decaying and allow the process of coal formation to begin. Today's swamp plants may eventually turn into coal millions of years from now.

The first step of coal formation is plant matter changing into peat. Peat is made mostly of plant material and water. Peat is not coal. In some parts of the world, peat is dried and burned for warmth or used as fuel. Peat that is buried by layers of sediment can turn into coal after millions of years.

Over time, pressure and high temperature force water and gases out of the peat. The peat gradually becomes harder, and its carbon content increases. The amount of heat and pressure determines the type of coal that forms. Lignite forms first, followed by bituminous coal and, finally, anthracite. Anthracite is highly valued because it has the highest carbon content and gives off the most energy as heat when burned.

Today, all three types of coal are mined around the world. When burned, coal releases energy as heat and pollutes the air. The greater the carbon content of the coal, the fewer pollutants are released and the cleaner the coal burns.

Visualize It!

10 Compare What is similar about the way petroleum and coal form? What is different?

_____

_____

_____

_____

_____

_____

_____

Power Trip

How are fossil fuels used as energy sources?

Active Reading

11 Identify As you read, underline the uses of fossil fuels.

In the United States, petroleum fuels are mainly used for transportation and heating. Airplanes, trains, boats, and cars all use petroleum for energy. Some people also use petroleum as a heating fuel. There are some oil-fired power plants in the United States, but most are found in other parts of the world.

Natural gas can be used as transportation fuel but is mainly used for heating and cooking. The use of natural gas as a source of electrical power is increasing. The U.S. Department of Energy projects that most power plants in the near future will use natural gas. Today, coal is mainly used in the U.S. to generate electricity, which we use for lighting and to power appliances and technology.

Burning coal heats water to produce steam. The steam turns the turbines to generate electricity. Scrubbers and filters in the smokestack help reduce air pollution.

Coal-Fired Power Plant

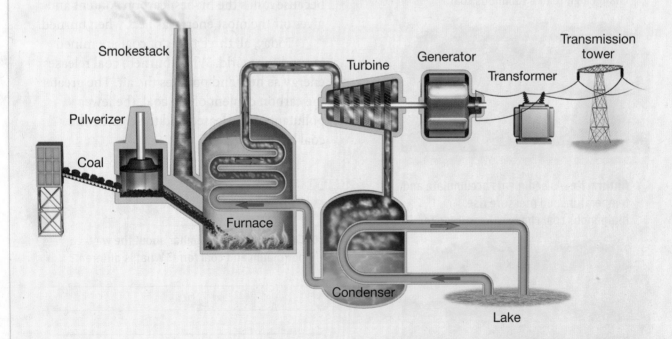

How is energy produced from nuclear fuels?

During **fission**, the nuclei of radioactive atoms are split into two or more fragments. A small particle called a neutron hits and splits an atom. This process releases large amounts of energy as heat and radiation. Fission also releases more neutrons that bombard other atoms. The process repeats as a chain reaction. Fission takes place inside a reactor core. Fuel rods containing uranium, shown in green below, provide the material for the chain reaction. Control rods that absorb neutrons are used to regulate the chain reaction. The energy is released, which is used to generate electrical power. A closed reactor system contains the radioactivity. Nuclear wastes are contained separately for disposal.

During nuclear reactions, energy in the form of heat is released, which turns water into steam. Steam turns the turbines to generate electricity.

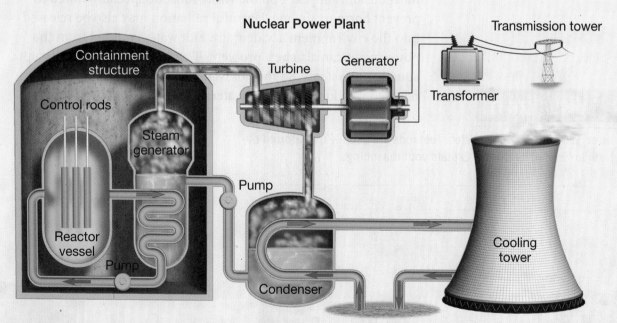

Nuclear Power Plant

12 Compare How are the two types of power plants similar? How are they different?

Similar	Different
_____	_____
_____	_____
_____	_____
_____	_____

The Pros and Cons

How can we evaluate nonrenewable energy resources?

There are advantages and disadvantages to using nonrenewable energy resources. Nonrenewable resources provide much of the energy that humans need to power transportation, warm homes, and produce electricity relatively cheaply. But the methods of obtaining and using these resources can have negative effects on the environment.

The Pros and Cons of Nuclear Fuel

Nuclear fission produces a large amount of energy and does not cause air pollution because no fuel is burned. Mining uranium also does not usually result in massive strip mines or large loss of habitats.

However, nuclear power does have drawbacks. Nuclear power plants produce dangerous wastes that remain radioactive for thousands of years. So the waste must be specially stored to prevent harm to anyone. Harmful radiation may also be released into the environment accidentally. Hot water released from the power plant can also be a problem. This heated water can disrupt aquatic ecosystems. So the hot water must be cooled before it is released into local bodies of water.

Active Reading

13 **Identify** As you read, underline the effects that nuclear power plants have on their surroundings.

Visualize It!

14 **Infer** Why do you think nuclear fuel rods are usually transported by train instead of by trucks? Explain your reasoning.

_____

_____

Used nuclear fuel rods must be transported in specially built steel containers.

The Pros and Cons of Fossil Fuels

Fossil fuels are relatively inexpensive to obtain and use. However, there are problems associated with their use. Burning coal can release sulfur dioxide, which combines with moisture in the air to form acid rain. Acid rain causes damage to structures and the environment. Coal mining also disturbs habitats, lowers water tables, and pollutes water.

Environmental problems are also associated with using oil. In 2010, a blown oil well spilled an estimated 126 million gallons of crude oil in the Gulf of Mexico for 87 days. The environmental costs may continue for years.

Burning fossil fuels can cause smog, especially in cities with millions of vehicles. Smog is a brownish haze that can cause respiratory problems and contribute to acid rain. Burning fossil fuels also releases carbon dioxide into the atmosphere. Increases in atmospheric carbon dioxide can lead to global warming.

Some coal is mined by removing the tops of mountains to expose the coal. This damages habitats and can cause water pollution as well.

15 Evaluate In the chart below, list the advantages and disadvantages of using nuclear fuel and fossil fuels.

Type of fuel	Pros	Cons
nuclear fuel		
fossil fuels		

Visual Summary

To complete this summary, check the box that indicates true or false. Then use the key below to check your answers. You can use this page to review the main concepts of the lesson.

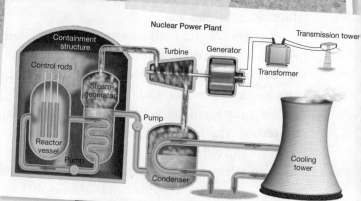

Nuclear Power Plant

Nuclear fuel is an energy resource that undergoes the process of fission to release energy for human use.

	T	F	
16	☐	☐	Uranium is often used as fuel in nuclear fission.
17	☐	☐	One disadvantage of nuclear fission is that it produces only a small amount of energy.

Nonrenewable Energy Resources

Most of the energy used today comes from fossil fuels, which include petroleum, natural gas, and coal.

	T	F	
18	☐	☐	Natural gas forms from microscopic marine organisms.
19	☐	☐	Most transportation fuels are products of coal.
20	☐	☐	Burning fossil fuels decreases the amount of carbon dioxide in the atmosphere.

Answers: 16 True; 17 False; 18 True; 19 False; 20 False

21 **Summarize** Identify the advantages and disadvantages for both fossil fuels and nuclear fuels.

Lesson Review

Vocabulary

Fill in the blank with the term that best completes the following sentences.

1 _____ is energy in an atom's nucleus.

2 Crude oil is a liquid kind of _____

3 _____ can be renewable or nonrenewable.

4 During the process of _____, the nuclei of radioactive atoms are split into two or more smaller nuclei.

Key Concepts

5 Describe Describe how fossil fuels are converted into usable energy.

_____

_____

_____

_____

6 Sequence Which of the following sequences of processes best describes how electricity is generated in a nuclear power plant?

A fission reaction, produce steam, turn turbine, generate electricity, cool water

B produce steam, fission reaction, turn turbine, generate electricity, cool water

C cool water, fission reaction, produce steam, turn turbine, generate electricity

D produce steam, turn turbine, cool water, fission reaction, generate electricity

7 Identify Which is an example of how people use nonrenewable energy resources?

A eating a banana

B sailing a boat

C walking to school

D driving a car

Critical Thinking

8 Hypothesize Why do some places in the United States have deposits of coal but others have deposits of petroleum and natural gas?

_____

_____

_____

_____

_____

Use the graph to answer the following questions.

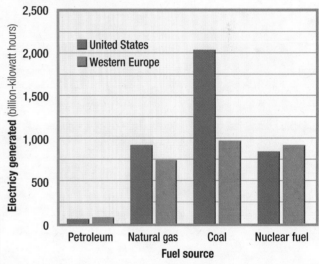

Electricity Produced from Nonrenewable Energy Resources in 2007

9 Calculate About how much more coal than petroleum is used to generate electricity in the United States and Western Europe?

_____

_____

_____

10 Analyze What patterns of energy resource use do you see in the graph?

_____

_____

_____

My Notes

Renewable Energy Resources

ESSENTIAL QUESTION

How do humans use renewable energy resources?

By the end of this lesson, you should be able to describe how humans use energy resources and the role of renewable energy resources in society.

S6E6.a Renewable and nonrenewable energy resources

Panels such as these can turn an unused city roof into a miniature solar energy plant.

Lesson Labs

Quick Labs
• Design a Turbine
• Understanding Solar Panels

S.T.E.M. Lab
• Modeling Geothermal Power

Engage Your Brain

1 Predict Check T or F to show whether you think each statement is true or false.

T	F	
☐	☐	Renewable energy resources can never run out.
☐	☐	Renewable energy resources do not cause any type of pollution.
☐	☐	Solar energy is the most widely used renewable energy resource in the United States.
☐	☐	Renewable energy resources include solar energy, wind energy, and geothermal energy.

2 Describe Write a caption to explain how the sun's energy is being used in this photo.

_____

_____

_____

_____

_____

Active Reading

3 Synthesize You can often define an unknown word if you know the meaning of its word parts. Use the word parts and sentence below to make an educated guess about the meaning of the word *geothermal*.

Word part	Meaning
geo-	Earth
therm-	heat

Example sentence

A <u>geothermal</u> power plant uses steam produced deep in the ground to generate electricity.

geothermal:

_____

_____

_____

Vocabulary Terms

• energy resource
• wind energy
• hydroelectric energy
• solar energy
• biomass
• geothermal energy
• photosynthesis

4 Apply As you learn the definition of each vocabulary term in this lesson, create your own definition or sketch to help you remember the meaning of the term.

Energy *Déjà Vu*

What are the two main sources of renewable energy?

An **energy resource** is a natural resource used to generate electricity and other forms of energy. Most of the energy used by humans comes from *nonrenewable resources*. These resources are used more quickly than they can be replaced. But *renewable resources* can be replaced almost as quickly as they are used. Most renewable energy resources come from the sun and some from Earth itself.

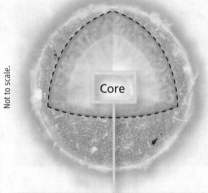

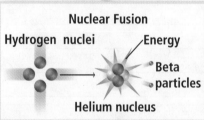

Nuclear Fusion
Hydrogen nuclei   Energy
                       Beta particles
Helium nucleus

When atomic nuclei fuse, energy is released.

The Sun

The sun's energy is a result of nuclear fusion. Fusion is the process by which two or more nuclei fuse together to form a larger nucleus. Fusion produces a large amount of energy, which is released into space as light and heat.

Solar energy warms Earth, causing the movement of air masses. Moving air masses form winds and some ocean currents. Solar energy also fuels plant growth. Animals get energy by eating plants. Humans can harness energy from wind, moving water, plant and animal materials, and directly from the light and heat that comes from the sun.

Earth

Energy from within Earth comes from two sources. One source is the decay of radioactive elements in Earth's mantle and crust, caused by nuclear fission. Fission is the splitting of the nuclei of radioactive atoms. The second source of energy within Earth is energy stored during Earth's formation. The heat produced from these sources radiates outward toward Earth's surface. Humans can harness this heat to use as an energy source.

---

5 Contrast Explain how energy production in the sun differs from energy production in Earth's interior.

_____

_____

_____

_____

_____

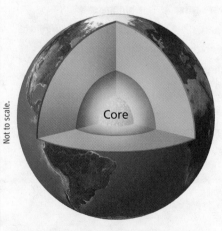

Earth's internal energy comes from the process of nuclear fission and the events that formed Earth.

How might a renewable energy resource become nonrenewable?

All of the energy resources you will learn about in this lesson are renewable. That doesn't mean that they can't become nonrenewable resources. Trees, for example, are a renewable resource. Some people burn wood from trees to heat their homes and cook food. However, some forests are being cut down but are not being replanted in a timely manner. Others are being cut down and replaced with buildings. If this process continues, eventually these forests will no longer be considered renewable resources.

6 Apply Read the caption below, then describe what might happen if the community uses too much of the water in the reservoir.

_____

_____

_____

_____

_____

7 Distinguish What is the difference between nonrenewable and renewable energy resources?

_____

_____

_____

_____

_____

Think Outside the Book

8 Apply Write an interview with a renewable resource that is afraid it might become nonrenewable. Be sure to include questions and answers.

A community uses this reservoir for water. The dam at the end of the reservoir uses moving water to produce electricity for the community.

Turn, Turn, Turn

How do humans use wind energy?

Wind is created by the sun's uneven heating of air masses in Earth's atmosphere. **Wind energy** uses the force of moving air to drive an electric generator or do other work. Wind energy is renewable because the wind will blow as long as the sun warms Earth. Wind energy is harnessed by machines called wind turbines. Electricity is generated when moving air turns turbine blades that drive an electric generator. Clusters of wind turbines, called wind farms, generate large amounts of electricity.

Although wind energy is a renewable energy resource, it has several disadvantages. Wind farms can be placed only in areas that receive large amounts of wind. The equipment required to collect and convert wind energy is also expensive to produce and maintain. And the production and maintenance of this equipment produces a small amount of pollution. The turbine blades can also be hazardous to birds.

Windmills such as these have been used for centuries to grind grain and pump surface water for irrigation.

A wind-powered water pump can pull water from deep underground when electricity is not available.

Wind farms are a form of clean energy, because they do not generate air pollution as they generate electricity.

9 Infer What is the main benefit of placing these turbines in open water?

_____

_____

_____

_____

How do humans get energy from moving water?

10 Identify Underline the kind of energy that is found in moving water.

Like wind, moving water has kinetic energy. People have harnessed the energy of falling or flowing water to power machines since ancient times. Some grain and saw mills still use water to power their equipment. Electrical energy produced by moving water is called **hydroelectric energy**. Hydroelectric energy is renewable because the water cycle is driven by the sun. Water that evaporates from oceans and lakes falls on higher elevations and flows downhill in streams, rivers, and waterfalls. The energy in flowing water is converted to electrical energy when it spins turbines connected to electric generators inside the dam.

Hydroelectric energy is a good source of energy only in locations where there are large, reliable amounts of flowing water. Another disadvantage of hydroelectric energy is that hydroelectric dams and their technology are expensive to build. The dams also can block the movement of fish between the sea and their spawning grounds. Special fish ladders must be built to allow fish to swim around the dam.

Visualize It!

11 Explain What is the purpose of the lake that is located behind the dam of a hydroelectric plant? Explain your reasoning.

_____

_____

_____

_____

_____

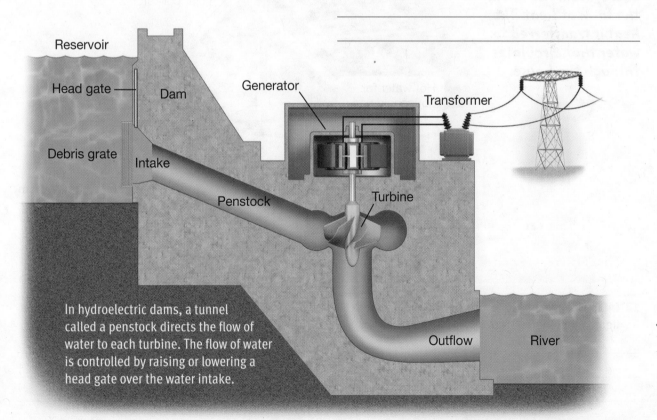

In hydroelectric dams, a tunnel called a penstock directs the flow of water to each turbine. The flow of water is controlled by raising or lowering a head gate over the water intake.

Let the Sunshine In

How do humans use solar energy?

Most forms of energy come from the sun—even fossil fuels begin with the sun as an energy resource. **Solar energy** is the energy received by Earth from the sun in the form of radiation. Solar energy can be used to warm buildings directly. Solar energy can also be converted into electricity by solar cells.

To Provide Energy as Heat

We can use liquids warmed by the sun to warm water and buildings. Some liquids, such as water, have a high capacity for absorbing and holding heat. When the heat is absorbed by the liquid in a solar collector, it can be transferred to water that circulates through a building. The hot water can be used for bathing or other household uses, or to warm the building. The only pollution generated by solar heating systems comes from the manufacture and maintenance of their equipment. Solar heating systems work best in areas with large amounts of sunlight.

Solar collectors absorb energy from the sun in the form of heat. The heat is transferred to water that circulates through the house.

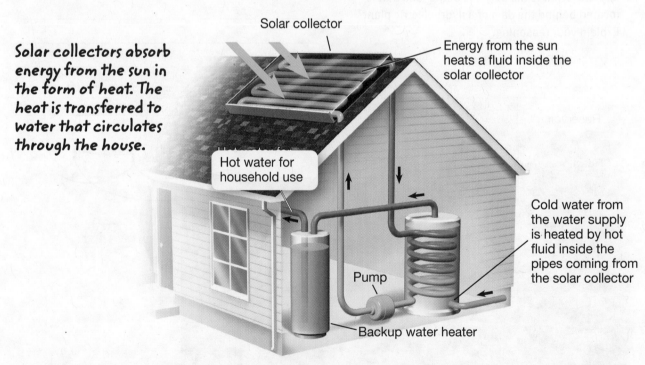

Solar collector

Energy from the sun heats a fluid inside the solar collector

Hot water for household use

Cold water from the water supply is heated by hot fluid inside the pipes coming from the solar collector

Pump

Backup water heater

12 Infer Not all solar collectors use water to absorb energy from the sun. Why might a solar heating system use a liquid other than water?

_____

_____

_____

Active Reading **13 Identify** As you read, underline the characteristics of a photovoltaic cell.

To Produce Electricity

Solar collectors can also be used to generate electricity. First, heated fluid is used to produce steam. Then, the steam turns a turbine connected to an electric generator.

Electricity can also be generated when sunlight is absorbed by a photovoltaic cell. A single photovoltaic cell produces a small amount of electricity. The electricity from joined photovoltaic cells can power anything from calculators to entire communities. Many cells must be joined together to form each solar panel, as shown in the solar power plant below. Solar power plants must be built in places with adequate space and abundant sunshine year-round. These requirements increase the costs of solar power.

This calculator is powered by solar cells instead of a battery.

Visualize It! (Inquiry)

14 Claims • Evidence • Reasoning Based on this image and your reading, what might be a disadvantage to using solar energy to supply electricity to a large community? Explain your reasoning.

_____

_____

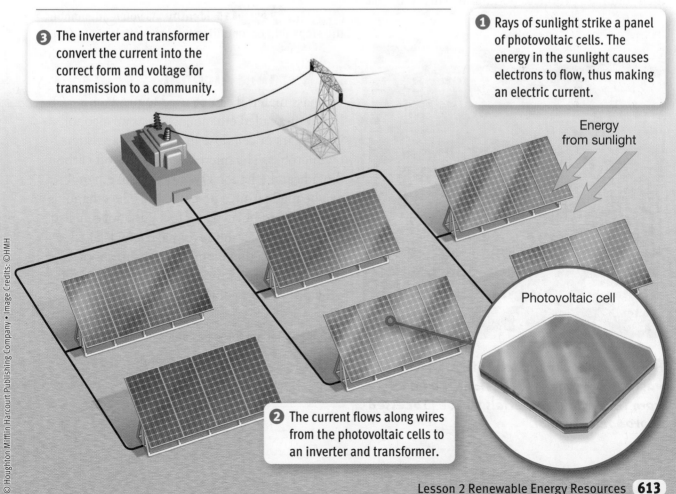

3 The inverter and transformer convert the current into the correct form and voltage for transmission to a community.

1 Rays of sunlight strike a panel of photovoltaic cells. The energy in the sunlight causes electrons to flow, thus making an electric current.

Energy from sunlight

Photovoltaic cell

2 The current flows along wires from the photovoltaic cells to an inverter and transformer.

How do humans get energy from living things?

Plants absorb light energy from the sun and convert it to chemical energy through photosynthesis. During **photosynthesis**, plants convert carbon dioxide and water to oxygen and glucose. This process allows plants to accumulate chemical energy in their leaves, stems, and roots. Chemical energy is also present in the dung of animals. These sources of energy make up biomass.

By Burning Biomass

Biomass is organic matter from plants and from animal waste that contains chemical energy. Biomass can be burned to release energy. This energy can be used to cook food, provide warmth, or power an engine. Biomass sources include trees, crops, animal waste, and peat.

Biomass is inexpensive and can usually be replaced relatively quickly, so it is considered to be a renewable resource. Some types of biomass renew more slowly than others. Peat renews so slowly in areas where it is used heavily that it is treated as a nonrenewable resource. Like fossil fuels, biomass produces pollutants when it burns.

These peat pellets will be used to generate steam in the power plant in the background. The steam will generate electricity by turning turbines.

Active Reading **15 Identify** As you read, number the steps that occur during the production of ethanol.

By Burning Alcohol

Biomass material can be used to produce a liquid fuel called ethanol, which is an alcohol. The sugars or cellulose in the plants are eaten by microbes. The microbes then give off carbon dioxide and ethanol. Over 1,000 L of ethanol can be made from 1 acre of corn. The ethanol is collected and burned as a fuel. Ethanol can also be mixed with gasoline to make a fuel called gasohol. The ethanol produced from about 40% of one corn harvest in the United States would provide only 10% of the fuel used in our cars!

16 List What are three examples of how biomass can be used for energy?

_____

_____

_____

These wagons are loaded with sugar cane wastes from sugar production. The cellulose from these plant materials will be processed to produce ethanol.

© Houghton Mifflin Harcourt Publishing Company • Image Credits: (t) ©Hank Morgan/Photo Researchers, Inc.; (b) ©Christian Tragni/Aurora Photos/Alamy Images

How do humans use geothermal energy?

The water in the geyser at right is heated by geothermal energy. **Geothermal energy** is energy produced by heat from Earth's interior. Geothermal energy heats rock formations deep within the ground. Groundwater absorbs this heat and forms hot springs and geysers where the water reaches Earth's surface. Geothermal energy is used to produce energy as heat and electricity.

To Provide Energy as Heat

Geothermal energy can be used to warm and cool buildings. A closed loop system of pipes runs from underground into the heating system of a home or building. Water pumped through these pipes absorbs heat from the ground and is used to warm the building. Hot groundwater can also be pumped in and used in a similar way. In warmer months, the ground is cooler than the air, so this system can also be used for cooling.

To Produce Electricity

Geothermal energy is also used to produce electricity. Wells are drilled into areas of superheated groundwater, allowing steam and hot water to escape. Geothermal power plants pump the steam or hot water from underground to spin turbines that generate electricity, as shown at right. A disadvantage of geothermal energy is pollution that occurs during production of the technology needed to capture it. The technology is also expensive to make and maintain.

Because Earth's core will be very hot for billions of years, geothermal energy will be available for a long time.

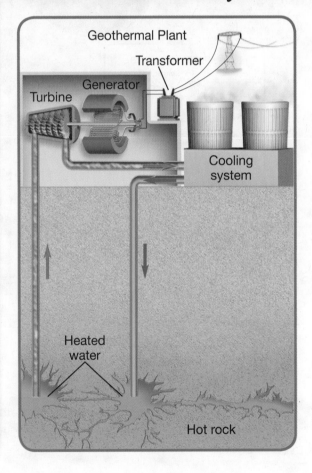

Geothermal Plant

Transformer

Generator

Turbine

Cooling system

Heated water

Hot rock

17 List What are some advantages and disadvantages to using geothermal energy?

Advantages	Disadvantages

Visual Summary

To complete this summary, fill in the blanks with the correct word or phrase. Then, use the key below to check your answers. You can use this page to review the main concepts of the lesson.

The source of geothermal energy is energy from within Earth.

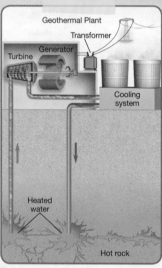

Geothermal Plant
Transformer
Generator
Turbine
Cooling system
Heated water
Hot rock

18 In geothermal power plants, hot water or _____ is pumped from within Earth's crust to produce electricity.

Renewable Energy Resources

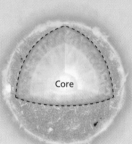

Most of the renewable energy resources that people use come from the sun.

19 Renewable resources that come from the sun include _____ _____ _____

Answers: 18 steam; 19 biomass, solar energy, wind energy, and hydroelectric energy

20 Synthesize Which type of renewable energy resource would be best to use to provide electricity for your town? Explain your reasoning.

Lesson Review

Vocabulary

Fill in the blanks with the term that best completes the following sentences.

1 Organic matter that contains stored energy is called _____

2 A resource that humans can use to produce energy is a(n) _____

3 _____ is an energy resource harnessed from flowing water.

Key Concepts

4 Describe Identify a major advantage and a major disadvantage of using renewable energy resources to produce electricity.

_____

_____

_____

_____

_____

_____

5 Explain If renewable energy resources can be replaced, why do we need to conserve them? Use an example to support your answer.

_____

_____

_____

_____

_____

_____

6 Describe What is the source of energy that powers wind and flowing water?

_____

_____

_____

_____

_____

Critical Thinking

Use this graph to answer the following questions.

Total Renewable Energy Resources Consumed in 2014 in the United States

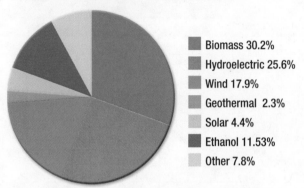

- Biomass 30.2%
- Hydroelectric 25.6%
- Wind 17.9%
- Geothermal 2.3%
- Solar 4.4%
- Ethanol 11.53%
- Other 7.8%

Source: EIA Short-Term Energy Outlook 2014

7 Evaluate Which is the most used renewable energy resource in the United States? Why do you think this is the case?

_____

_____

_____

_____

8 Evaluate Which is the least used renewable energy resource in the United States? Why do you think this is the case?

_____

_____

_____

_____

_____

9 Relate Suppose someone gave you a mystery natural resource. Which questions would you ask to help you define it as a nonrenewable or renewable resource?

_____

_____

_____

_____

My Notes

S6E6.b Quality and supply of natural resources

Analyzing Technology

Skills
Identify risks
✓ Identify benefits
✓ Evaluate cost of technology
✓ Evaluate environmental impact
✓ Propose improvements
Propose risk reduction
Plan for technology failures
Compare technology
✓ Communicate results

Objectives
• Describe the effects of making paper cups on Earth's resources.
• Estimate the carbon dioxide saved by recycling paper cups.
• Propose improvements for the life cycle of a paper cup.

Analyzing the Life Cycle of a Paper Cup

A product's life cycle includes all of the phases in its "life," from getting raw materials to disposing of it once it has served its purpose. Most steps in the life cycle of a paper product affects the environment in some way.

Newspapers awaiting recycling

These paper cups probably will not be recycled.

Impact of a Paper Cup

A life cycle analysis of a paper cup shows that making it requires trees, water, ink, and plastic for a waterproof lining. The process also uses several different kinds of fuel, such as natural gas and diesel truck fuel for energy to make and transport the cups. The whole process releases about 110 grams (about ¼ pound) of carbon dioxide (KAR•buhn dy•AHK•syd) per cup into the atmosphere. This amount is 3 to 4 times the weight of a cup itself. And because of the plastic lining, paper cups are difficult to recycle.

1 Estimate Assume that a recycled paper cup is made up of only paper, and that paper could be recycled 5 times. About how much carbon dioxide would this prevent from being released into the atmosphere?

_____

_____

_____

Recycling Paper Products

Many paper products are more easily recycled than paper cups are. Over 70% of newspaper is recycled to make various products such as cereal boxes, egg cartons, and tissue paper. Many paper products can be recycled 5 to 7 times, after which the paper fibers are too short and no longer stick together well enough to make paper. Recycling paper products not only saves trees but also saves a lot of water, electricity, and gas and reduces air pollution.

The life of a paper product starts with trees. Loggers cut the tree, and a paper mill grinds it into pulp.

Most newspapers are recycled, saving trees and energy used in logging.

The mill mixes the pulp with water and other chemicals to make paper, which is used to make paper products such as paper cups.

Most paper cups end up in a landfill.

2 Infer Most newspaper is recycled. Most paper cups are not. What is one difference in environmental impact between burial and incineration for used paper products?

_____

_____

_____

These products are used by all of us and then either recycled, incinerated, or buried in a landfill.

🖐 You Try It! ⟶

Now it's your turn to analyze the life cycle of a paper cup.

621

You Try It!

Now it's your turn to analyze the life cycle of a paper cup. You'll consider things such as the benefits of paper cups and their cost in both money and environmental impact. Then you can suggest some ways to improve the cycle.

1 Identify Benefits

With your class, research the benefits of making and using paper cups. List those benefits below.

Benefits

_____

2 Evaluate Cost of Technology

A A paper mill uses about 16,000 gallons of water and about 400 kWh of electricity to produce one ton of paper cups. Using the information shown here, what is the cost of the water and electricity that are used to make one ton of paper cups?

_____

_____

_____

B A modern paper mill costs around $1 billion to build. How many cups would a company need to sell to pay for the cost of the plant, the water, and the electricity?

_____

_____

_____

- Water costs about $0.0007 per gallon.

- Electricity costs about $0.072/kWh.

- 33,000 cups weighs about a ton.

- One ton of cups sells for $2,000.

③ Evaluate Environmental Impact

With a partner, discuss possible impacts of the life cycle of a paper cup on the environment. Consider things such as the harvesting of trees, the use of chlorine-based chemicals to bleach the pulp, the energy required by the paper mill, problems associated with disposal of paper cups after their use, etc.

_____

_____

_____

_____

_____

④ Propose Improvements

With a partner, propose some improvements to the process of making or disposing of paper cups that might help make the life cycle of paper cups more environmentally friendly.

_____

_____

_____

_____

_____

⑤ Communicate Results

With your partner, tell the class the most important thing you have learned about the life cycle of a paper cup, and explain why you think it is important.

_____

_____

_____

_____

_____

_____

Managing Resources

ESSENTIAL QUESTION

Why should natural resources be managed?

By the end of this lesson, you should be able to explain the consequences of society's use of natural resources and the importance of managing these resources wisely.

Bauxite is a mineral that is mined to make aluminum. The company that removed the bauxite replanted the mined area with trees. Replanting restores habitat and helps to prevent erosion.

S6E6.a Renewable and nonrenewable energy resources

S6E6.b Quality and supply of natural resources

Engage Your Brain

1 Predict Check T or F to show whether you think each statement is true or false.

T F

☐ ☐ Renewable resources cannot be replaced at the same rate that they are used.

☐ ☐ Resource use always results in the pollution of natural areas.

☐ ☐ Placing limits on the amount of fish that can be caught can cause fish populations to increase.

☐ ☐ Recycling nonrenewable resources can cause them to be used up more quickly.

2 Describe What natural resources could be obtained from the areas in the picture?

_____

_____

_____

_____

Active Reading

3 Apply Some words have similar meanings. Use context clues to write your own definitions for the words *conservation* and *stewardship*.

Example sentence

Hotels practice water <u>conservation</u> by installing water-saving showerheads.

conservation:

_____

_____

Example sentence

Fertilizers can run off into lakes and cause algae to bloom. People who live near lakes can practice good <u>stewardship</u> of the lake by not using lawn fertilizers.

stewardship:

_____

_____

Vocabulary Terms

- natural resource
- renewable resource
- nonrenewable resource
- stewardship
- conservation
- ozone

4 Identify This list shows vocabulary terms you'll learn in this lesson. As you read, underline the definition of each term.

Useful Stuff

What are the two main types of resources?

Any natural material that is used by people is a **natural resource**. Water, trees, minerals, air, and oil are just a few examples of Earth's resources. Resources can be divided into renewable and nonrenewable resources.

Renewable Resources

A natural resource that can be replaced as quickly as the resource is used is a **renewable resource**. Water, trees, and fish are examples of renewable resources. Renewable resources can become nonrenewable resources if they are used too quickly. For example, trees in a forest can become nonrenewable if they are cut down faster than new trees can grow to replace them.

Nonrenewable Resources

A natural resource that is used much faster than it can be replaced is a **nonrenewable resource**. Coal is an example of a nonrenewable resource. It takes millions of years for coal to form. Once coal is used up, it is no longer available. Minerals, oil, and natural gas are other examples of nonrenewable resources.

5 Compare How is a renewable resource different from a nonrenewable resource?

_____
_____
_____
_____
_____
_____
_____

Visualize It!

6 Identify Label each picture as a renewable resource or nonrenewable resource.

A

B

salt mine

C

_____   _____   _____

What can happen when we use resources?

Natural resources can make people's lives easier. Natural resources allow us to heat and cool buildings, produce and use electricity, transport people and goods, and make products.

While natural resources are helpful, the way they are used can cause harm. Mining and oil spills can damage ecosystems. Oil spills can also harm local fishing or tourism industries. Burning coal or other fossil fuels can cause air and water pollution. Used products can fill landfills or litter beaches and other natural areas. Overuse of resources can make them hard to find. When resources are hard to find, they become more expensive.

Active Reading

7 Identify As you read, underline the possible effects of resource use by people.

Visualize It!

8 List What are three ways that natural resources are making life easier for this family?

_____

_____

_____

_____

_____

9 Explain How can the extraction of natural resources damage the environment? Explain your reasoning.

_____

_____

_____

_____

_____

10 Describe How can human use of natural resources pollute the environment?

_____

_____

_____

_____

Best Practices

What are some effective ways to manage resources?

As human populations continue to grow, we will need more and more resources in order to survive. People can make sure that resources continue to be available by practicing stewardship and conservation. **Stewardship** is the careful and responsible management of resources. **Conservation** is the protection and wise use of natural resources.

Conserving Renewable Resources

Stewardship of renewable resources involves a variety of conservation practices. Limits on fishing or logging can increase fish populations and protect forest ecosystems. Fish can be restocked in lakes and rivers. Logged areas can be replanted with trees. Water conservation can reduce the amount of water used in an area, so that rain can renew the water supply. Reducing the use of chemicals and energy resources can reduce the amount of pollution in air and water, and on land.

Active Reading

11 Identify As you read, underline the ways that resources can be managed effectively.

Visualize It!

12 Identify Describe the ways that each activity in the picture shows stewardship of natural resources.

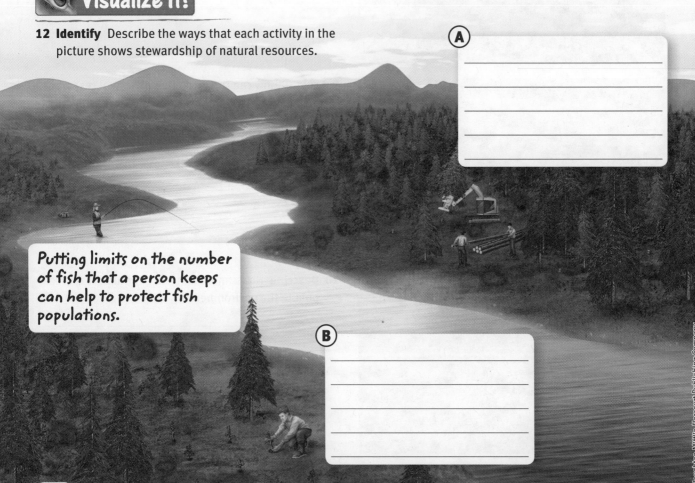

Ⓐ

Putting limits on the number of fish that a person keeps can help to protect fish populations.

Ⓑ

Reducing the Use of Nonrenewable Resources

Nonrenewable resources last longer if they are used efficiently. For example, compact fluorescent light bulbs, or CFLs, use much less energy to produce the same amount of light as incandescent light bulbs do. By using less electrical energy, fewer resources like coal are needed to produce electricity. Reducing, reusing, and recycling also reduce the amount of natural resources that must be obtained from Earth. Although recycling materials requires energy, it takes much less energy to recycle an aluminum can than it does to make a new one!

You can reuse a plastic water bottle instead of buying bottled water. Reusing conserves water and oil.

13 Apply How can you reduce the use of nonrenewable resources? Write your ideas in the table below.

Resource	Is used to...	Ways to reduce
oil	Make plastic objects. Provide energy.	Use reusable containers. Recycle plastics. Drive less.
coal		
metal		

Compact fluorescent bulbs last longer than incandescent bulbs and use a lot less energy.

Cans, wires, and other objects made of metal can be collected and recycled into new objects.

Pluses and Minuses

What are the disadvantages and advantages of managing resources?

Managing resources has disadvantages. Developing new technologies that use fewer resources is expensive. Changing how people use resources can be difficult, because some people have a hard time breaking old habits. Recycling resources can sometimes be expensive and inconvenient.

Managing resources also has many advantages. Management can reduce the loss of a valuable resource. It can also reduce waste. Less waste means less space is needed for landfills. Many resources produce pollution as they are gathered or used, so resource management can lead to less pollution.

Active Reading

14 Identify As you read, underline the advantages of managing resources.

Visualize It!

15 Place a (−) next to each property of the hybrid electric car that is a disadvantage. Place a (+) next to each property of the car that is an advantage.

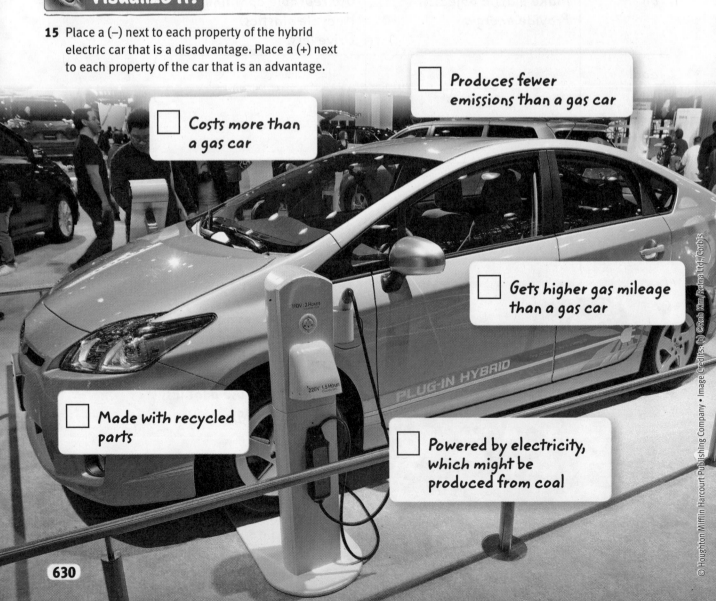

☐ Produces fewer emissions than a gas car

☐ Costs more than a gas car

☐ Gets higher gas mileage than a gas car

☐ Made with recycled parts

☐ Powered by electricity, which might be produced from coal

What kinds of changes can we make to manage resources?

Managing natural resources takes place on global, national, state, local, and individual levels. On the global level, countries make agreements to help manage international resources. For example, countries agreed to stop using chemicals called CFCs after scientists discovered that CFCs were causing damage to the ozone layer. **Ozone** is a molecule that is made up of three oxygen atoms. The ozone layer contains ozone gas in addition to other atmospheric gases. The ozone layer is a resource that protects Earth from harmful radiation. Eliminating the use of CFCs has slowed the breakdown of the ozone layer.

Change Laws

On the national level, countries pass laws to manage resources. Many nations have laws that determine where, when, and how many trees can be harvested for timber. Laws also govern how materials must be disposed of to prevent and reduce harm to land and water. Governments spend money to promote recycling programs. In addition, government funding allows scientists to develop technologies for using resources more efficiently.

Change Habits

Think about all the things you do every day. Changing some of your habits can help to conserve resources. You can conserve water by taking shorter showers and turning off the faucet while brushing your teeth. You can use reusable lunch containers and water bottles. You can recycle disposable materials, such as plastic bottles or newspaper, instead of throwing them away. You can bike or walk instead of riding in a car. You can save energy by turning off lights or TV sets when they are not being used. Families can buy energy-efficient appliances to save even more energy.

Think Outside the Book Inquiry

16 Apply With a partner, suggest laws that could be enacted in your community to protect resources.

Visualize It!

17 List What are some of the ways these students are conserving resources in their school lunchroom?

_____

_____

_____

_____

_____

_____

You can conserve resources in your school lunchroom.

ALUMINUM   MILK CARTONS   PLASTIC

Visual Summary

To complete this summary, write the answer to each question. Then use the key below to check your answers. You can use this page to review the main concepts of the lesson.

Managing Resources

Humans use natural resources to carry out daily activities.

18 What is a negative impact of resource use?

_____

_____

Managing resources has advantages and disadvantages.

Managing resources can allow resources to be conserved.

19 List two ways that resources can be managed effectively.

_____

_____

20 What is one advantage of developing energy-efficient technologies?

_____

_____

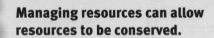

Answers: 18 Using resources can cause pollution and damage to ecosystems;
19 Sample answers: practicing water conservation; limiting logging to protect forests;
20 a reduction in pollution

21 Claims • Evidence • Reasoning What would a scientist need to consider when developing biofuels from plants like sugar cane and corn to use instead of fossil fuels? State your claim. Summarize evidence to support your claim and explain your reasoning.

Lesson Review

Vocabulary

Circle the term that best completes the following sentence.

1 *Conservation/Stewardship* is the protection and wise use of resources.

2 Anything that can be used to take care of a need is a *renewable resource/natural resource*.

3 A *renewable resource/nonrenewable resource* is used more quickly than it can be replaced.

Key Concepts

4 Identify Which of the following is a renewable resource?

A oil

B sunlight

C gold

D natural gas

5 Describe How does reusing, reducing, and recycling conserve energy?

_____

_____

_____

_____

6 Explain How can technology be used to conserve nonrenewable resources?

_____

_____

_____

_____

7 Compare What is the relationship between stewardship and conservation?

_____

_____

_____

_____

_____

Critical Thinking

8 Contrast How might the management of nonrenewable resources be different from the management of renewable resources?

_____

_____

_____

_____

Use the photo below to answer the following questions.

9 Predict Could the resource in the picture become nonrenewable? Explain your reasoning.

_____

_____

_____

_____

10 Apply How can individuals help to conserve the resource in the picture?

_____

_____

_____

_____

_____

My Notes

Lesson 4

Human Impact on Land

ESSENTIAL QUESTION

What impact can human activities have on land resources?

By the end of this lesson, you should be able to identify the impact that human activity has on Earth's land.

Human activities can carve up land features. A tunnel was cut into this mountain in Zion National Park, Utah, so that people may move around easily.

S6E5.e Effect of natural processes and human activity on Earth's surface

🧠 Engage Your Brain

1 Predict Check T or F to show whether you think each statement is true or false.

T   F

☐ ☐ Urban areas have more open land than rural areas do.

☐ ☐ Many building materials are made from land resources.

☐ ☐ Soil provides habitat for plants but not animals.

☐ ☐ Soil can erode when trees are removed from an area.

2 Illustrate Draw a picture of an object or material that is taken from the land and that is commercially important.

✏️ Active Reading

3 Synthesize You can often define an unknown word if you know the meaning of its word parts. Use the word parts to make an educated guess about the meaning of the words *land degradation* and *deforestation*.

Word part	Meaning
degrade	to damage something
deforest	to remove trees from an area
-ation	action or process

Vocabulary Terms

- urbanization
- land degradation
- desertification
- deforestation

4 Apply As you learn the definition of each vocabulary term in this lesson, create your own definition or sketch to help you remember the meaning of the term.

land degradation:

_____

_____

deforestation:

_____

_____

Land of Plenty

Why is land important?

It is hard to imagine human life without land. Land supplies a solid surface for buildings and roads. The soil in land provides nutrients for plants and hiding places for animals. Minerals below the land's surface can be used for construction materials. Fossil fuels underground can be burned to provide energy. Land and its resources affect every aspect of human life.

Recreational

Residential

Commercial/Industrial

Transport

Visualize It! Inquiry **5 Relate** Imagine you live in this area. Choose two land uses shown here and describe why they are important to you. Explain your reasoning.

_____

_____

_____

_____

_____

Agricultural

What are the different types of land use?

We live on land in urban or rural areas. Cities and towns are urban areas. Rural areas are open lands that may be used for farming. Humans use land in many ways. We use natural areas for *recreation*. We use roads that are built on land for *transport*. We grow crops and raise livestock on *agricultural* land. We live in *residential* areas. We build *commercial* businesses on land and extract resources such as metals and water from the land.

Recreational

Natural areas are places that humans have left alone or restored to a natural state. These wild places include forests, grasslands, and desert areas. People use natural areas for hiking, bird-watching, mountain-biking, hunting, and other fun or recreational activities.

Transport

A large network of roads and train tracks connect urban and rural areas all across the country. Roads in the U.S. highway system cover 4 million miles of land. Trucks carry goods on these highways and smaller vehicles carry passengers. Railroads carrying freight or passengers use over 120,000 miles of land for tracks. Roads and train tracks are often highly concentrated in urban areas.

Agricultural

Much of the open land in rural areas is used for agriculture. Crops such as corn, soybeans, and wheat are grown on large, open areas of land. Land is also needed to raise and feed cattle and other livestock. Agricultural land is open, but very different from the natural areas that it has replaced. Farmland generally contains only one or two types of plants, such as corn or cotton. Natural grasslands, forests, and other natural areas contain many species of plants and animals.

Residential

Where do you call home? People live in both rural and urban areas. Rural areas have large areas of open land and low densities of people. Urban areas have dense human populations and small areas of open land. This means that more people live in a square km of an urban area than live in a square km of a rural area. **Urbanization** is the growth of urban areas caused by people moving into cities. When cities increase in size, the population of rural areas near the city may decrease. When an area becomes urbanized, its natural land surface is replaced by buildings, parking lots, and roads. City parks, which contain natural surfaces, may also be built in urban areas.

Commercial and Industrial

As cities or towns expand, commercial businesses are built too, and replace rural or natural areas. Industrial businesses also use land resources. For example, paper companies and furniture manufacturers use wood from trees harvested on forest land. Cement companies, fertilizer manufacturers, and steel manufacturers use minerals that are mined from below the land's surface. Commercial and industrial development usually includes development of roads or railways. Transporting goods to market forms the basis of commerce.

7 Identify What effects does urbanization have on land?

_____

_____

_____

_____

_____

Why is soil important?

Soil is a mixture of mineral fragments, organic material, water, and air. Soil forms when rocks break down and dead organisms decay. There are many reasons why soil is important. Soil provides habitat for organisms such as plants, earthworms, fungi, and bacteria. Many plants get the water and nutrients they need from the soil. Because plants form the base of food webs, healthy soil is important for most land ecosystems. Healthy soil is also important for agricultural land, which supplies humans with food.

Active Reading

8 Identify As you read, underline the ways that soil is important to plants.

It Is a Habitat for Organisms

Earthworms, moles, badgers, and other burrowing animals live in soil. These animals also find food underground. *Decomposers* are organisms that break down dead animal and plant material, releasing the nutrients into the soil. Decomposers such as fungi and bacteria live in soil. Soil holds plant roots in place, providing support for the plant. In turn, plants are food for herbivores and are habitats for organisms such as birds and insects. Many animals on Earth depend on soil for shelter or food.

It Stores Water and Nutrients

Falling rain soaks into soil and is stored between soil particles. Different types of soil can store different amounts of water. Wetland soils, for example, store large amounts of water and reduce flooding. Soils are also part of the nutrient cycle. Plants take up nutrients and water stored in soil. Plants and animals that eat them die and are broken down by decomposers such as bacteria and earthworms. Nutrients are released back into the soil and the cycle starts again.

Visualize It!

Nutrients Cycle between Soil and Organisms

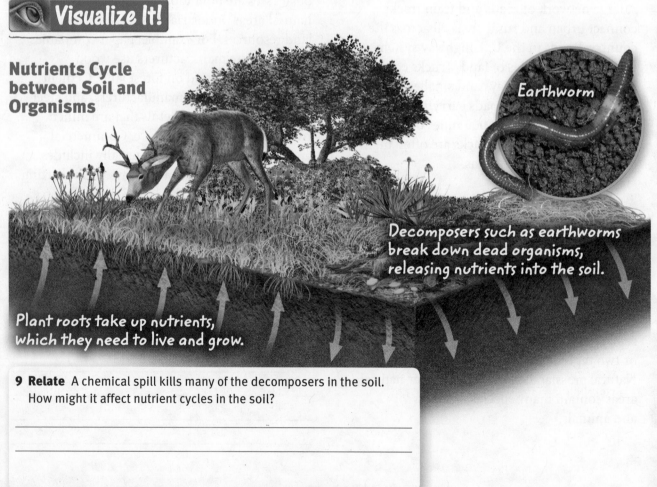

Earthworm

Decomposers such as earthworms break down dead organisms, releasing nutrients into the soil.

Plant roots take up nutrients, which they need to live and grow.

9 Relate A chemical spill kills many of the decomposers in the soil. How might it affect nutrient cycles in the soil?

_____

_____

© Houghton Mifflin Harcourt Publishing Company • Image Credits: ©Valerie Giles/Photo Reasearchers, Inc.

Dust Bowl

In the 1930s, huge clouds of dusty soil rolled across the southern Great Plains of the United States. Areas that were once farmlands and homesteads were wiped out. What caused the soil to blow away?

Drought and Overuse

Farmers who settled in the southern Great Plains overplowed and overgrazed their land. When severe drought hit in 1931, topsoil dried out. Winds lifted the soil and carried it across the plains in huge storms that farmers called "black blizzards." The drought and dust storms continued for years.

Modern Day Dust Bowl

Today in northwest China another dust bowl is forming. Large areas of farmland were made there by clearing the natural vegetation and plowing the soil. Herds of sheep and cattle are overgrazing the land, and large dust storms are common.

Extend

Inquiry

10 Identify What type of land use by people contributed to the Dust Bowl? Does it remain a common use of land today?

11 Compare Research another area under threat from overuse that differs from the feature. What type of land use is causing the problem?

12 Illustrate Do one of the following to show how the Dust Bowl or the area you researched affected society: make a poster, write a play, write a song, or draw a cartoon strip. Present your findings to the class.

Footprints

How can human activities affect land and soil?

Human activities can have positive and negative effects on land and soil. Some activities restore land to its natural state, or increase the amount of fertile soil on land. Other activities can degrade land. **Land degradation** is the process by which human activity and natural processes damage land to the point that it can no longer support the local ecosystem. Urbanization, deforestation, and poor farming practices can all lead to land degradation.

Active Reading

14 **Identify** As you read, underline the effects that urbanization can have on land.

Urban Sprawl

When urbanization occurs at the edge of a city or town, it is called *urban sprawl*. Urban sprawl replaces forests, fields, and grasslands with houses, roads, schools, and shopping areas. Urban sprawl decreases the amount of farmland that is available for growing crops. It decreases the amount of natural areas that surround cities. It increases the amount of asphalt and concrete that covers the land. Rainwater runs off hard surfaces and into storm drains instead of soaking into the ground and filling aquifers. Rainwater runoff from urban areas can increase the erosion of nearby soils.

Erosion

Erosion (ih•ROH•zhuhn) is the process by which wind, water, or gravity transports soil and sediment from one place to another. Some type of erosion occurs on most land. However, erosion can speed up when land is degraded. Roots of trees and plants act as anchors to the soil. When land is cleared for farming, the trees and plants are removed and the soil is no longer protected. This exposes soil to blowing wind and running water that can wash away the soil, as shown in this photo.

Nutrient Depletion and Land Pollution

Crops use soil nutrients to grow. If the same crops are planted year after year, the same soil nutrients get used up. Plants need the right balance of nutrients to grow. Farmers can plant a different crop each year to reduce nutrient loss. Pollution from industrial activities can damage land. Mining wastes, gas and petroleum leaks, and chemical wastes can kill organisms in the soil. U.S. government programs such as Superfund help to clean up polluted land.

Desertification

When too many livestock are kept in one area, they can overgraze the area. Overgrazing removes the plants and roots that hold topsoil together. Overgrazing and other poor farming methods can cause desertification. **Desertification** (dih•zer•tuh•fih•KAY•shuhn) is the process by which land becomes more desertlike and unable to support life. Without plants, soil becomes dusty and prone to wind erosion. Deforestation and urbanization can also lead to desertification.

Deforestation

The removal of trees and other vegetation from an area is called **deforestation**. Logging for wood can cause deforestation. Surface mining causes deforestation by removing vegetation and soil to get to the minerals below. Deforestation also occurs in rain forests, as shown in the photo, when farmers cut or burn down trees so they can grow crops. Urbanization can cause deforestation when forests are replaced with buildings. Deforestation leads to increased soil erosion.

👁 Visualize It!

15 Relate How has human activity affected the forest in this photo? Explain the evidence that supports your claim.

_____

_____

_____

_____

643

Visual Summary

To complete this summary, circle the correct word or phrase. Then use the key below to check your answers. You can use this page to review the main concepts of the lesson.

Humans use land in different ways.

16 Crops are grown on recreational/agricultural land.

Soil is important to all organisms, including humans.

17 Decomposers/plants that live in soil break down dead matter in the soil.

Human Impact on Land

Human activities can affect land and soil.

18 Poor farming practices and drought can lead to desertification/urbanization.

Answers: 16 agricultural; 17 decomposers; 18 desertification

19 **Claims • Evidence • Reasoning** How could concentrating human populations in cities help to conserve agricultural and recreational lands? State your claim. Summarize evidence to support your claim and explain your reasoning.

Lesson Review

Vocabulary

Draw a line to connect the following terms to their definitions.

1 urbanization

2 deforestation

3 land degradation

4 desertification

A the removal of trees and other vegetation from an area

B the process by which land becomes more desertlike

C the process by which human activity can damage land

D the formation and growth of cities

Key Concepts

5 Contrast How are natural areas different from rural areas?

_____

_____

_____

_____

6 Relate How might deforestation lead to desertification?

_____

_____

_____

7 Relate Think of an animal that eats other animals. Why would soil be important to this animal? Explain your reasoning.

_____

_____

_____

_____

Critical Thinking

Use this photo to answer the following questions.

8 Analyze What type of land degradation is occurring in this photo?

_____

_____

9 Predict This type of soil damage can happen in urban areas too. Outline how urbanization could lead to this type of degradation.

_____

_____

_____

_____

_____

_____

10 Apply What kinds of land uses are around your school? Write down each type of land use. Then describe how one of these land uses might affect natural systems.

_____

_____

_____

_____

_____

_____

My Notes

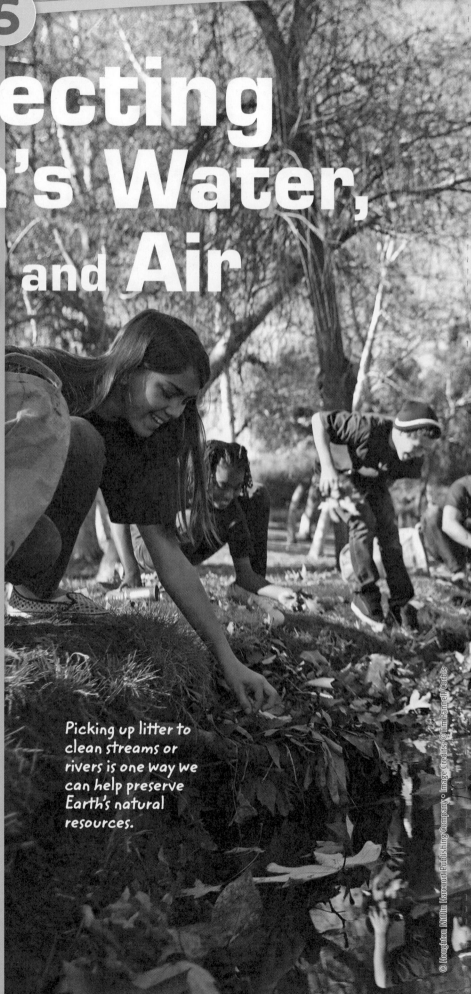

Protecting Earth's Water, Land, and Air

ESSENTIAL QUESTION

How can Earth's resources be used wisely?

By the end of this lesson, you should be able to summarize the value of conserving Earth's resources and the effect that wise stewardship has on land, water, and air resources.

Picking up litter to clean streams or rivers is one way we can help preserve Earth's natural resources.

 S6E6.b Quality and supply of natural resources

Lesson Labs

Quick Labs
• Soil Erosion
• Investigate the Value of Recycling

Exploration Lab
• Filtering Water

Engage Your Brain

1 Predict Check T or F to show whether you think each statement is true or false.

T	F	
☐	☐	Conservation is the overuse of natural resources.
☐	☐	It is everybody's job to be a good steward of Earth's resources.
☐	☐	Reforestation is the planting of trees to repair degraded lands.
☐	☐	Alternative energy sources, like solar power, increase the amount of pollution released into the air.

2 Describe Have you ever done something to protect a natural resource? Draw a picture showing what you did. Include a caption.

Active Reading

3 Synthesize You can often guess the meaning of a word from its context, or how it is used in a sentence. Use the sentence below to guess the meaning of the word *stewardship*.

Example sentence

Stewardship of water resources will ensure that there is plenty of clean water for future generations.

stewardship:

_____

_____

Vocabulary Terms

• conservation   • stewardship

4 Apply As you learn the definition of each vocabulary term in this lesson, create your own definition or sketch to help remember the meaning of the term.

Keeping It Clean

What are conservation and stewardship?

In the past, some people used Earth's resources however they wanted, without thinking about the consequences. They thought it didn't matter if they cut down hundreds of thousands of trees or caught millions of fish. They also thought it didn't matter if they dumped trash into bodies of water. Now we know that it does matter how we use resources. Humans greatly affect the land, water, and air. If we wish to keep using our resources in the future, we need to conserve and care for them.

Conservation: Wise Use of Resources

Conservation (kahn•sur•VAY•shuhn) is the wise use of natural resources. By practicing conservation, we can help make sure that resources will still be around for future generations. It is up to everybody to conserve and protect resources. When we use energy or create waste, we can harm the environment. If we conserve whenever we can, we reduce the harm we do to the environment. We can use less energy by turning off lights, computers, and appliances. We can reuse shopping bags, as in the picture below. We can recycle whenever possible, instead of just throwing things away. By doing these things, we take fewer resources from Earth and put less pollution into the water, land, and air.

Active Reading

5 Identify As you read, underline the definitions of *conservation* and *stewardship*.

Visualize It!

6 Identify How are the people in the picture below practicing conservation?

_____

_____

_____

This old tire is being used as a planter instead of being thrown away.

Stewardship: Managing Resources

Stewardship (stoo•urd•SHIP) is the careful and responsible management of a resource. If we are not good stewards, we will use up a resource or pollute it. Stewardship of Earth's resources will ensure that the environment stays clean enough to help keep people and other living things healthy. Stewardship is everybody's job. Governments pass laws that protect water, land, and air. These laws determine how resources can be used and what materials can be released into the environment. Individuals can also act as stewards. For example, you can plant trees or help clean up a habitat in your community. Any action that helps to maintain or improve the environment is an act of stewardship.

7 Compare Fill in the Venn diagram to compare and contrast conservation and stewardship.

Stewardship

Both

Conservation

Turning empty lots into gardens improves the environment and provides people with healthy food.

👁 Visualize It!

8 Identify How is the person in the picture to the right practicing stewardship?

_____

_____

_____

Sea turtles are endangered. Scientists help sea turtles that have just hatched find their way to the sea.

Water Wise!

How can we preserve water resources?

Most of the Earth's surface is covered by water, so you might think there is lots of water for humans to use. However, there is actually very little fresh water on Earth, so people should use freshwater resources very carefully. People should also be careful to avoid polluting water, because the quality of water is important to the health of both humans and ecosystems. Because water is so important to our health, we need to keep it clean!

By Conserving Water

If we want to make sure there is enough water for future generations, we need to reduce the amount of water we use. In some places, if people aren't careful about using water wisely, there soon won't be enough water for everyone. There are many ways to reduce water usage. We can use low-flow toilets and showerheads. We can take shorter showers. In agriculture and landscaping, we can reduce water use by installing efficient irrigation systems. We can also use plants that don't need much water. Only watering lawns the amount they need and following watering schedules saves water. The photo below shows a simple way to use less water—just turn off the tap while brushing your teeth!

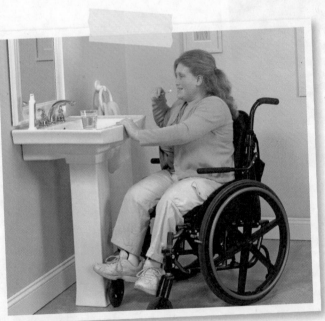

Do the Math

You Try It

9 Calculate How much fresh water is on Earth?

Solve

Each square on the grid equals 1%. Use the grid to fill in the percentage of each type of water found on Earth.

Earth's Water

▢ Salt water _____

■ Ice (fresh water) _____

■ Fresh liquid water _____

10 Identify What are some ways you can reduce the amount of water you use?

• *Turn off the tap when brushing my teeth.*

• _____
_____

• _____
_____

• _____
_____

With Water Stewardship

Humans and ecosystems need clean water. The diagram below shows how a community keeps its drinking water clean. The main way to protect drinking water is to keep pollution from entering streams, lakes, and other water sources. Laws like the Clean Water Act and Safe Drinking Water Act were passed to protect water sources. These laws indicate how clean drinking water must be and limit the types of chemicals that businesses and private citizens can release into water. These laws also help finance water treatment facilities. We can help protect water by not throwing chemicals in the trash or dumping them down the drain. We can also use nontoxic chemicals whenever possible. Reducing the amount of fertilizer we use on our gardens also reduces water pollution.

For healthy ecosystems and safe drinking water, communities need to protect water sources. The first step to protecting water sources is keeping them from becoming polluted.

Protecting Water Resources

Water testing makes sure water is safe for people to drink. It also helps us find out if there is a pollution problem that needs to be fixed.

Without clean water to drink, people can get sick. Clean water is also important for agriculture and natural ecosystems.

Water treatment plants remove pollution from wastewater before it is reused or put back into the environment.

Visualize It!

11 Claims • Evidence • Reasoning
What steps should a community take to manage its water resources? Explain your reasoning.

_____

_____

_____

_____

This Land Is Your Land

How can we preserve land resources?

People rely on land resources for recreation, agriculture, transportation, commerce, industry, and housing. If we manage land resources carefully, we can make sure that these resources will be around for generations and continue to provide resources for humans to use. We also need to make sure that there are habitats for wild animals. To do all these things, we must protect land resources from overuse and pollution. Sometimes we need to repair damage that is already done.

Through Preservation

Preservation of land resources is very important. *Preservation* means protecting land from being damaged or changed. Local, state, and national parks protect many natural areas. These parks help ensure that many species survive. Small parks can protect some species. Other species, such as predators, need larger areas. For example, wolves roam over hundreds of miles and would not be protected by small parks. By protecting areas big enough for large predators, we also protect habitats for many other species.

Active Reading

12 Identify As you read this page and the next, underline ways that we can protect land resources.

Yosemite National Park is one of the oldest national parks in the country. Like other national, state, and local parks, Yosemite was formed to preserve natural habitats.

Think Outside the Book

13 Apply Plant and animal species depend on land resources. Find out which endangered plant or animal species live in your area. Write a paragraph explaining how your community can help protect those species. Explain the reasoning behind each of your suggestions.

Through Reforestation

People use the wood from trees for many things. We use it to make paper and to build houses. We also use wood to heat homes and cook food. In many places, huge areas of forest were cut down to use the wood and nothing was done to replant the forests. Now when we cut trees down, they are often replanted, as in the picture at right. We also plant trees in areas where forests disappeared many years ago in order to help bring the forests back. The process of planting trees to reestablish forestland is called *reforestation*. Reforestation is important, but we can't cut down all forests and replant them. It is important to keep some old forests intact for the animals that need them to survive.

Reforestation

Through Reclamation

In order to use some resources, such as coal, metal, and minerals, the resources first have to be dug out of the ground. In the process, the land is damaged. Sometimes, large areas of land are cleared and pits are dug to reach the resource. Land can also be damaged in other ways, including by development and agriculture. *Reclamation* is the process by which a damaged land area is returned to nearly the condition it was in before people used it. Land reclamation, shown in the lower right photo, is required for mines in many states once the mines are no longer in use. Many national and state laws, such as the Surface Mining and Reclamation Act and the Resource Conservation and Recovery Act, guide land reclamation.

A mine being reclaimed

Visualize It!

14 Compare What are the similarities between reforestation and reclamation?

_____

_____

_____

_____

© Houghton Mifflin Harcourt Publishing Company • Image Credits: (bkgd) ©David Davis/Fotolia; (t) ©David R. Frazier/Photo Researchers, Inc.; (br) ©Photoshot Holdings Ltd/Alamy

One way to reduce urban sprawl is to locate homes and businesses close together.

Through Reducing Urban Sprawl

Urban sprawl is the outward spread of suburban areas around cities. As we build more houses and businesses across a wider area, there is less land for native plants and animals. Reducing urban sprawl helps to protect land resources. One way to reduce sprawl is to locate more people and businesses in a smaller area. A good way to do this is with vertical development—that means constructing taller buildings. Homes, businesses, and even recreational facilities can be placed within high-rise buildings. We also can reduce sprawl using mixed-use development. This development creates communities with businesses and houses very close to one another. Mixed-use communities are also better for the environment, because people can walk to work instead of driving.

Through Recycling

Recycling is one of the most important things we can do to preserve land resources. *Recycling* is the process of recovering valuable materials from waste or scrap. We can recycle many of the materials that we use. By recycling materials like metal, plastic, paper, and glass, we use fewer raw materials. Recycling aluminum cans reduces the amount of bauxite that is mined. We use bauxite in aluminum smelting. Everyone can help protect land resources by recycling. Lots of people throw away materials that can be recycled. Find out what items you can recycle!

Bauxite mine

15 Apply Aluminum is mined from the ground. Recycling aluminum cans decreases the need for mining bauxite. Paper can also be recycled. How does recycling paper preserve trees?

_____

_____

Through Using Soil Conservation Methods

Soil conservation protects soil from erosion or degradation by overuse or pollution. For example, farmers change the way they plow in order to conserve soil. Contour plowing creates ridges of soil across slopes. The small ridges keep water from eroding soils. In strip cropping, two types of crops are planted in rows next to each other to reduce erosion. Terracing is used on steep hills to prevent erosion. Areas of the hill are flattened to grow crops. This creates steps down the side of the hill. *Crop rotation* means that crops with different needs are planted in alternating seasons. This reduces the prevalence of plant diseases and makes sure there are nutrients for each crop. It also ensures that plants are growing in the soil almost year-round. In no-till farming, soils are not plowed between crop plantings. Stalks and cover crops keep water in the soils and reduce erosion by stopping soil from being blown away.

Active Reading

16 Identify As you read this page, underline five methods of soil conservation.

Visualize It!

Terracing involves building leveled areas, or steps, to grow crops on.

In contour plowing, crop rows are planted in curved lines along land's natural contours.

Strip cropping prevents erosion by creating natural dams that stop water from rushing over a field.

17 Analyze Which two soil conservation techniques would be best to use on gentle slopes?

☐ contour plowing

☐ crop terracing

☐ strip cropping

18 Analyze Which soil conservation technique would be best to use on very steep slopes?

☐ contour plowing

☐ crop terracing

☐ strip cropping

Into Thin Air

How can we reduce air pollution?

Polluted air can make people sick and harm organisms. Air pollution can cause the atmosphere to change in ways that are harmful to the environment and to people. There are many ways that we can reduce air pollution. We can use less energy. Also, we can develop new ways to get energy that produces less pollution. Everybody can help reduce air pollution in many different ways.

Through Energy Conservation

Energy conservation is one of the most important ways to reduce air pollution. Fossil fuels are currently the most commonly used energy resource. When they are burned, they release pollution into the air. If we use less energy, we burn fewer fossil fuels.

There are lots of ways to conserve energy. We can turn off lights when we don't need them. We can use energy-efficient lightbulbs and appliances. We can use air conditioners less in the summer and heaters less in the winter. We can unplug electronics when they are not in use. Instead of driving ourselves to places, we can use public transportation. We can also develop alternative energy sources that create less air pollution. Using wind, solar, and geothermal energy will help us burn less fossil fuel.

Using public transportation, riding a bike, sharing rides, and walking reduce the amount of air pollution produced by cars.

Many cities, such as Los Angeles, California, have air pollution problems.

Energy can be produced with very little pollution. These solar panels help us use energy from the sun and replace the use of fossil fuels.

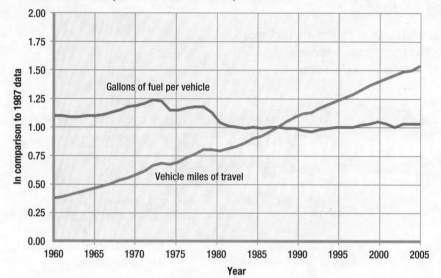

Vehicle Fuel Consumption and Miles Traveled, 1960–2005

In comparison to 1987 data

Gallons of fuel per vehicle

Vehicle miles of travel

Year

Source: U.S. Department of Transportation

20 Claims • Evidence • Reasoning
How has vehicle fuel consumption in comparison to miles traveled changed since 1960? What is the likely cause for this change? Explain your reasoning.

Through Technology

There are lots of ways to generate energy without creating much air pollution. By developing these alternative energy sources, we can reduce the amount of pollution created by burning fossil fuels. Wind turbines generate clean power. So do solar panels that use energy from the sun. We also can use power created by water flowing through rivers or moving with the tides. Geothermal energy from heat in Earth's crust can be used to generate electricity. Hybrid cars get energy from their brakes and store it in batteries. They burn less gas and release less pollution. Driving smaller cars that can go farther on a gallon of gas also reduces air pollution.

New technologies, such as this compact fluorescent lightbulb (CFL), help limit air pollution. CFL bulbs use less energy to make the same amount of light.

Through Laws

Governments in many countries work independently and together to reduce air pollution. They monitor air quality and set limits on what can be released into the air. In the United States, the Clean Air Act limits the amount of toxic chemicals and other pollutants that can be released into the atmosphere by factories and vehicles. It is up to the Environmental Protection Agency to make sure that these limits are enforced. Because air isn't contained by borders, some solutions must be international. The Kyoto Protocol is a worldwide effort to limit the release of greenhouse gases—pollution that can warm the atmosphere.

21 Summarize List three ways air pollution can be reduced.

-
-
-

Visual Summary

To complete this summary, fill in the blanks with the correct word or phrase. Then use the key below to check your answers. You can use this page to review the main concepts of the lesson.

Protecting Water, Land, and Air

Water resources are important to our health.

22 A community's water supply can be protected by:

- conserving water
- preventing pollution
- _____
- treating wastewater

Land resources are used to grow food and make products.

23 Land resources can be protected by:

- preservation
- reclamation and reforestation
- reducing urban sprawl
- _____
- soil conservation

Everybody needs clean air to breathe.

24 The main way to reduce air pollution is to:

_____

_____

_____

_____

_____

25 Relate How can you personally act as a steward of water, land, and air resources?

© Houghton Mifflin Harcourt Publishing Company • Image Credits: (c) ©photka/Shutterstock; (r) ©Ekaterina Pokrovsky/Shutterstock

Lesson Review

Vocabulary

Fill in the blank with the term that best completes the following sentences.

1 _____ is the wise use of natural resources.

2 _____ is the careful and responsible management of a resource.

Key Concepts

3 Describe How can water pollution be prevented?

_____

_____

_____

Fill in the table below.

Example	Type of land resource conservation
4 Identify A county creates a park to protect a forest.	
5 Identify A mining company puts soil back in the hole and plants grass seeds on top of it.	
6 Identify A logging company plants new trees after it has cut some down.	
7 Identify A plastic milk bottle is turned into planks for a boardwalk to the beach.	
8 Identify Instead of building lots of single houses, a city builds an apartment building with a grocery store.	

9 Determine How has technology helped decrease air pollution in recent years?

_____

_____

_____

_____

10 Explain Why is it important to protect Earth's water, land, and air resources?

_____

_____

_____

Critical Thinking

11 Explain Land reclamation can be expensive. Why might recycling materials lead to spending less money on reclamation?

_____

_____

_____

Use the graph to answer the following question.

Average Water Usage of U.S. Household

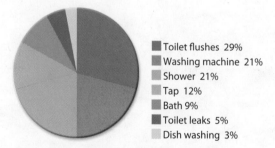

- Toilet flushes 29%
- Washing machine 21%
- Shower 21%
- Tap 12%
- Bath 9%
- Toilet leaks 5%
- Dish washing 3%

Source: U.S. Environmental Protection Agency

12 Analyze The graph above shows water use in the average U.S. household. Using the graph, identify three effective ways a household could conserve water.

_____

_____

My Notes

Unit 7 (Big Idea)

Humans use natural resources for materials and energy, and also affect the environment with their population growth.

Lesson 1

ESSENTIAL QUESTION

How do we use nonrenewable energy resources?

Describe how humans use energy resources and the role of nonrenewable energy resources in society.

Lesson 2

ESSENTIAL QUESTION

How do humans use renewable energy resources?

Describe how humans use energy resources and the role of renewable energy resources in society.

Lesson 3

ESSENTIAL QUESTION

Why should natural resources be managed?

Explain the consequences of society's use of natural resources and the importance of managing these resources wisely.

Lesson 4

ESSENTIAL QUESTION

What impact can human activities have on land resources?

Identify the impact that human activity has on Earth's land.

Lesson 5

ESSENTIAL QUESTION

How can Earth's resources be used wisely?

Summarize the value of conserving Earth's resources and the effect that wise stewardship has on land, water, and air resources.

Connect ESSENTIAL QUESTIONS

Lessons 3, 4, and 5

1 Explain How do humans affect natural resources and their environment?

_____

_____

_____

_____

Think Outside the Book

2 Synthesize Choose one of these activities to help synthesize what you have learned in this unit.

☐ Using what you learned in Lessons 1 and 2, create a poster presentation that compares and contrasts one renewable resource and one nonrenewable resource. Include a discussion of at least one drawback for each resource type.

☐ Using what you learned in Lessons 4 and 5, create an informational poster that explains what humans can do to protect Earth's environment.

Unit 7 Review

Name _____

Vocabulary

Check the box to show whether each statement is true or false.

T	F	
☐	☐	**1** <u>Land degradation</u> is the process by which humans restore damaged land so that it can support the local ecosystem.
☐	☐	**2** <u>Conservation</u> is the wise use of natural resources.
☐	☐	**3** <u>Stewardship</u> is the application of various methods that use up natural resources.
☐	☐	**4** <u>Biomass</u> energy comes from organic matter such as plant material and manure.
☐	☐	**5** Rocks, water, air, minerals, forests, wildlife, and soil are all examples of a <u>natural resource</u>.

Key Concepts

Read each question below, and circle the best answer.

6 Humans use land in many ways. How is an area described if it contains few people, has large areas of open space, and is a mix of natural land, farmland, and parks?

A rural area

B urban area

C natural area

D industrial area

7 Sometimes, a renewable resource can be considered nonrenewable because it is used up faster than it can be replenished. Which of the following choices is an example of this?

A coal supply getting smaller because it takes millions of years to form

B forests being cut down at a quicker rate than they can grow

C solar energy being used to provide electricity to a home

D water in streams replaced by rainfall from the atmosphere

8 The picture below shows a common human activity.

Carboni   7_CFLAEAG366012_238A   2nd pass

Reducing this activity would likely have an effect on which of the following?

A urban sprawl

B global warming

C land degradation

D water pollution

9 Which of the following is a disadvantage of managing resources?

A less of the natural resource is wasted

B reduction in pollution due to less manufacturing

C expense of recycling materials

D more resources extracted from Earth

10 What is a major reason solar energy is not used everywhere on a large scale?

A It is too difficult to purchase and install solar panels.

B Solar energy is not very effective at producing electricity.

C The manufacture of solar panels produces too much pollution.

D Solar panels are most efficient in places that receive lots of sunlight.

11 The chemicals released by burning petroleum in car engines contribute to what local and global effects?

A smog and global warming   **C** acid rain and fusion

B fog and radioactivity   **D** sulfur dioxide decrease and ozone buildup

12 Which of the following correctly explains why soil is important?

A It is a resource that cannot be depleted.   **C** It breaks down dead organisms.

B It provides a habitat for fungi.   **D** It increases land degradation.

13 Nuclear energy is best described as what type of energy resource?

A renewable   **C** renewable and inexhaustible

B nonrenewable   **D** nonrenewable because it is used up so rapidly

14 Which of the following is a way to reduce air pollution?

A increase the burning of fossil fuels   **C** use public transportation

B reduce development of renewable energy sources   **D** remove laws that limit toxic chemicals

15 Which of these is not a soil conservation method?

A crop rotation   **C** contour plowing

B terracing   **D** reforestation

Critical Thinking

Answer the following questions in the space provided.

16 Below is an example of a technology used for alternative energy.

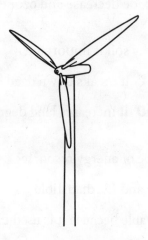

What type of energy does the equipment in the picture harness? _____

Is the type of energy harnessed by this equipment renewable or nonrenewable?
Explain your answer. _____

_____

Name one advantage and one disadvantage of using this type of energy.

_____

_____

17 Urbanization has major effects on Earth's land and water. Natural vegetation is
removed in order to make room for buildings, roads, and parking lots. How does
removing vegetation affect the land?

_____

_____

_____

_____

_____

_____

_____

_____

_____

_____

18 What are three ways that urban populations can positively affect water quality?

_____

_____

_____

_____

19 Can land be considered a natural resource? Explain.

_____

_____

Give two examples of how land is important to life on Earth.

_____

_____

_____

_____

20 How do paved parking lots and roads with concrete or asphalt affect water flow on the land?

_____

_____

_____

_____

_____

Connect **ESSENTIAL QUESTIONS**
Lessons 1 and 3

Answer the following questions in the space provided.

21 Below is a graph of the production and use of petroleum in the United States in the past, present, and likely usage in the future.

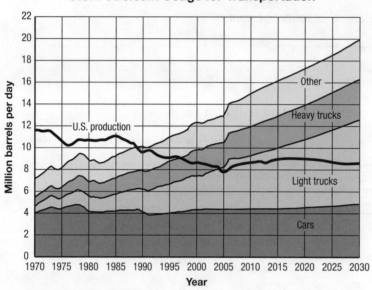

Summarize how current production and usage of petroleum compare.

_____

_____

_____

_____

Name two risks linked to offshore drilling and transporting petroleum.

_____

_____

_____

_____

Resources

Glossary

Pronunciation Key							
Sound	**Symbol**	**Example**	**Respelling**	**Sound**	**Symbol**	**Example**	**Respelling**
ă	a	pat	PAT	ŏ	ah	bottle	BAHT'l
ā	ay	pay	PAY	ō	oh	toe	TOH
âr	air	care	KAIR	ô	aw	caught	KAWT
ä	ah	father	FAH•ther	ôr	ohr	roar	ROHR
är	ar	argue	AR•gyoo	oi	oy	noisy	NOYZ•ee
ch	ch	chase	CHAYS	o͝o	u	book	BUK
ĕ	e	pet	PET	o͞o	oo	boot	BOOT
ĕ (at end of a syllable)	eh	settee lessee	seh•TEE leh•SEE	ou	ow	pound	POWND
ĕr	ehr	merry	MEHR•ee	s	s	center	SEN•ter
ē	ee	beach	BEECH	sh	sh	cache	CASH
g	g	gas	GAS	ŭ	uh	flood	FLUHD
ĭ	i	pit	PIT	ûr	er	bird	BERD
ĭ (at end of a syllable)	ih	guitar	gih•TAR	z	z	xylophone	ZY•luh•fohn
ī	y eye (only for a complete syllable)	pie island	PY EYE•luhnd	z	z	bags	BAGZ
				zh	zh	decision	dih•SIZH•uhn
				ə	uh	around broken focus	uh•ROWND BROH•kuhn FOH•kuhs
îr	ir	hear	HIR	ər	er	winner	WIN•er
j	j	germ	JERM	th	th	thin they	THIN THAY
k	k	kick	KIK				
ng	ng	thing	THING	w	w	one	WUHN
ngk	ngk	bank	BANGK	wh	hw	whether	HWETH•er

abrasion (uh·BRAY·zhuhn) the process by which rock is reduced in size by the scraping action of other rocks driven by water, wind, and gravity (389)
abrasión proceso por el cual se reduce el tamaño de las rocas debido al efecto de desgaste de otras rocas arrastradas por el agua, el viento o la gravedad

acid precipitation (AS·id prih·sip·ih·TAY·shuhn) rain, sleet, or snow that contains a high concentration of acids (390)
precipitación ácida lluvia, aguanieve o nieve que contiene una alta concentración de ácidos

air mass (AIR MAS) a large body of air throughout which temperature and moisture content are similar (294)
masa de aire gran volumen de aire, cuya temperatura y cuyo contenido de humedad son similares en toda su extensión

air pressure (AIR PRESH·er) the measure of the force with which air molecules push on a surface (251, 290)
presión atmosférica la medida de la fuerza con la que las moléculas del aire empujan contra una superficie

alluvial fan (uh·LOO·vee·uhl FAN) a fan-shaped mass of material deposited by a stream when the slope of the land decreases sharply (401)
abanico aluvial masa en forma de abanico de materiales depositados por un arroyo cuando la pendiente del terreno disminuye bruscamente

aphelion (uh·FEE·lee·uhn) in the orbit of a planet or other body in the solar system, the point that is farthest from the sun (45)
afelio punto más alejado del Sol en la órbita de un planeta u otros cuerpos en el sitema solar

aquifer (AH·kwuh·fer) a body of rock or sediment that stores groundwater and allows the flow of groundwater (184)
acuífero masa rocosa o sedimentaria que almacena agua subterránea y permite que fluya

asteroid (AS·tuh·royd) a small, rocky object that orbits the sun; most asteroids are located in a band between the orbits of Mars and Jupiter (96)
asteroide cuerpo pequeño y rocoso que se encuentra en órbita alrededor del Sol; la mayoría de los asteroides se ubican en una banda entre las órbitas de Marte y Júpiter

asthenosphere (as·THEN·uh·sfir) the soft layer of the mantle on which the tectonic plates move (502)
astenosfera capa viscosa del manto sobre la que se mueven las placas tectónicas

astronomical unit (as·truh·NAHM·ih·kuhl YOO·nit) the average distance between Earth and the sun; approximately 150 million kilometers (symbol, AU) (60)
unidad astronómica distancia promedio entre la Tierra y el Sol; aproximadamente 150 millones de kilómetros (símbolo: UA)

atmosphere (AT·muh·sfir) a mixture of gases that surrounds a planet, moon, or other celestial body (250)
atmósfera mezcla de gases que rodea un planeta, una luna, u otras cuerpos celestes

atom (AT·uhm) the smallest unit of an element that maintains the properties of that element (442)
átomo unidad más pequeña de un elemento que conserva las propiedades de ese elemento

barrier island (BAIR·ee·er EYE·luhnd) a long ridge of sand or narrow island that lies parallel to the shore (406)
isla barrera largo arrecife de arena o isla angosta ubicada paralela a la costa

beach (BEECH) an area of the shoreline that is made up of deposited sediment (406)
playa área de la costa que está formada por sedimento depositado

Big Bang theory (BIG BANG THEE·uh·ree) the theory that all matter and energy in the universe was compressed into an extremely small volume that 13 billion to 15 billion years ago exploded and began expanding in all directions (32)
teoría del Big Bang teoría que establece que toda la materia y la energía del universo estaban comprimidas en un volumen extremadamente pequeño que explotó hace aproximadamente 13 a 15 mil millones de años y empezó a expandirse en todas direcciones

biomass (BY·oh·mas) plant material, manure, or any other organic matter that is used as an energy source (614)
biomasa materia vegetal, estiércol o cualquier otra materia orgánica que se usa como fuente de energía

centripetal force (sehn·TRIP·ih·tuhl FOHRS) the inward force required to keep a particle or an object moving in a circular path (48)
fuerza centrípeta la fuerza hacia adentro que se requiere para mantener en movimiento una partícula o un cuerpo en una trayectoria circular

channel (CHAN·uhl) the path that a stream follows (182)
canal trayectoria que sigue un arroyo

chemical weathering (KEM·ih·kuhl WETH·er·ing) the chemical breakdown and decomposition of rocks by natural processes in the environment (390)
desgaste químico la descomposición química que sufren las rocas por procesos naturales del entorno

cleavage (KLEE·vij) in geology, the tendency of a mineral to split along specific planes of weakness to form smooth, flat surfaces (449)
crucero geología, la tendencia de un mineral a agrietarse a lo largo de planos débiles específicos y formar superficies lisas y planas

climate (KLY·mit) the weather conditions in an area over a long period of time (342, 518)
clima condiciones del tiempo en un área durante un largo período de tiempo

cloud (KLOWD) a collection of small water droplets or ice crystals suspended in the air, which forms when the air is cooled and condensation occurs (166, 292)

nube conjunto de pequeñas gotitas de agua o cristales de hielo suspendidos en el aire, que se forma cuando el aire se enfría y ocurre condensación

comet (KAHM·it) a small body that gives off gas and dust as it passes close to the sun; a typical comet moves in an elliptical orbit around the sun and is made of dust and frozen gases (94)
cometa cuerpo pequeño que libera gas y polvo al pasar cerca del Sol; un cometa típico está formado por polvo y gases congelados y sigue una órbita elíptica alrededor del Sol

composition (kahm·puh·ZISH·uhn) the chemical makeup of a rock; describes either the minerals or other materials in the rock (476)
composición constitución química de una roca; describe los minerales u otros materiales presentes en ella

compound (KAHM·pownd) a substance made up of atoms of two or more different elements joined by chemical bonds (442)
compuesto sustancia formada por átomos de dos o más elementos diferentes unidos por enlaces químicos

compression (kuhm·PRESH·uhn) stress that occurs when forces act to squeeze an object (545)
compresión estrés que se produce cuando distintas fuerzas actúan para apretar un objeto

condensation (kahn·den·SAY·shuhn) the change of state from a gas to a liquid (165)
condensación cambio de estado de gas a líquido

conduction (kuhn·DUHK·shuhn) the transfer of energy as heat through a material (268)
conducción transferencia de energía en forma de calor a través de un material

conservation (kahn·ser·VAY·shuhn) the wise use of and preservation of natural resources (628, 650)
conservación uso inteligente y preservación de los recursos naturales

continental margin (kahn·tuh·NEN·tl MAR·jin) the shallow seafloor that is located between the shoreline and the deep-ocean bottom (199)
margen continental suelo marino poco profundo que se ubica entre la costa y el fondo profundo del océano

convection (kuhn·VEK·shuhn) the movement of matter due to differences in density; the transfer of energy due to the movement of matter (266, 501, 534)
convección movimiento de la materia debido a diferencias en densidad; la transferencia de energía debido al movimiento de la materia

convection current (kuhn·VEK·shuhn KER·uhnt) any movement of matter that results from differences in density; may be vertical, circular, or cyclical (229)
corriente de convección cualquier movimiento de la materia que se produce como resultado de diferencias en densidad; puede ser vertical, circular o cíclico

convergent boundary (kuhn·VER·juhnt BOWN·duh·ree) the boundary between tectonic plates that are colliding (532)

límite convergente límite entre placas tectónicas que chocan

core (KOHR) the central part of Earth below the mantle (501)
núcleo parte central de la Tierra debajo del manto

Coriolis effect (kohr·ee·OH·lis ih·FEKT) the curving of the path of a moving object from an otherwise straight path due to Earth's rotation (225, 277)
efecto de Coriolis desviación de la trayectoria recta que experimentan los cuerpos en movimiento debido a la rotación de la Tierra

Cosmic Microwave Background (CMB) (KAHZ·mik MY·kroh·wayv BAK·grownd) the electromagnetic radiation left over from the formation of the universe (33)
Radiación de fondo de microondas (RFM) residuo de radiación electromagnética que quedó cuando se formó el universo

creep (KREEP) the slow downhill movement of weathered rock material (420)
arrastre movimiento lento y descendente de materiales rocosos desgastados

crest (KREST) the highest point of a wave (210)
cresta punto más alto de una onda

crust (KRUHST) the thin and solid outermost layer of Earth above the mantle (501)
corteza capa más externa, delgada y sólida de la Tierra, que se encuentra sobre el manto

crystal (KRIS·tuhl) a solid whose atoms, ions, or molecules are arranged in a regular, repeating pattern (443)
cristal sólido cuyos átomos, iones o moléculas están ordenados en un patrón regular y repetitivo

day (DAY) the time required for Earth to rotate once on its axis (116)
día tiempo que se requiere para que la Tierra rote una vez sobre su eje

deep current (DEEP KER·uhnt) a streamlike movement of ocean water far below the surface (228)
corriente profunda movimiento del agua del océano es similar a una corriente y que ocurre debajo de la superficie

deep-ocean basin (DEEP·oh·shuhn BAY·sin) the ocean floor under the deep-ocean water (199)
cuenca oceánica profunda fondo del océano, que se encuentra bajo aguas profundas

deforestation (dee·fohr·ih·STAY·shuhn) the removal of trees and other vegetation from an area (643)
deforestación eliminación de árboles y otras plantas de un área

deformation (dee·fohr·MAY·shuhn) the bending, tilting, and breaking of Earth's crust; the change in the shape of rock in response to stress (542, 569)
deformación proceso de doblar, inclinar y romper la corteza de la Tierra; el cambio en la forma de una roca en respuesta a la tensión

delta (DEL·tuh) a mass of material deposited in a triangular or fan shape at the mouth of a river or stream (401)
delta depósito de materiales en forma de triángulo o abanico ubicado en la desembocadura de un río

deposition (dep·uh·ZISH·uhn) the process in which material is laid down (398, 459)
depositación proceso por medio del cual un material se deposita

desertification (dih·zer·tuh·fih·KAY·shuhn) the process by which human activities or climatic changes make arid or semiarid areas more desertlike (643)
desertificación proceso por medio del cual las actividades humanas o los cambios climáticos transforman un área árida o semiárida en desierto

dew point (DOO POYNT) at constant pressure and water vapor content, the temperature at which the rate of condensation equals the rate of evaporation (167, 291)
punto de rocío a presión y contenido de vapor de agua constantes, la temperatura a la que la tasa de condensación es igual a la tasa de evaporación

divergent boundary (dy·VER·juhnt BOWN·duh·ree) the boundary between two tectonic plates that are moving away from each other (533)
límite divergente límite entre dos placas tectónicas que se están separando una de la otra

divide (dih·VYD) the boundary between drainage areas that have streams that flow in opposite directions (183)
división límite entre áreas de drenaje que tienen corrientes que fluyen en direcciones opuestas

dune (DOON) a mound of wind-deposited sand that moves as a result of the action of wind (415)
duna montículo formado por arena que se desplaza y acumula debido a la acción del viento

dwarf planet (DWOHRF PLAN·it) a celestial body that orbits the sun, is round because of its own gravity, but has not cleared its orbital path (91)
planeta enano cuerpo celeste que orbita alrededor del Sol, es redondo debido a su propia fuerza de gravedad, pero no ha despejado los alrededores de su trayectoria orbital

earthquake (ERTH·kwayk) a movement or trembling of the ground that is caused by a sudden release of energy when rocks along a fault move (568)
terremoto movimiento o temblor del suelo causado por una liberación súbita de energía que se produce cuando se mueven las rocas ubicadas a lo largo de una falla

eclipse (ih·KLIPS) an event in which the shadow of one celestial body falls on another (134)
eclipse suceso en el que la sombra de un cuerpo celeste cubre otro cuerpo celeste

elastic rebound (ee·LAS·tik REE·bownd) the sudden return of elastically deformed rock to its undeformed shape (569)

rebote elástico ocurre cuando una roca deformada elásticamente vuelve súbitamente a su forma no deformada

electromagnetic spectrum (ee·lek·troh·mag·NET·ik SPEK·truhm) all of the frequencies or wavelengths of electromagnetic radiation (28)
espectro electromagnético todas las frecuencias o longitudes de onda de la radiación electromagnética

element (EL·uh·muhnt) a substance that cannot be separated or broken down into simpler substances by chemical means (442)
elemento sustancia que no se puede separar o descomponer en sustancias más simples por medio de métodos químicos

elevation (el·uh·VAY·shuhn) the height of an object above sea level (346)
elevación altura de un objeto sobre el nivel del mar

energy resource (EN·er·jee REE·sohrs) a natural resource that humans use to generate energy (594, 608)
recurso energético recurso natural que utilizan los humanos para generar energía

epicenter (EP·ih·sen·ter) the point on Earth's surface directly above an earthquake's starting point, or focus (568)
epicentro punto situado directamente sobre la superficie de la Tierra en punto de inicio, o foco, de un terremoto

equinox (EE·kwuh·nahks) the moment when the sun appears to cross the celestial equator (120)
equinoccio momento en que el Sol parece cruzar el ecuador celeste

erosion (ih·ROH·zhuhn) the process by which wind, water, ice, or gravity transports soil and sediment from one location to another (398, 459)
erosión proceso por medio del cual el viento, el agua, el hielo o la gravedad transporta tierra y sedimentos de un lugar a otro

evaporation (ee·vap·uh·RAY·shuhn) the change of state from a liquid to a gas that usually occurs at the surface of a liquid over a wide range of temperatures (164)
evaporación cambio de estado de líquido a gaseoso que ocurre generalmente en la superficie de un líquido en un amplio rango de temperaturas

fault (FAWLT) a break in a body of rock along which one block moves relative to another (544, 569)
falla grieta en un cuerpo rocoso a lo largo de la cual un bloque se mueve respecto de otro

fission (FISH·uhn) the process by which a nucleus splits into two or more fragments and releases neutrons and energy (599)
fisión proceso por medio del cual un núcleo se divide en dos o más fragmentos y libera neutrones y energía

floodplain (FLUHD·playn) an area along a river that forms from sediments deposited when the river overflows its banks (401)

terreno aluvial área a lo largo de un río formada por sedimentos que se depositan cuando el río se desborda

focus (FOH·kuhs) the location within Earth along a fault at which the first motion of an earthquake occurs (568)
foco lugar dentro de la Tierra a lo largo de una falla donde ocurre el primer movimiento de un terremoto

fog (FAWG) a cloud that forms near the ground and results in a reduction in visibility (169, 292)
niebla nube que se forma cerca del suelo y causa una reducción de la visibilidad

folding (FOHLD·ing) the bending of rock layers due to stress (543)
plegamiento fenómeno que ocurre cuando las capas de roca se doblan debido a la compresión

fossil (FAHS·uhl) the trace or remains of an organism that lived long ago, most commonly preserved in sedimentary rock (511)
fósil indicios o restos de un organismo que vivió hace mucho tiempo, comúnmente preservados en las rocas sedimentarias

fossil fuel (FAHS·uhl FYOO·uhl) a nonrenewable energy resource formed from the remains of organisms that lived long ago; examples include oil, coal, and natural gas (594)
combustible fósil recurso energético no renovable formado a partir de los restos de organismos que vivieron hace mucho tiempo; algunos ejemplos incluyen el petróleo, el carbón y el gas natural

front (FRUHNT) the boundary between air masses of different densities and usually different temperatures (294)
frente límite entre masas de aire de diferentes densidades y, normalmente, diferentes temperaturas

galaxy (GAL·uhk·see) a collection of stars, dust, and gas bound together by gravity (8)
galaxia conjunto de estrellas, polvo y gas unidos por la gravedad

gas giant (GAS JY·uhnt) a planet that has a deep, massive atmosphere, such as Jupiter, Saturn, Uranus, or Neptune (76)
gigante gaseoso planeta con una atmósfera masiva y profunda, como por ejemplo, Júpiter, Saturno, Urano o Neptuno

geocentric (jee·oh·SEN·trik) describes something that uses Earth as the reference point (10)
geocéntrico término que describe algo que usa a la Tierra como punto de referencia

geothermal energy (jee·oh·THER·muhl EN·er·jee) the energy produced by heat within Earth (615)
energía geotérmica energía producida por el calor del interior de la Tierra

glacial drift (GLAY·shuhl DRIFT) the rock material carried and deposited by glaciers (416)

deriva glacial el material rocoso que los glaciares transportan y depositan

glacier (GLAY·sher) a large mass of ice that exists year-round and moves over land (416)
glaciar masa grande de hielo que existe durante todo el año y se mueve sobre el terreno

global warming (GLOH·buhl WOHR·ming) a gradual increase in average global temperature (364)
calentamiento global aumento gradual de la temperatura global promedio

global wind (GLOH·buhl WIND) the movement of air over Earth's surface in patterns that are worldwide (278)
viento global movimiento del aire sobre la superficie terrestre según patrones globales

gravity (GRAV·ih·tee) a force of attraction between objects that is due to their masses (44, 130)
gravedad fuerza de atracción entre dos cuerpos debido a sus masas

greenhouse effect (GREEN·hows ih·FEKT) the warming of the surface and lower atmosphere of Earth that occurs when water vapor, carbon dioxide, and other gases absorb and reradiate thermal energy (254, 362)
efecto invernadero calentamiento de la superficie y de la parte más baja de la atmósfera, el cual se produce cuando el vapor de agua, el dióxido de carbono y otros gases absorben y vuelven a irradiar la energía térmica

groundwater (GROWND·waw·ter) the water that is beneath Earth's surface (180, 402)
agua subterránea agua que está debajo de la superficie de la Tierra

heat (HEET) the energy transferred between objects that are at different temperatures (263)
calor transferencia de energía entre cuerpos que están a temperaturas diferentes

heliocentric (hee·lee·oh·SEN·trik) sun-centered (10)
heliocéntrico centrado en el Sol

hot spot (HAHT SPAHT) a volcanically active area of Earth's surface, commonly far from a tectonic plate boundary (560)
mancha caliente área volcánicamente activa de la superficie de la Tierra que comúnmente se encuentra lejos de un límite entre placas tectónicas

humidity (hyoo·MID·ih·tee) the amount of water vapor in the air (291)
humedad cantidad de vapor de agua que hay en el aire

humus (HYOO·muhs) dark, organic material formed in soil from the decayed remains of plants and animals (429)
humus material orgánico obscuro que se forma en el suelo a partir de restos de plantas y animales en descomposición

hurricane (HER·ih·kayn) a severe storm that develops over tropical oceans and whose strong winds of more than 119 km/h spiral in toward the intensely low-pressure storm center (310)

huracán tormenta violenta que se desarrolla sobre océanos tropicales, con vientos fuertes que soplan a más de 119 km/h y que se mueven en espiral hacia el centro de presión extremadamente baja de la tormenta

hydroelectric energy (hy·droh·ee·LEK·trik EN·er·jee) electrical energy produced by the flow of water (611)
energía hidroeléctrica energía eléctrica producida por el flujo del agua

ice age (EYES AYJ) a long period of climatic cooling during which the continents are glaciated repeatedly (361)
edad de hielo largo período de enfriamiento del clima, durante el cual los continentes se ven repetidamente sometidos a la glaciación

ice core (EYES KOHR) a long cylinder of ice obtained from drilling through ice caps or ice sheets; used to study past climates (519)
testigo de hielo cilindro largo de hielo que se obtiene al perforar casquetes glaciares o capas de hielo; se usa para estudiar los climas del pasado

igneous rock (IG·nee·uhs RAHK) rock that forms when magma cools and solidifies (460)
roca ígnea roca que se forma cuando el magma se enfría y se solidifica

jet stream (JET STREEM) a narrow band of strong winds that blow in the upper troposphere (280, 299)
corriente en chorro franja estrecha de vientos fuertes que soplan en la parte superior de la troposfera

Kuiper Belt (KY·per BELT) a region of the solar system that starts just beyond the orbit of Neptune and that contains dwarf planets and other small bodies made mostly of ice (92)
cinturón de Kuiper región del sistema solar que comienza justo después de la órbita de Neptuno y que contiene planetas enanos y otros cuerpos pequeños formados principalmente de hielo

Kuiper Belt object (KY·per BELT AHB·jekt) one of the hundreds or thousands of small bodies that orbit the sun in a flat belt beyond Neptune's orbit; also includes dwarf planets located in the Kuiper Belt (92)
cuerpo del cinturón de Kuiper uno de los cientos o miles de cuerpos pequeños que orbitan alrededor del Sol en un cinturón plano, más allá de la órbita de Neptuno; también incluye los planetas enanos ubicados en el cinturón de Kuiper

land degradation (LAND deg·ruh·DAY·shuhn) the process by which human activity and natural processes damage land to the point that it can no longer support the local ecosystem (642)
degradación del suelo proceso por el cual la actividad humana y los procesos naturales dañan el suelo hasta el punto de que el ecosistema local no puede subsistir

landslide (LAND·slyd) the sudden movement of rock and soil down a slope (421)
derrumbamiento movimiento súbito de rocas y suelo por una pendiente

latitude (LAT·ih·tood) the distance north or south from the equator; expressed in degrees (344)
latitud distancia hacia el norte o hacia el sur del ecuador; se expresa en grados

lava (LAH·vuh) magma that flows onto Earth's surface; the rock that forms when lava cools and solidifies (554)
lava magma que fluye a la superficie terrestre; la roca que se forma cuando la lava se enfría y se solidifica

lightning (LYT·ning) an electric discharge that takes place between two oppositely charged surfaces, such as between a cloud and the ground, between two clouds, or between two parts of the same cloud (309)
relámpago descarga eléctrica que ocurre entre dos superficies que tienen carga opuesta, como por ejemplo, entre una nube y el suelo, entre dos nubes o entres dos partes de la misma nube

light-year (LYT·yir) the distance that light travels in one year; about 9.46 trillion kilometers (15)
año luz distancia que viaja la luz en un año; aproximadamente 9.46 billones de kilómetros

lithosphere (LITH·uh·sfir) the solid, outer layer of Earth that consists of the crust and the rigid upper part of the mantle (502)
litosfera capa externa y sólida de la Tierra que está formada por la corteza y la parte superior y rígida del manto

local wind (LOH·kuhl WIND) the movement of air over short distances; occurs in specific areas as a result of certain geographical features (282)
viento local movimiento del aire a través de distancias cortas; se produce en áreas específicas como resultado de ciertas características geográficas

loess (LUHS) fine-grained sediments of quartz, feldspar, hornblende, mica, and clay deposited by the wind (415)
loess sedimentos de grano fino de cuarzo, feldespato, horneblenda, mica y arcilla depositados por el viento

lunar phases (LOO·ner FAYZ·iz) the different appearances of the moon from Earth throughout the month (132)
fases lunares diferente apariencia que tiene la Luna cuando se ve desde la Tierra a lo largo del mes

luster (LUHS·ter) the way in which a mineral reflects light (449)
brillo forma en que un mineral refleja la luz

magma (MAG·muh) the molten or partially molten rock material containing trapped gases produced under Earth's surface (554)
magma material rocoso total o parcialmente fundido que contiene gases atrapados que se producen debajo de la superficie terrestre

mantle (MAN·tl) the layer of rock between Earth's crust and core (501)
manto capa de roca que se encuentra entre la corteza terrestre y el núcleo

marsh (marsh) an area of wetland dominated by plants such as grasses, sedges, and rushes (401)
ciénaga zona de humedales donde predominan plantas tales como pastos, ciperáceas y juncos

matter (MAT·er) anything that has mass and takes up space (442)
materia cualquier cosa que tiene masa y ocupa un lugar en el espacio

mechanical wave (mih·KAN·ih·kuhl WAYV) a wave that requires a medium through which to travel (212)
onda mecánica onda que requiere un medio para desplazarse

mesosphere (MEZ·uh·sfir) the layer of the atmosphere between the stratosphere and the thermosphere and in which temperature decreases as altitude increases (252, 502)
mesosfera capa de la atmósfera que se encuentra entre la estratosfera y la termosfera, en la cual la temperatura disminuye al aumentar la altitud

metamorphic rock (met·uh·MOHR·fik RAHK) a rock that forms from other rocks as a result of intense heat, pressure, or chemical processes (460)
roca metamórfica roca que se forma a partir de otras rocas como resultado de calor intenso, presión o procesos químicos

meteor (MEE·tee·er) a bright streak of light that results when a meteoroid burns up in Earth's atmosphere (98)
meteoro rayo de luz brillante que se produce cuando un meteoroide se quema en la atmósfera de la Tierra

meteorite (MEE·tee·uh·ryt) a meteoroid that reaches Earth's surface without burning up completely (98)
meteorito meteoroide que llega a la superficie de la Tierra sin quemarse por completo

meteorology (mee·tee·uh·RAHL·uh·jee) the scientific study of Earth's atmosphere, especially in relation to weather and climate (324)
meteorología estudio científico de la atmósfera de la Tierra, sobre todo en lo que se relaciona al tiempo y al clima

meteoroid (MEE·tee·uh·royd) a relatively small, rocky body that travels through space (98)
meteoroide cuerpo rocoso relativamente pequeño que viaja en el espacio

mid-ocean ridge (MID·oh·shuhn RIJ) a long, undersea mountain chain that forms along the floor of the major oceans (200)

dorsal oceánica larga cadena submarina de montañas que se forma en el suelo de los principales océanos

mineral (MIN·er·uhl) a natural, usually inorganic solid that has a characteristic chemical composition and an orderly internal structure (442)
mineral sólido natural, normalmente inorgánico, que tiene una composición química característica y una estructura interna ordenada

mudflow (MUHD·floh) the flow of a mass of mud or rock and soil mixed with a large amount of water (421)
flujo de lodo flujo de una masa de lodo o roca y suelo mezclados con una gran cantidad de agua

natural resource (NACH·uh·ruhl REE·sohrs) any natural material that is used by humans, such as water, petroleum, minerals, forests, and animals (594, 626)
recurso natural cualquier material natural que utilizan los seres humanos, como agua, petróleo, minerales, bosques, y animales

neap tide (NEEP TYD) a tide of minimum range that occurs during the first and third quarters of the moon (145)
marea muerta marea que tiene un rango mínimo y que ocurre durante el primer y el tercer cuartos de la Luna

nebula (NEB·yuh·luh) a large cloud of gas and dust in interstellar space; a region in space where stars are born (9)
nebulosa nube grande de gas y polvo en el espacio interestelar; una región en el espacio donde nacen las estrellas

nonrenewable resource (nahn·rih·NOO·uh·buhl REE·sohrs) a resource that forms at a rate that is much slower than the rate at which the resource is consumed (594, 626)
recurso no renovable recurso que se forma a una tasa que es mucho más lenta que la tasa a la que se consume

nuclear energy (NOO·klee·er EN·er·jee) the energy released by a fission or fusion reaction; the binding energy of the atomic nucleus (594)
energía nuclear energía liberada por una reacción de fisión o fusión; la energía de enlace del núcleo atómico

nuclear fusion (NOO·klee·er FYOO·zhuhn) the process by which nuclei of small atoms combine to form a new, more massive nucleus; the process releases energy (8)
fusión nuclear proceso por medio del cual los núcleos de átomos pequeños se combinan y forman un núcleo nuevo con mayor masa; el proceso libera energía

ocean current (OH·shuhn KER·uhnt) a movement of ocean water that follows a regular pattern (224)
corriente oceánica movimiento del agua del océano que sigue un patrón regular

ocean trench (OH·shuhn TRENCH) a long, narrow, and steep depression on the ocean floor that forms when one tectonic plate subducts beneath another plate;

trenches run parallel to volcanic island chains or to the coastlines of continents; also called a trench or a deep-ocean trench (201)

fosa oceánica depresión larga, angosta y empinada que se encuentra en el fondo del océano y se forma cuando una placa tectónica se subduce bajo otra; las fosas submarinas corren en forma paralela a cadenas de islas volcánicas o a las costas continentales; también denominada fosa o fosa oceánica profunda

ocean wave (OH·shuhn WAYV) a disturbance on the ocean that transmits energy and takes the shape of a swell or ridge (210)

ola marítima de alteración del océano que transmite energía y adopta la forma de onda o cresta

Oort cloud (OHRT KLOWD) a spherical region that surrounds the solar system, that extends from the Kuiper Belt to almost halfway to the nearest star, and that contains billions of comets (95)

nube de Oort región esférica que rodea al sistema solar y que se extiende desde el cinturón de Kuiper hasta la mitad del camino hacia la estrella más cercana y contiene miles de millones de cometas

orbit (OHR·bit) the path that a body follows as it travels around another body in space (44)

órbita trayectoria que sigue un cuerpo al desplazarse alrededor de otro cuerpo en el espacio

oxidation (ahk·sih·DAY·shuhn) a chemical reaction in which a material combines with oxygen to form new material; in geology, oxidation is a form of chemical weathering (390)

oxidación reacción química en la que un material se combina con oxígeno para formar un material nuevo; en geología, la oxidación es una forma de desgaste químico

ozone (OH·zohn) a gas molecule that is made up of three oxygen atoms (631)

ozono molécula de gas que está formada por tres átomos de oxígeno

ozone layer (OH·zohn LAY·er) the layer of the atmosphere at an altitude of 15 to 40 km in which ozone absorbs ultraviolet solar radiation (254)

capa de ozono capa de la atmósfera ubicada a una altitud de 15 a 40 km, en la cual el ozono absorbe la ultravioleta radiación solar

Pangaea (pan·JEE·uh) the supercontinent that formed 300 million years ago and that began to break up 200 million years ago (516, 527)

Pangea supercontinente que se formó hace 300 millones de años y que comenzó a separarse hace 200 millones de años

parallax (PAIR·uh·laks) an apparent shift in the position of an object when viewed from different locations (10)

paralaje cambio aparente en la posición de un objeto cuando se ve desde lugares distintos

penumbra (pih·NUHM·bruh) the outer part of a shadow such as the shadow cast by Earth or the moon in which sunlight is only partially blocked (134)

penumbra parte exterior de la sombra (como la sombra producida por la Tierra o la Luna) en la que la luz solar solamente se encuentra bloqueada parcialmente

perihelion (pehr·ih·HEE·lee·uhn) in the orbit of a planet or other body in the solar system, the point that is closest to the sun (45)

perihelio en la órbita de un planeta u otros cuerpos en el sistema solar, el punto que está más cerca del Sol

photosynthesis (foh·toh·SIN·thih·sis) the process by which plants, algae, and some bacteria use sunlight, carbon dioxide, and water to make food (614)

fotosíntesis proceso por medio del cual las plantas, las algas y algunas bacterias utilizan la luz solar, el dióxido de carbono y el agua para producir alimento

physical weathering (FIZ·ih·kuhl WETH·er·ing) the mechanical breakdown of rocks into smaller pieces that is caused by natural processes and that does not change the chemical composition of the rock material (386)

desgaste físico rompimiento mecánico de una roca en fragmentos más pequeños que ocurre por procesos naturales y que no modifica la composición química del material rocoso

planet (PLAN·it) a relatively large spherical body that orbits a star (7)

planeta cuerpo esférico relativamente grande que orbita alrededor de una estrella

planetary ring (PLAN·ih·tehr·ee RING) a disk of matter that encircles a planet that consists of numerous particles in orbit, which range in size from dust grains up to objects tens of meters across (78)

anillo planetario disco de materia que rodea un planeta y está compuesto por numerosas partículas en órbita que pueden ser desde motas de polvo hasta objetos de decenas de metros

planetesimal (plan·ih·TES·uh·muhl) a small body from which a planet originated in the early stages of development of the solar system (51)

planetesimal cuerpo pequeño a partir del cual se originó un planeta en las primeras etapas de desarrollo del sistema solar

plate tectonics (PLAYT tek·TAHN·iks) the theory that explains how large pieces of Earth's outermost layer, called tectonic plates, move and change shape (530)

tectónica de placas teoría que explica cómo se mueven y cambian de forma las placas tectónicas, las cuales son grandes porciones de la capa más externa de la Tierra

precipitation (prih·sip·ih·TAY·shuhn) any form of water that falls to Earth's surface from the clouds (165, 292)

precipitación cualquier forma de agua que cae de las nubes a la superficie de la Tierra

radiation (ray·dee·AY·shuhn) the transfer of energy as electromagnetic waves (264)
radiación transferencia de energía en forma de ondas electromagnéticas

redshift (RED·shift) a shift toward the red end of the spectrum; occurs in the spectrum of an object when the object is moving away from the observer (31)
corrimiento al rojo corrimiento hacia el extremo rojo del espectro; ocurre en el espectro de un objeto cuando el objeto se está alejando del observador

relative humidity (REL·uh·tiv hyoo·MID·ih·tee) the ratio of the amount of water vapor in the air to the amount of water vapor needed to reach saturation at a given temperature (291)
humedad relativa proporción de la cantidad de vapor de agua que hay en el aire respecto a la cantidad de vapor de agua que se necesita para alcanzar la saturación a una temperatura dada

renewable resource (rih·NOO·uh·buhl REE·sohrs) a natural resource that can be replaced at the same rate at which the resource is consumed (594, 626)
recurso renovable recurso natural que puede reemplazarse a la misma tasa a la que se consume

revolution (rev·uh·LOO·shuhn) the motion of a body that travels around another body in space; one complete trip along an orbit (117)
revolución movimiento de un cuerpo que viaja alrededor de otro cuerpo en el espacio; un viaje completo a lo largo de una órbita

rift zone (RIFT ZOHN) an area of deep cracks that forms between two tectonic plates that are pulling away from each other (464)
zona de rift área de grietas profundas que se forma entre dos placas tectónicas que se están alejando una de la otra

rock (RAHK) a naturally occurring solid mixture of one or more minerals or organic matter (476)
roca mezcla sólida de uno o más minerales o de materia orgánica que se produce de forma natural

rock cycle (RAHK SY·kuhl) the series of processes in which rock forms, changes from one type to another, is broken down or melted, and forms again by geologic processes (462)
ciclo de las rocas serie de procesos por medio de los cuales una roca se forma, cambia de un tipo a otro, se descompone o funde y se forma nuevamente por procesos geológicos

rockfall (RAHK·fawl) the rapid mass movement of rock down a steep slope or cliff (421)
desprendimiento de rocas movimiento rápido y masivo de rocas por una pendiente empinada o un precipicio

rotation (roh·TAY·shuhn) the spin of a body on its axis (116)
rotación giro de un cuerpo alrededor de su eje

salinity (suh·LIN·ih·tee) a measure of the amount of dissolved salts in a given amount of liquid (194)
salinidad medida de la cantidad de sales disueltas en una cantidad determinada de líquido

sandbar (SAND·bar) a low ridge of sand deposited along the shore of a lake or sea (406)
barra de arena arrecife bajo de arena depositado a lo largo de la orilla de un lago o del mar

satellite (SAT'l·yt) a natural or artificial body that revolves around a celestial body that is greater in mass (130)
satélite cuerpo natural o artificial que gira alrededor de un cuerpo celeste que tiene mayor masa

seafloor spreading (SEE·flohr SPRED·ing) the process by which new oceanic lithosphere (seafloor) forms when magma rises to Earth's surface at mid-ocean ridges and solidifies, as older, existing seafloor moves away from the ridge (528)
expansión del suelo marino proceso por medio del cual se forma nueva litósfera oceánica (suelo marino) cuando el magma sube a la superficie de la Tierra en las dorsales oceánicas y se solidifica, a medida que el antiguo suelo marino existente se aleja de la dorsal oceánica

season (SEE·zuhn) a division of the year that is characterized by recurring weather conditions and determined by both Earth's tilt relative to the sun and Earth's position in its orbit around the sun (120)
estación de las partes en que se divide el año que se caracteriza por condiciones climáticas recurrentes y que está determinada tanto por la inclinación de la Tierra con relación al Sol como por la posición que ocupa en su órbita alrededor del Sol

sedimentary rock (sed·uh·MEN·tuh·ree RAHK) a rock that forms from compressed or cemented layers of sediment (460)
roca sedimentaria roca que se forma a partir de capas comprimidas o cementadas de sedimento

shear stress (SHIR STRES) stress that occurs when forces act in parallel but opposite directions, pushing parts of a solid in opposite directions (544)
tensión de corte estrés que se produce cuando dos fuerzas actúan en direcciones paralelas pero opuestas, lo que empuja las partes de un sólido en direcciones opuestas

shoreline (SHOHR·lyn) the boundary between land and a body of water (403)
litoral límite entre la tierra y una masa de agua

soil (SOYL) a loose mixture of rock fragments, organic material, water, and air that can support the growth of vegetation (428)
suelo mezcla suelta de fragmentos de roca, material orgánico, agua y aire en la que puede crecer vegetación

soil horizon (SOYL huh·RY·zuhn) each layer of soil within a soil profile (431)
horizonte del suelo cada capa del suelo dentro de un perfil del suelo

soil profile (SOYL PROH·fyl) a vertical section of soil that shows the layers, or horizons (431)

perfil del suelo sección vertical de suelo que muestra las capas u horizontes

solar energy (SOH·ler EN·er·jee) the energy received by Earth from the sun in the form of radiation (612)

energía solar energía que la Tierra recibe del Sol en forma de radiación

solar nebula (SOH·ler NEB·yuh·luh) a rotating cloud of gas and dust from which the sun and planets formed (49)

nebulosa solar nube de gas y polvo en rotación a partir de la cual se formaron el Sol y los planetas

solar system (SOH·ler SIS·tuhm) the sun and all of the planets and other bodies that travel around it (7)

sistema solar Sol y todos los planetas y otros cuerpos que se desplazan alrededor de él

solstice (SOHL·stis) the point at which the sun is as far north or as far south of the equator as possible (120)

solsticio punto en el que el Sol está tan lejos del ecuador como es posible, ya sea hacia el norte o hacia el sur

spectrum (SPEK·truhm) a range of electromagnetic radiation that is ordered by wavelength or frequency, such as the band of colors that is produced when white light passes through a prism (28)

espectro gama de radiación electromagnética ordenada por longitud de onda o frecuencia, como la banda de colores que se produce cuando la luz blanca pasa a través de un prisma

spring tide (SPRING TYD) a tide of increased range that occurs two times a month, at the new and full moons (144)

marea viva marea de mayor rango que ocurre dos veces al mes, durante la luna nueva y la luna llena

star (STAR) a large celestial body that is composed of gas and that emits light; the sun is a typical star (8)

estrella cuerpo celeste grande que está compuesto de gas y emite luz; el Sol es una estrella típica

station model (STAY·shuhn MAHD·l) a pattern of meteorological symbols that represents the weather at a particular observing station and that is recorded on a weather map (328)

modelo de estación modelo de símbolos meteorológicos que representan el tiempo en una estación de observación determinada y que se registra en un mapa meteorológico

stewardship (STOO·erd·ship) the careful and responsible management of a resource (628, 651)

gestión ambiental responsable manejo cuidadoso y responsable de un recurso

storm surge (STOHRM SERJ) a local rise in sea level near the shore that is caused by strong winds from a storm, such as those from a hurricane (311)

marea de tempestad levantamiento local del nivel del mar cerca de la costa, el cual es resultado de los fuertes vientos de una tormenta, como por ejemplo, los vientos de un huracán

stratosphere (STRAT·uh·sfir) the layer of the atmosphere that is above the troposphere and in which temperature increases as altitude increases (252)

estratosfera capa de la atmósfera que se encuentra encima de la troposfera y en la que la temperatura aumenta al aumentar la altitud

streak (STREEK) the color of a mineral in powdered form (448)

veta color de un mineral en forma de polvo

sublimation (suhb·luh·MAY·shuhn) the change of state from a solid directly to a gas (164)

sublimación cambio de estado por el cual un sólido se convierte directamente en un gas

subsidence (suhb·SYD·ns) the sinking of regions of Earth's crust to lower elevations (464)

subsidencia hundimiento de regiones de la corteza terrestre a elevaciones más bajas

supernova (soo·per·NOH·vuh) a gigantic explosion in which a massive star collapses and throws its outer layers into space (9)

supernova explosión gigantesca en la que una estrella masiva se colapsa y lanza sus capas externas hacia el espacio

surface current (SER·fuhs KER·uhnt) a horizontal movement of ocean water that is caused by wind and that occurs at or near the ocean's surface (224, 349)

corriente superficial movimiento horizontal del agua del océano que es producido por el viento y que ocurre en la superficie del océano o cerca de ella

surface water (SER·fuhs WAW·ter) all the bodies of fresh water, salt water, ice, and snow that are found above the ground (180)

agua superficial todas las masas de agua dulce, agua salada, hielo y nieve que se encuentran en la superficie del suelo

tectonic plate (tek·TAHN·ik PLAYT) a block of lithosphere that consists of the crust and the rigid, outermost part of the mantle (530, 557)

placa tectónica bloque de litosfera formado por la corteza y la parte rígida y más externa del manto

tectonic plate boundary (tek·TAHN·ik PLAYT BOWN·duh·ree) the edge between two or more plates, classified as divergent, convergent, or transform by the movement taking place between the plates (569)

límite de las placas tectónica borde entre dos o más placas clasificado como divergente, convergente o transformante por el movimiento que se produce entre las placas

temperature (TEM·per·uh·chur) a measure of how hot (or cold) something is; specifically, a measure of the average kinetic energy of the particles in an object (262)

temperatura grado de calor (o frío) de un cuerpo; específicamente, una medida de la energía cinética promedio de las partículas de un cuerpo

tension (TEN·shuhn) stress that occurs when forces act to stretch an object (545)

tensión estrés que se produce cuando distintas fuerzas actúan para estirar un objeto

terrestrial planet (tuh·RES·tree·uhl PLAN·it) one of the highly dense planets nearest to the sun; Mercury, Venus, Mars, and Earth (60)

planeta terrestre de los planetas muy densos que se encuentran más cerca del Sol; Mercurio, Venus, Marte y la Tierra

texture (TEKS·cher) the quality of a rock that is based on the sizes, shapes, and positions of the rock's grains (477)

textura cualidad de una roca que se basa en el tamaño, la forma y la posición de los granos que la forman

thermal energy (THER·muhl EN·er·jee) the kinetic energy of a substance's atoms (262)

energía térmica energía cinética de los átomos de una sustancia

thermal expansion (THER·muhl ek·SPAN·shuhn) an increase in the size of a substance in response to an increase in the temperature of the substance (262)

expansión térmica aumento en el tamaño de una sustancia en respuesta a un aumento en la temperatura de la sustancia

thermocline (THER·muh·klyn) a layer in a body of water in which water temperature drops with increased depth faster than it does in other layers (195)

termoclina capa en una masa de agua en la que, al aumentar la profundidad, la temperatura del agua disminuye más rápido de lo que lo hace en otras capas

thermosphere (THER·muh·sfir) the uppermost layer of the atmosphere, in which temperature increases as altitude increases (252)

termosfera capa más alta de la atmósfera, en la cual la temperatura aumenta a medida que aumenta la altitud

thunder (THUHN·der) the sound caused by the rapid expansion of air along an electrical strike (309)

trueno sonido producido por la expansión rápida del aire a lo largo de una descarga eléctrica

thunderstorm (THUHN·der·stohrm) a usually brief, heavy storm that consists of rain, strong winds, lightning, and thunder (308)

tormenta eléctrica tormenta fuerte y normalmente breve que consiste en lluvia, vientos fuertes, relámpagos y truenos

tidal range (TYD·l RAYNJ) the difference in levels of ocean water at high tide and low tide (144)

rango de marea diferencia en los niveles del agua del océano entre la marea alta y la marea baja

tide (TYD) the periodic rise and fall of the water level in the oceans and other large bodies of water (142)

marea ascenso y descenso periódico del nivel del agua en los océanos y otras masas grandes de agua

topography (tuh·PAHG·ruh·fee) the size and shape of the land surface features of a region, including its relief (346)

topografía tamaño y forma de las características de la superficie de una terreno, incluido su relieve

tornado (tohr·NAY·doh) a destructive, rotating column of air that has very high wind speeds and that may be visible as a funnel-shaped cloud (312)

tornado columna destructiva de aire en rotación cuyos vientos se mueven a velocidades muy altas y que puede verse como una nube con forma de embudo

trace fossil (TRAYS FAHS·uhl) a fossilized structure, such as a footprint or a coprolite, that formed in sedimentary rock by animal activity on or within soft sediment (513)

fósil traza estructura fosilizada, como una huella o un coprolito, que se formó en una roca sedimentaria por la actividad de un animal sobre sedimento blando o dentro de éste

transform boundary (TRANS·fohrm BOWN·duh·ree) the boundary between tectonic plates that are sliding past each other horizontally (533)

límite de transformación límite entre placas tectónicas que se deslizan horizontalmente una sobre otra

transpiration (tran·spuh·RAY·shuhn) the process by which plants release water vapor into the air through stomata; also the release of water vapor into the air by other organisms (164)

transpiración proceso por medio del cual las plantas liberan vapor de agua al aire por medio de los estomas; también, la liberación de vapor de agua al aire por otros organismos

tributary (TRIB·yuh·tehr·ee) a stream that flows into a lake or into a larger stream (182)

afluente arroyo que desemboca en un lago o en otro arroyo más grande

troposphere (TROH·puh·sfir) the lowest layer of the atmosphere, in which temperature decreases at a constant rate as altitude increases (252)

troposfera capa inferior de la atmósfera, en la que la temperatura disminuye a una tasa constante a medida que la altitud aumenta

trough (TRAWF) the lowest point of a wave (210)

seno punto más bajo de una onda

tsunami (tsoo·NAH·mee) a giant ocean wave that forms after a volcanic eruption, submarine earthquake, or landslide (217)

tsunami ola gigante del océano que se forma después de una erupción volcánica, terremoto submarino o un derrumbamiento

umbra (UHM·bruh) a shadow that blocks sunlight, such as the conical section in the shadow of Earth or the moon (134)

umbra sombra que bloquea la luz solar, como por ejemplo, la sección cónica en la sombra de la Tierra o la Luna

uniformitarianism (yoo·nuh·fohr·mih·TAIR·ee·uh·niz·uhm) a principle that geologic processes that occurred in the past can be explained by current geologic processes (510)

uniformitarianismo principio que establece que es posible explicar los procesos geológicos que ocurrieron en el pasado en función de los procesos geológicos actuales

universe (YOO·nuh·vers) space and all the matter and energy in it (6, 26)
universo espacio y toda la materia y energía que hay dentro de él

uplift (UHP·lift) the rising of regions of Earth's crust to higher elevations (464)
levantamiento elevación de regiones de la corteza terrestre a elevaciones más altas

upwelling (UHP·well·ing) the movement of deep, cold, and nutrient-rich water to the surface (230)
surgencia movimiento de las aguas profundas, frías y ricas en nutrientes hacia la superficie

urbanization (er·buh·nih·ZAY·shuhn) an increase in the proportion of a population living in urban areas rather than in rural areas (639)
urbanización aumento la proporción de población en las áreas urbanas

vent (VENT) an opening at the surface of Earth through which volcanic material passes (554)
chimenea abertura en la superficie de la Tierra a través de la cual pasa material volcánico

visibility (viz·uh·BIL·ih·tee) the distance at which a given standard object can be seen and identified with the unaided eye (292)
visibilidad distancia a la que un objeto dado es perceptible e identificable para el ojo humano

volcano (vahl·KAY·noh) a vent or fissure in Earth's surface through which magma and gases are expelled (554)
volcán chimenea o fisura en la superficie de la Tierra a través de la cual se expulsan magma y gases

water cycle (WAW·ter SY·kuhl) the continuous movement of water between the atmosphere, the land, the oceans, and living things (162)
ciclo del agua movimiento continuo del agua entre la atmósfera, la tierra, los océanos y los seres vivos

water table (WAW·ter TAY·buhl) the upper surface of underground water; the upper boundary of the zone of saturation (180)
capa freática nivel más alto del agua subterránea; el límite superior de la zona de saturación

watershed (WAW·ter·shed) the area of land that is drained by a river system (183)
cuenca hidrográfica área del terreno que es drenada por un sistema de ríos

wave (WAYV) a disturbance that transfers energy from one place to another; a wave can be a single cycle, or it can be a repeating pattern (210)
onda alteración que transfiere energía de un lugar a otro; una onda puede ser un ciclo único o un patrón repetido

wave period (WAYV PIR·ee·uhd) the time required for corresponding points on consecutive waves to pass a given point (211)
período de onda tiempo que se requiere para que los puntos correspondientes de ondas consecutivas pasen por un punto dado

wavelength (WAYV·lengkth) the distance from any point on a wave to the corresponding point on the next wave (28, 210)
longitud de onda distancia entre cualquier punto de una onda y el punto correspondiente de la siguiente onda

weather (WETH·er) the short-term state of the atmosphere, including temperature, humidity, precipitation, wind, and visibility (290, 342)
tiempo estado de la atmósfera a corto plazo que incluye la temperatura, la humedad, la precipitación, el viento y la visibilidad

weather forecasting (WETH·er FOHR·kast·ing) the process of predicting atmospheric conditions by collecting and analyzing atmospheric data (324)
pronóstico del tiempo proceso de predecir las condiciones atmosféricas recopilando y analizando datos atmosféricos

weathering (WETH·er·ing) the natural process by which atmospheric and environmental agents, such as wind, rain, and temperature changes, disintegrate and decompose rocks (386, 459)
meteorización proceso natural por medio del cual los agentes atmosféricos o ambientales, como el viento, la lluvia y los cambios de temperatura, desintegran y descomponen las rocas

wind (WIND) the movement of air caused by differences in air pressure (276, 290)
viento movimiento de aire producido por diferencias en la presión barométrica

wind energy (WIND EN·er·jee) the use of the force of moving air to drive an electric generator (610)
energía eólica uso de la fuerza del aire en movimiento para hacer funcionar un generador eléctrico

year (YIR) the time required for Earth to orbit once around the sun (117)
año tiempo que se requiere para que la Tierra gire alrededor del Sol una vez

Index

Italic page numbers represent illustrative material, such as figures, tables, margin elements, photographs, and illustrations. Boldface page numbers represent page numbers for definitions.

equinox, **120**, *120–121*
erratics, *418*
Eris (dwarf), 91
Eros (asteroid), *97*
erosion, 382–383, *383*, **398–405**, *398, 403, 404, 405,* 417, 418, *459,* 642, *642*
ethanol, 614, *614*
Europa (moon), 77, *77*
evaporation, **164**, *164,* 167, 168

fairy chimneys, *459*
faults, 542, **544**, 568, 569
 normal, **545**, *545,* 571
 reverse, **545**, *545,* 571
 strike-slip, **544**, *544,* 571
fissure, *556*
flood, **314**
floodplain, **401**, *401*
Florida, *381*
folds, **543**, *543*
fossils, *508,* 511–514, *511, 512, 513*
fossil fuels, **594**, 601, 638
 coal, **595**, *595,* 597, 601
 formation, 596–597, *596, 597*
 natural gas, **595**, *595,* 596
 petroleum, **595**, *595,* 596
fog, **169**, *169,* 291, 292
frequency, 28

galaxy, *3, 4,* **6, 8,** 17, 26, *26, 27*
 dwarf, **8**
 elliptical, **8**
 irregular, **8**
 spiral, *3,* **8**
 Whirlpool, 22, *22*
galaxy cluster, 26, *27*
Galaxy Zoo, 2, 3
Galileo, 10, *77*
gamma ray, 28, *29*
Gamow, George, 31, *31*
Ganymede (moon), *76,* 77
gas giant planets, 7, 52, *52,* 74–84
Gehry, Frank, *451*
general relativity, **30**
geocentric model, **10**, *12*
geothermal energy, **615**, *615*
Gila Cliff Dwellings, *465*
glaciers, 170, 171, 416, *416,* 417, *417,* 418, *418*
glass, 472–473
global warming, 362, **364**
gneiss, *461*
Göreme, Turkey, *459*
Grand Canyon, 400
gravity, 42–54, **130**, *157,* 162, *162*
 mass movement, **420**–421
 tidal force, **142**, 144
Great Dark Spot, 82, *82*
Great Red Spot, 77
Great Rift Valley, *558*

Great Salt Lake, *480*
Great Sphinx, *458*
greenhouse effect, 254, *255,* 362, 367, 659
Guggenheim Museum, *451*
Gulf Stream, *224,* 348

Hale-Bopp (comet), 88
Haleakala, Maui (volcano), 347
Haumea (dwarf), 91
heat, 263, 317
Hebes Chasma, *67*
heliocentric model, **10**, *11, 13*
hot spot, **560**, *560*
Hubble, Edwin, 31, *31,* 33
Hubble Space Telescope, *4, 6, 22,* 77
humidity, **291**
humus, **429**
hurricane, **310–311**, *310, 311,* 315
Hurricane Hunters, 325, *325*
Huygens (probe), 79
hydroelectric energy, *609,* **611**, *611*

ice age, **361**, 419, *419*
ice core, **519**, *519*
igneous rock, 460, 461, *461,* 462, *462,* 464, 478–479, *478, 479*
inflation, **34**
infrared, 28, *29*
International Astronomical Union (IAU), **127**
Io (moon), *77,* 77
Itokawa (asteroid), *97, 97*

jet stream, **280**, *280, 299, 299*
Jupiter, **76–77**, 80, 91, 96

Kepler, Johannes, 45; laws of planetary motion, 45–46
kettle lakes, *418*
Kilauea volcano, 560, *560*
Kuiper Belt, 90, 92, 93, *93,* 95
Kuiper Belt objects (KBO), 92–93
Kyoto Protocol, 367, 659

La Brea Tar Pits, 511
Lake Missoula, 419, *419*
landslide, **421**, *421*
land use, 636–644, *638*
 deforestation, **643**, *643,* 368
 degradation, **642**, *642*
 desertification, **643**, *643*

La Niña, 360
latitude, **344**
lava, **554**, *554*
lava plateau, **556**, *556*
law of universal gravitation, 47, 54
laws of planetary motion, 45–46
Lemaître, Georges, 31, *31*
light-year (ly), **15**, 16, 22
lightning, *306,* 308, **309**, *309*
lithosphere, **502**, 530, 532, 533
Local Group, 16, *16*
loess, 415

magma, 444, 462, *462,* 464, 478, *478,* **554**, 559
Makemake (dwarf), 91
mammoth, *512*
mantle (Earth), 500, *500,* **501**, *501*
mantle convection, **534**, *534*
Mariana Trench, 201, *206*
Mars, 58, **66–68**, *66,* 91, 96, 99
 Exploration Rovers, 69
 Global Surveyor, 68
 volcanoes, 67
marsh, 401
Mercury, 58, **60–61**, *60,* 63
mesosphere, **252**, 502
metamorphic rock, 460, 461, *461,* 462, *463,* 464, 482–483, *482, 483*
meteors, **98**
meteorites, **98**–99, *98,* 213
meteoroids, *90,* **98**
meteorology, **324**
microwave, **28**
midnight sun, **119**, *119*
Mid-Atlantic Ridge, 558
mid-ocean ridge, **200**, *200,* 558, 571
Milky Way, 8, 16, *16*
minerals, *381,* 426, 434, 440, **441–453**, 476
 chemical composition, 442–443, *442*
 classification, **446**, *446, 447*
 crystals, 440, 443, 478, *478*
 formation, 444–445, *444, 445*
 identification, 448–450
Miranda (moon), 81, *81*
Mississippi River watershed, 183
Mont Blanc, *540*
moon, 7, 65, **128**, 130–131, *131*
 eclipses, **134**, *134,* 135
 phases, **132**, *132–133*
 tides, **142**–148
mountains,
 fault-block, **547**, *547*
 folded, **546**, *546*
 volcanic, **547**, *547*
Mount Everest, *251*
Mount Kilimanjaro, 347
Mt. Griggs, **547**, *547*
Mt. Pinatubo, *358,* 359, *359*
Mt. St. Helens, 559
mudflow, 421